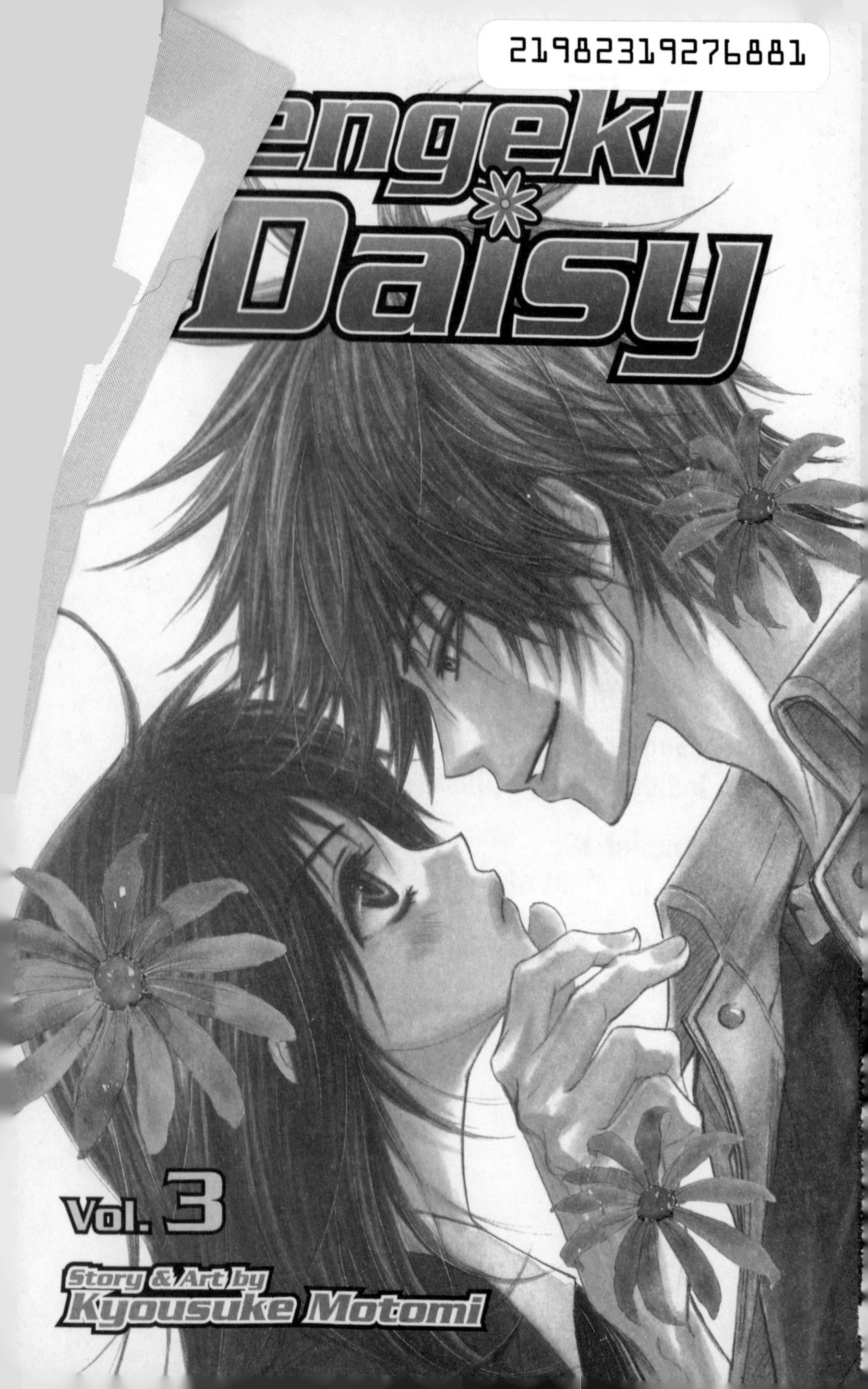
engeki
Daisy
Vol. 3
Story & Art by
Kyousuke Motomi

Dengeki Daisy

Volume 3 CONTENTS

DAISY

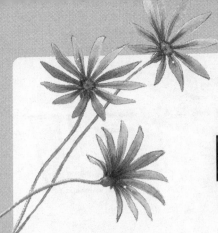

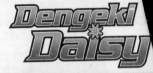

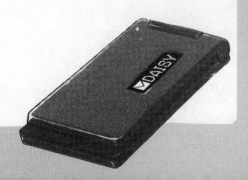

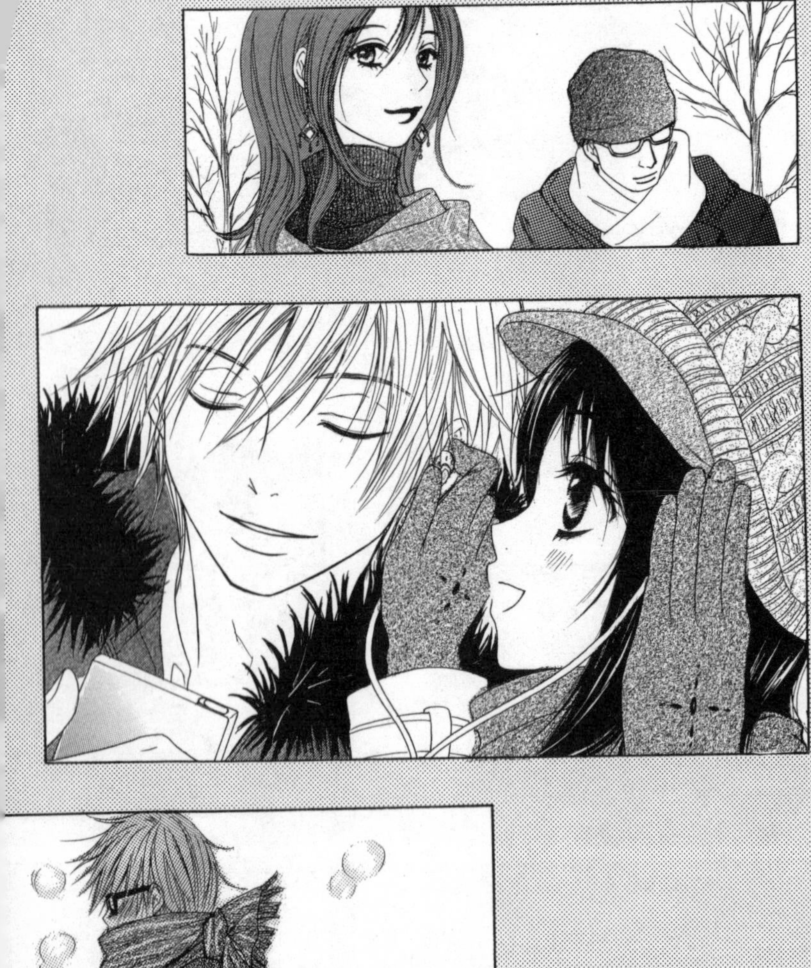

CHAPTER 10: YOU WON'T BE HERE.

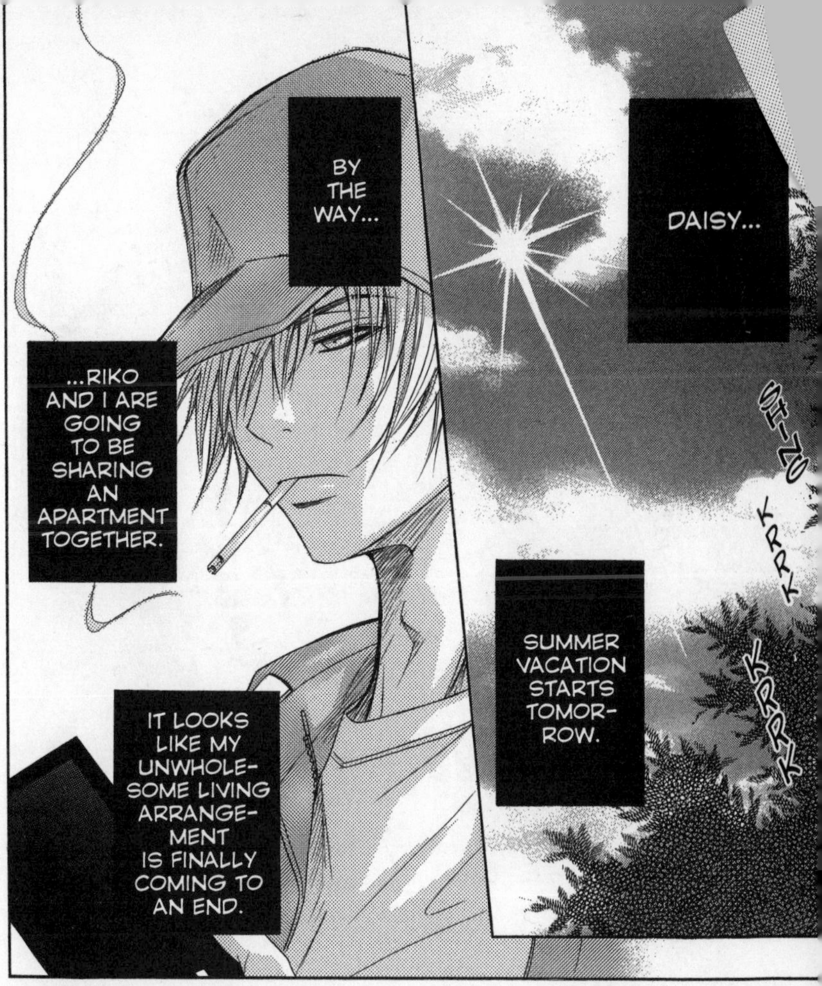
DAISY...
KRRK
KRRK
SUMMER VACATION STARTS TOMOR-ROW.
BY THE WAY...
...RIKO AND I ARE GOING TO BE SHARING AN APARTMENT TOGETHER.
IT LOOKS LIKE MY UNWHOLE-SOME LIVING ARRANGE-MENT IS FINALLY COMING TO AN END.

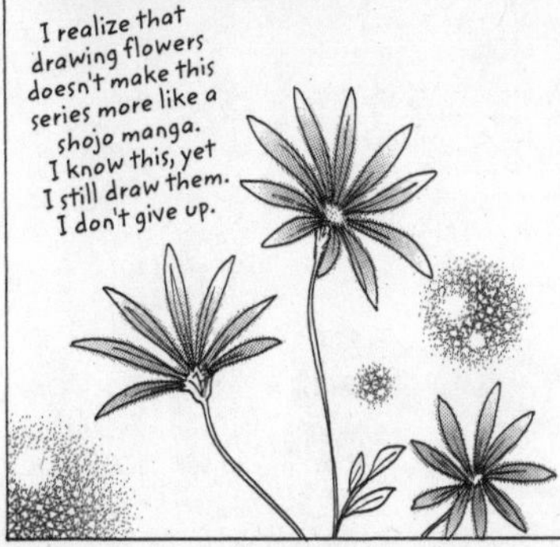
I realize that drawing flowers doesn't make this series more like a shojo manga. I know this, yet I still draw them. I don't give up.

HELLO, EVERYONE! IT'S KYOUSUKE MOTOMI.

HERE IS VOLUME 3 OF *DENGEKI DAISY*.

THANK YOU FOR PICKING IT UP!

I HOPE YOU ENJOY IT.

PLEASE, PLEASE READ IT UNTIL THE LAST PAGE.

THANK YOU.

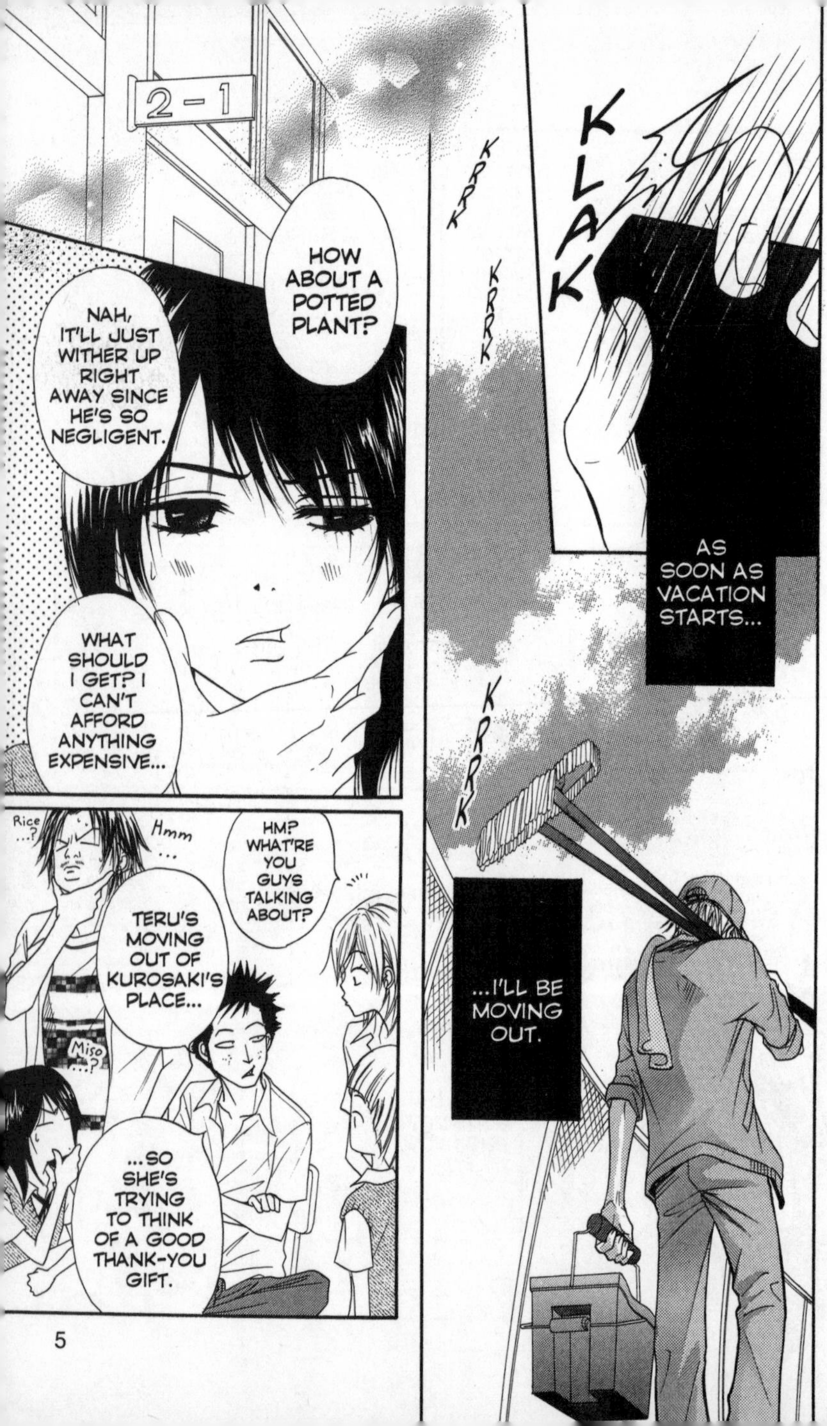
KLAK
KRRK
KRRK
AS SOON AS VACATION STARTS...
KRRK
...I'LL BE MOVING OUT.
HOW ABOUT A POTTED PLANT?
NAH, IT'LL JUST WITHER UP RIGHT AWAY SINCE HE'S SO NEGLIGENT.
WHAT SHOULD I GET? I CAN'T AFFORD ANYTHING EXPENSIVE...
HM? WHAT'RE YOU GUYS TALKING ABOUT?
Hmm...
Rice...?
TERU'S MOVING OUT OF KUROSAKI'S PLACE...
Miso...?
...SO SHE'S TRYING TO THINK OF A GOOD THANK-YOU GIFT.

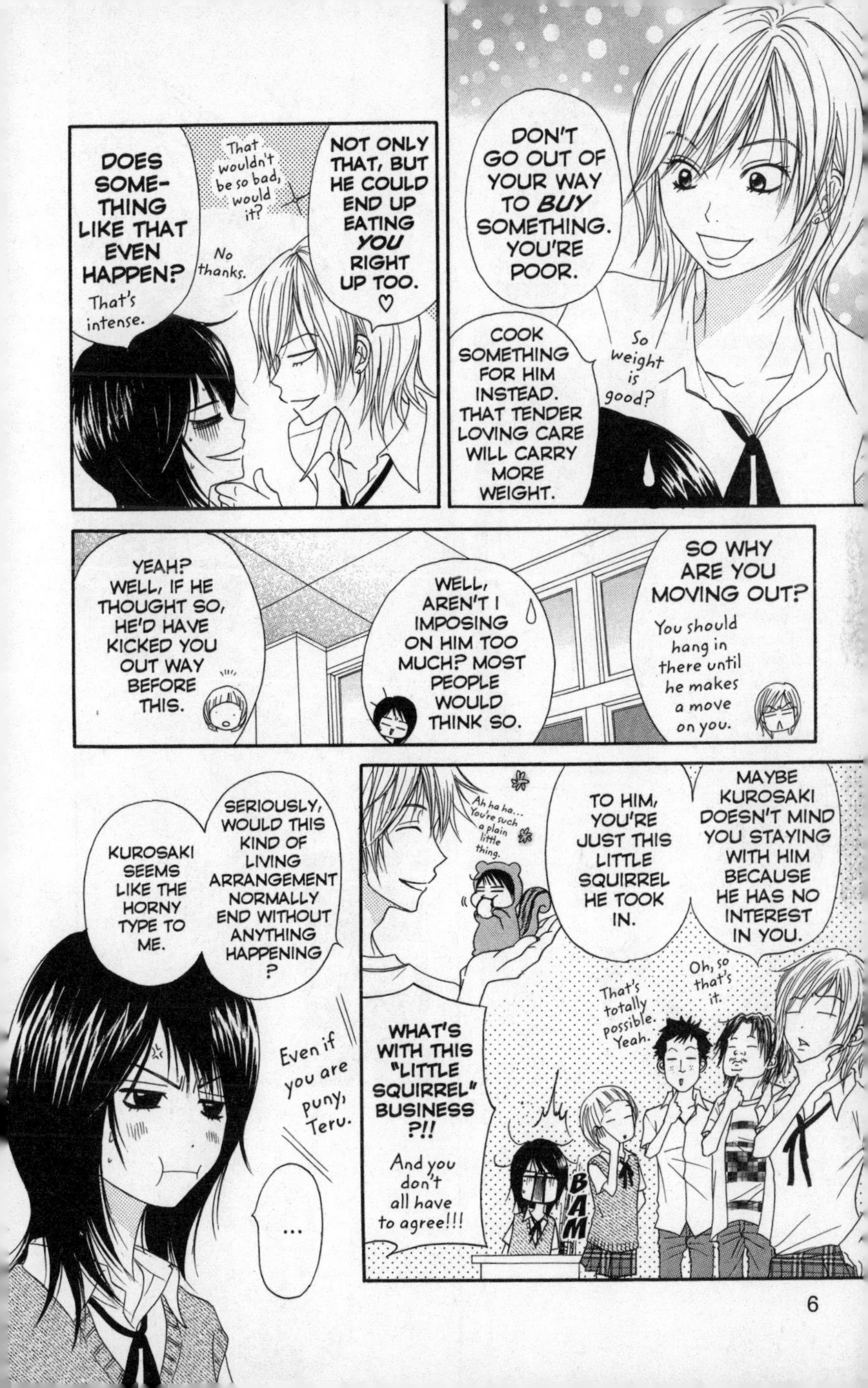
DON'T GO OUT OF YOUR WAY TO *BUY* SOMETHING. YOU'RE POOR.
COOK SOMETHING FOR HIM INSTEAD. THAT TENDER LOVING CARE WILL CARRY MORE WEIGHT.
So weight is good?
NOT ONLY THAT, BUT HE COULD END UP EATING *YOU* RIGHT UP TOO. ♡
That wouldn't be so bad, would it?
No thanks.
DOES SOMETHING LIKE THAT EVEN HAPPEN?
That's intense.
SO WHY ARE YOU MOVING OUT?
You should hang in there until he makes a move on you.
WELL, AREN'T I IMPOSING ON HIM TOO MUCH? MOST PEOPLE WOULD THINK SO.
YEAH? WELL, IF HE THOUGHT SO, HE'D HAVE KICKED YOU OUT WAY BEFORE THIS.
MAYBE KUROSAKI DOESN'T MIND YOU STAYING WITH HIM BECAUSE HE HAS NO INTEREST IN YOU.
TO HIM, YOU'RE JUST THIS LITTLE SQUIRREL HE TOOK IN.
Ah ha ha... You're such a plain little thing.
Oh, so that's it.
That's totally possible. Yeah.
WHAT'S WITH THIS "LITTLE SQUIRREL" BUSINESS?!!
And you don't all have to agree!!!
BAM
SERIOUSLY, WOULD THIS KIND OF LIVING ARRANGEMENT NORMALLY END WITHOUT ANYTHING HAPPENING?
KUROSAKI SEEMS LIKE THE HORNY TYPE TO ME.
Even if you are puny, Teru.
...

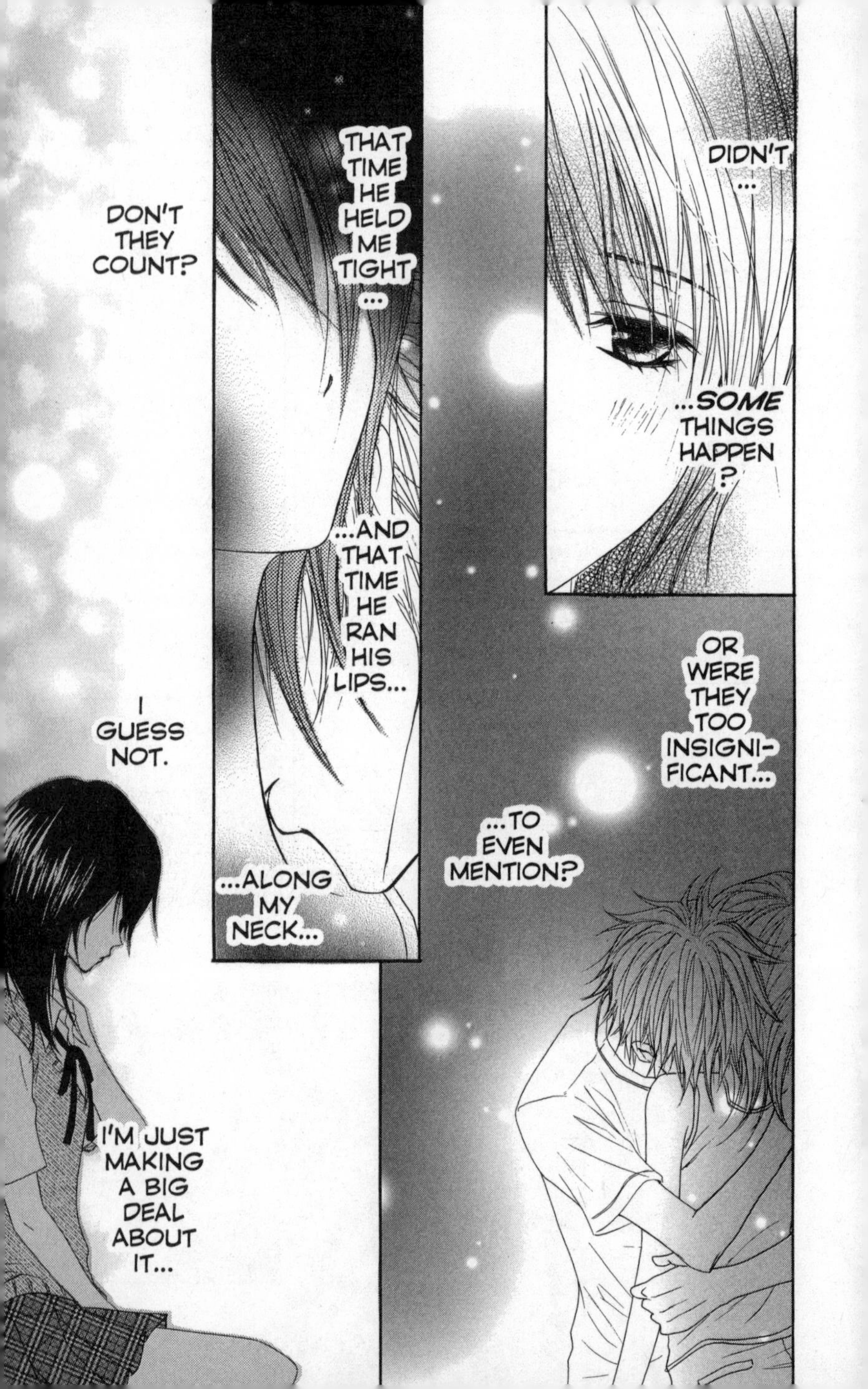
DIDN'T ...
...SOME THINGS HAPPEN?
THAT TIME HE HELD ME TIGHT ...
...AND THAT TIME HE RAN HIS LIPS...
...ALONG MY NECK...
OR WERE THEY TOO INSIGNIFICANT...
...TO EVEN MENTION?
DON'T THEY COUNT?
I GUESS NOT.
I'M JUST MAKING A BIG DEAL ABOUT IT...

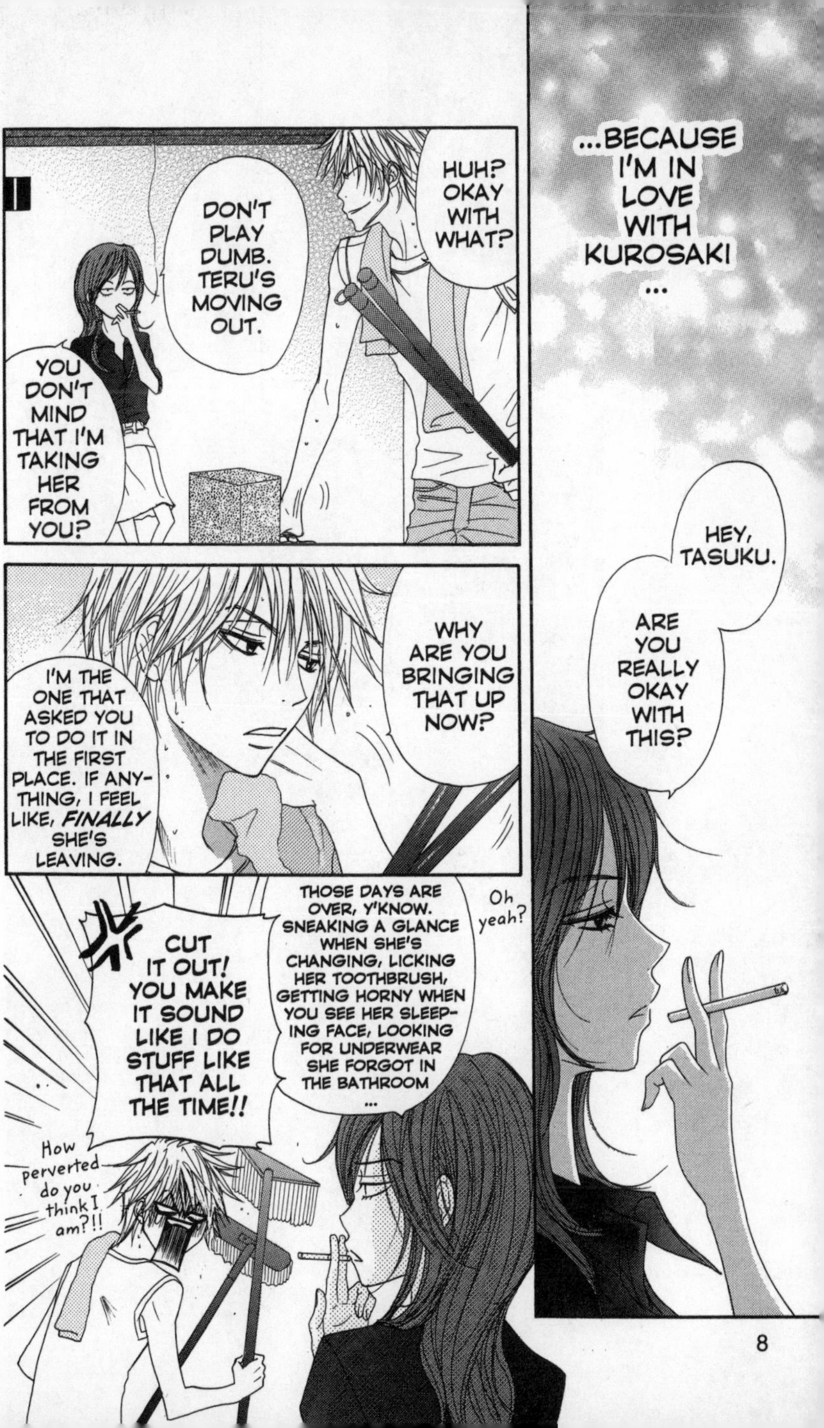
...BECAUSE I'M IN LOVE WITH KUROSAKI ...
HEY, TASUKU.
ARE YOU REALLY OKAY WITH THIS?
HUH? OKAY WITH WHAT?
DON'T PLAY DUMB. TERU'S MOVING OUT.
YOU DON'T MIND THAT I'M TAKING HER FROM YOU?
WHY ARE YOU BRINGING THAT UP NOW?
I'M THE ONE THAT ASKED YOU TO DO IT IN THE FIRST PLACE. IF ANY-THING, I FEEL LIKE, *FINALLY* SHE'S LEAVING.
Oh yeah?
THOSE DAYS ARE OVER, Y'KNOW. SNEAKING A GLANCE WHEN SHE'S CHANGING, LICKING HER TOOTHBRUSH, GETTING HORNY WHEN YOU SEE HER SLEEP-ING FACE, LOOKING FOR UNDERWEAR SHE FORGOT IN THE BATHROOM ...
CUT IT OUT! YOU MAKE IT SOUND LIKE I DO STUFF LIKE THAT ALL THE TIME!!
How perverted do you think I am?!!

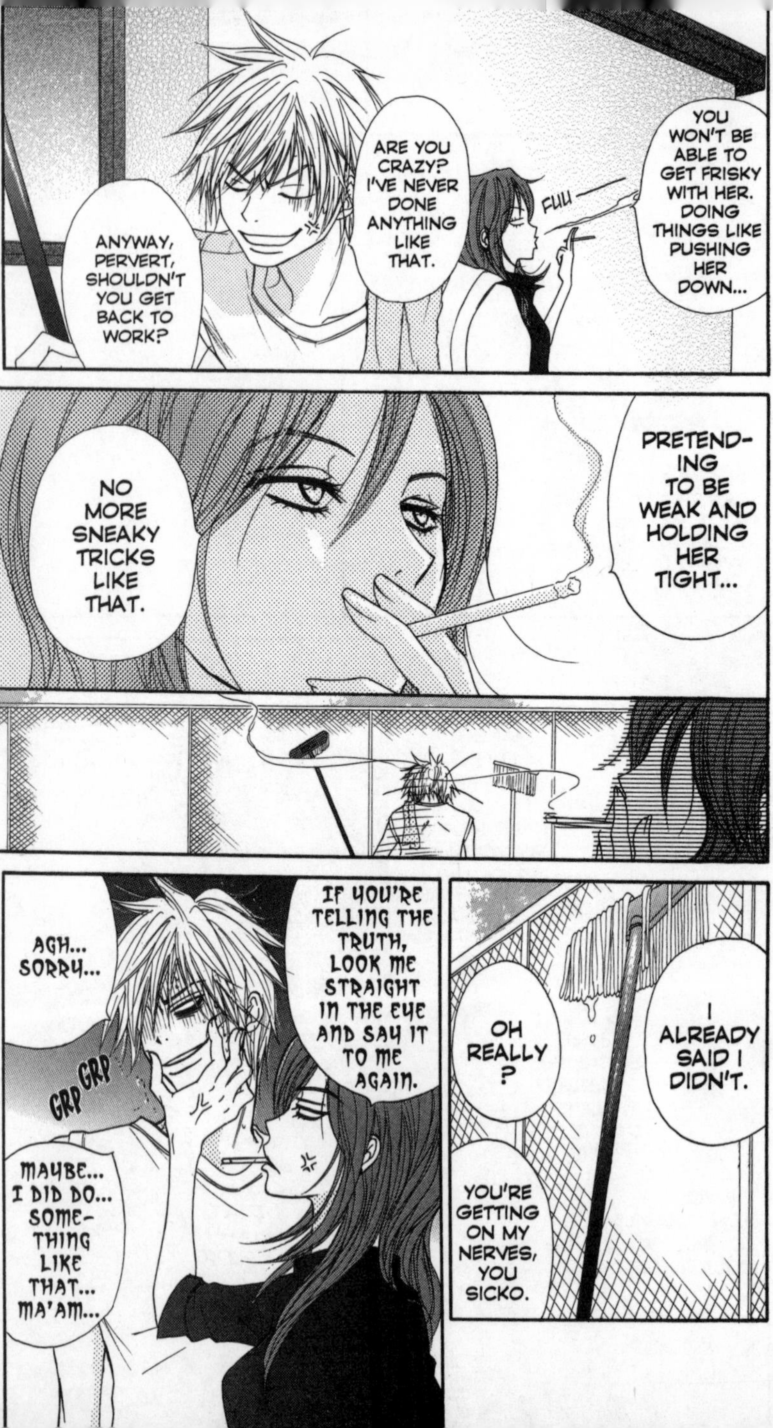
YOU WON'T BE ABLE TO GET FRISKY WITH HER. DOING THINGS LIKE PUSHING HER DOWN...
FUU
ARE YOU CRAZY? I'VE NEVER DONE ANYTHING LIKE THAT.
ANYWAY, PERVERT, SHOULDN'T YOU GET BACK TO WORK?
PRETEND-ING TO BE WEAK AND HOLDING HER TIGHT...
NO MORE SNEAKY TRICKS LIKE THAT.
I ALREADY SAID I DIDN'T.
OH REALLY?
YOU'RE GETTING ON MY NERVES, YOU SICKO.
IF YOU'RE TELLING THE TRUTH, LOOK ME STRAIGHT IN THE EYE AND SAY IT TO ME AGAIN.
AGH... SORRY...
GRP GRP
MAYBE... I DID DO... SOME-THING LIKE THAT... MA'AM...

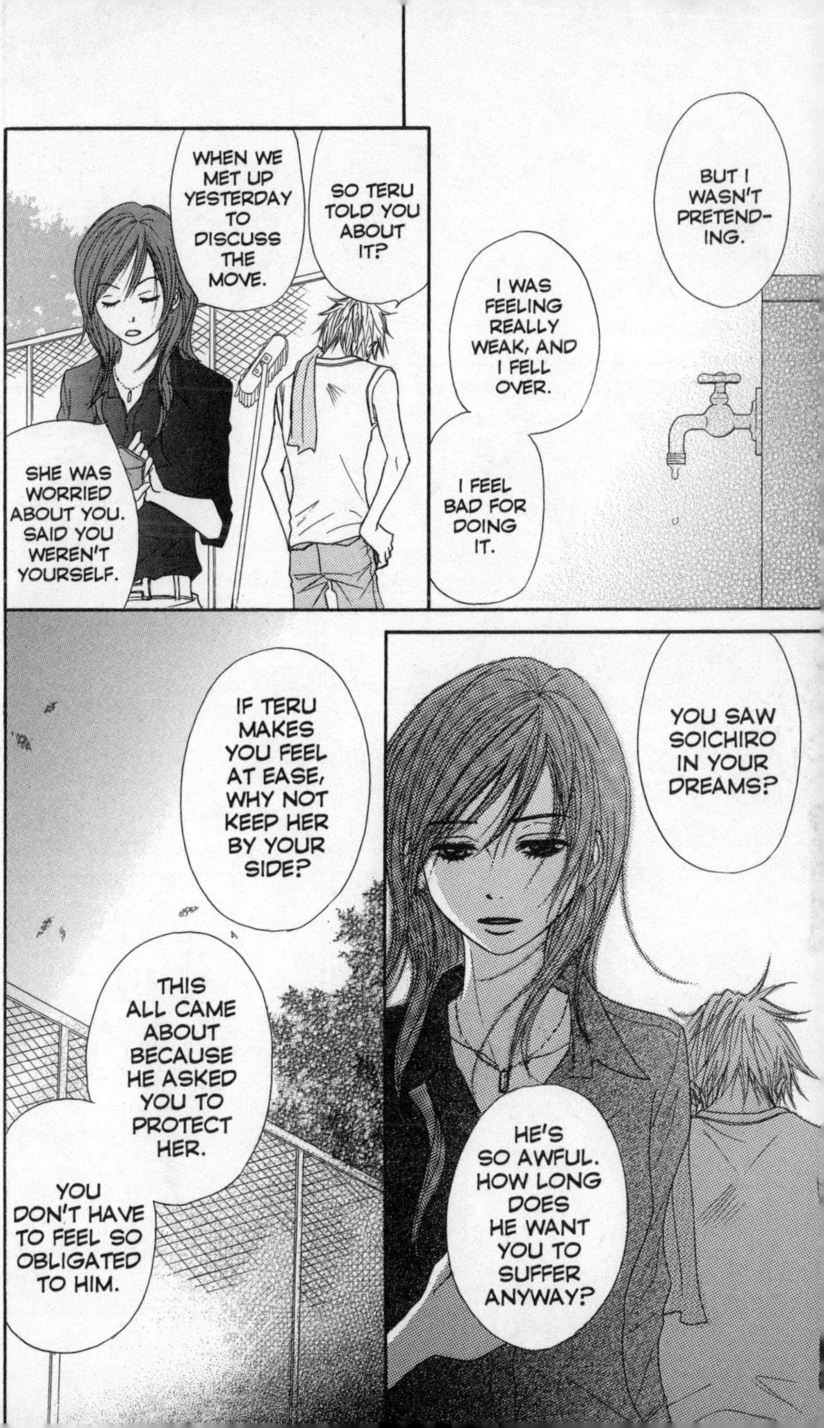
BUT I WASN'T PRETEND-ING.
I WAS FEELING REALLY WEAK, AND I FELL OVER.
I FEEL BAD FOR DOING IT.
SO TERU TOLD YOU ABOUT IT?
WHEN WE MET UP YESTERDAY TO DISCUSS THE MOVE.
SHE WAS WORRIED ABOUT YOU. SAID YOU WEREN'T YOURSELF.
YOU SAW SOICHIRO IN YOUR DREAMS?
HE'S SO AWFUL. HOW LONG DOES HE WANT YOU TO SUFFER ANYWAY?
IF TERU MAKES YOU FEEL AT EASE, WHY NOT KEEP HER BY YOUR SIDE?
THIS ALL CAME ABOUT BECAUSE HE ASKED YOU TO PROTECT HER.
YOU DON'T HAVE TO FEEL SO OBLIGATED TO HIM.

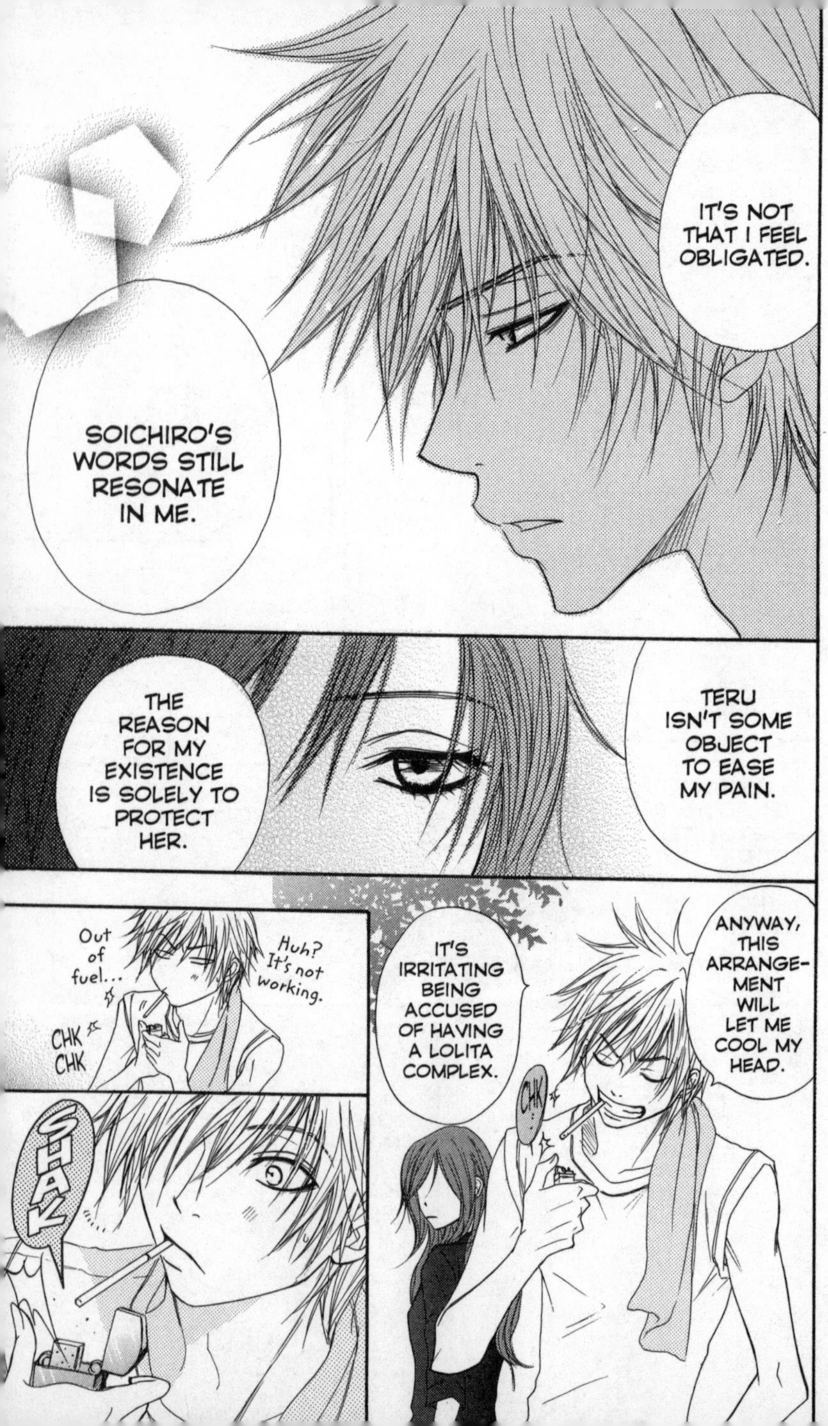
IT'S NOT THAT I FEEL OBLIGATED.
SOICHIRO'S WORDS STILL RESONATE IN ME.
TERU ISN'T SOME OBJECT TO EASE MY PAIN.
THE REASON FOR MY EXISTENCE IS SOLELY TO PROTECT HER.
ANYWAY, THIS ARRANGE-MENT WILL LET ME COOL MY HEAD.
IT'S IRRITATING BEING ACCUSED OF HAVING A LOLITA COMPLEX.
CHK
Huh? It's not working.
Out of fuel...
CHK CHK
SHAK

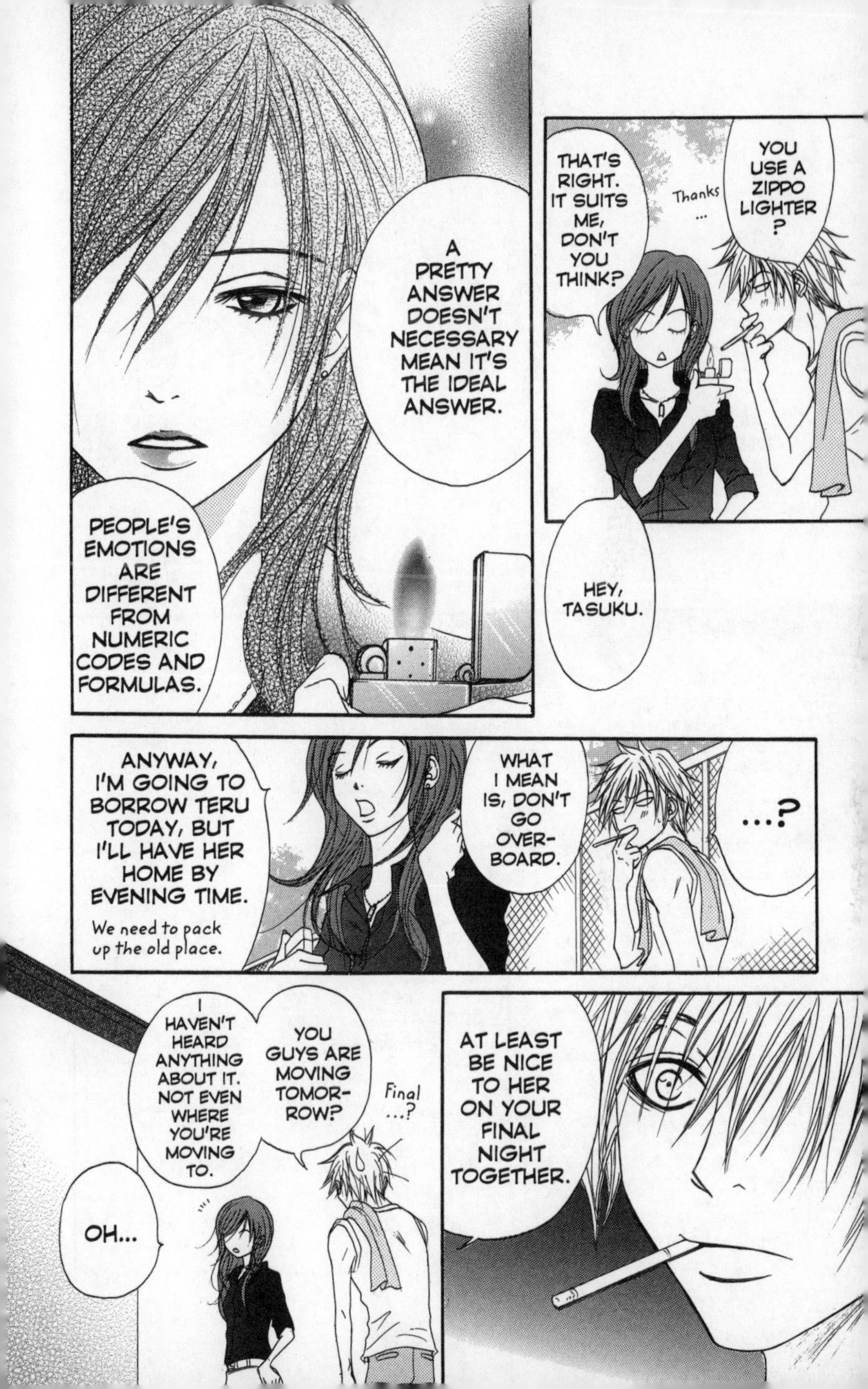
YOU USE A ZIPPO LIGHTER?
Thanks...
THAT'S RIGHT. IT SUITS ME, DON'T YOU THINK?
HEY, TASUKU.
A PRETTY ANSWER DOESN'T NECESSARY MEAN IT'S THE IDEAL ANSWER.
PEOPLE'S EMOTIONS ARE DIFFERENT FROM NUMERIC CODES AND FORMULAS.
...?
WHAT I MEAN IS, DON'T GO OVER-BOARD.
ANYWAY, I'M GOING TO BORROW TERU TODAY, BUT I'LL HAVE HER HOME BY EVENING TIME.
We need to pack up the old place.
AT LEAST BE NICE TO HER ON YOUR FINAL NIGHT TOGETHER.
Final ...?
YOU GUYS ARE MOVING TOMOR-ROW?
I HAVEN'T HEARD ANYTHING ABOUT IT. NOT EVEN WHERE YOU'RE MOVING TO.
OH...

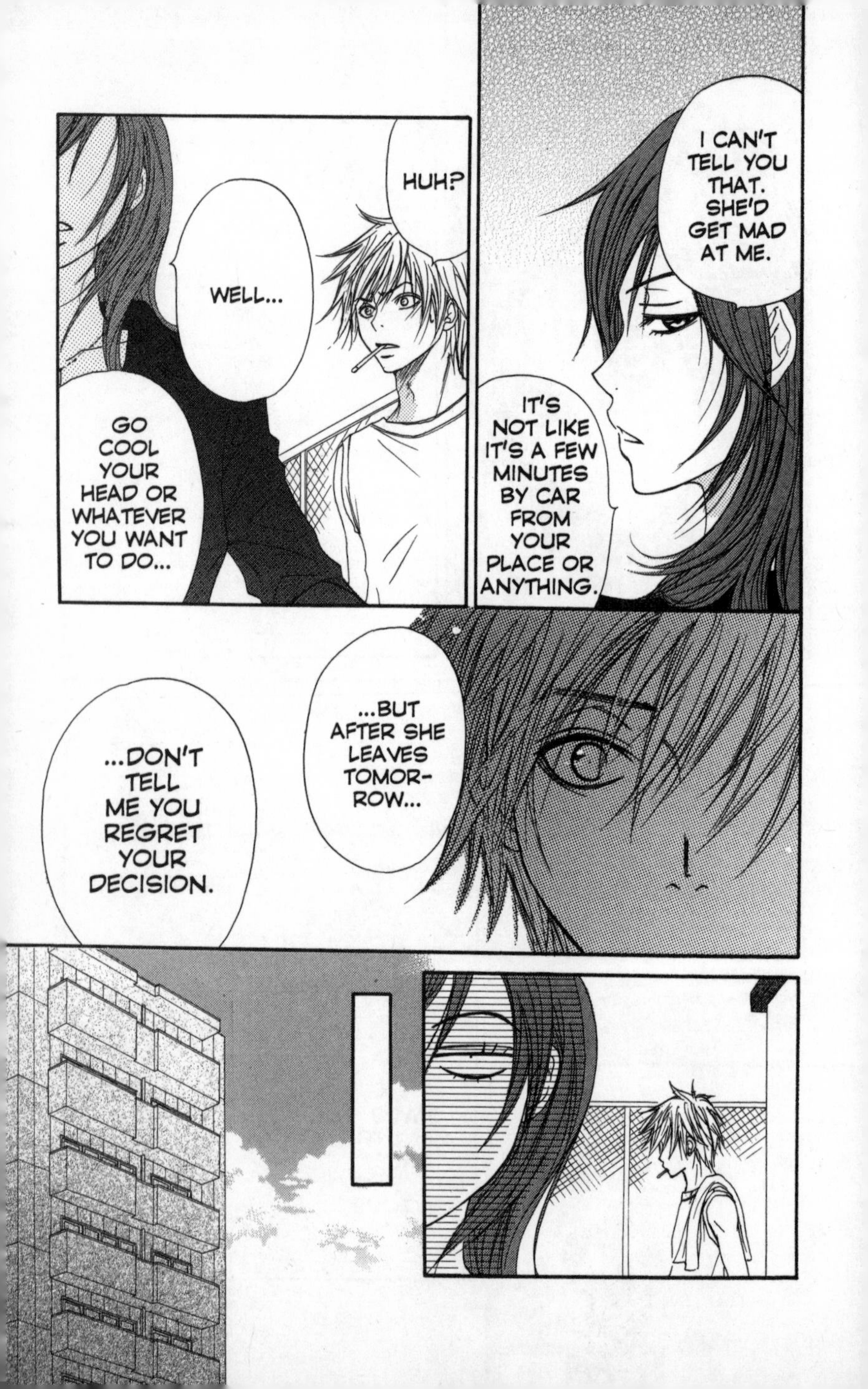
I CAN'T TELL YOU THAT. SHE'D GET MAD AT ME.
IT'S NOT LIKE IT'S A FEW MINUTES BY CAR FROM YOUR PLACE OR ANYTHING.
HUH?
WELL...
GO COOL YOUR HEAD OR WHATEVER YOU WANT TO DO...
...BUT AFTER SHE LEAVES TOMOR-ROW...
...DON'T TELL ME YOU REGRET YOUR DECISION.

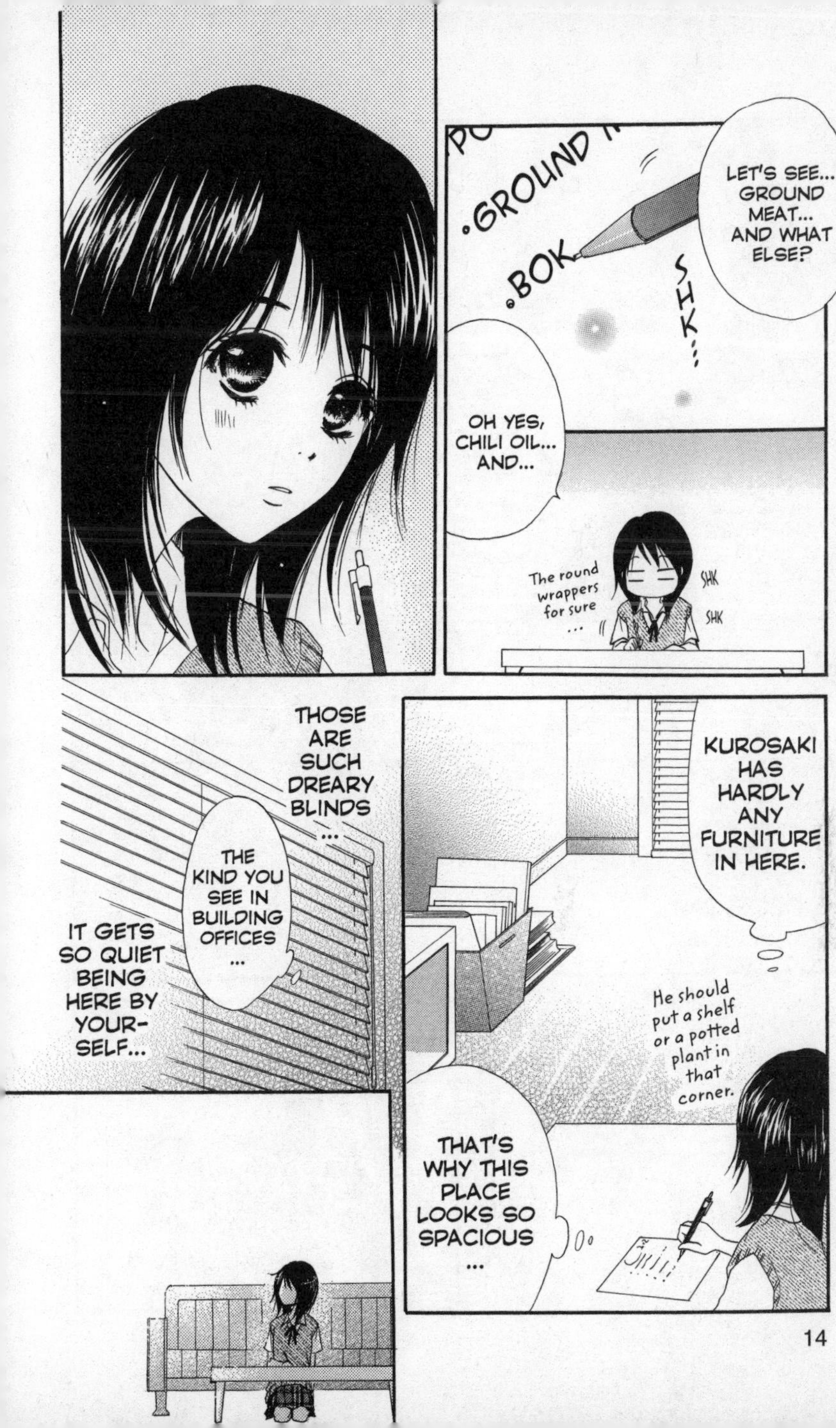

LET'S SEE... GROUND MEAT... AND WHAT ELSE?
GROUND
BOK
SHK...
OH YES, CHILI OIL... AND...
The round wrappers for sure ...
SHK
SHK
KUROSAKI HAS HARDLY ANY FURNITURE IN HERE.
He should put a shelf or a potted plant in that corner.
THAT'S WHY THIS PLACE LOOKS SO SPACIOUS ...
THOSE ARE SUCH DREARY BLINDS ...
THE KIND YOU SEE IN BUILDING OFFICES ...
IT GETS SO QUIET BEING HERE BY YOURSELF...

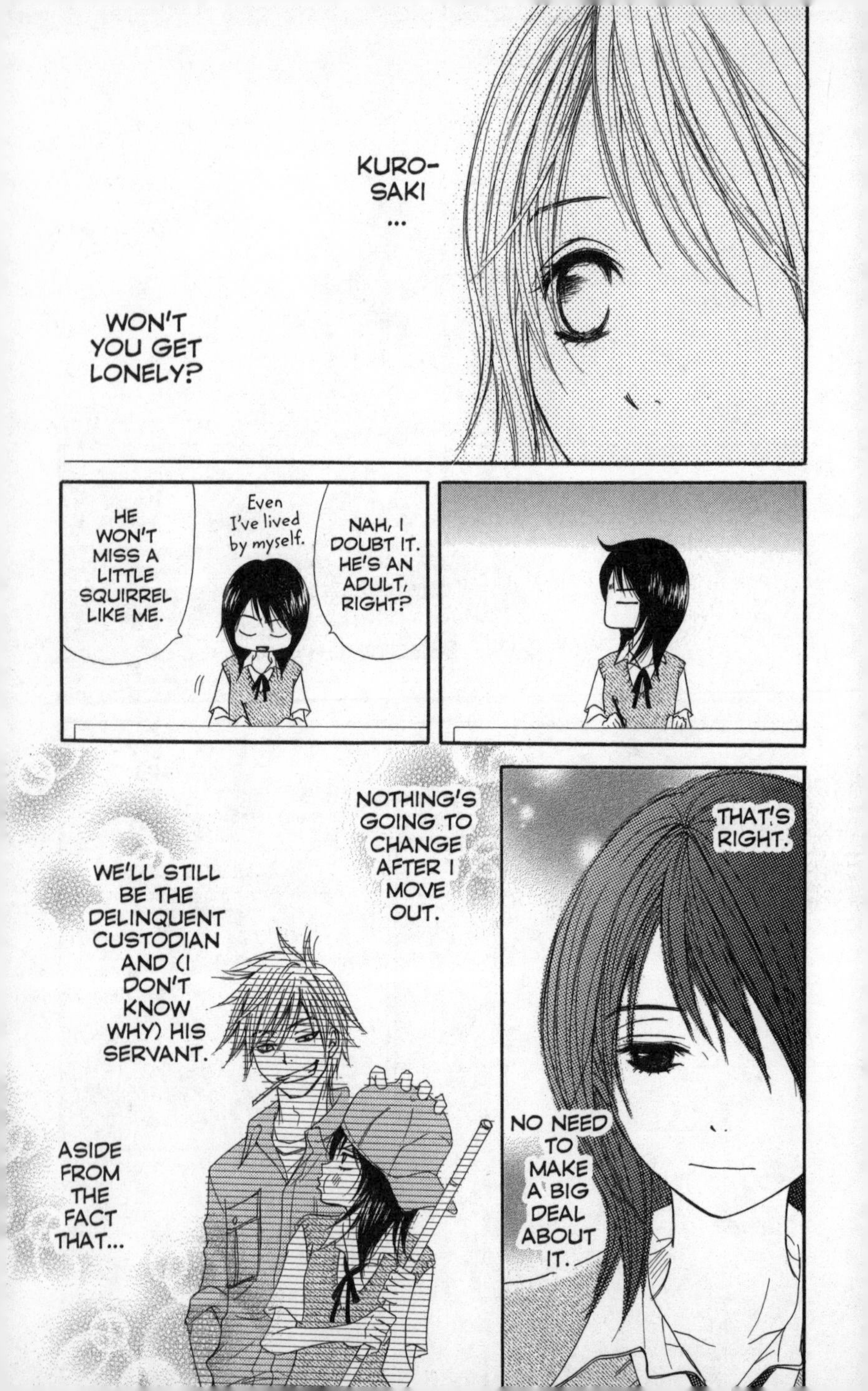

KURO-SAKI...
WON'T YOU GET LONELY?
NAH, I DOUBT IT. HE'S AN ADULT, RIGHT?
Even I've lived by myself.
HE WON'T MISS A LITTLE SQUIRREL LIKE ME.
THAT'S RIGHT.
NO NEED TO MAKE A BIG DEAL ABOUT IT.
NOTHING'S GOING TO CHANGE AFTER I MOVE OUT.
WE'LL STILL BE THE DELINQUENT CUSTODIAN AND (I DON'T KNOW WHY) HIS SERVANT.
ASIDE FROM THE FACT THAT...

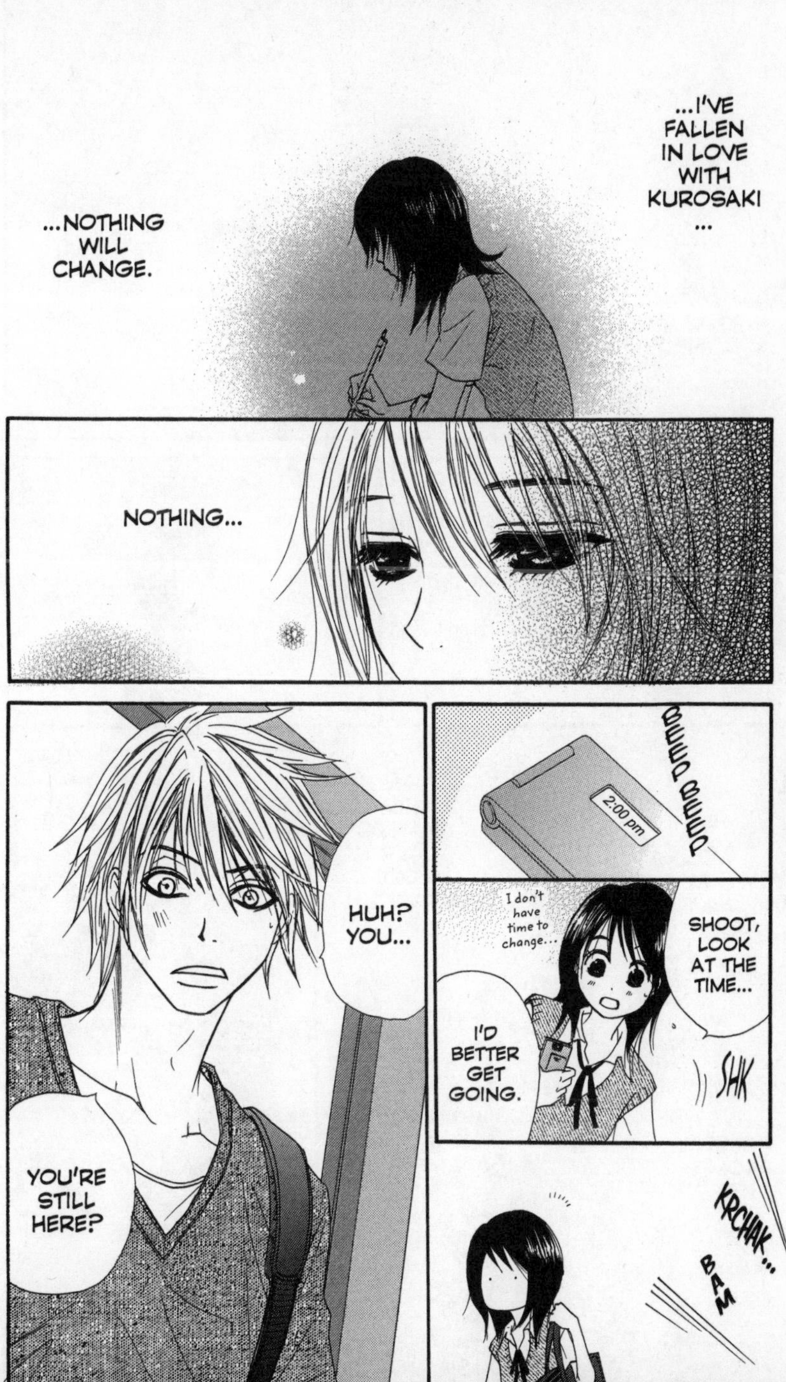
...I'VE FALLEN IN LOVE WITH KUROSAKI ...
...NOTHING WILL CHANGE.
NOTHING...
BEEP BEEP
2:00 pm
SHOOT, LOOK AT THE TIME...
I don't have time to change...
I'D BETTER GET GOING.
SHK
KRCHAK...
BAM
HUH? YOU...
YOU'RE STILL HERE?

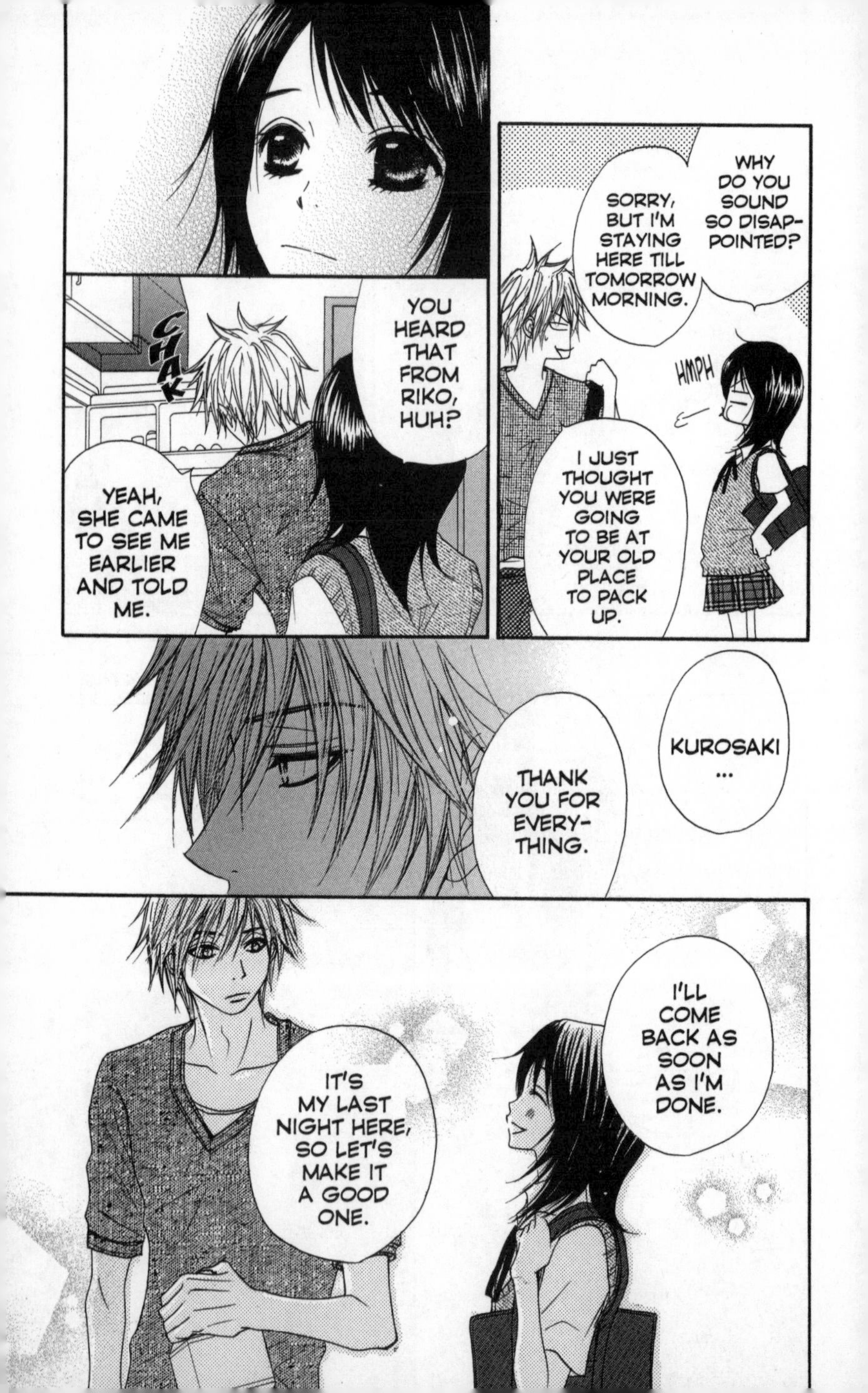
WHY DO YOU SOUND SO DISAPPOINTED?
SORRY, BUT I'M STAYING HERE TILL TOMORROW MORNING.
HMPH
I JUST THOUGHT YOU WERE GOING TO BE AT YOUR OLD PLACE TO PACK UP.
CHAK
YOU HEARD THAT FROM RIKO, HUH?
YEAH, SHE CAME TO SEE ME EARLIER AND TOLD ME.
KUROSAKI...
THANK YOU FOR EVERYTHING.
I'LL COME BACK AS SOON AS I'M DONE.
IT'S MY LAST NIGHT HERE, SO LET'S MAKE IT A GOOD ONE.

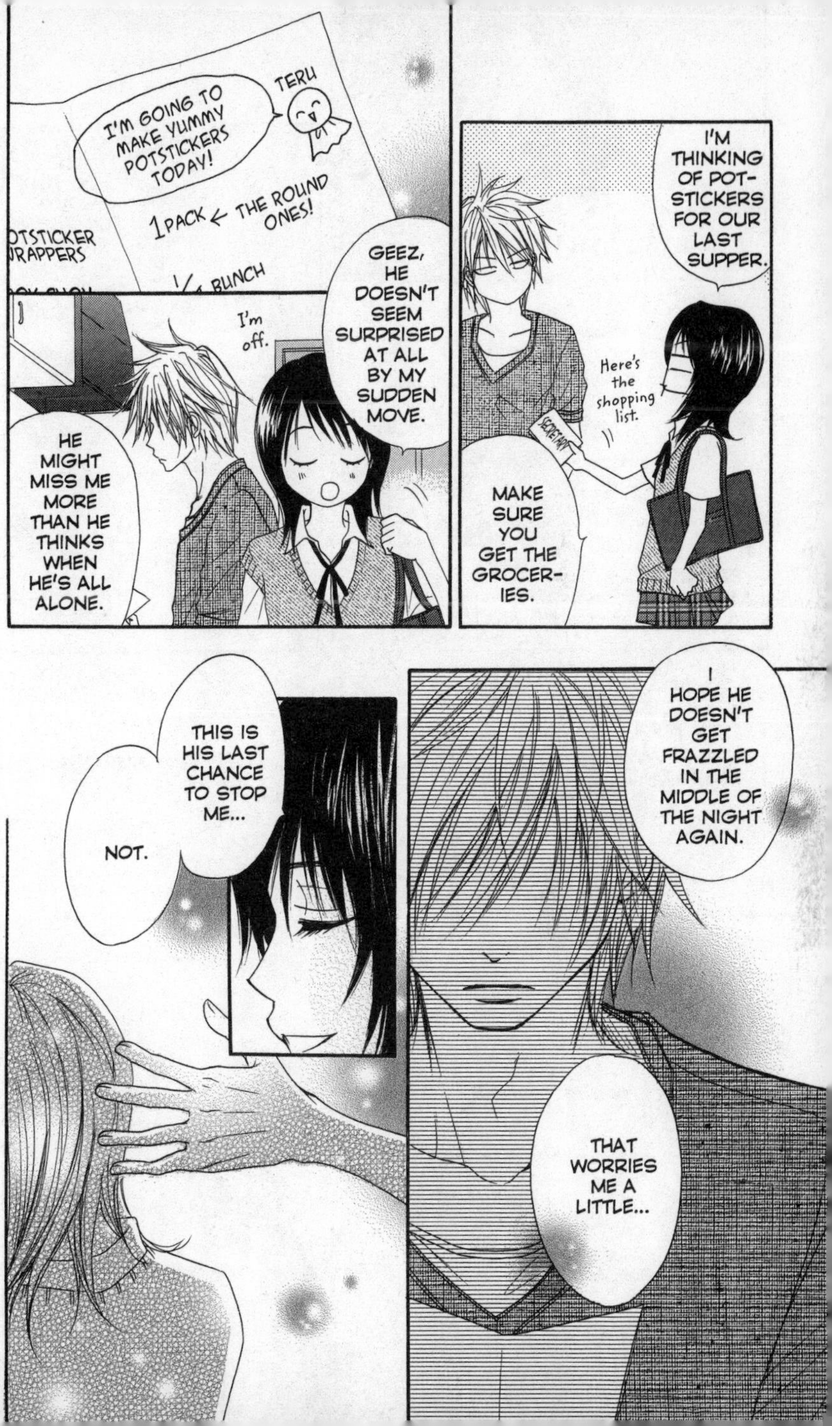
I'M THINKING OF POT-STICKERS FOR OUR LAST SUPPER.
Here's the shopping list.
SECRETARY
MAKE SURE YOU GET THE GROCER-IES.
TERU
I'M GOING TO MAKE YUMMY POTSTICKERS TODAY!
1PACK ← THE ROUND ONES!
OTSTICKER
RAPPERS
1/4 BUNCH
GEEZ, HE DOESN'T SEEM SURPRISED AT ALL BY MY SUDDEN MOVE.
I'm off.
HE MIGHT MISS ME MORE THAN HE THINKS WHEN HE'S ALL ALONE.
I HOPE HE DOESN'T GET FRAZZLED IN THE MIDDLE OF THE NIGHT AGAIN.
THAT WORRIES ME A LITTLE...
THIS IS HIS LAST CHANCE TO STOP ME...
NOT.

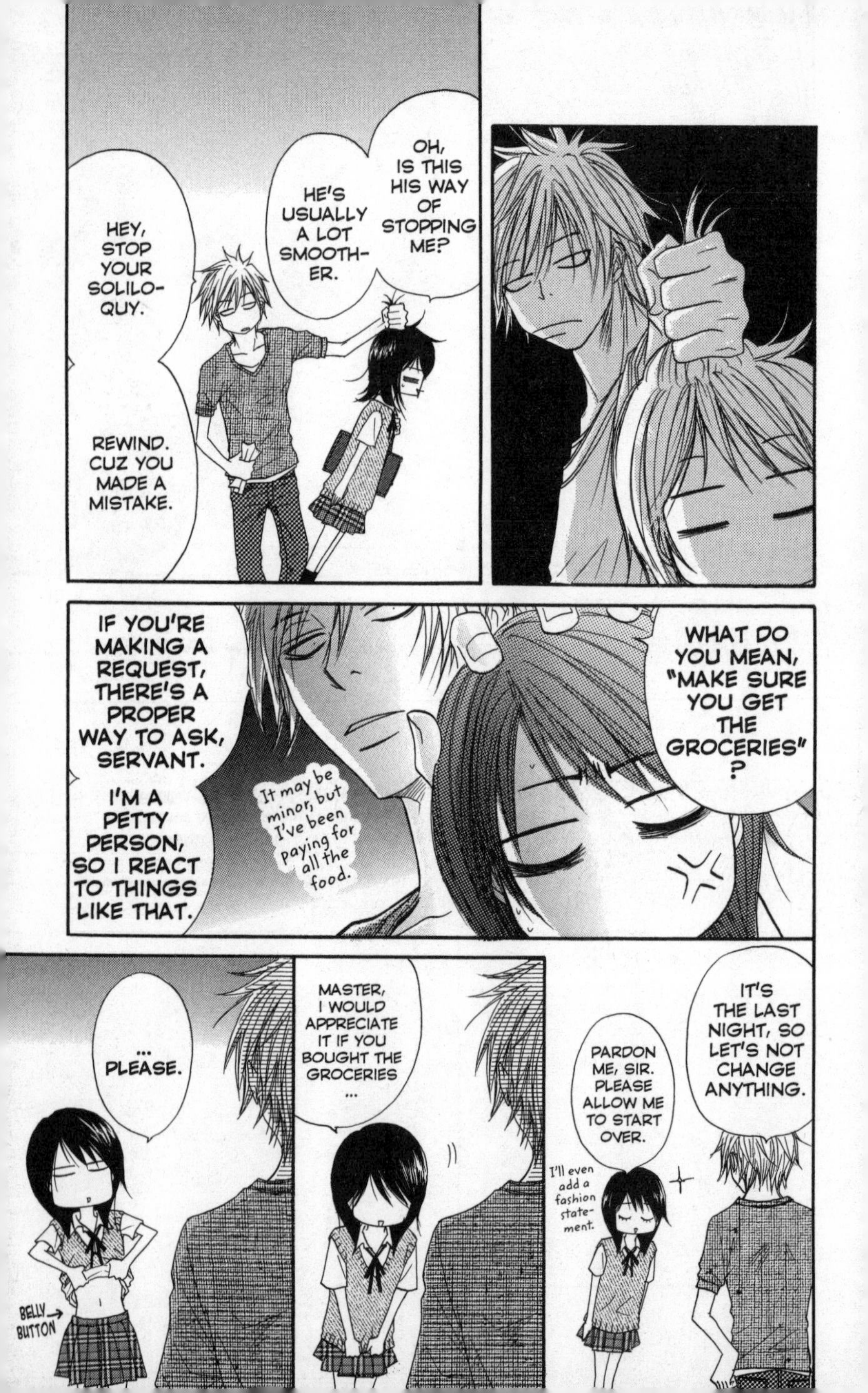
OH, IS THIS HIS WAY OF STOPPING ME?
HE'S USUALLY A LOT SMOOTH-ER.
HEY, STOP YOUR SOLILO-QUY.
REWIND. CUZ YOU MADE A MISTAKE.
WHAT DO YOU MEAN, "MAKE SURE YOU GET THE GROCERIES"?
IF YOU'RE MAKING A REQUEST, THERE'S A PROPER WAY TO ASK, SERVANT.
It may be minor, but I've been paying for all the food.
I'M A PETTY PERSON, SO I REACT TO THINGS LIKE THAT.
IT'S THE LAST NIGHT, SO LET'S NOT CHANGE ANYTHING.
PARDON ME, SIR. PLEASE ALLOW ME TO START OVER.
I'll even add a fashion state-ment.
MASTER, I WOULD APPRECIATE IT IF YOU BOUGHT THE GROCERIES...
... PLEASE.
BELLY BUTTON

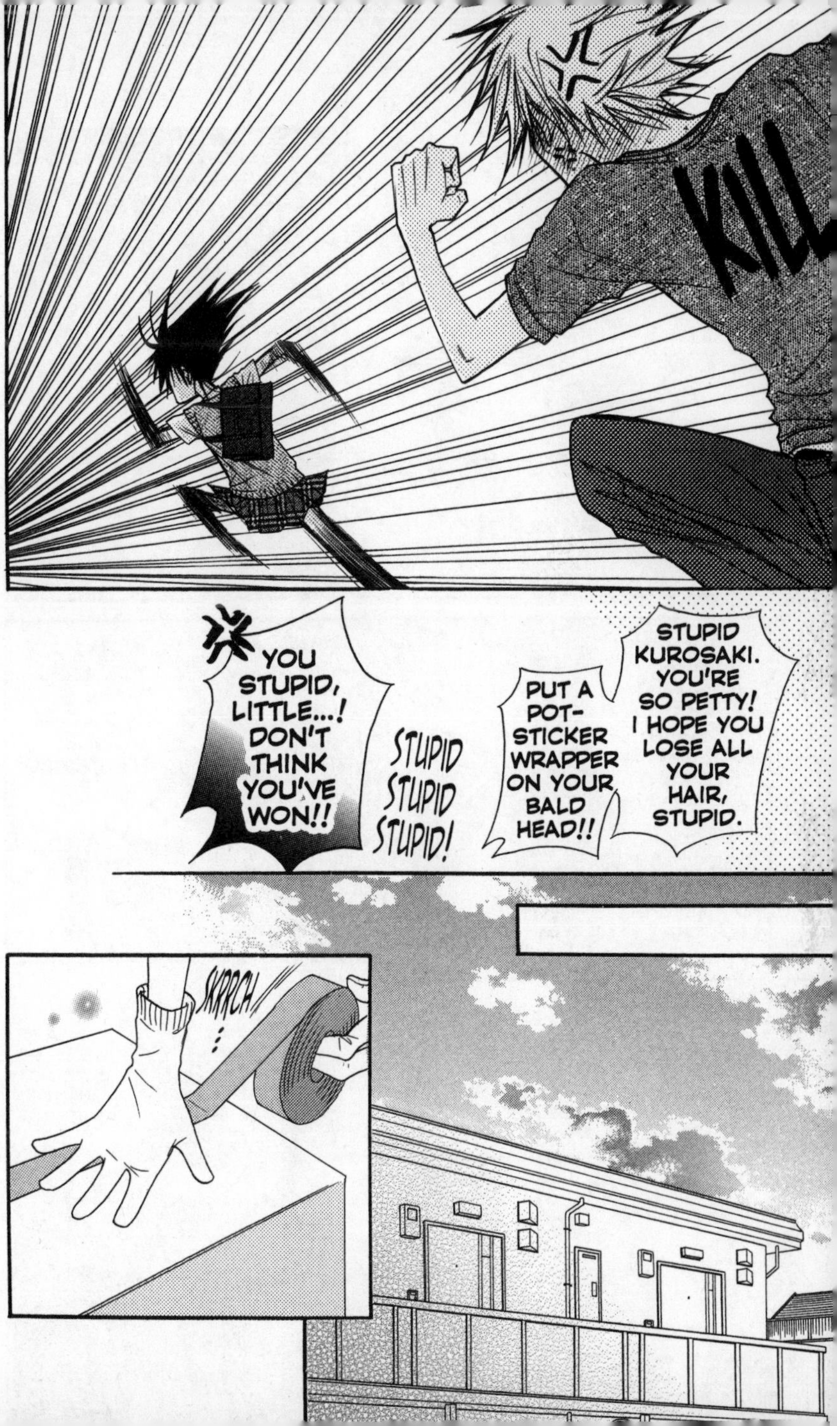
KILL
STUPID KUROSAKI. YOU'RE SO PETTY! I HOPE YOU LOSE ALL YOUR HAIR, STUPID.
PUT A POT-STICKER WRAPPER ON YOUR BALD HEAD!!
STUPID STUPID STUPID!
YOU STUPID, LITTLE...! DON'T THINK YOU'VE WON!!
SKRRCH

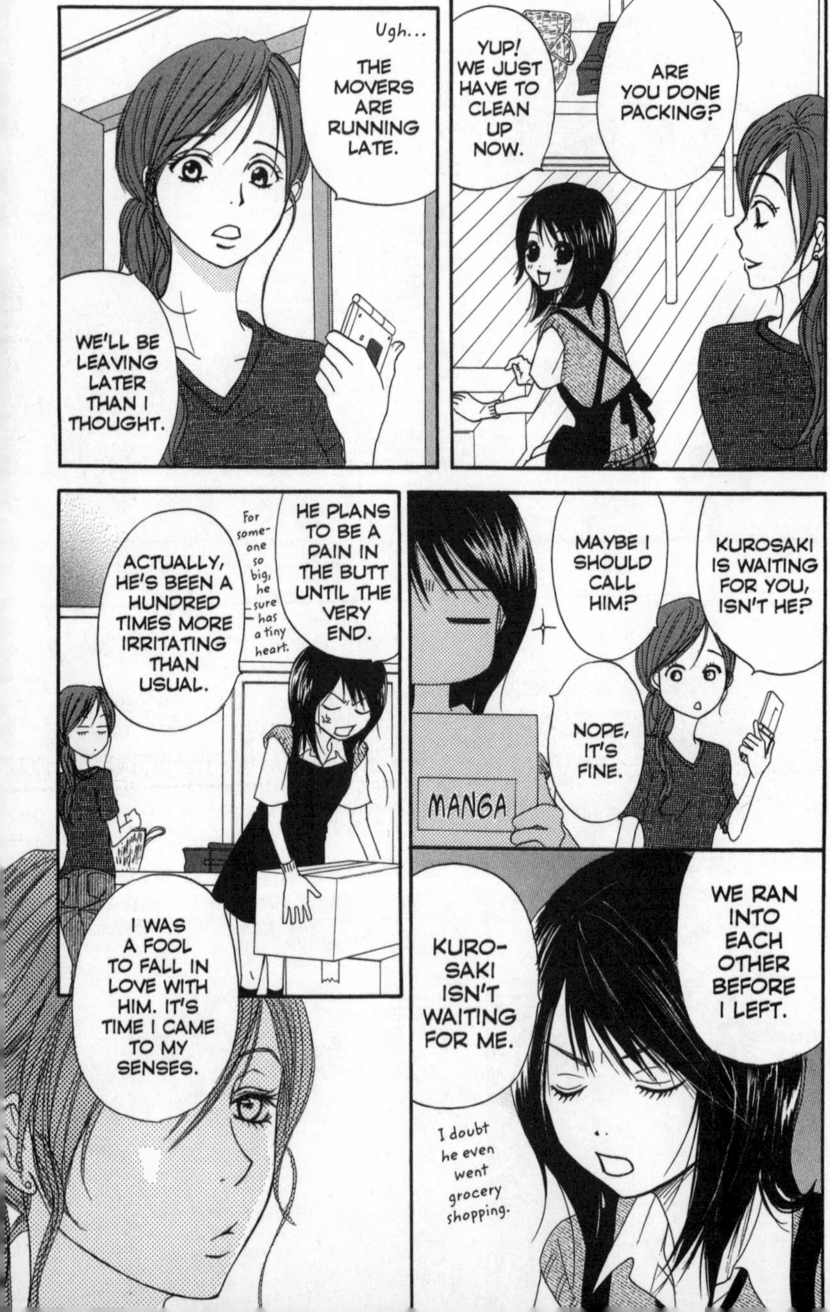
ARE YOU DONE PACKING?
YUP! WE JUST HAVE TO CLEAN UP NOW.
Ugh...
THE MOVERS ARE RUNNING LATE.
WE'LL BE LEAVING LATER THAN I THOUGHT.
KUROSAKI IS WAITING FOR YOU, ISN'T HE?
MAYBE I SHOULD CALL HIM?
NOPE, IT'S FINE.
MANGA
WE RAN INTO EACH OTHER BEFORE I LEFT.
KURO-SAKI ISN'T WAITING FOR ME.
I doubt he even went grocery shopping.
HE PLANS TO BE A PAIN IN THE BUTT UNTIL THE VERY END.
For someone so big, he sure has a tiny heart.
ACTUALLY, HE'S BEEN A HUNDRED TIMES MORE IRRITATING THAN USUAL.
I WAS A FOOL TO FALL IN LOVE WITH HIM. IT'S TIME I CAME TO MY SENSES.

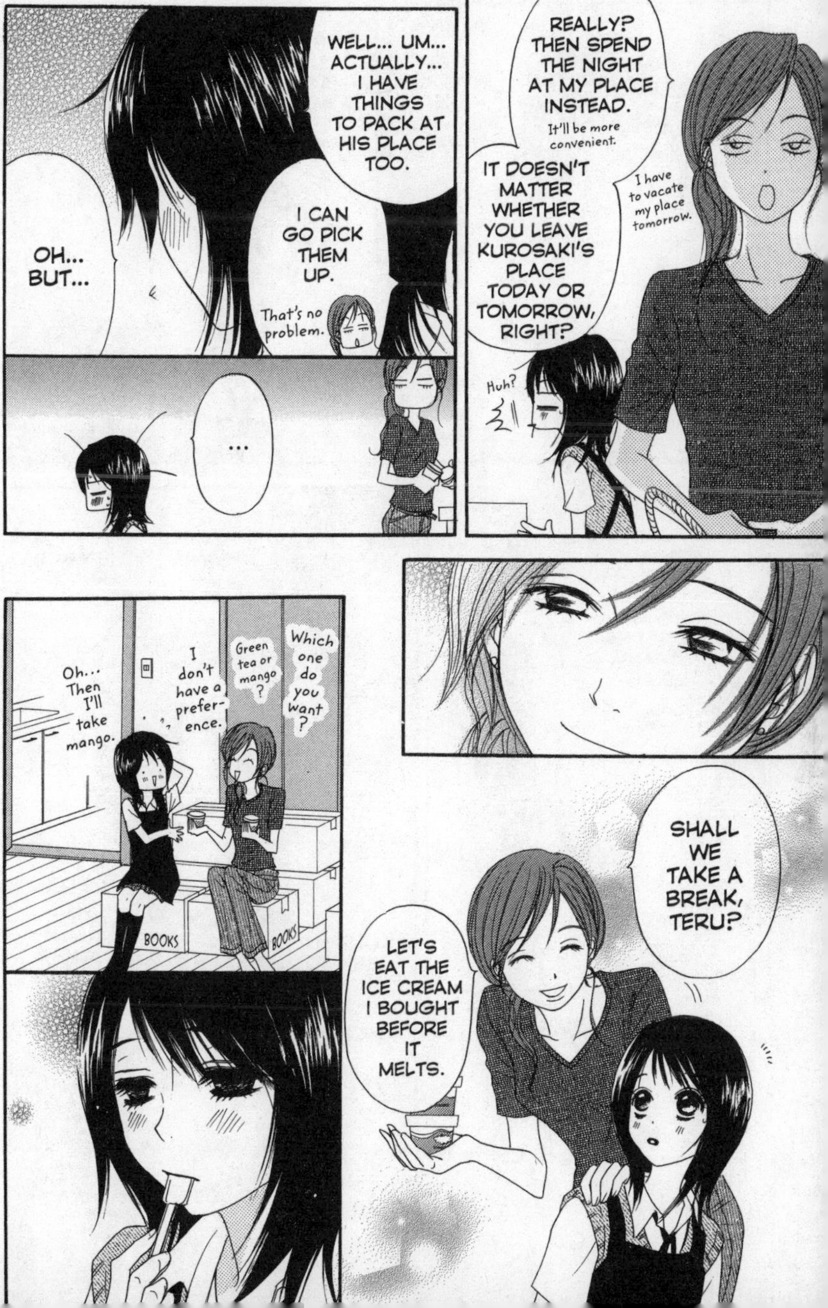
REALLY? THEN SPEND THE NIGHT AT MY PLACE INSTEAD.
It'll be more convenient.
I have to vacate my place tomorrow.
IT DOESN'T MATTER WHETHER YOU LEAVE KUROSAKI'S PLACE TODAY OR TOMORROW, RIGHT?
Huh?
WELL... UM... ACTUALLY... I HAVE THINGS TO PACK AT HIS PLACE TOO.
I CAN GO PICK THEM UP.
That's no problem.
OH... BUT...
...
SHALL WE TAKE A BREAK, TERU?
LET'S EAT THE ICE CREAM I BOUGHT BEFORE IT MELTS.
Which one do you want?
Green tea or mango?
I don't have a preference.
Oh... Then I'll take mango.
BOOKS
BOOKS

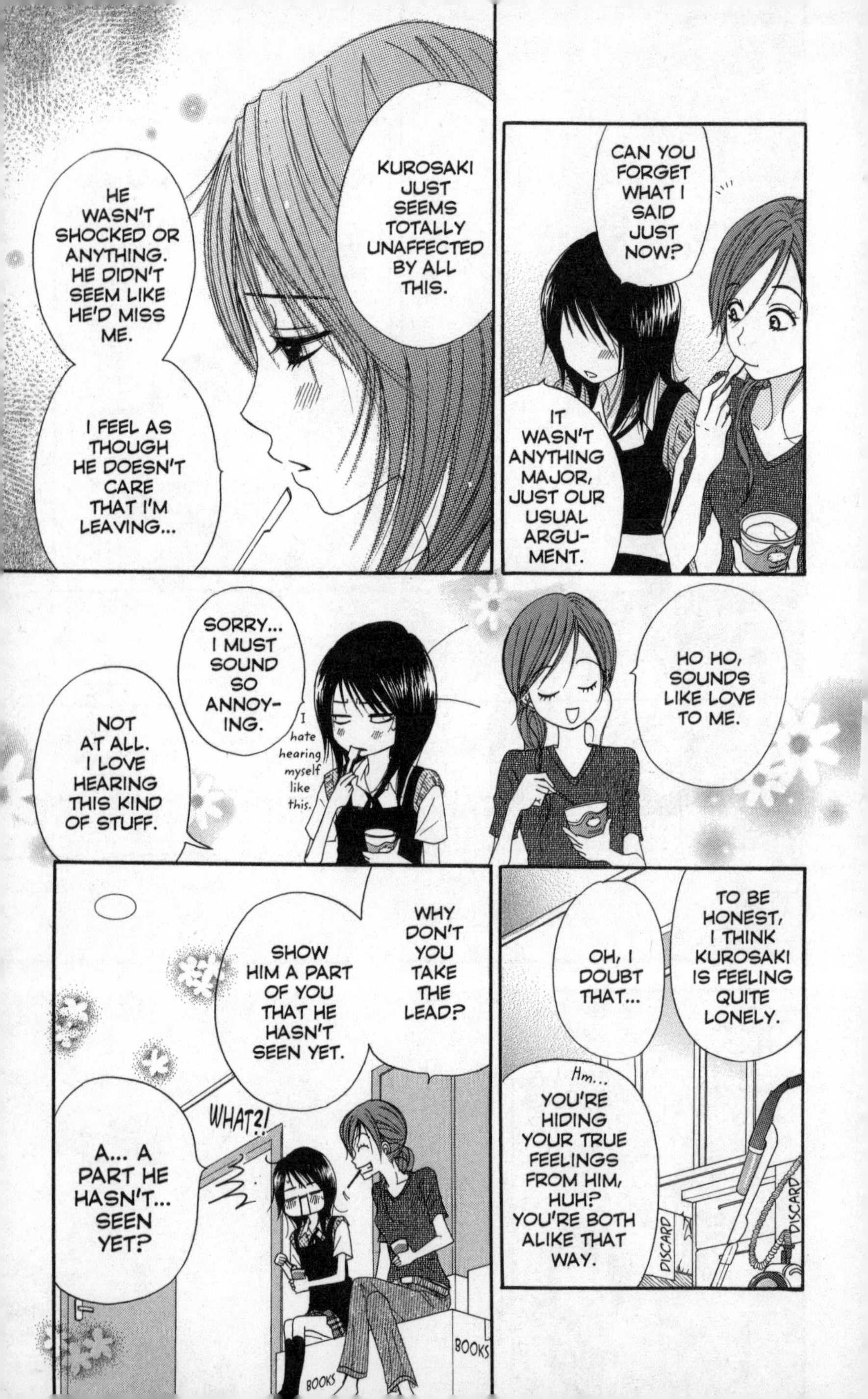
CAN YOU FORGET WHAT I SAID JUST NOW?
IT WASN'T ANYTHING MAJOR, JUST OUR USUAL ARGUMENT.
KUROSAKI JUST SEEMS TOTALLY UNAFFECTED BY ALL THIS.
HE WASN'T SHOCKED OR ANYTHING. HE DIDN'T SEEM LIKE HE'D MISS ME.
I FEEL AS THOUGH HE DOESN'T CARE THAT I'M LEAVING...
HO HO, SOUNDS LIKE LOVE TO ME.
SORRY... I MUST SOUND SO ANNOY-ING.
I hate hearing myself like this.
NOT AT ALL. I LOVE HEARING THIS KIND OF STUFF.
TO BE HONEST, I THINK KUROSAKI IS FEELING QUITE LONELY.
OH, I DOUBT THAT...
Hm...
YOU'RE HIDING YOUR TRUE FEELINGS FROM HIM, HUH? YOU'RE BOTH ALIKE THAT WAY.
DISCARD
DISCARD
WHY DON'T YOU TAKE THE LEAD?
SHOW HIM A PART OF YOU THAT HE HASN'T SEEN YET.
WHAT?!
A... A PART HE HASN'T... SEEN YET?
BOOKS
BOOKS

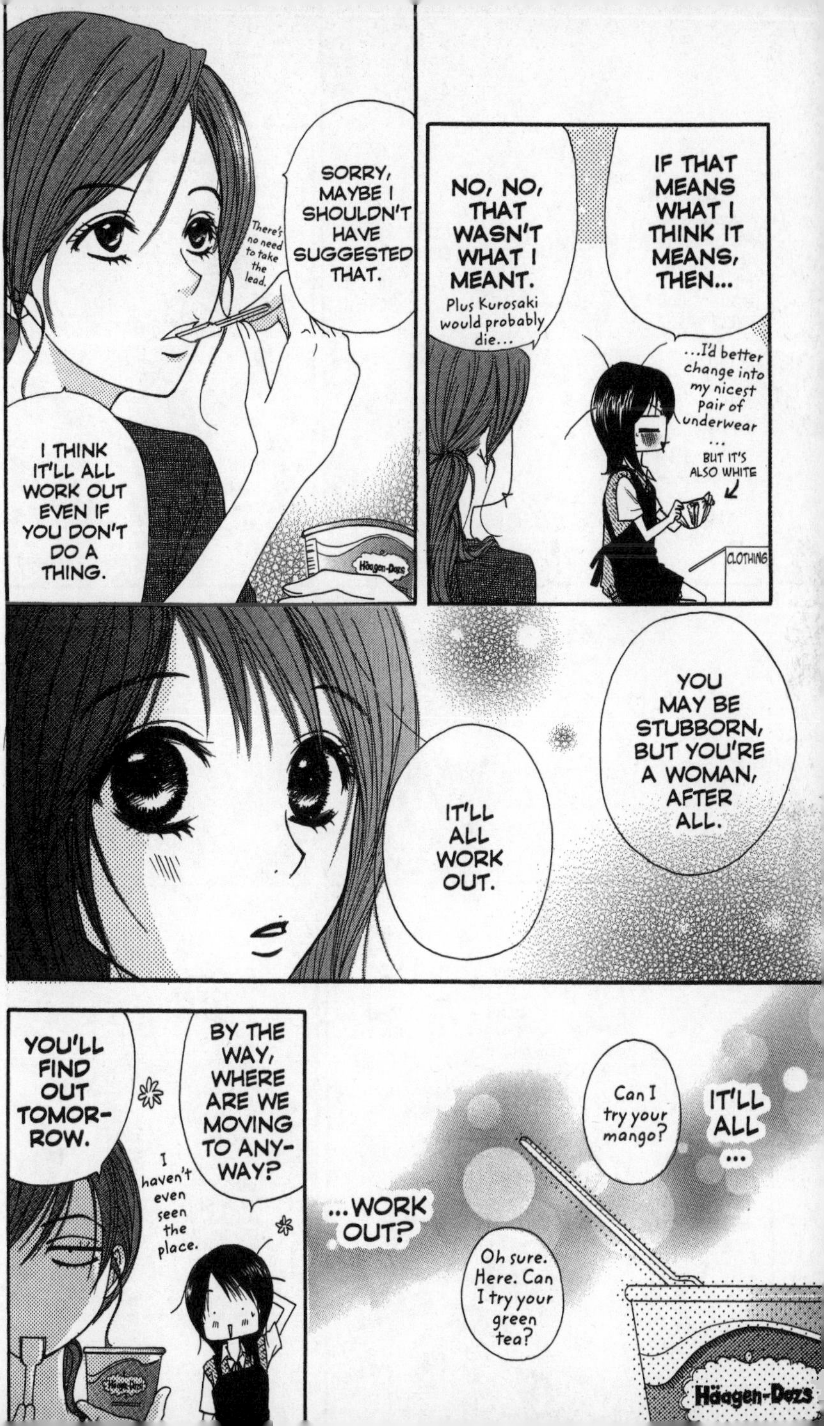
IF THAT MEANS WHAT I THINK IT MEANS, THEN...
NO, NO, THAT WASN'T WHAT I MEANT.
Plus Kurosaki would probably die...
...I'd better change into my nicest pair of underwear...
BUT IT'S ALSO WHITE
CLOTHING
SORRY, MAYBE I SHOULDN'T HAVE SUGGESTED THAT.
There's no need to take the lead.
I THINK IT'LL ALL WORK OUT EVEN IF YOU DON'T DO A THING.
Häagen-Dazs
YOU MAY BE STUBBORN, BUT YOU'RE A WOMAN, AFTER ALL.
IT'LL ALL WORK OUT.
IT'LL ALL...
Can I try your mango?
...WORK OUT?
Oh sure. Here. Can I try your green tea?
Häagen-Dazs
BY THE WAY, WHERE ARE WE MOVING TO ANYWAY?
YOU'LL FIND OUT TOMORROW.
I haven't even seen the place.

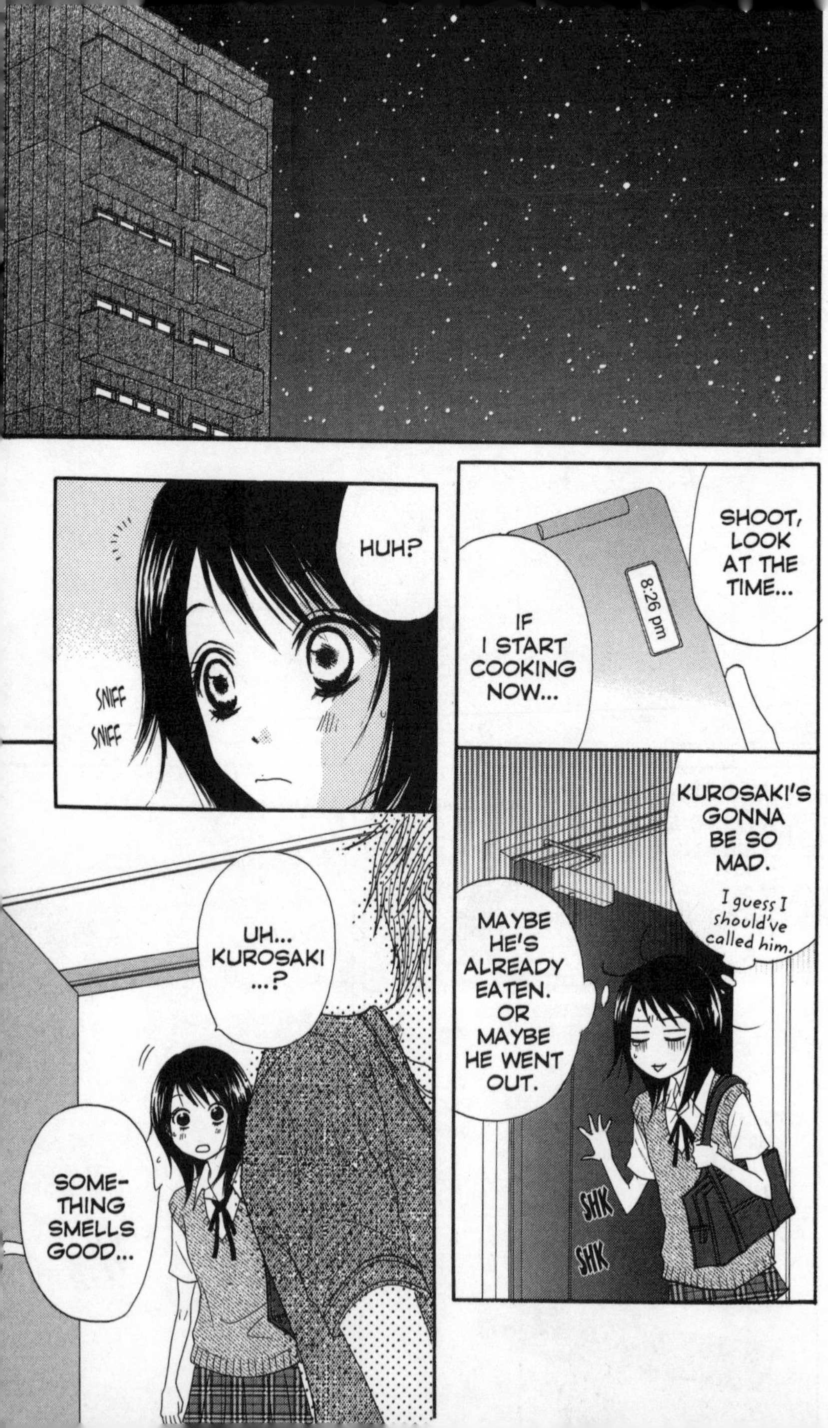
SHOOT, LOOK AT THE TIME...
8:26 pm
IF I START COOKING NOW...
HUH?
SNIFF SNIFF
KUROSAKI'S GONNA BE SO MAD.
I guess I should've called him.
MAYBE HE'S ALREADY EATEN. OR MAYBE HE WENT OUT.
SHK SHK
UH... KUROSAKI ...?
SOME-THING SMELLS GOOD...

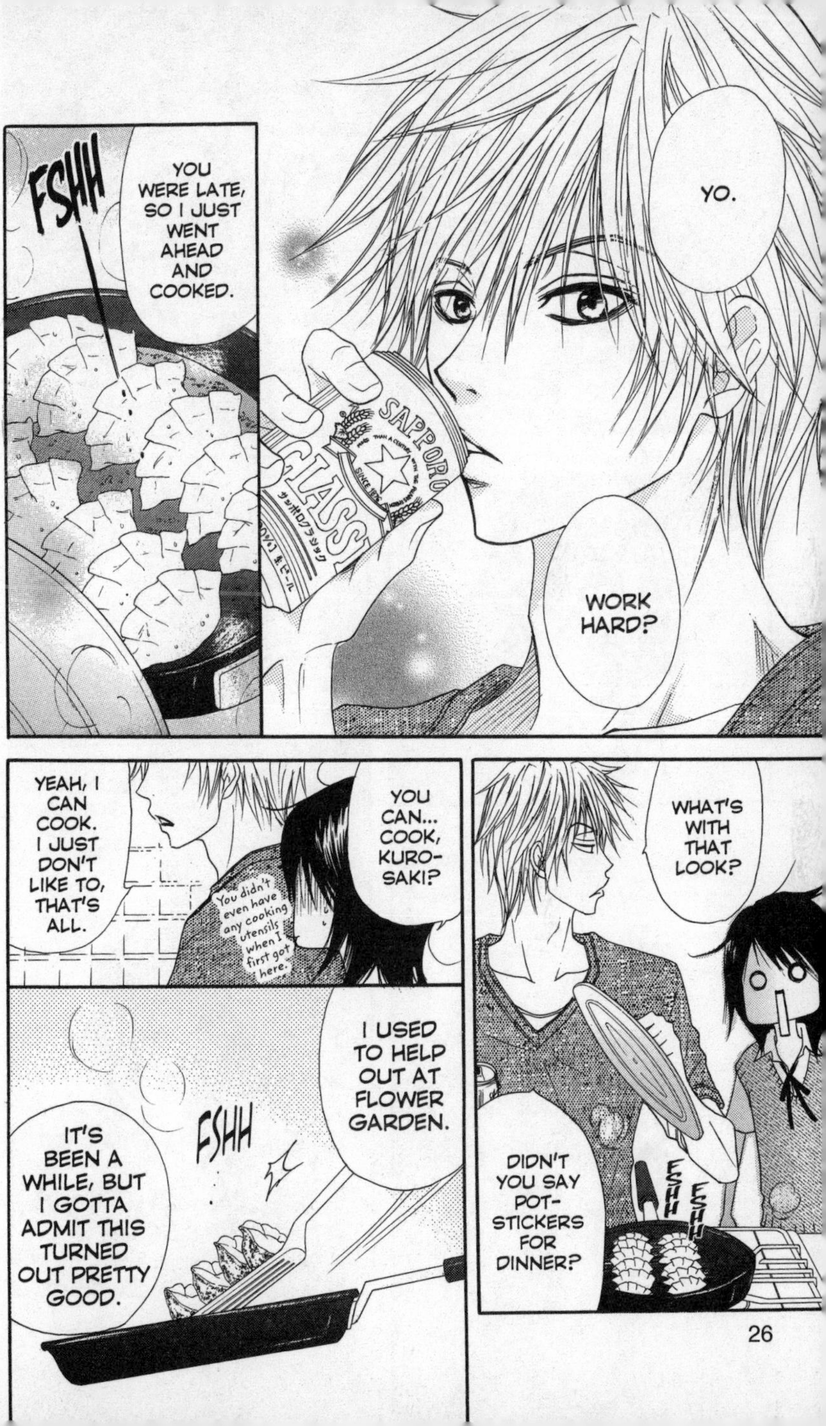
YO.
WORK HARD?
YOU WERE LATE, SO I JUST WENT AHEAD AND COOKED.
FSHH
WHAT'S WITH THAT LOOK?
DIDN'T YOU SAY POT-STICKERS FOR DINNER?
FSHH FSHH
YOU CAN... COOK, KURO-SAKI?
You didn't even have any cooking utensils when I first got here.
YEAH, I CAN COOK. I JUST DON'T LIKE TO, THAT'S ALL.
I USED TO HELP OUT AT FLOWER GARDEN.
FSHH
IT'S BEEN A WHILE, BUT I GOTTA ADMIT THIS TURNED OUT PRETTY GOOD.

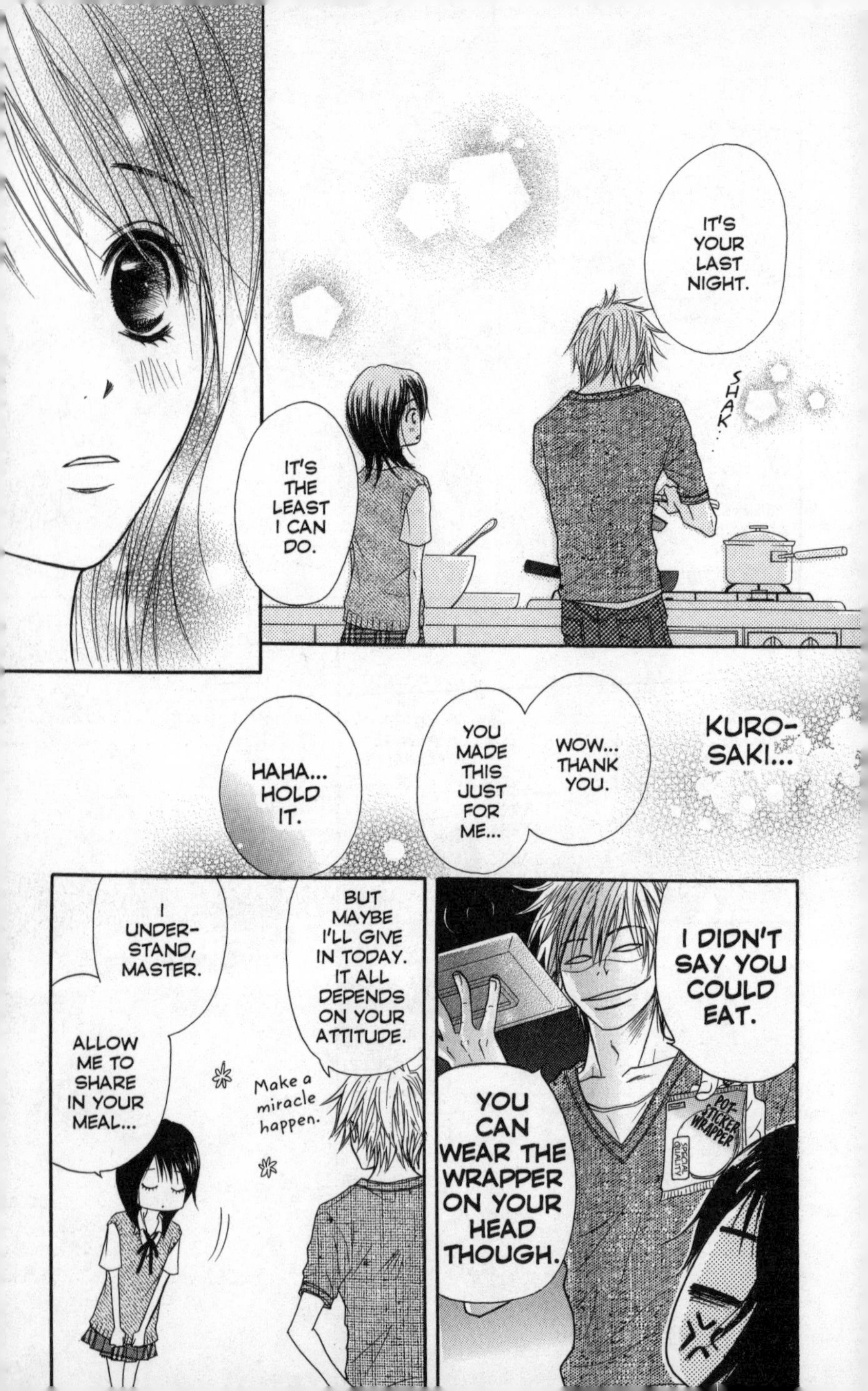
IT'S YOUR LAST NIGHT.
SHAK...
IT'S THE LEAST I CAN DO.
KURO-SAKI...
WOW... THANK YOU.
YOU MADE THIS JUST FOR ME...
HAHA... HOLD IT.
I DIDN'T SAY YOU COULD EAT.
POT-STICKER WRAPPER
SPECIAL QUALITY
YOU CAN WEAR THE WRAPPER ON YOUR HEAD THOUGH.
BUT MAYBE I'LL GIVE IN TODAY. IT ALL DEPENDS ON YOUR ATTITUDE.
I UNDER-STAND, MASTER.
ALLOW ME TO SHARE IN YOUR MEAL...
Make a miracle happen.

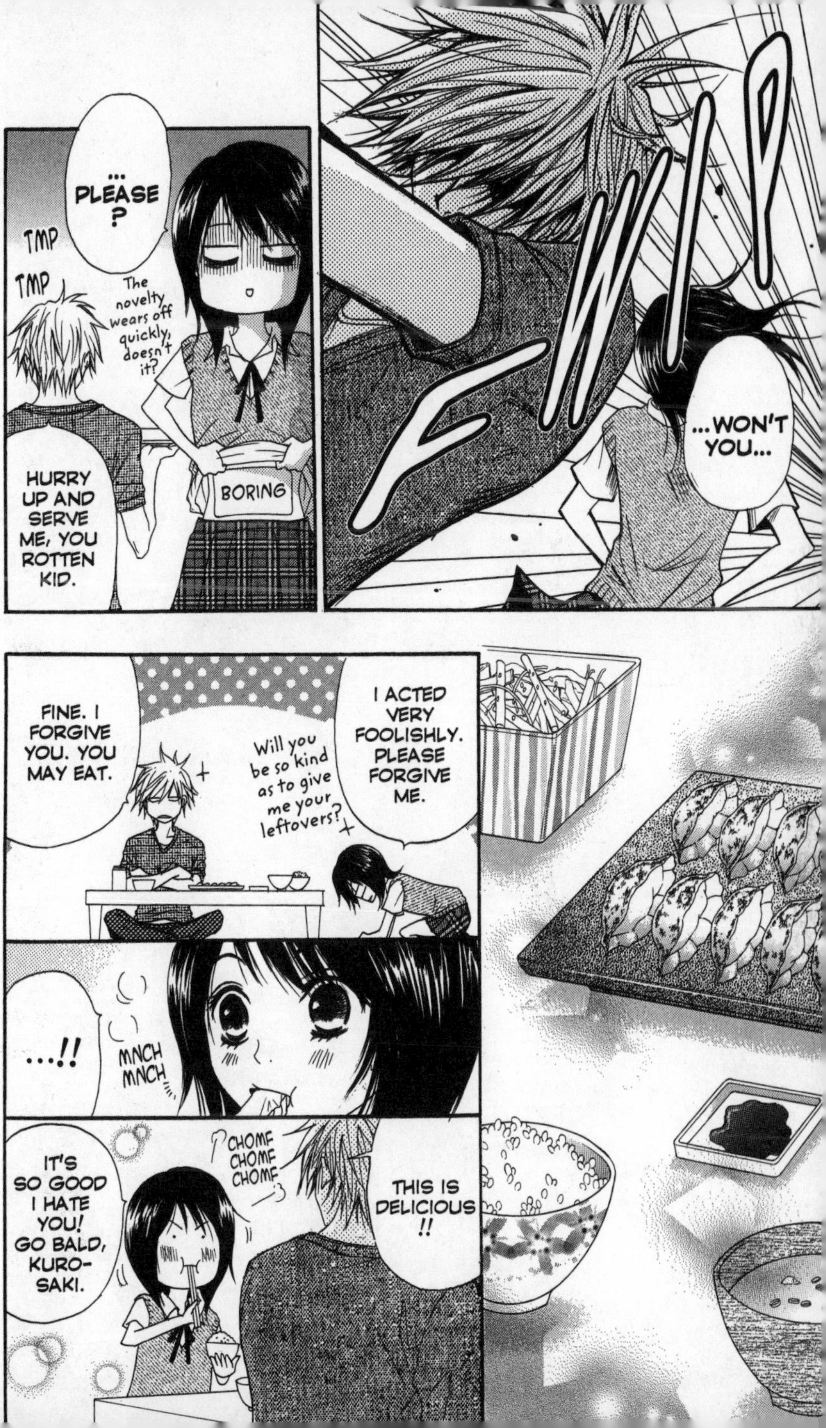
FWIP
...WON'T YOU...
...PLEASE?
The novelty wears off quickly, doesn't it?
TMP TMP
BORING
HURRY UP AND SERVE ME, YOU ROTTEN KID.
I ACTED VERY FOOLISHLY. PLEASE FORGIVE ME.
Will you be so kind as to give me your leftovers?
FINE. I FORGIVE YOU. YOU MAY EAT.
MNCH MNCH
...!!
THIS IS DELICIOUS!!
CHOMF CHOMF CHOMF
IT'S SO GOOD I HATE YOU! GO BALD, KURO-SAKI.

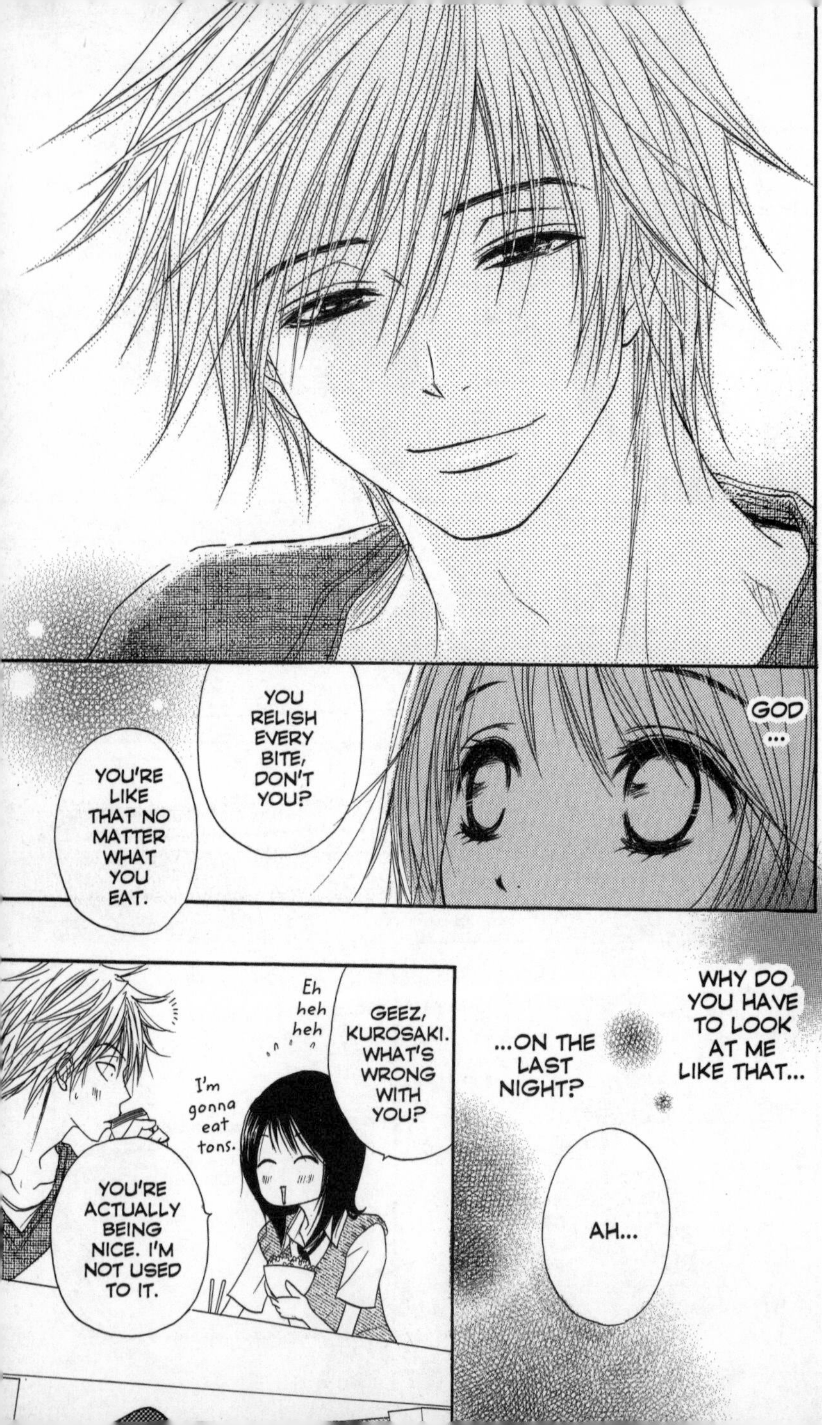
GOD...
YOU RELISH EVERY BITE, DON'T YOU?
YOU'RE LIKE THAT NO MATTER WHAT YOU EAT.
WHY DO YOU HAVE TO LOOK AT ME LIKE THAT...
...ON THE LAST NIGHT?
AH...
GEEZ, KUROSAKI. WHAT'S WRONG WITH YOU?
Eh heh heh
I'm gonna eat tons.
YOU'RE ACTUALLY BEING NICE. I'M NOT USED TO IT.

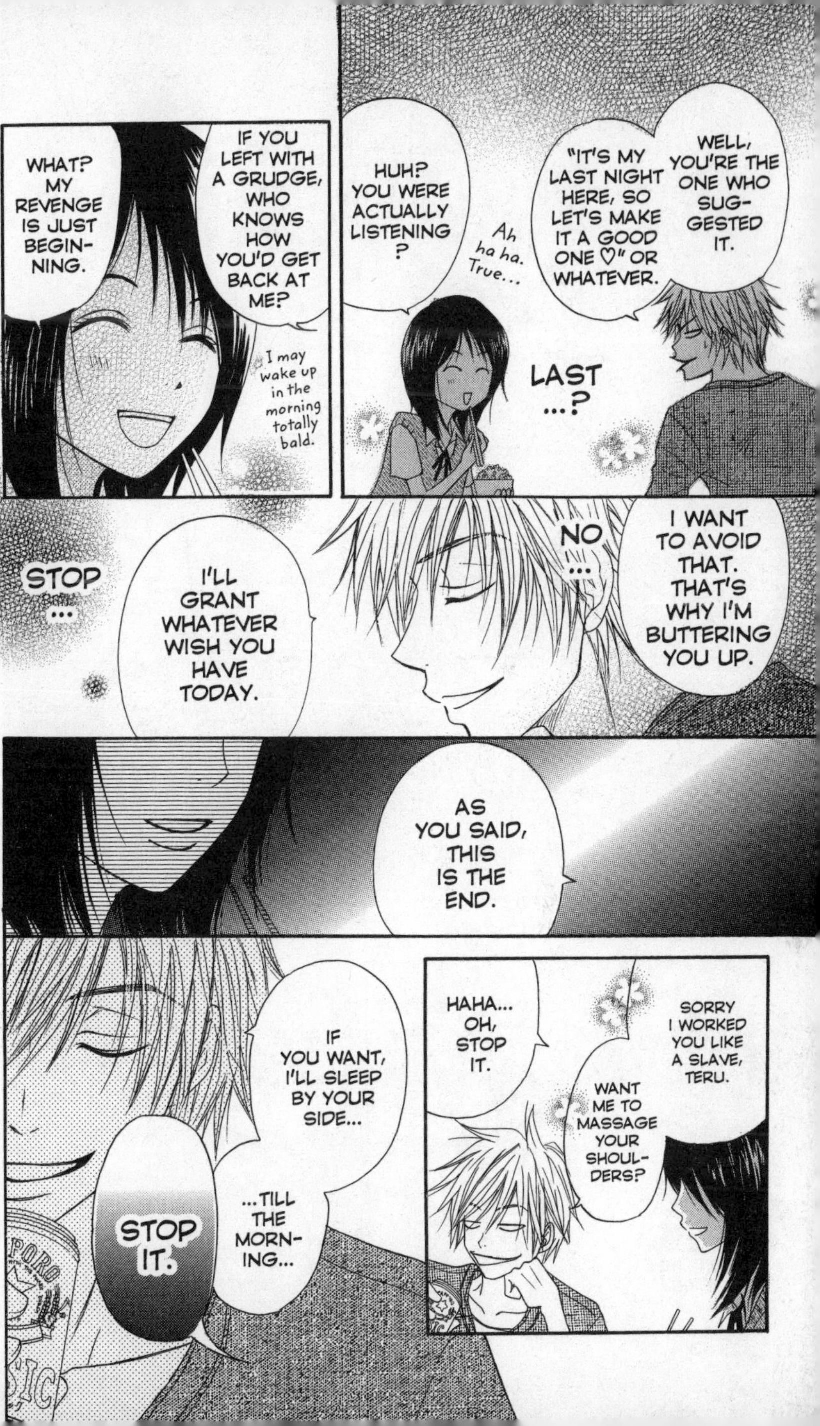
WELL, YOU'RE THE ONE WHO SUG-GESTED IT.
"IT'S MY LAST NIGHT HERE, SO LET'S MAKE IT A GOOD ONE ♡" OR WHATEVER.
Ah ha ha. True...
HUH? YOU WERE ACTUALLY LISTENING?
LAST ...?
IF YOU LEFT WITH A GRUDGE, WHO KNOWS HOW YOU'D GET BACK AT ME?
I may wake up in the morning totally bald.
WHAT? MY REVENGE IS JUST BEGIN-NING.
I WANT TO AVOID THAT. THAT'S WHY I'M BUTTERING YOU UP.
NO ...
I'LL GRANT WHATEVER WISH YOU HAVE TODAY.
STOP ...
AS YOU SAID, THIS IS THE END.
SORRY I WORKED YOU LIKE A SLAVE, TERU.
HAHA... OH, STOP IT.
WANT ME TO MASSAGE YOUR SHOUL-DERS?
IF YOU WANT, I'LL SLEEP BY YOUR SIDE...
...TILL THE MORN-ING...
STOP IT.

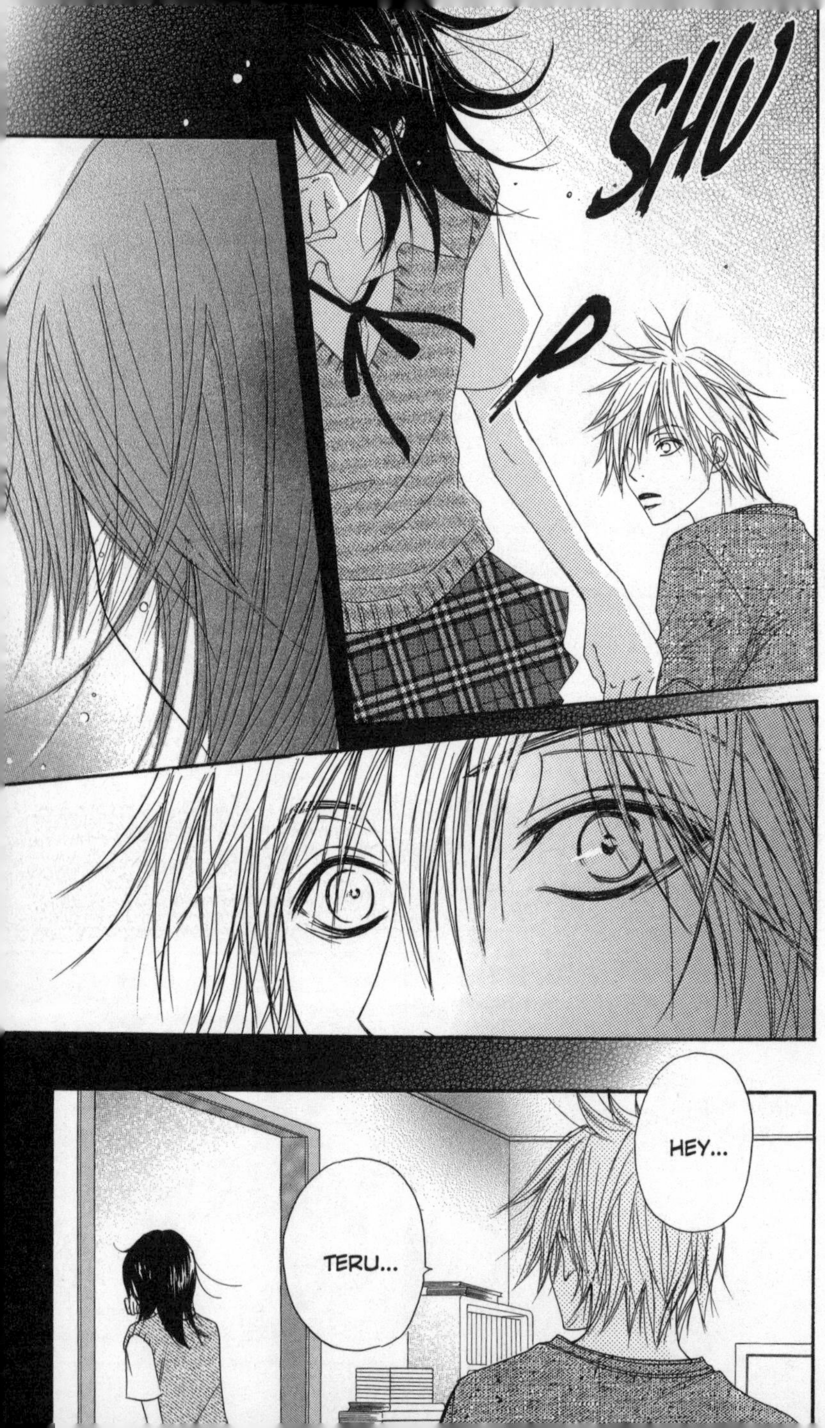
SHUP
HEY...
TERU...

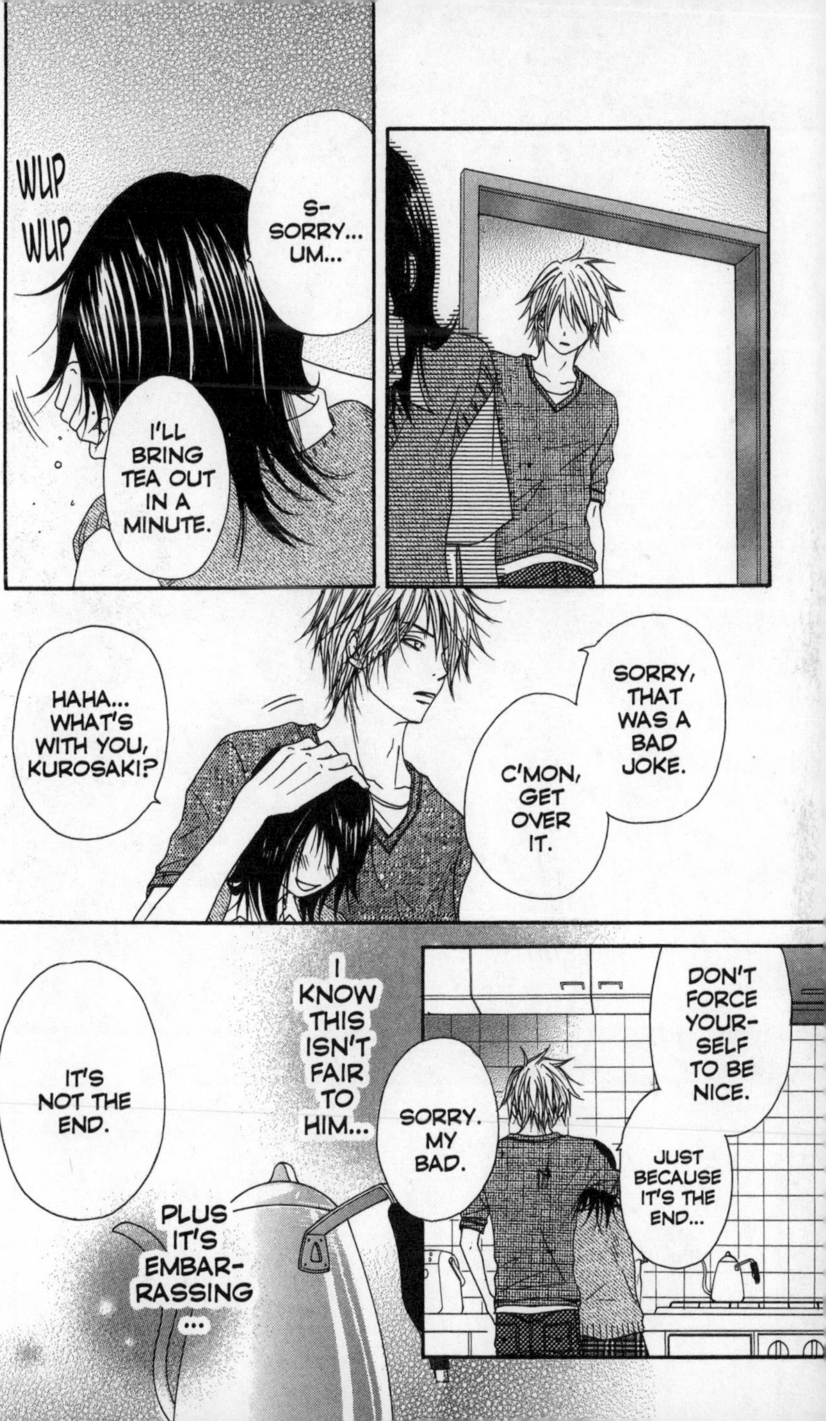
S-SORRY... UM...
WUP WUP
I'LL BRING TEA OUT IN A MINUTE.
SORRY, THAT WAS A BAD JOKE.
C'MON, GET OVER IT.
HAHA... WHAT'S WITH YOU, KUROSAKI?
DON'T FORCE YOURSELF TO BE NICE.
JUST BECAUSE IT'S THE END...
SORRY. MY BAD.
I KNOW THIS ISN'T FAIR TO HIM...
IT'S NOT THE END.
PLUS IT'S EMBARRASSING...

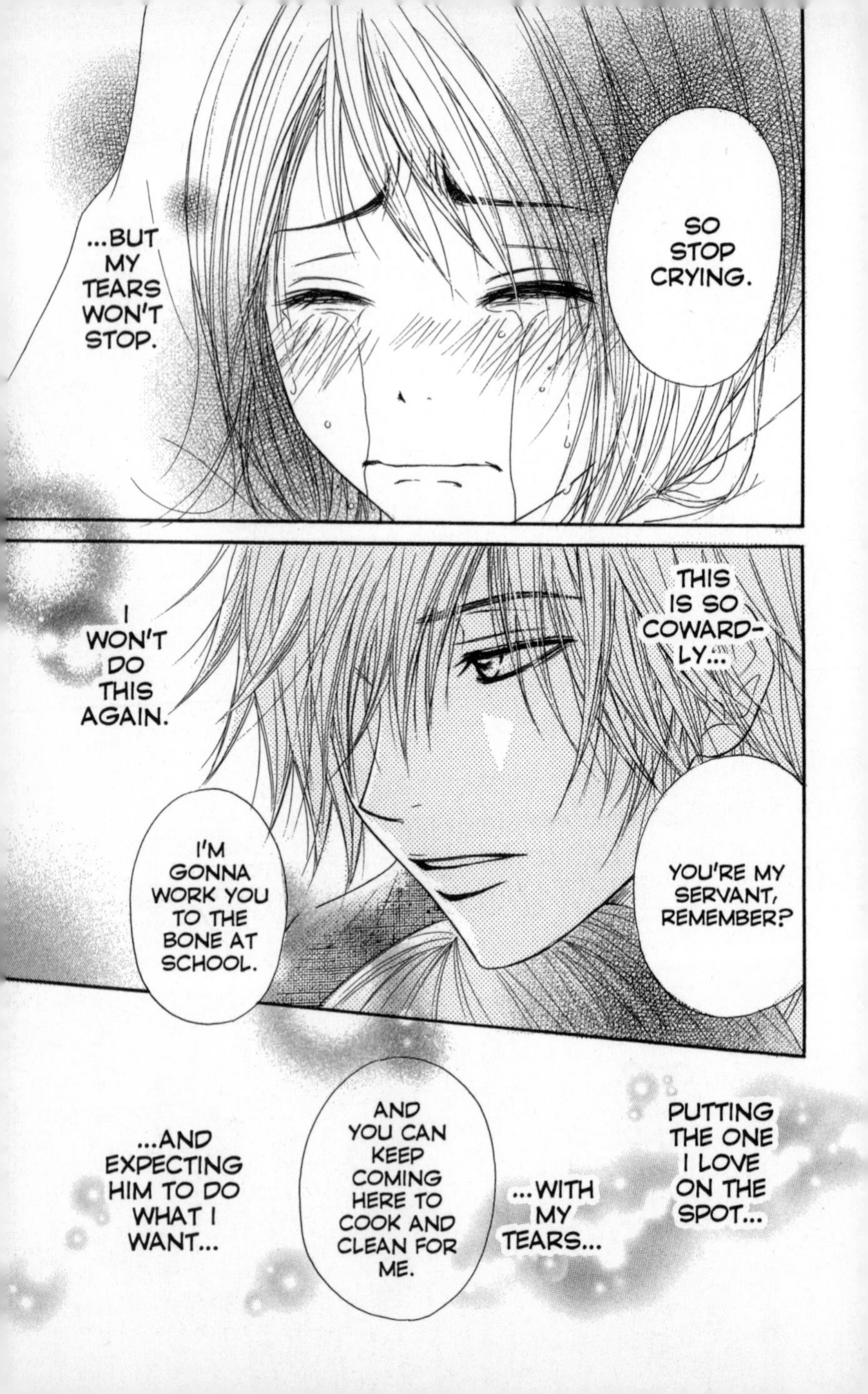
SO STOP CRYING.
...BUT MY TEARS WON'T STOP.
THIS IS SO COWARD-LY...
I WON'T DO THIS AGAIN.
YOU'RE MY SERVANT, REMEMBER?
I'M GONNA WORK YOU TO THE BONE AT SCHOOL.
PUTTING THE ONE I LOVE ON THE SPOT...
...WITH MY TEARS...
AND YOU CAN KEEP COMING HERE TO COOK AND CLEAN FOR ME.
...AND EXPECTING HIM TO DO WHAT I WANT...

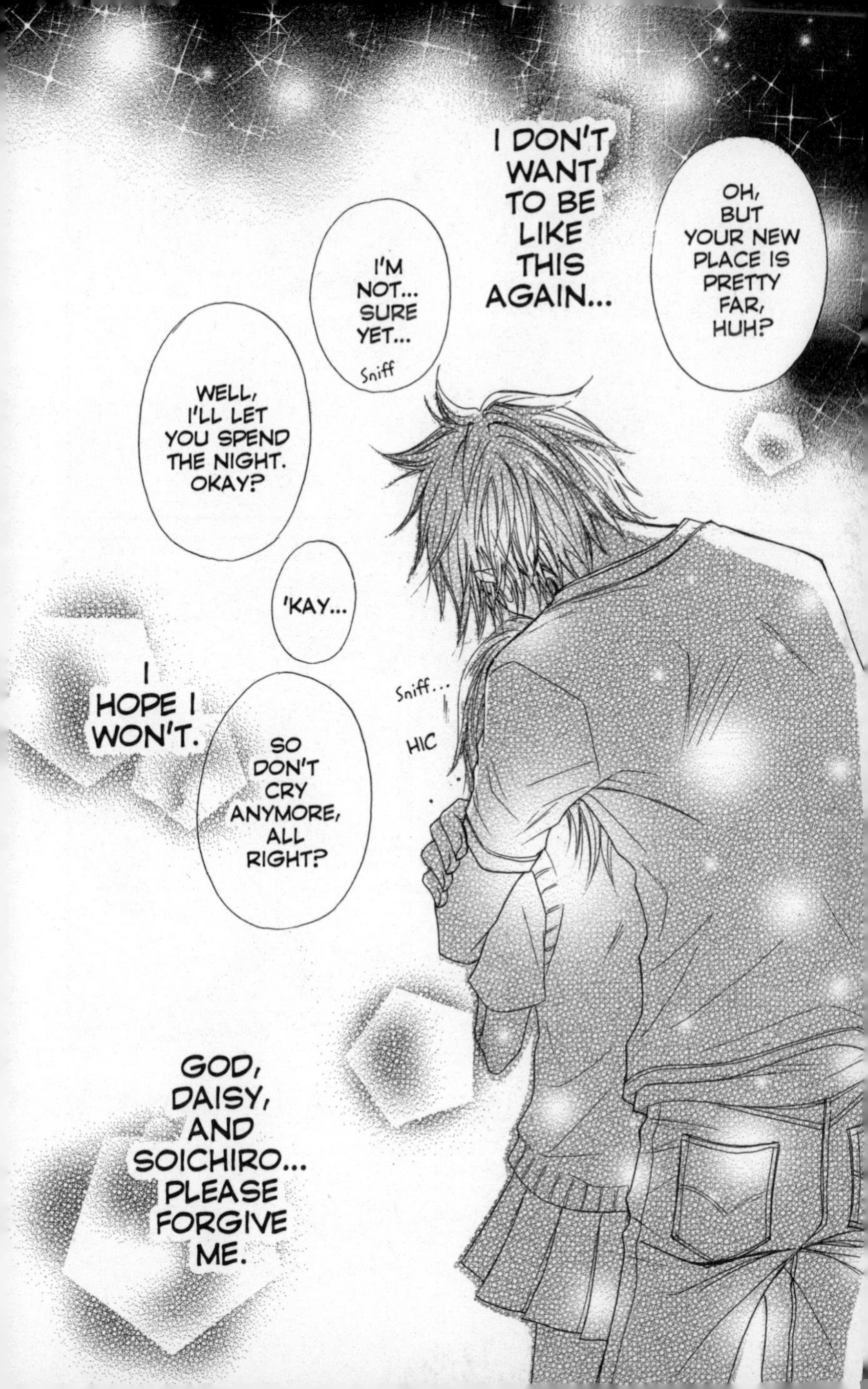

OH, BUT YOUR NEW PLACE IS PRETTY FAR, HUH?
I DON'T WANT TO BE LIKE THIS AGAIN...
I'M NOT... SURE YET...
Sniff
WELL, I'LL LET YOU SPEND THE NIGHT. OKAY?
'KAY...
Sniff...
HIC
SO DON'T CRY ANYMORE, ALL RIGHT?
I HOPE I WON'T.
GOD, DAISY, AND SOICHIRO... PLEASE FORGIVE ME.

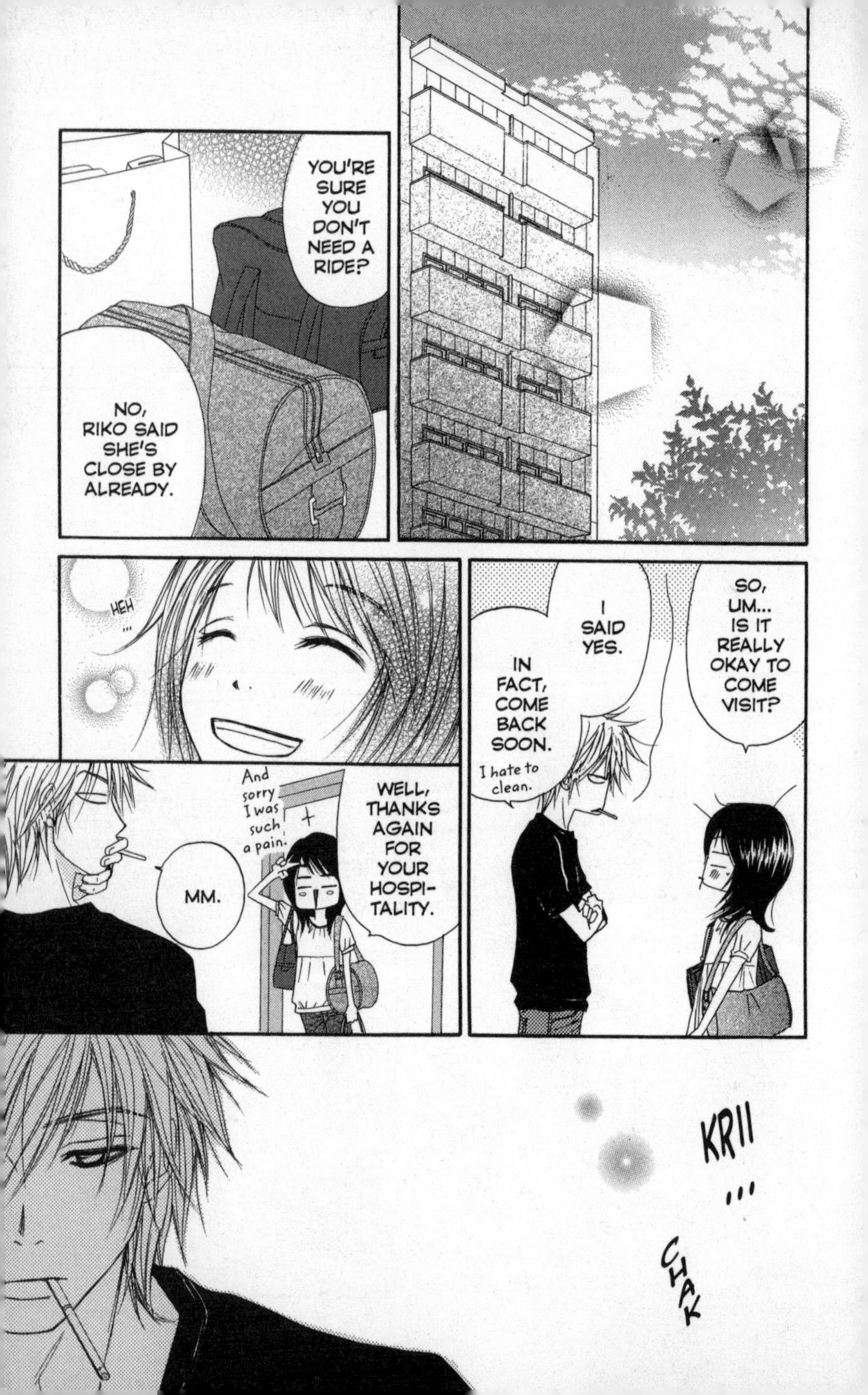
YOU'RE SURE YOU DON'T NEED A RIDE?
NO, RIKO SAID SHE'S CLOSE BY ALREADY.
SO, UM... IS IT REALLY OKAY TO COME VISIT?
I SAID YES.
IN FACT, COME BACK SOON.
I hate to clean.
HEH...
WELL, THANKS AGAIN FOR YOUR HOSPITALITY.
And sorry I was such a pain.
MM.
KRII...
CHAK

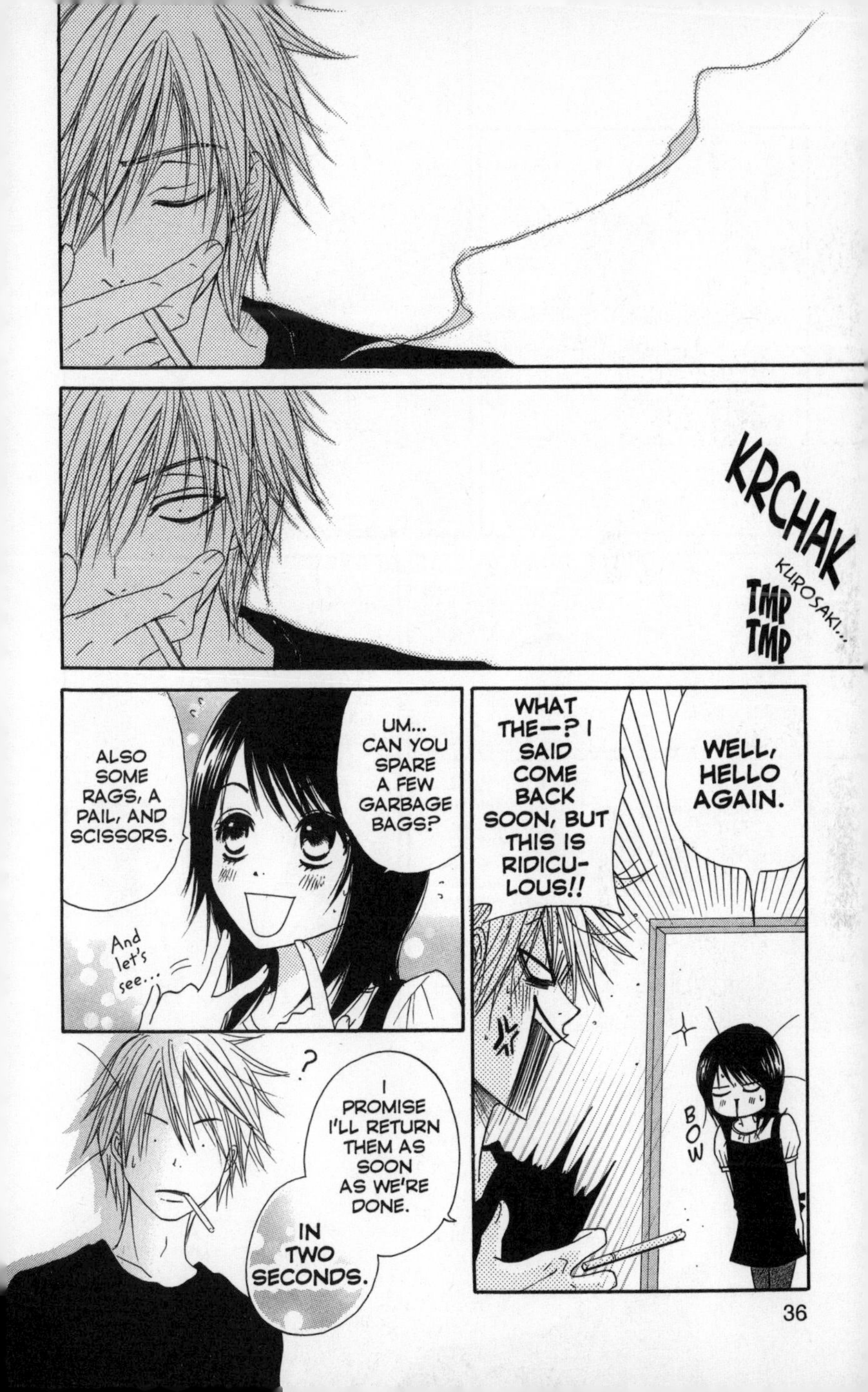
KRCHAK
KUROSAKI...
TMP TMP
WELL, HELLO AGAIN.
WHAT THE—? I SAID COME BACK SOON, BUT THIS IS RIDICULOUS!!
BOW
UM... CAN YOU SPARE A FEW GARBAGE BAGS?
ALSO SOME RAGS, A PAIL, AND SCISSORS.
And let's see...
?
I PROMISE I'LL RETURN THEM AS SOON AS WE'RE DONE.
IN TWO SECONDS.

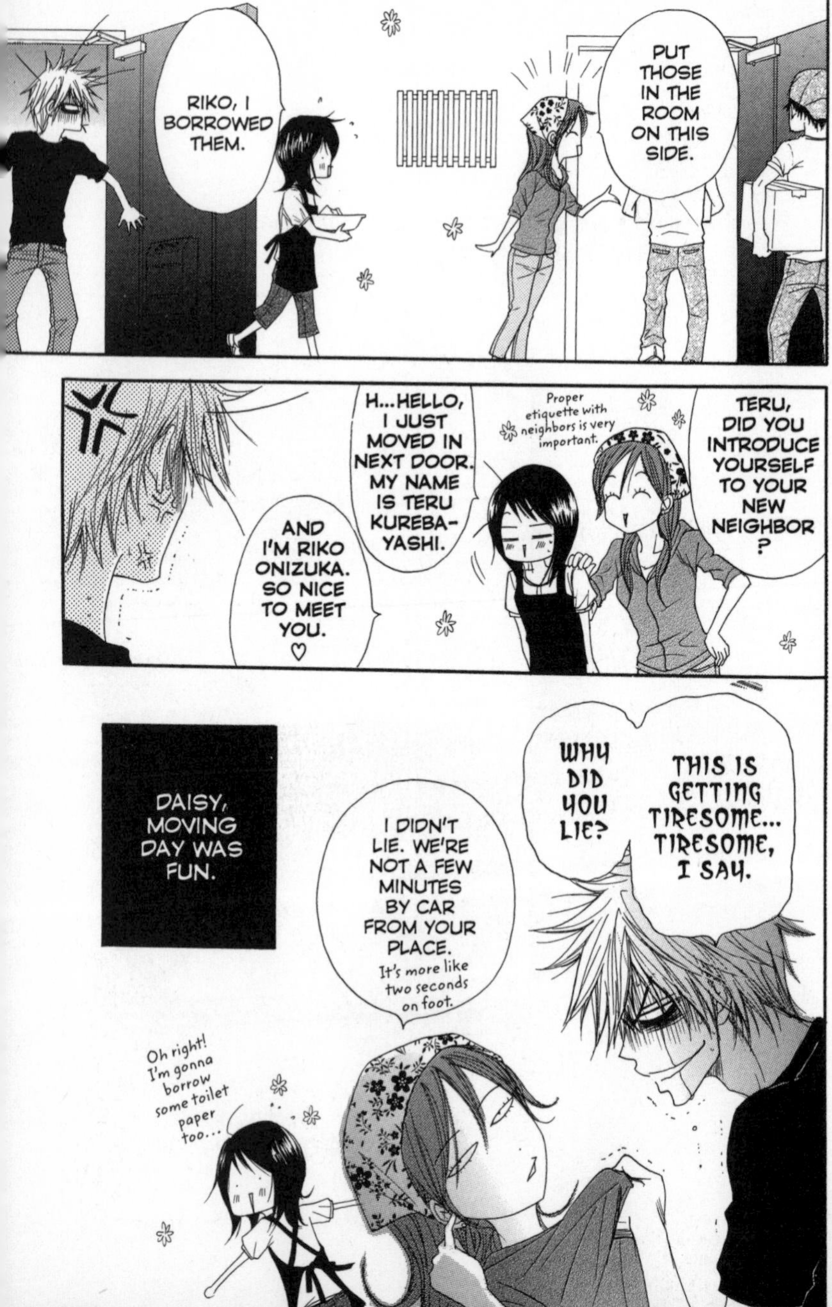
PUT THOSE IN THE ROOM ON THIS SIDE.
RIKO, I BORROWED THEM.
TERU, DID YOU INTRODUCE YOURSELF TO YOUR NEW NEIGHBOR?
Proper etiquette with neighbors is very important.
H...HELLO, I JUST MOVED IN NEXT DOOR. MY NAME IS TERU KUREBAYASHI.
AND I'M RIKO ONIZUKA. SO NICE TO MEET YOU. ♡
THIS IS GETTING TIRESOME... TIRESOME, I SAY.
WHY DID YOU LIE?
I DIDN'T LIE. WE'RE NOT A FEW MINUTES BY CAR FROM YOUR PLACE.
It's more like two seconds on foot.
DAISY, MOVING DAY WAS FUN.
Oh right! I'm gonna borrow some toilet paper too...

I'M SO THRILLED THAT ***DENGEKI DAISY*** HAS BEEN TRANSLATED AND PUBLISHED IN TAIWAN!!

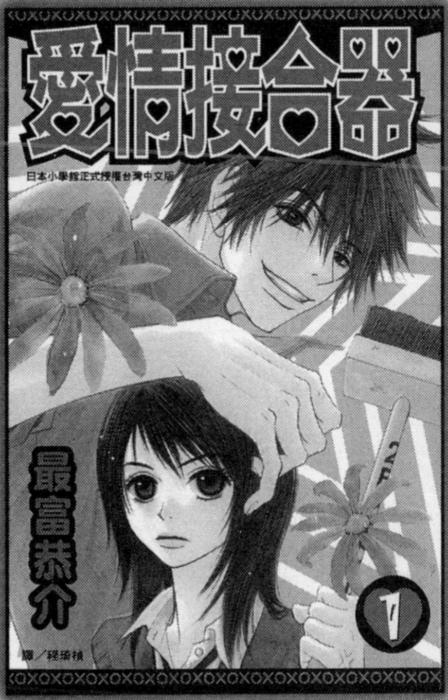
愛情接合器
日本小學館正式授權台灣中文版
最富恭介
1

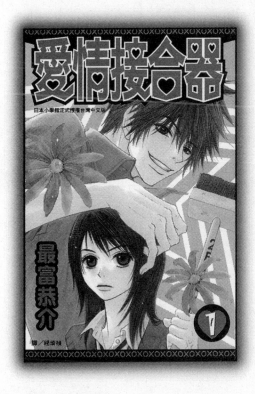

IT'S CALLED ***INSTRUMENT...***
...OF LOVE OVER THERE, HUH?

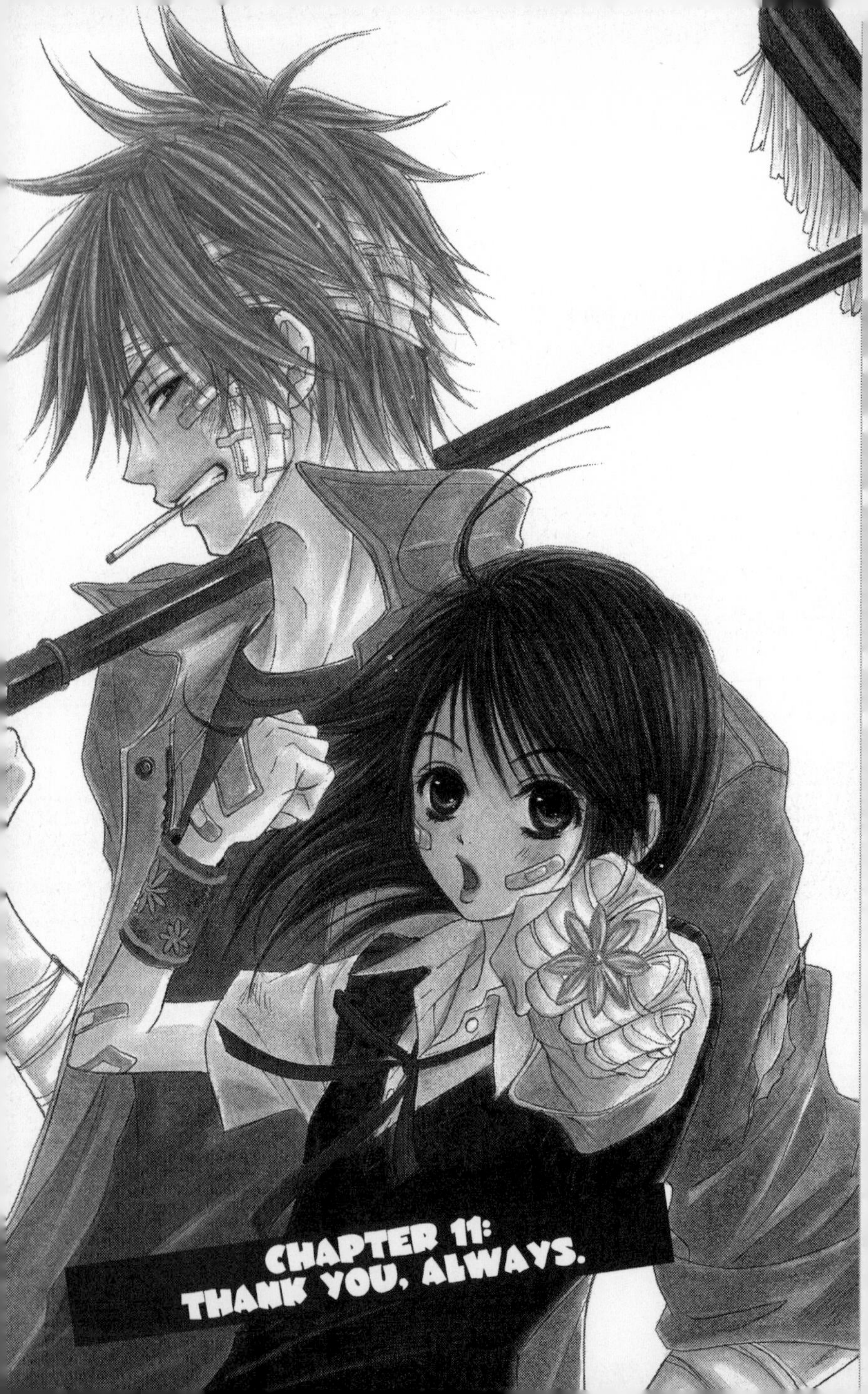
CHAPTER 11:
THANK YOU, ALWAYS.

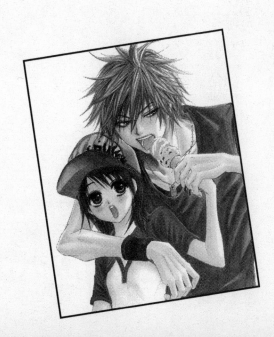

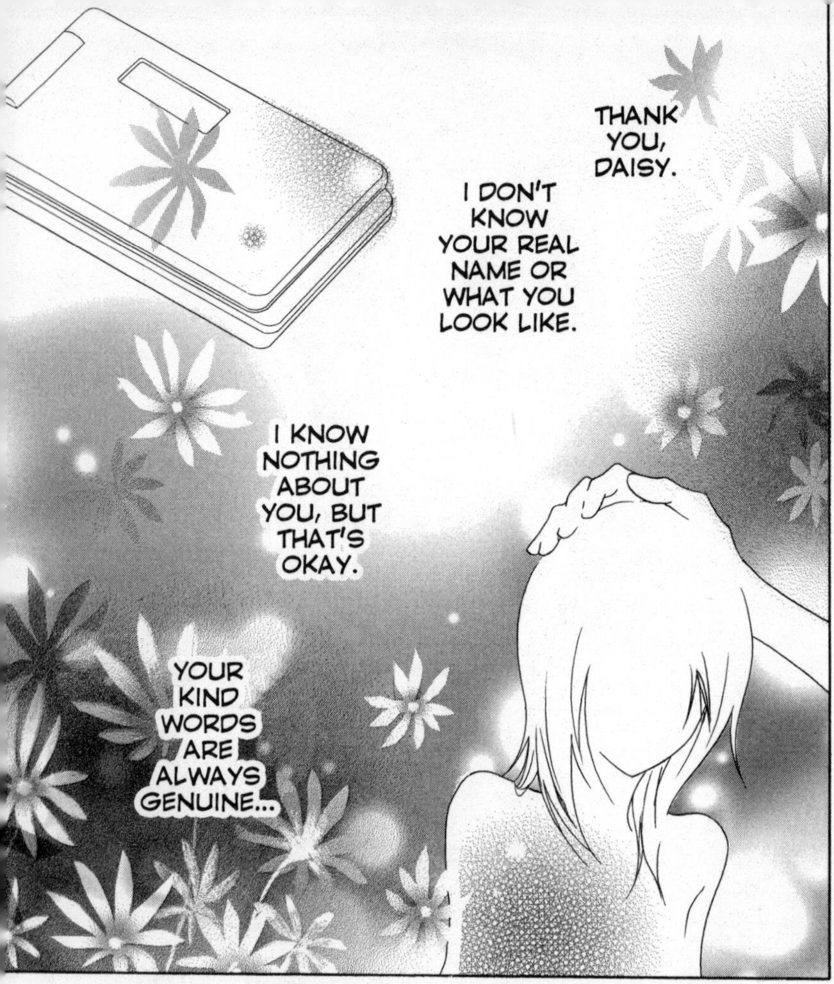
THANK YOU, DAISY.
I DON'T KNOW YOUR REAL NAME OR WHAT YOU LOOK LIKE.
I KNOW NOTHING ABOUT YOU, BUT THAT'S OKAY.
YOUR KIND WORDS ARE ALWAYS GENUINE...

I'VE BEEN GETTING MORE AND MORE QUESTIONS ABOUT THE CHARACTERS IN *DENGEKI DAISY* (LIKE THEIR PROFILES). RECENTLY, ONE OF THE FREQUENTLY ASKED QUESTIONS IS HOW OLD KUROSAKI IS. THIS WILL PROBABLY BE REVEALED IN A LATER VOLUME, SO PLEASE WAIT A WHILE LONGER.

OTHER QUESTIONS INCLUDE "WHAT COLOR IS KUROSAKI'S CELL PHONE?" (BLACK), "DOES KUROSAKI DISLIKE TOMATOES?" (VERY OBSERVANT OF YOU), "WHEN WILL KUROSAKI LOSE HIS HAIR?" AND "DOES KUROSAKI WEAR A WIG?" TO BE HONEST, 80 PERCENT OF THE MAIL AND EMAIL I GET ARE RELATED TO BALDNESS.

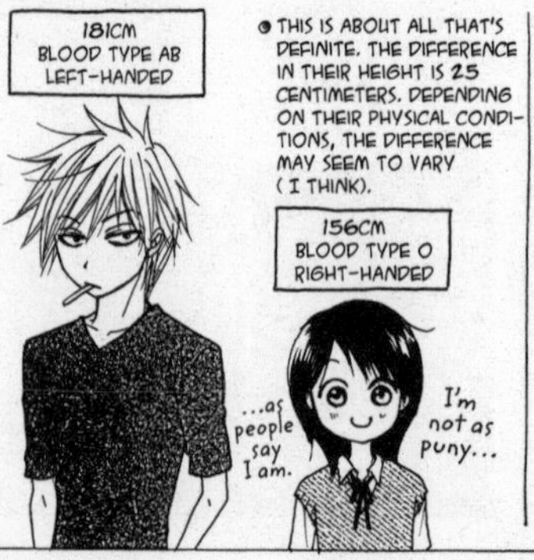
181CM
BLOOD TYPE AB
LEFT-HANDED
THIS IS ABOUT ALL THAT'S DEFINITE. THE DIFFERENCE IN THEIR HEIGHT IS 25 CENTIMETERS. DEPENDING ON THEIR PHYSICAL CONDITIONS, THE DIFFERENCE MAY SEEM TO VARY (I THINK).
156CM
BLOOD TYPE O
RIGHT-HANDED
I'm not as puny...
...as people say I am.

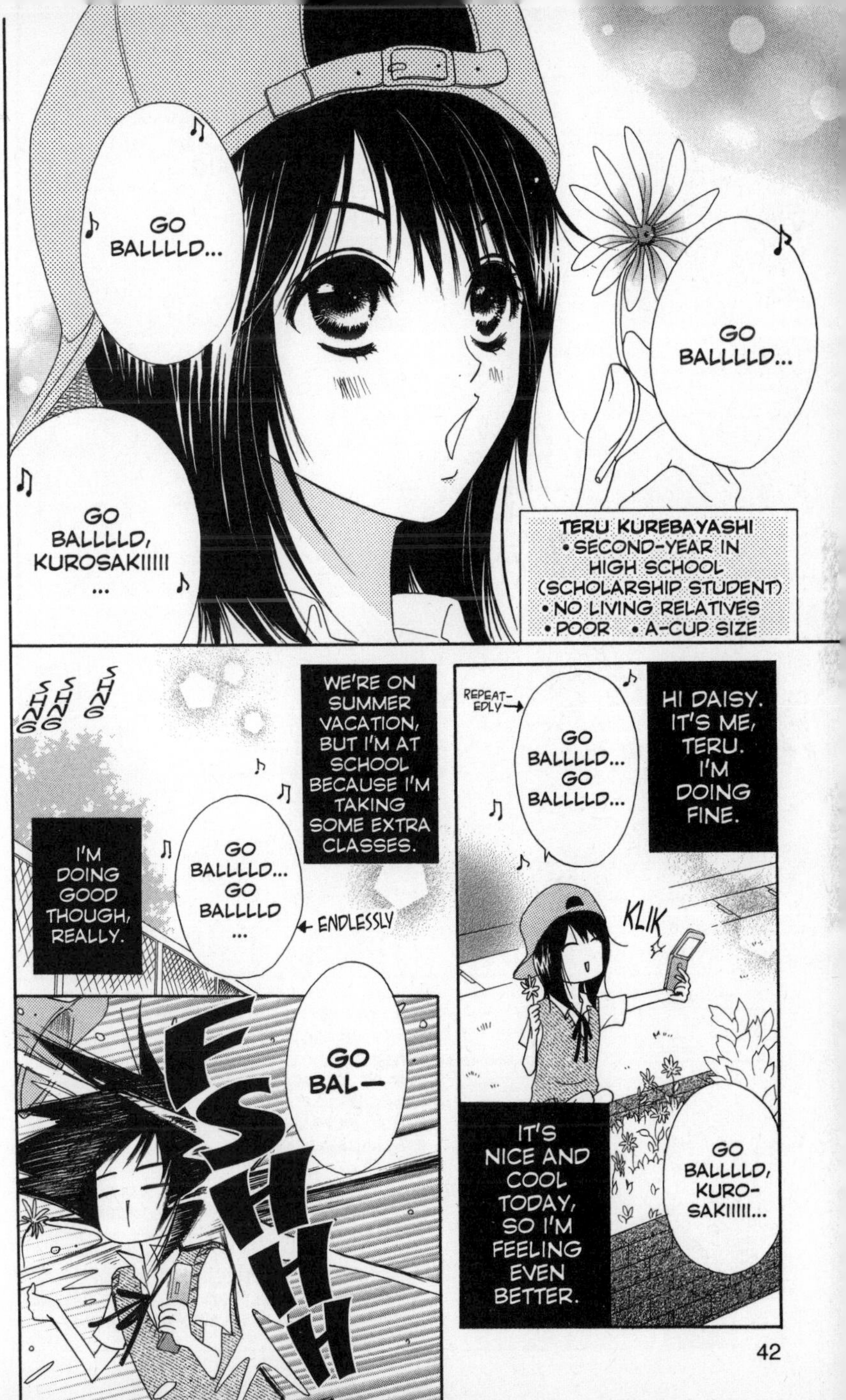
GO BALLLLD...
GO BALLLLD...
TERU KUREBAYASHI
• SECOND-YEAR IN HIGH SCHOOL (SCHOLARSHIP STUDENT)
• NO LIVING RELATIVES
• POOR • A-CUP SIZE
GO BALLLLD, KUROSAKIIIII ...
HI DAISY. IT'S ME, TERU. I'M DOING FINE.
REPEAT-EDLY
GO BALLLLD... GO BALLLLD...
KLIK
GO BALLLLD, KURO-SAKIIIII...
IT'S NICE AND COOL TODAY, SO I'M FEELING EVEN BETTER.
SHNG SHNG SHNG
WE'RE ON SUMMER VACATION, BUT I'M AT SCHOOL BECAUSE I'M TAKING SOME EXTRA CLASSES.
GO BALLLLD... GO BALLLLD ...
ENDLESSLY
I'M DOING GOOD THOUGH, REALLY.
GO BAL—
FSHHHH

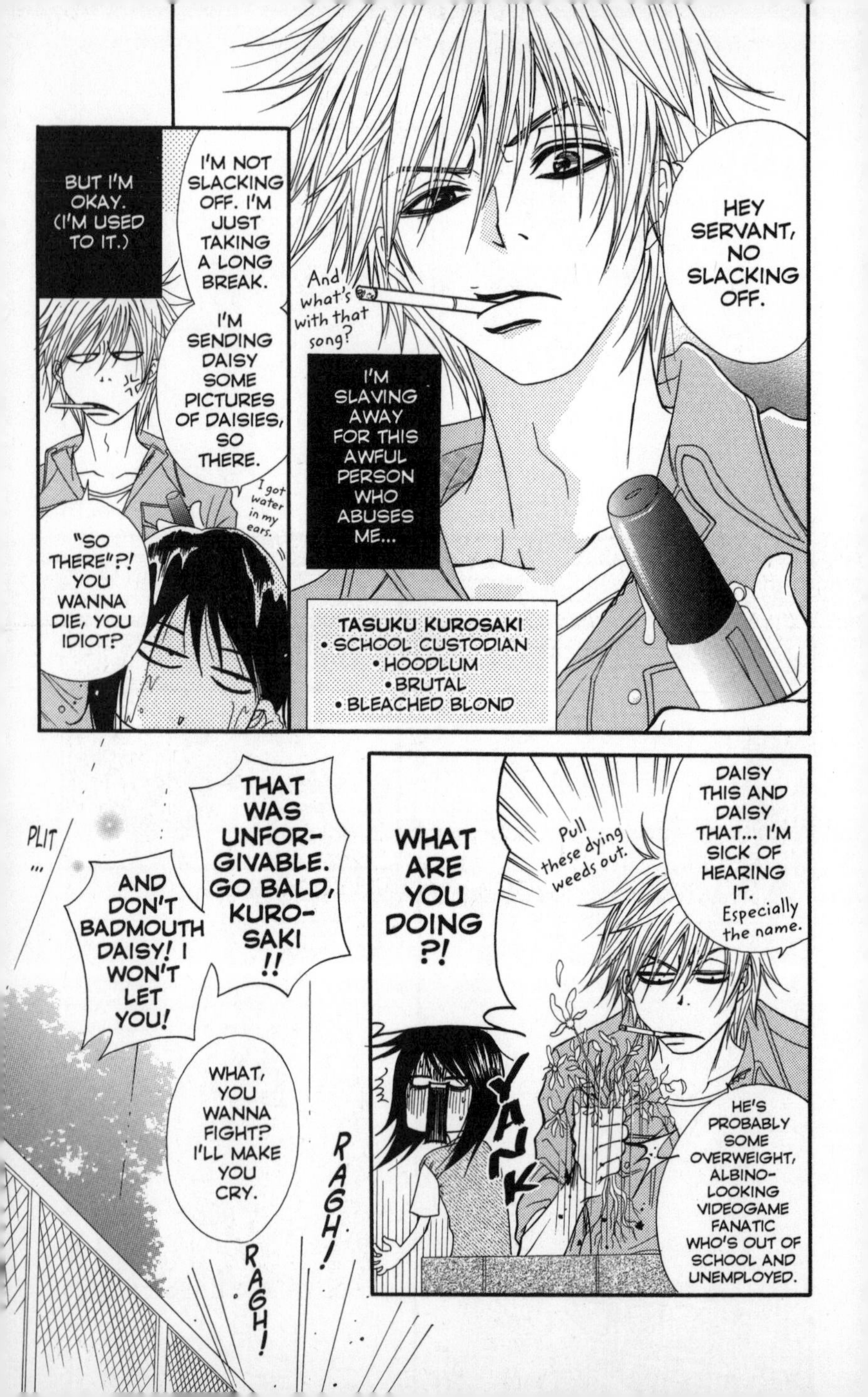
HEY SERVANT, NO SLACKING OFF.
And what's with that song?
I'M SLAVING AWAY FOR THIS AWFUL PERSON WHO ABUSES ME...
TASUKU KUROSAKI
• SCHOOL CUSTODIAN
• HOODLUM
• BRUTAL
• BLEACHED BLOND
I'M NOT SLACKING OFF. I'M JUST TAKING A LONG BREAK.
I'M SENDING DAISY SOME PICTURES OF DAISIES, SO THERE.
I got water in my ears.
BUT I'M OKAY. (I'M USED TO IT.)
"SO THERE"?! YOU WANNA DIE, YOU IDIOT?
DAISY THIS AND DAISY THAT... I'M SICK OF HEARING IT. Especially the name.
Pull these dying weeds out.
WHAT ARE YOU DOING?!
YANK
HE'S PROBABLY SOME OVERWEIGHT, ALBINO-LOOKING VIDEOGAME FANATIC WHO'S OUT OF SCHOOL AND UNEMPLOYED.
THAT WAS UNFORGIVABLE. GO BALD, KUROSAKI!!
AND DON'T BADMOUTH DAISY! I WON'T LET YOU!
PLIT
WHAT, YOU WANNA FIGHT? I'LL MAKE YOU CRY.
RAGH!
RAGH!

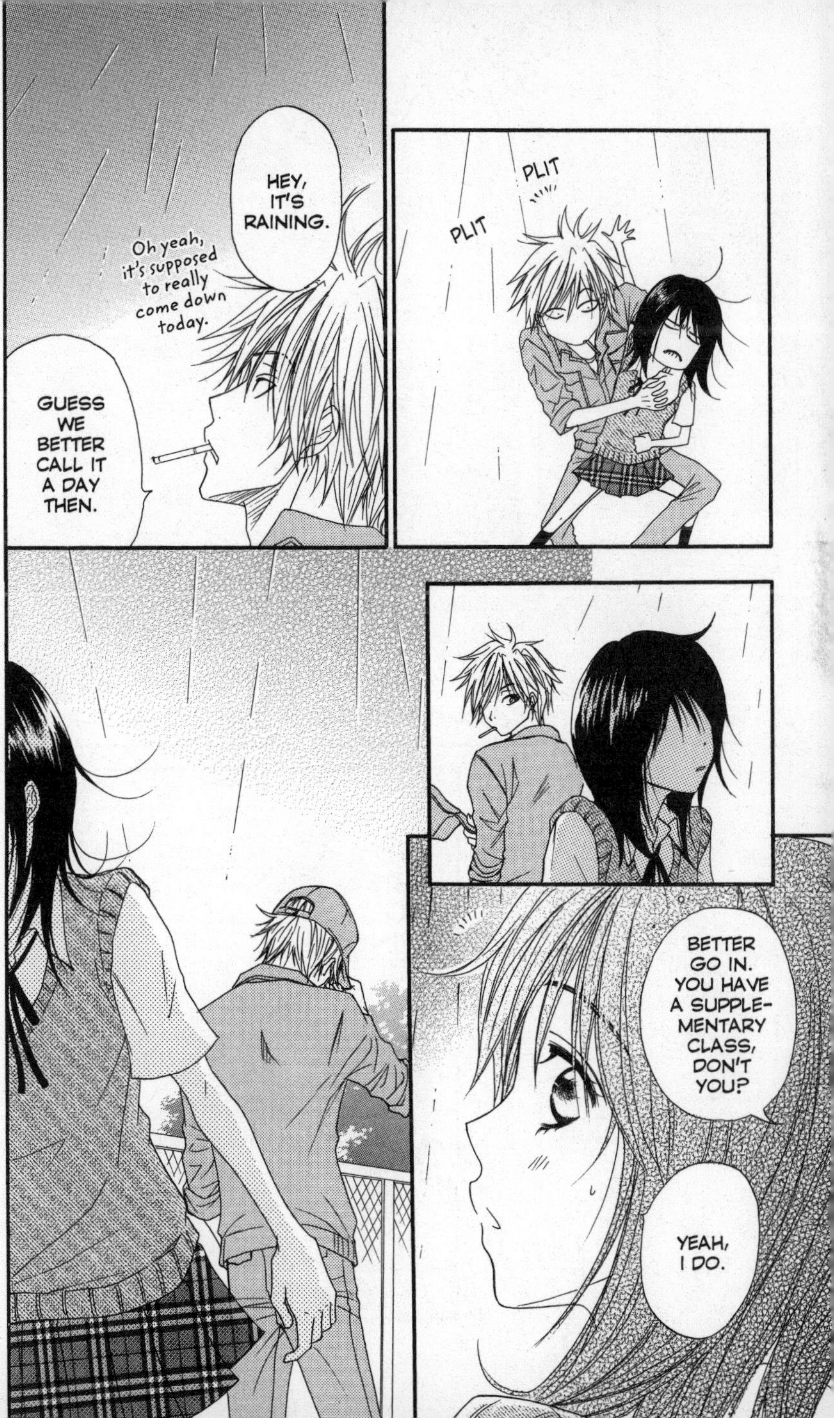
PLIT
PLIT
HEY, IT'S RAINING.
Oh yeah, it's supposed to really come down today.
GUESS WE BETTER CALL IT A DAY THEN.
BETTER GO IN. YOU HAVE A SUPPLE-MENTARY CLASS, DON'T YOU?
YEAH, I DO.

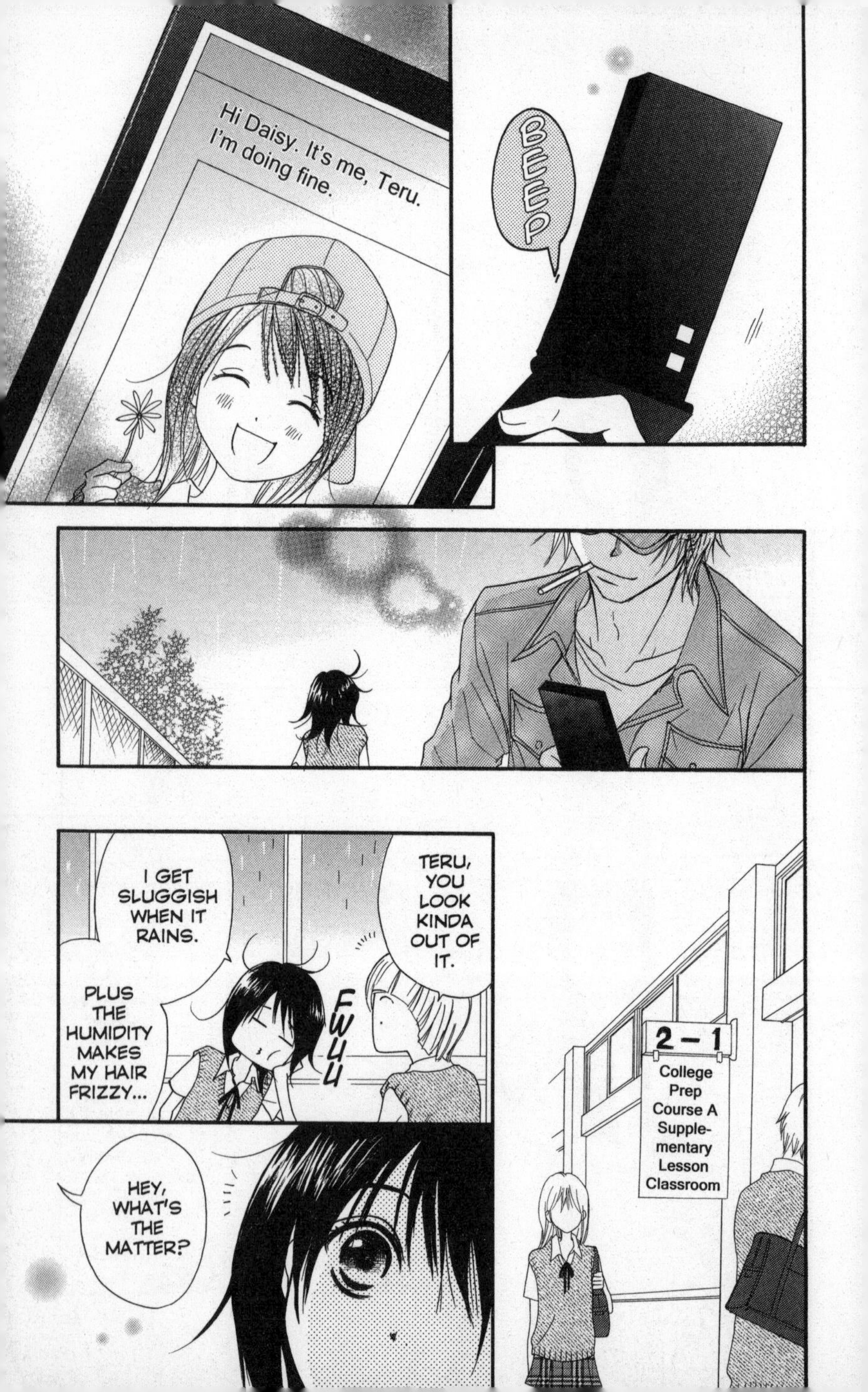
BEEP
Hi Daisy. It's me, Teru. I'm doing fine.
2 – 1
College Prep Course A Supplementary Lesson Classroom
TERU, YOU LOOK KINDA OUT OF IT.
I GET SLUGGISH WHEN IT RAINS.
FWUU
PLUS THE HUMIDITY MAKES MY HAIR FRIZZY...
HEY, WHAT'S THE MATTER?

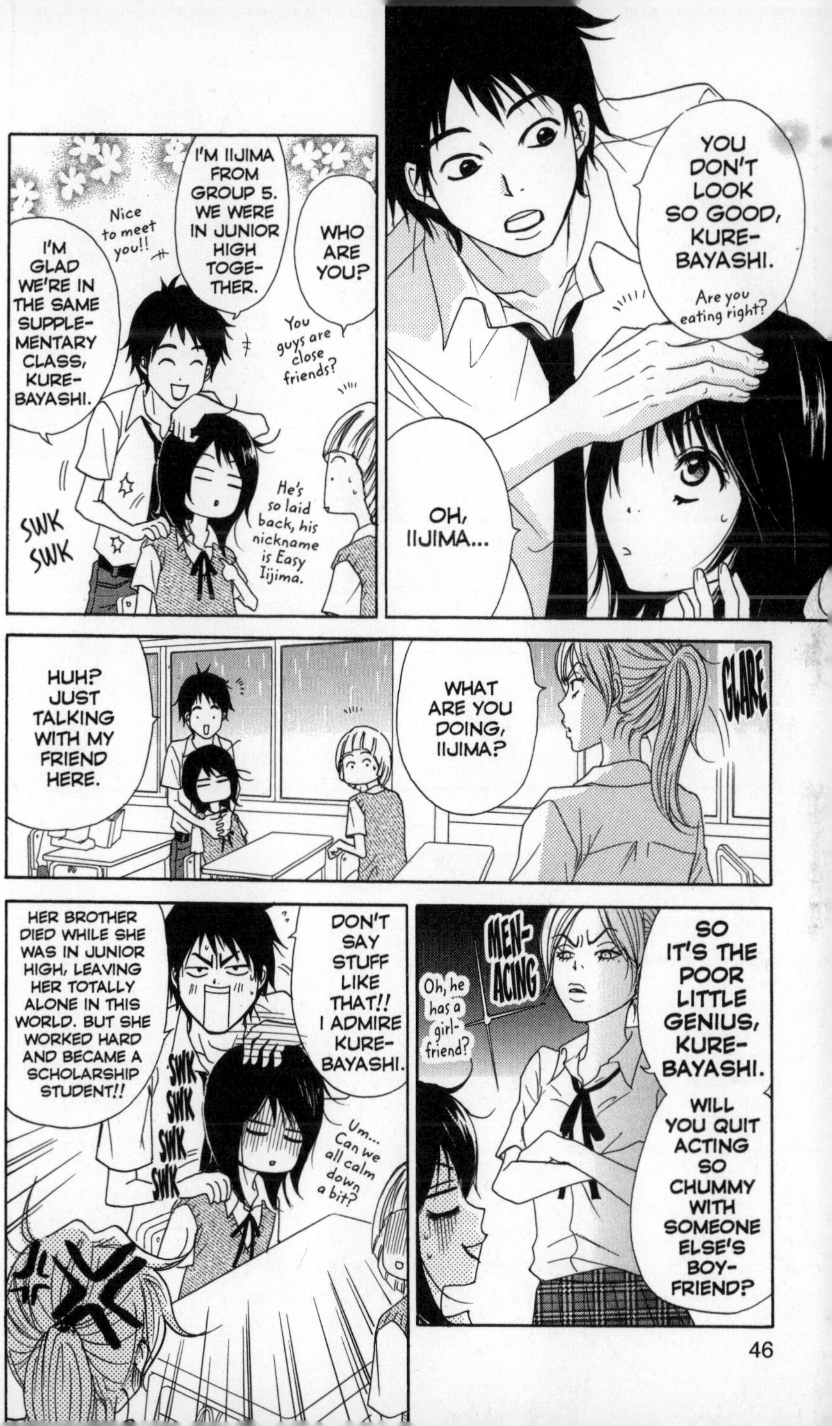
YOU DON'T LOOK SO GOOD, KURE-BAYASHI.
Are you eating right?
OH, IIJIMA...
WHO ARE YOU?
I'M IIJIMA FROM GROUP 5. WE WERE IN JUNIOR HIGH TOGE-THER.
Nice to meet you!!
I'M GLAD WE'RE IN THE SAME SUPPLE-MENTARY CLASS, KURE-BAYASHI.
You guys are close friends?
He's so laid back, his nickname is Easy Iijima.
SWK SWK
GLARE
WHAT ARE YOU DOING, IIJIMA?
HUH? JUST TALKING WITH MY FRIEND HERE.
SO IT'S THE POOR LITTLE GENIUS, KURE-BAYASHI.
WILL YOU QUIT ACTING SO CHUMMY WITH SOMEONE ELSE'S BOY-FRIEND?
MEN-ACING
Oh, he has a girl-friend?
DON'T SAY STUFF LIKE THAT!! I ADMIRE KURE-BAYASHI.
HER BROTHER DIED WHILE SHE WAS IN JUNIOR HIGH, LEAVING HER TOTALLY ALONE IN THIS WORLD. BUT SHE WORKED HARD AND BECAME A SCHOLARSHIP STUDENT!!
SWK SWK SWK SWK
Um... Can we all calm down a bit?

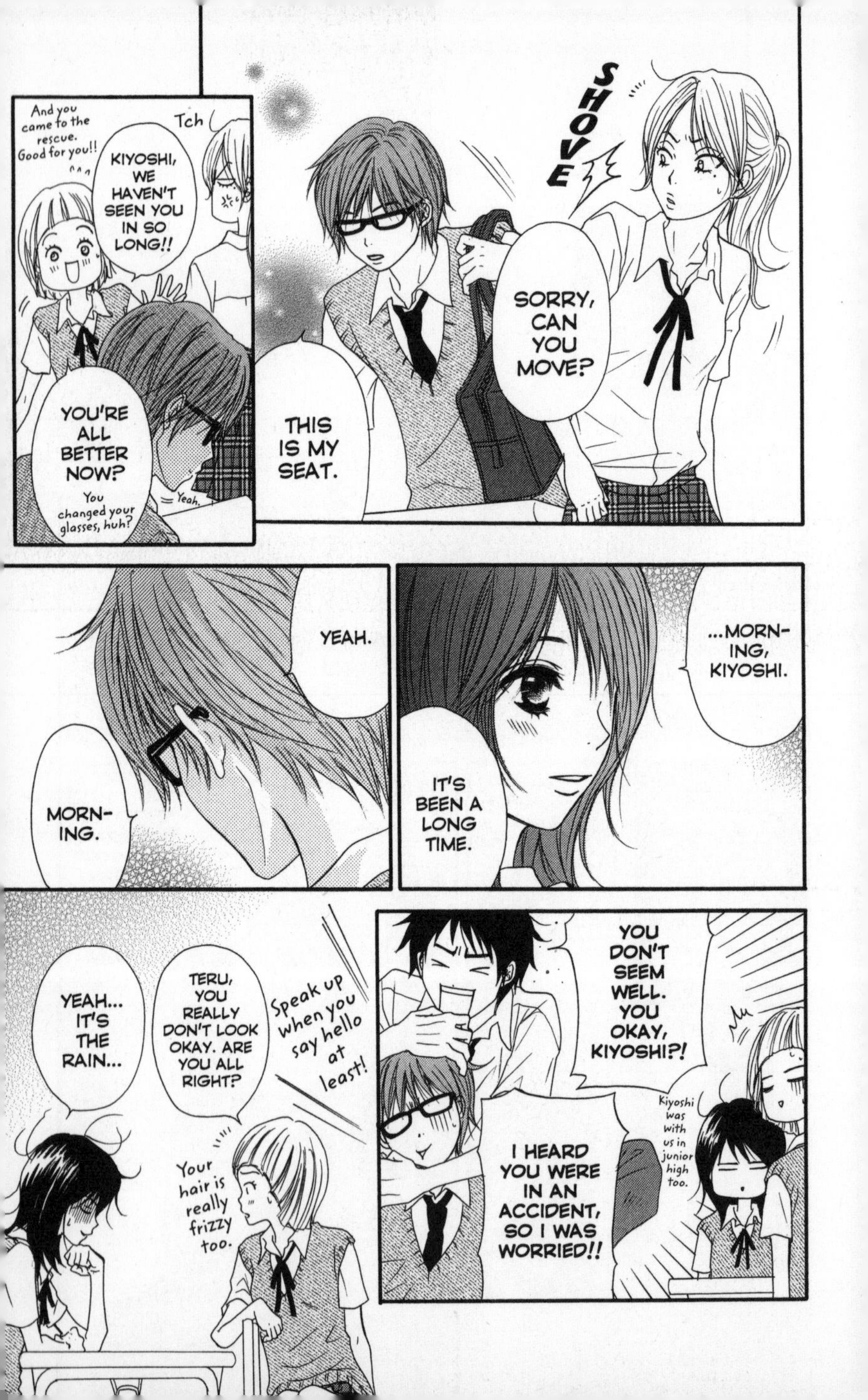
SHOVE
SORRY, CAN YOU MOVE?
THIS IS MY SEAT.
Tch
KIYOSHI, WE HAVEN'T SEEN YOU IN SO LONG!!
And you came to the rescue. Good for you!!
YOU'RE ALL BETTER NOW?
You changed your glasses, huh?
Yeah.
...MORN-ING, KIYOSHI.
IT'S BEEN A LONG TIME.
YEAH.
MORN-ING.
YOU DON'T SEEM WELL. YOU OKAY, KIYOSHI?!
Kiyoshi was with us in junior high too.
I HEARD YOU WERE IN AN ACCIDENT, SO I WAS WORRIED!!
Speak up when you say hello at least!
TERU, YOU REALLY DON'T LOOK OKAY. ARE YOU ALL RIGHT?
YEAH... IT'S THE RAIN...
Your hair is really frizzy too.

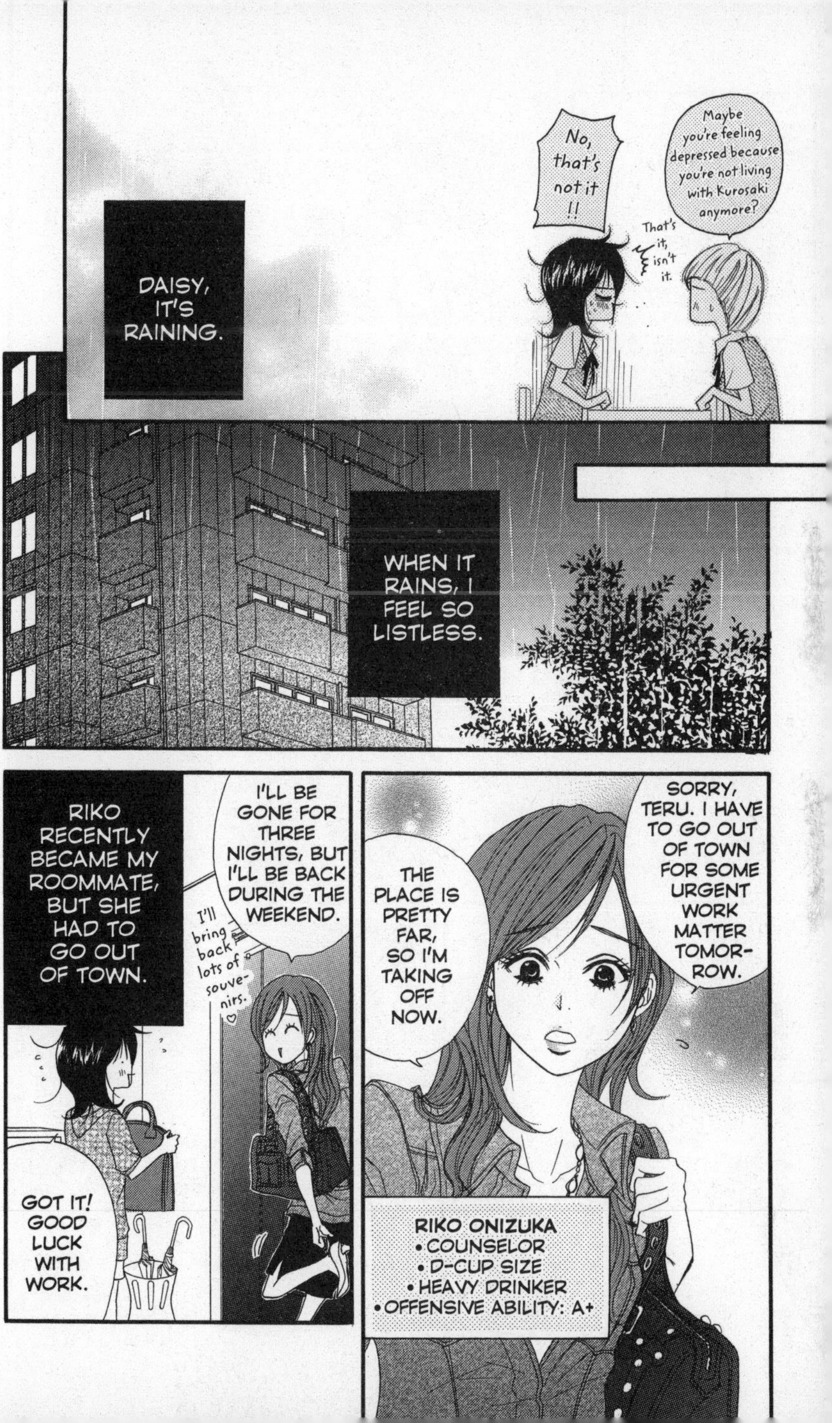
Maybe you're feeling depressed because you're not living with Kurosaki anymore?
That's it, isn't it.
No, that's not it !!
DAISY, IT'S RAINING.
WHEN IT RAINS, I FEEL SO LISTLESS.
SORRY, TERU. I HAVE TO GO OUT OF TOWN FOR SOME URGENT WORK MATTER TOMORROW.
THE PLACE IS PRETTY FAR, SO I'M TAKING OFF NOW.
RIKO ONIZUKA
•COUNSELOR
•D-CUP SIZE
•HEAVY DRINKER
•OFFENSIVE ABILITY: A+
I'LL BE GONE FOR THREE NIGHTS, BUT I'LL BE BACK DURING THE WEEKEND.
I'll bring back lots of souvenirs. ♡
RIKO RECENTLY BECAME MY ROOMMATE, BUT SHE HAD TO GO OUT OF TOWN.
GOT IT! GOOD LUCK WITH WORK.

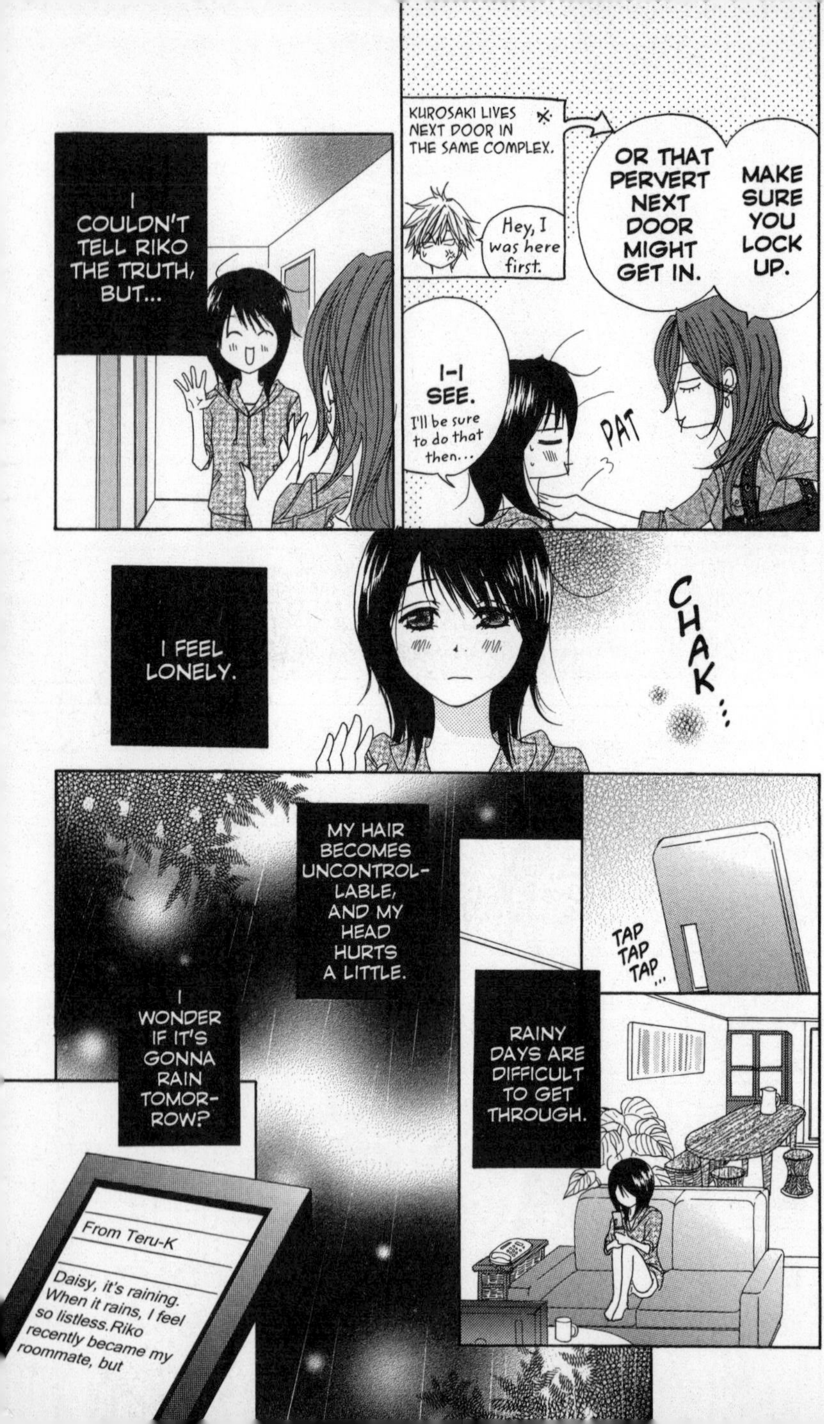
MAKE SURE YOU LOCK UP.
OR THAT PERVERT NEXT DOOR MIGHT GET IN.
KUROSAKI LIVES NEXT DOOR IN THE SAME COMPLEX. ※
Hey, I was here first.
PAT
I-I SEE.
I'll be sure to do that then...
I COULDN'T TELL RIKO THE TRUTH, BUT...
CHAK...
I FEEL LONELY.
TAP TAP TAP...
MY HAIR BECOMES UNCONTROL-LABLE, AND MY HEAD HURTS A LITTLE.
RAINY DAYS ARE DIFFICULT TO GET THROUGH.
I WONDER IF IT'S GONNA RAIN TOMOR-ROW?
From Teru-K
Daisy, it's raining. When it rains, I feel so listless.Riko recently became my roommate, but

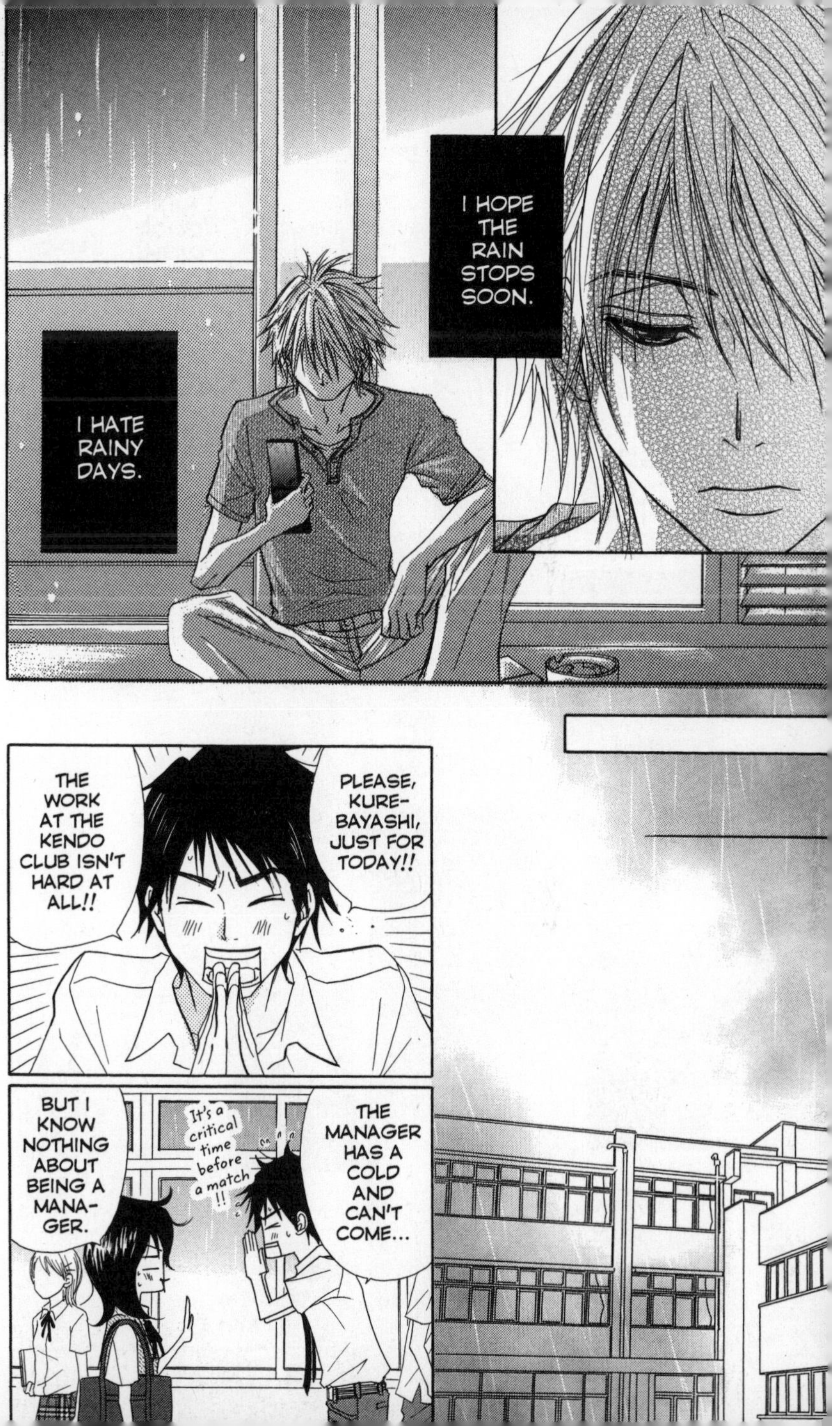

I HOPE THE RAIN STOPS SOON.
I HATE RAINY DAYS.
PLEASE, KURE-BAYASHI, JUST FOR TODAY!!
THE WORK AT THE KENDO CLUB ISN'T HARD AT ALL!!
THE MANAGER HAS A COLD AND CAN'T COME...
It's a critical time before a match!!
BUT I KNOW NOTHING ABOUT BEING A MANA-GER.

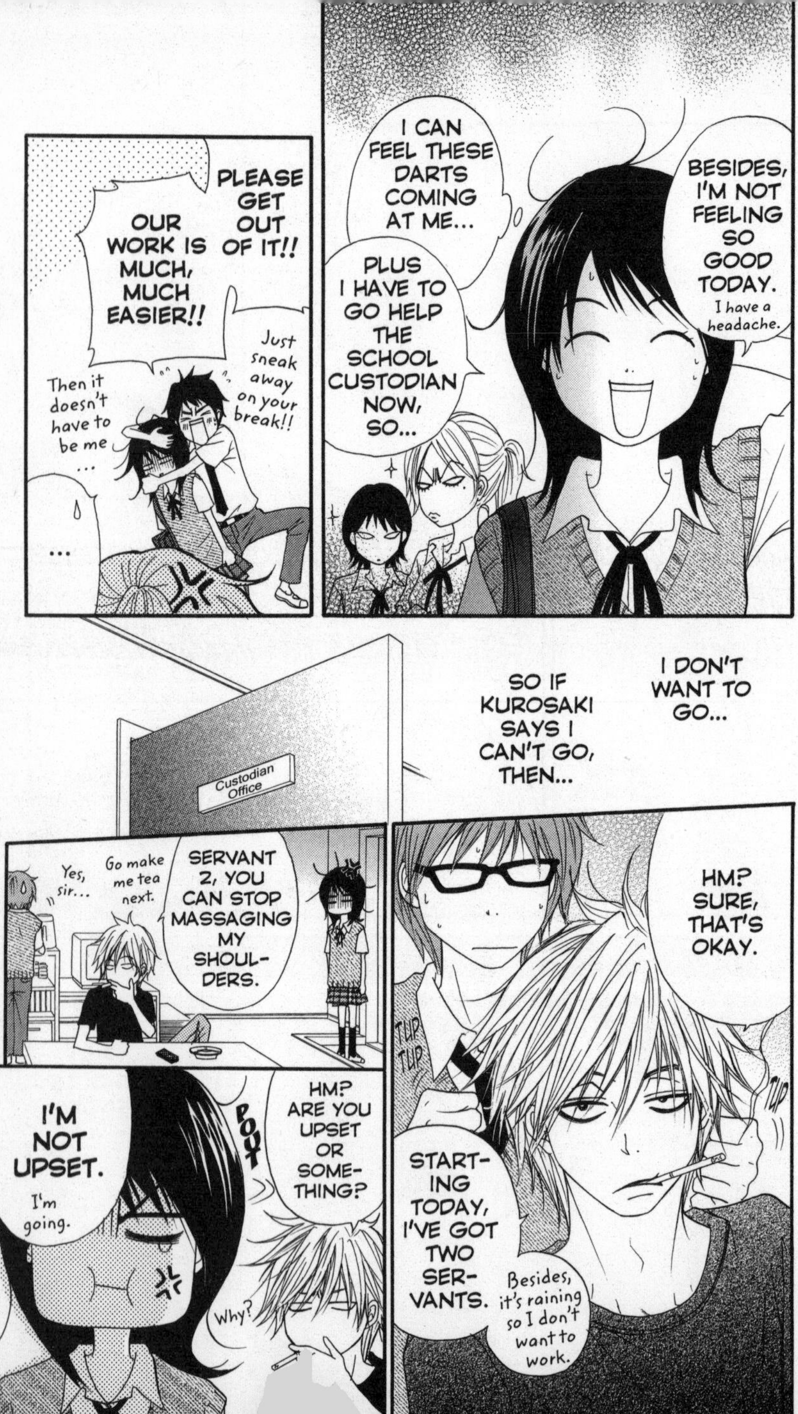
BESIDES, I'M NOT FEELING SO GOOD TODAY.
I have a headache.
I CAN FEEL THESE DARTS COMING AT ME...
PLUS I HAVE TO GO HELP THE SCHOOL CUSTODIAN NOW, SO...
PLEASE GET OUT OF IT!!
OUR WORK IS MUCH, MUCH EASIER!!
Just sneak away on your break!!
Then it doesn't have to be me ...
...
I DON'T WANT TO GO...
SO IF KUROSAKI SAYS I CAN'T GO, THEN...
Custodian Office
HM? SURE, THAT'S OKAY.
TUP TUP
TUP
STARTING TODAY, I'VE GOT TWO SERVANTS.
Besides, it's raining so I don't want to work.
SERVANT 2, YOU CAN STOP MASSAGING MY SHOULDERS.
Go make me tea next.
Yes, sir...
HM? ARE YOU UPSET OR SOMETHING?
POUT
Why?
I'M NOT UPSET.
I'm going.

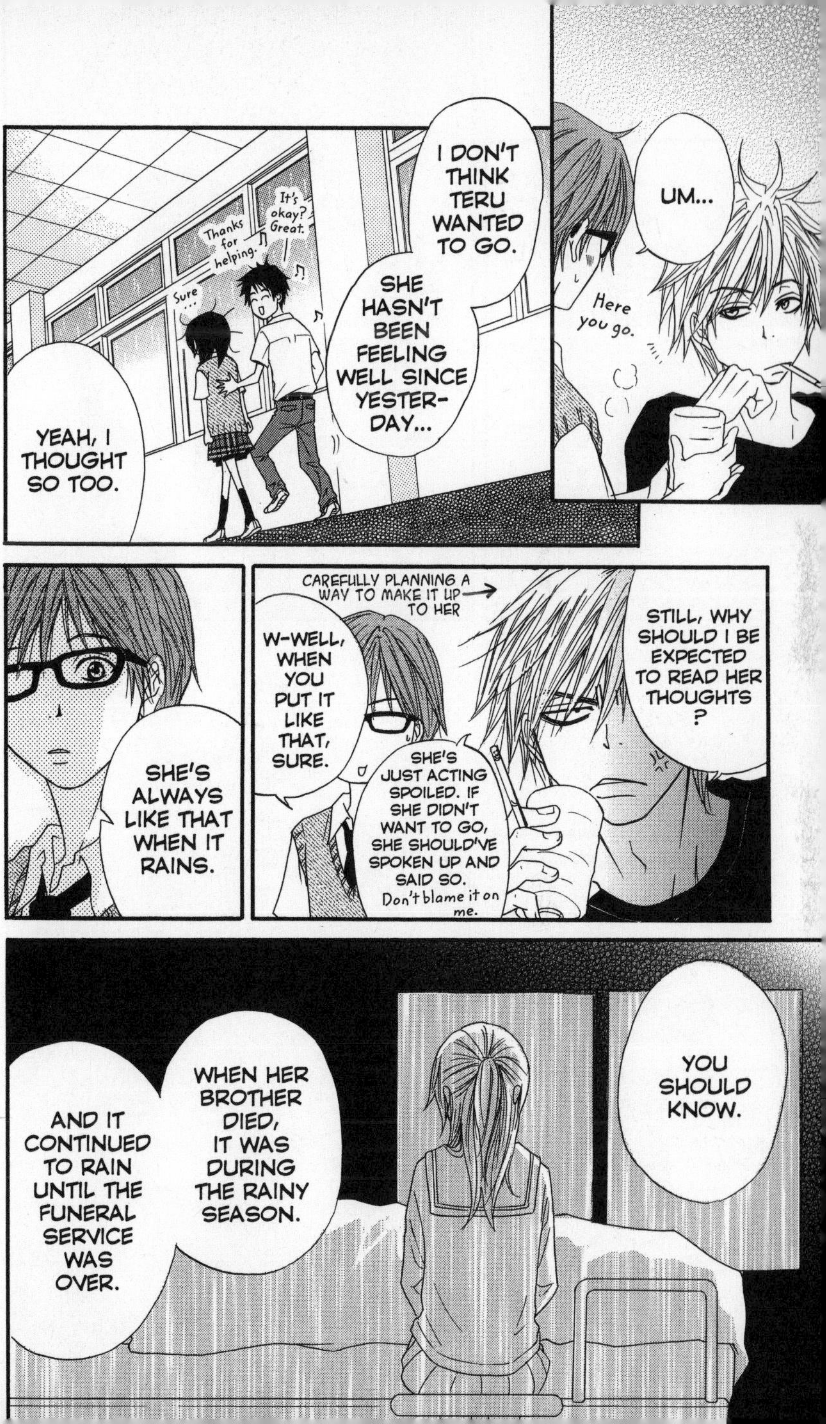
UM...
Here you go.
I DON'T THINK TERU WANTED TO GO.
SHE HASN'T BEEN FEELING WELL SINCE YESTER-DAY...
It's okay? Great.
Thanks for helping.
Sure...
YEAH, I THOUGHT SO TOO.
CAREFULLY PLANNING A WAY TO MAKE IT UP TO HER
STILL, WHY SHOULD I BE EXPECTED TO READ HER THOUGHTS?
SHE'S JUST ACTING SPOILED. IF SHE DIDN'T WANT TO GO, SHE SHOULD'VE SPOKEN UP AND SAID SO.
Don't blame it on me.
W-WELL, WHEN YOU PUT IT LIKE THAT, SURE.
SHE'S ALWAYS LIKE THAT WHEN IT RAINS.
YOU SHOULD KNOW.
WHEN HER BROTHER DIED, IT WAS DURING THE RAINY SEASON.
AND IT CONTINUED TO RAIN UNTIL THE FUNERAL SERVICE WAS OVER.

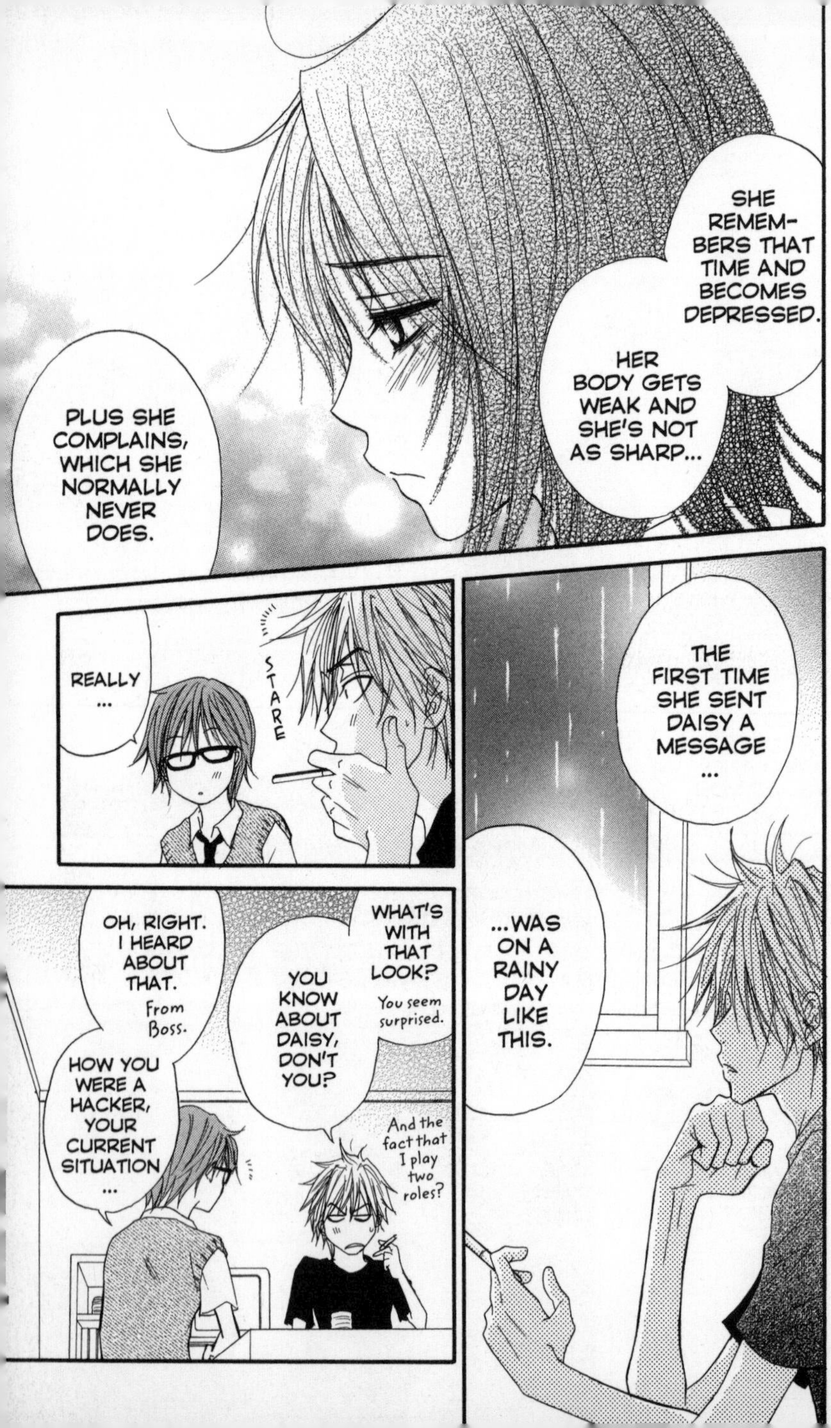
SHE REMEMBERS THAT TIME AND BECOMES DEPRESSED.
HER BODY GETS WEAK AND SHE'S NOT AS SHARP...
PLUS SHE COMPLAINS, WHICH SHE NORMALLY NEVER DOES.
THE FIRST TIME SHE SENT DAISY A MESSAGE ...
...WAS ON A RAINY DAY LIKE THIS.
STARE
REALLY ...
WHAT'S WITH THAT LOOK?
You seem surprised.
YOU KNOW ABOUT DAISY, DON'T YOU?
And the fact that I play two roles?
OH, RIGHT. I HEARD ABOUT THAT.
From Boss.
HOW YOU WERE A HACKER, YOUR CURRENT SITUATION ...

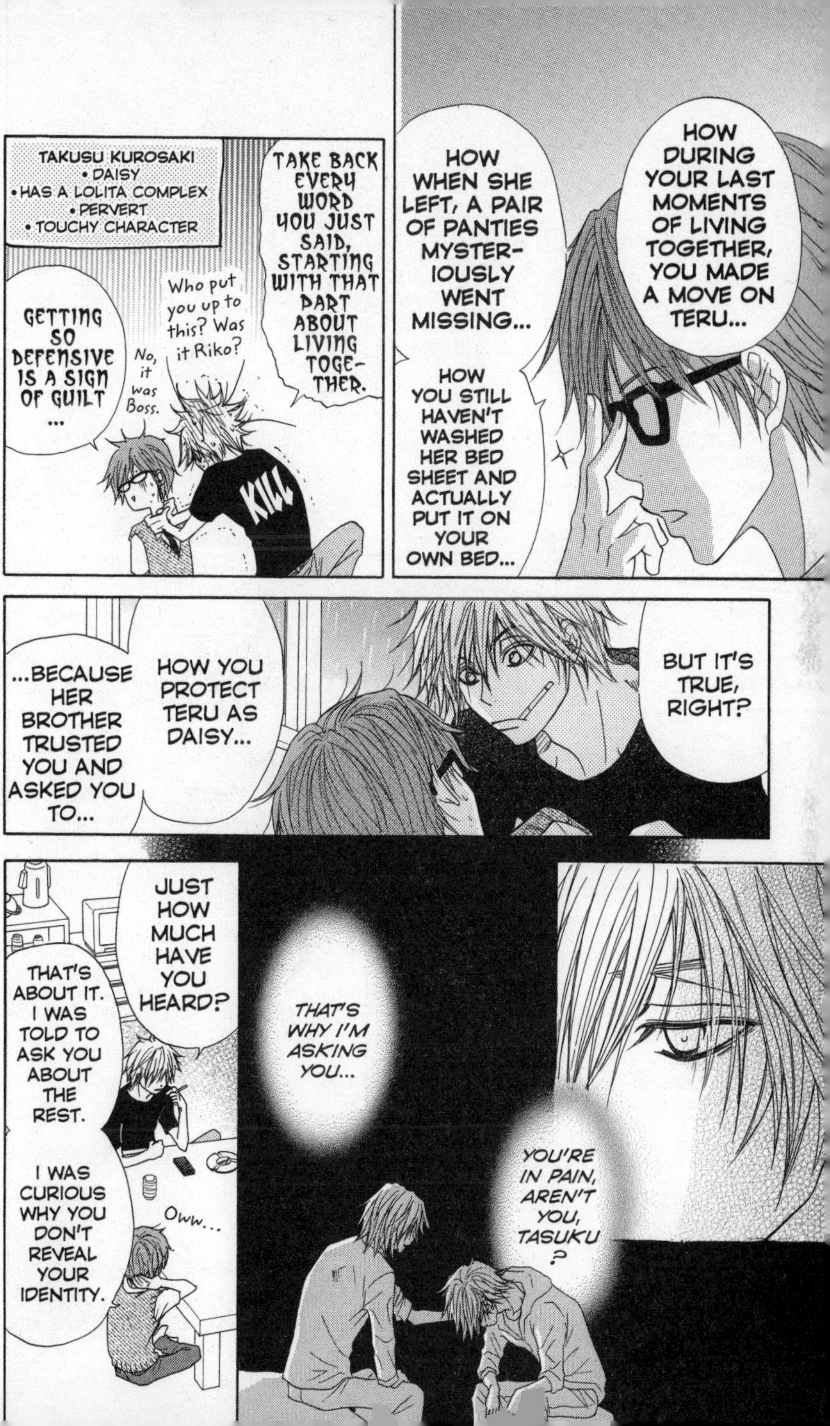
HOW DURING YOUR LAST MOMENTS OF LIVING TOGETHER, YOU MADE A MOVE ON TERU...
HOW WHEN SHE LEFT, A PAIR OF PANTIES MYSTER-IOUSLY WENT MISSING...
HOW YOU STILL HAVEN'T WASHED HER BED SHEET AND ACTUALLY PUT IT ON YOUR OWN BED...
TAKE BACK EVERY WORD YOU JUST SAID, STARTING WITH THAT PART ABOUT LIVING TOGE-THER.
TAKUSU KUROSAKI • DAISY • HAS A LOLITA COMPLEX • PERVERT • TOUCHY CHARACTER
Who put you up to this? Was it Riko?
No, it was Boss.
GETTING SO DEFENSIVE IS A SIGN OF GUILT ...
KILL
BUT IT'S TRUE, RIGHT?
HOW YOU PROTECT TERU AS DAISY...
...BECAUSE HER BROTHER TRUSTED YOU AND ASKED YOU TO...
THAT'S WHY I'M ASKING YOU...
YOU'RE IN PAIN, AREN'T YOU, TASUKU ?
JUST HOW MUCH HAVE YOU HEARD?
THAT'S ABOUT IT. I WAS TOLD TO ASK YOU ABOUT THE REST.
I WAS CURIOUS WHY YOU DON'T REVEAL YOUR IDENTITY.
Oww...

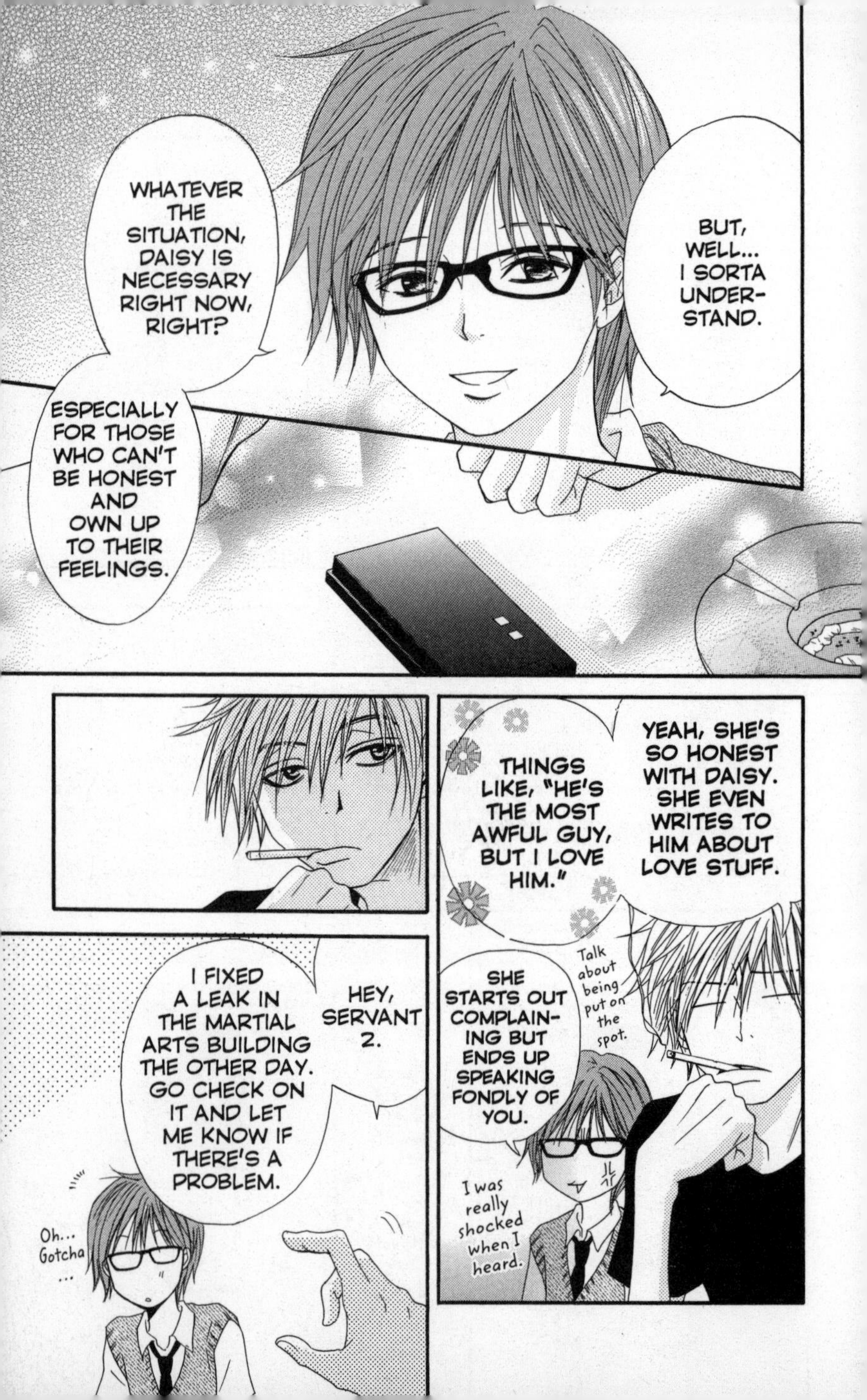
BUT, WELL... I SORTA UNDER-STAND.
WHATEVER THE SITUATION, DAISY IS NECESSARY RIGHT NOW, RIGHT?
ESPECIALLY FOR THOSE WHO CAN'T BE HONEST AND OWN UP TO THEIR FEELINGS.
YEAH, SHE'S SO HONEST WITH DAISY. SHE EVEN WRITES TO HIM ABOUT LOVE STUFF.
THINGS LIKE, "HE'S THE MOST AWFUL GUY, BUT I LOVE HIM."
Talk about being put on the spot.
SHE STARTS OUT COMPLAIN-ING BUT ENDS UP SPEAKING FONDLY OF YOU.
I was really shocked when I heard.
HEY, SERVANT 2.
I FIXED A LEAK IN THE MARTIAL ARTS BUILDING THE OTHER DAY. GO CHECK ON IT AND LET ME KNOW IF THERE'S A PROBLEM.
Oh... Gotcha...

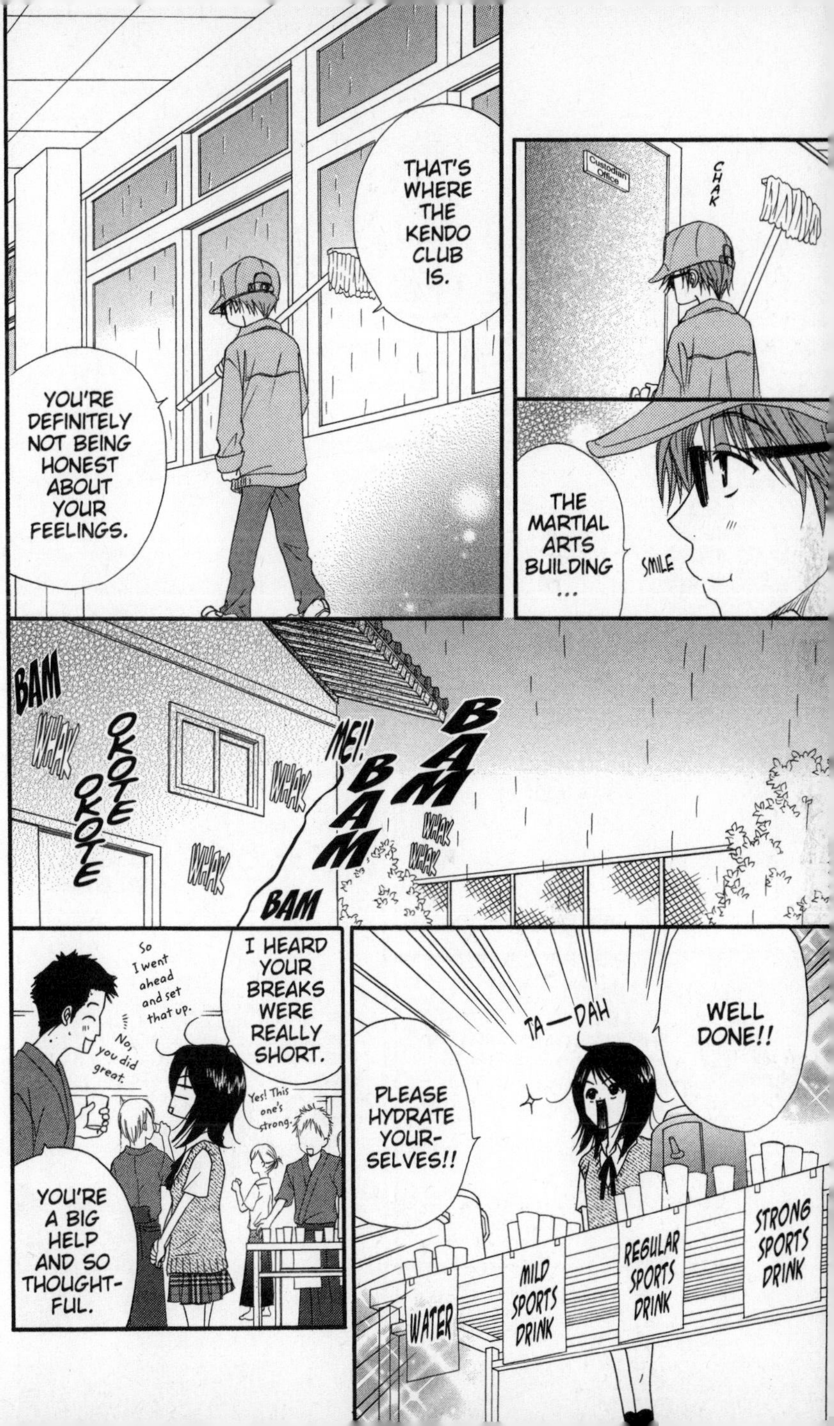
Custodian Office
CHAK
THE MARTIAL ARTS BUILDING ...
SMILE
THAT'S WHERE THE KENDO CLUB IS.
YOU'RE DEFINITELY NOT BEING HONEST ABOUT YOUR FEELINGS.
BAM
BAM
BAM
MEI!
WHAK
WHAK
WHAK
OKOTE OKOTE
WHAK
WHAK
BAM
BAM
WELL DONE!!
TA—DAH
PLEASE HYDRATE YOURSELVES!!
STRONG SPORTS DRINK
REGULAR SPORTS DRINK
MILD SPORTS DRINK
WATER
I HEARD YOUR BREAKS WERE REALLY SHORT.
So I went ahead and set that up.
No, you did great.
Yes! This one's strong.
YOU'RE A BIG HELP AND SO THOUGHTFUL.

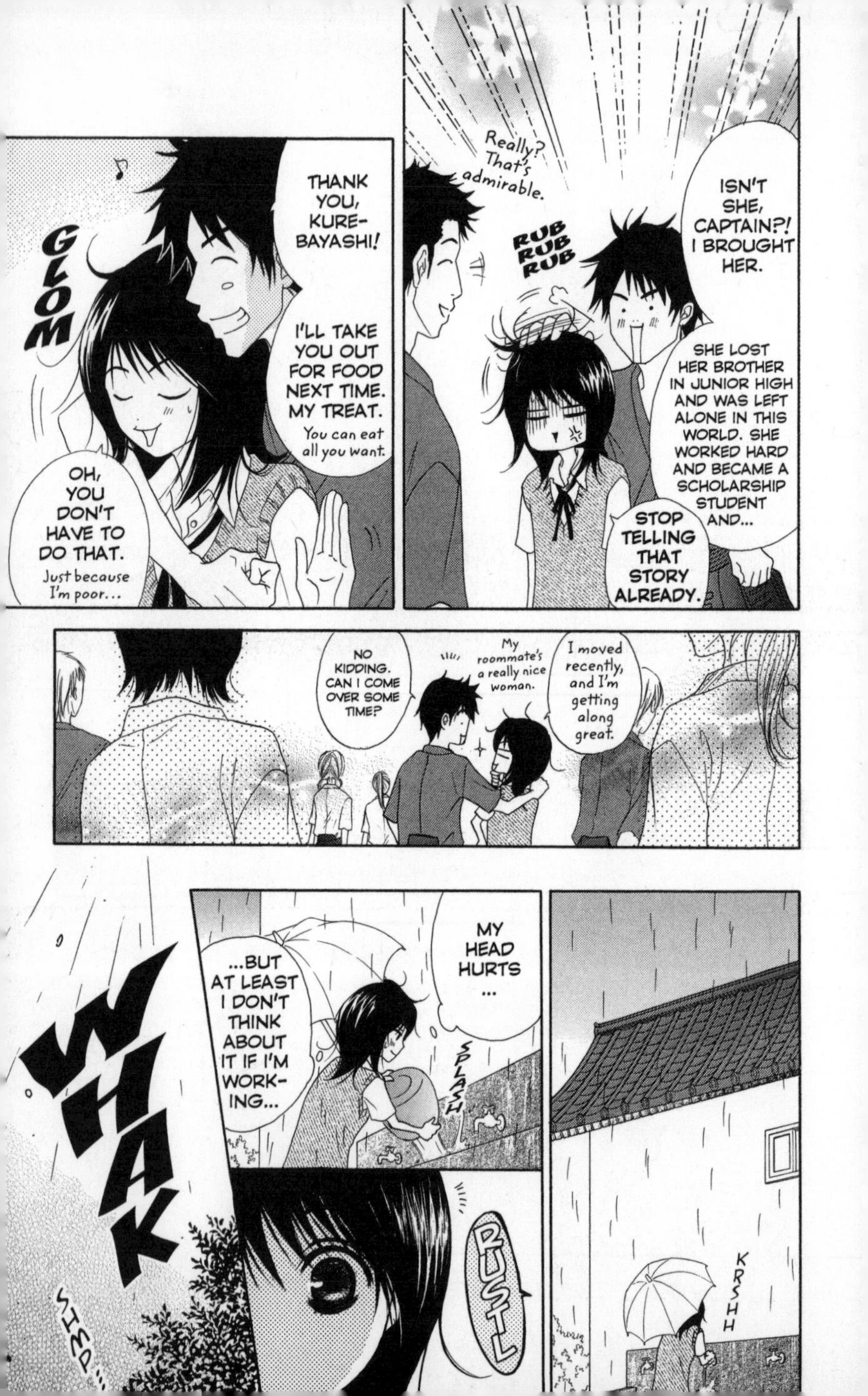

ISN'T SHE, CAPTAIN?! I BROUGHT HER.
Really? That's admirable.
RUB RUB RUB
SHE LOST HER BROTHER IN JUNIOR HIGH AND WAS LEFT ALONE IN THIS WORLD. SHE WORKED HARD AND BECAME A SCHOLARSHIP STUDENT AND...
STOP TELLING THAT STORY ALREADY.
THANK YOU, KURE-BAYASHI!
I'LL TAKE YOU OUT FOR FOOD NEXT TIME. MY TREAT.
You can eat all you want.
GLOM
OH, YOU DON'T HAVE TO DO THAT.
Just because I'm poor...
I moved recently, and I'm getting along great.
My roommate's a really nice woman.
NO KIDDING. CAN I COME OVER SOME TIME?
KRSHH
MY HEAD HURTS...
...BUT AT LEAST I DON'T THINK ABOUT IT IF I'M WORK-ING...
SPLASH
RUSTL
WHAK
SHMP...

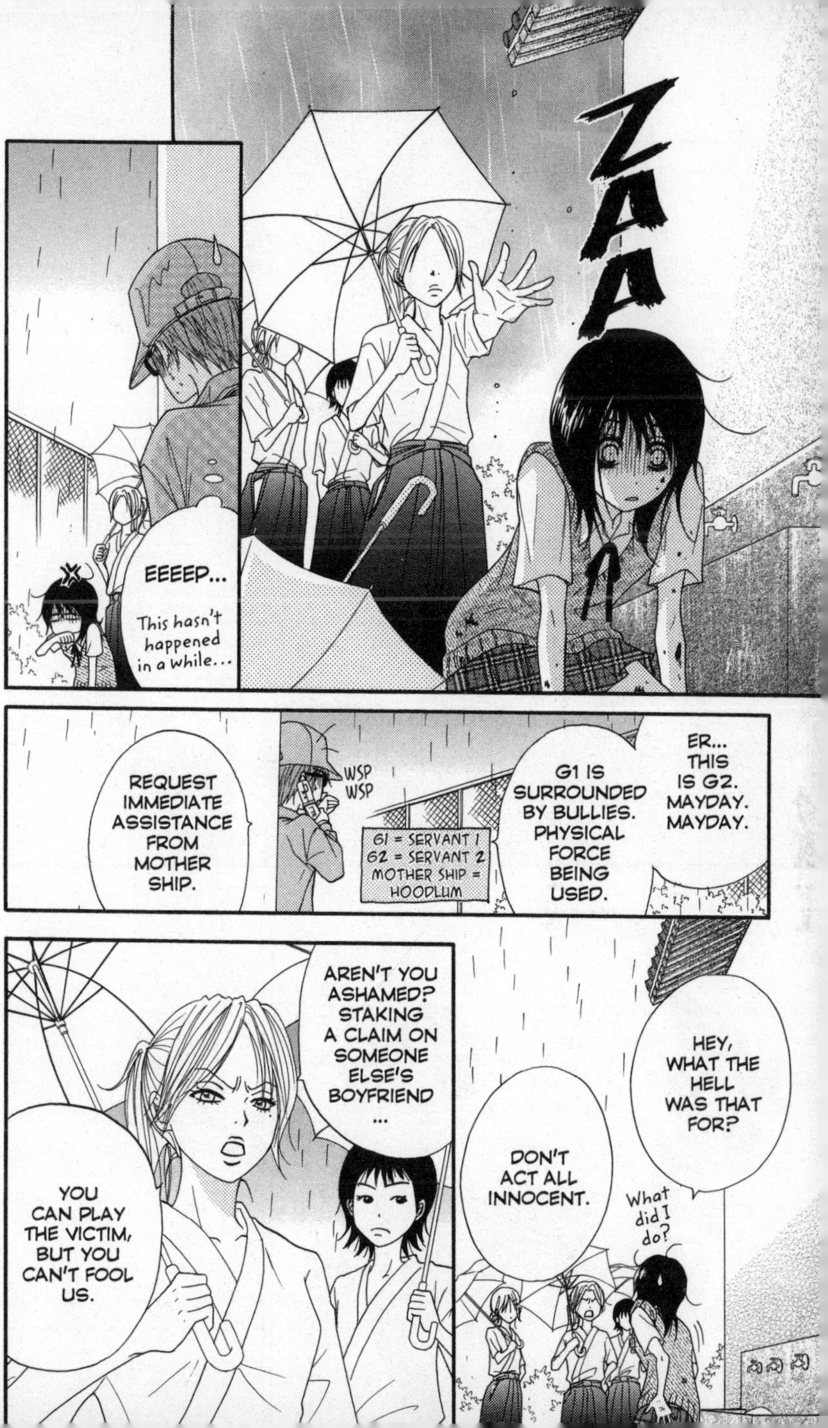
ZAA
EEEEP...
This hasn't happened in a while...
ER... THIS IS G2. MAYDAY. MAYDAY.
G1 IS SURROUNDED BY BULLIES. PHYSICAL FORCE BEING USED.
WSP WSP
G1 = SERVANT 1 G2 = SERVANT 2 MOTHER SHIP = HOODLUM
REQUEST IMMEDIATE ASSISTANCE FROM MOTHER SHIP.
HEY, WHAT THE HELL WAS THAT FOR?
What did I do?
DON'T ACT ALL INNOCENT.
AREN'T YOU ASHAMED? STAKING A CLAIM ON SOMEONE ELSE'S BOYFRIEND ...
YOU CAN PLAY THE VICTIM, BUT YOU CAN'T FOOL US.

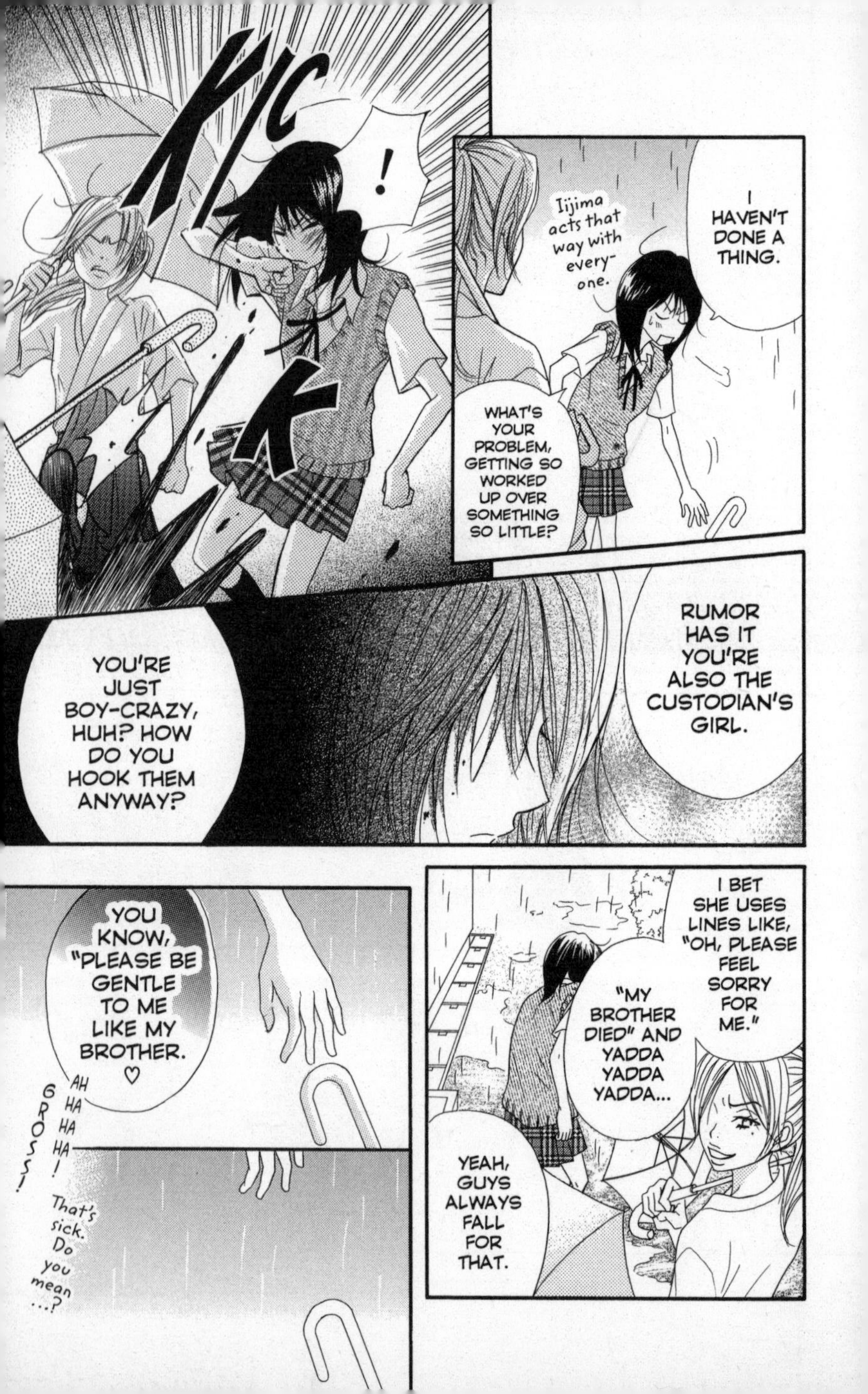
I HAVEN'T DONE A THING.
Iijima acts that way with every-one.
WHAT'S YOUR PROBLEM, GETTING SO WORKED UP OVER SOMETHING SO LITTLE?
!
KICK
RUMOR HAS IT YOU'RE ALSO THE CUSTODIAN'S GIRL.
YOU'RE JUST BOY-CRAZY, HUH? HOW DO YOU HOOK THEM ANYWAY?
I BET SHE USES LINES LIKE, "OH, PLEASE FEEL SORRY FOR ME."
"MY BROTHER DIED" AND YADDA YADDA YADDA...
YEAH, GUYS ALWAYS FALL FOR THAT.
YOU KNOW, "PLEASE BE GENTLE TO ME LIKE MY BROTHER. ♡
AH HA HA HA!
GROSS!
That's sick. Do you mean ...?

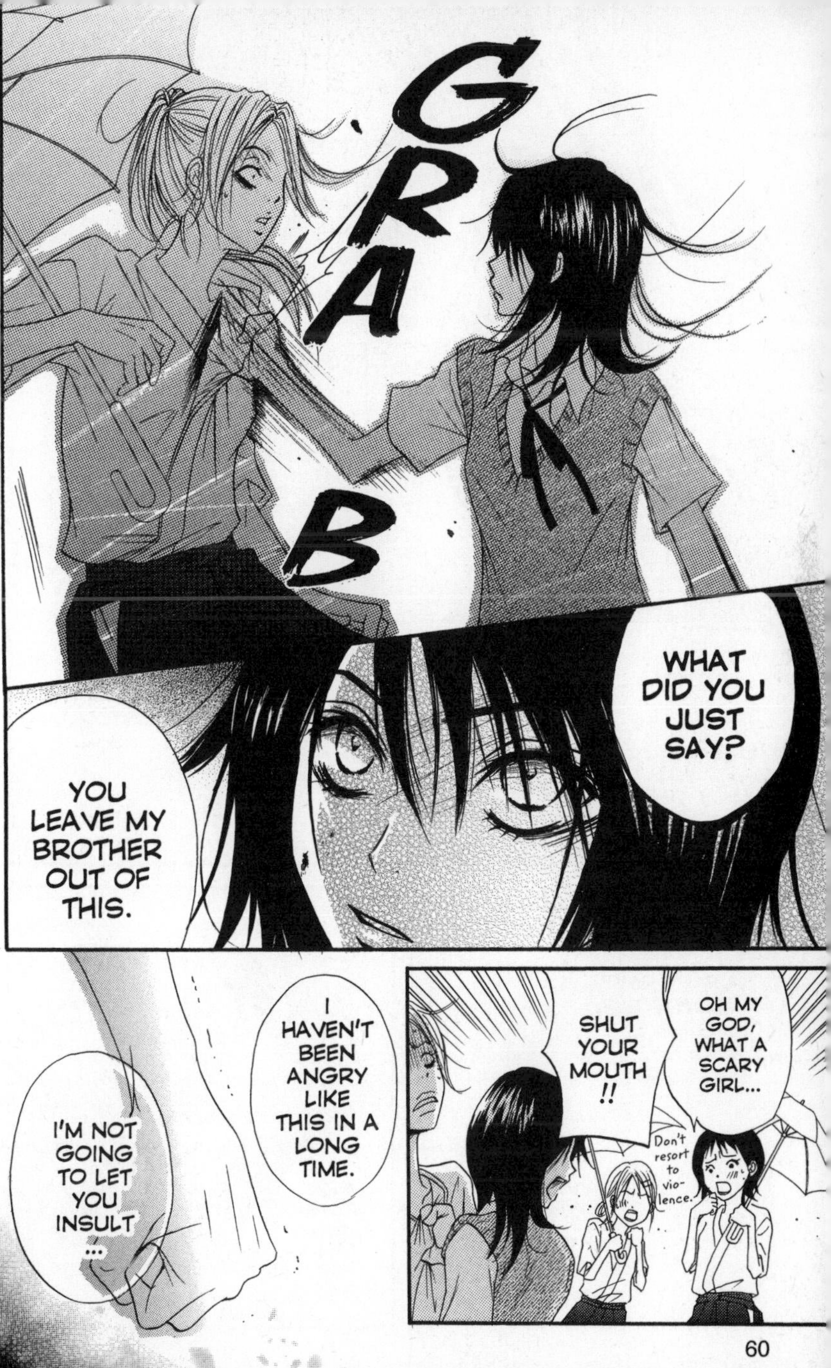
GRAB
WHAT DID YOU JUST SAY?
YOU LEAVE MY BROTHER OUT OF THIS.
OH MY GOD, WHAT A SCARY GIRL...
SHUT YOUR MOUTH !!
Don't resort to vio-lence.
I HAVEN'T BEEN ANGRY LIKE THIS IN A LONG TIME.
I'M NOT GOING TO LET YOU INSULT ...

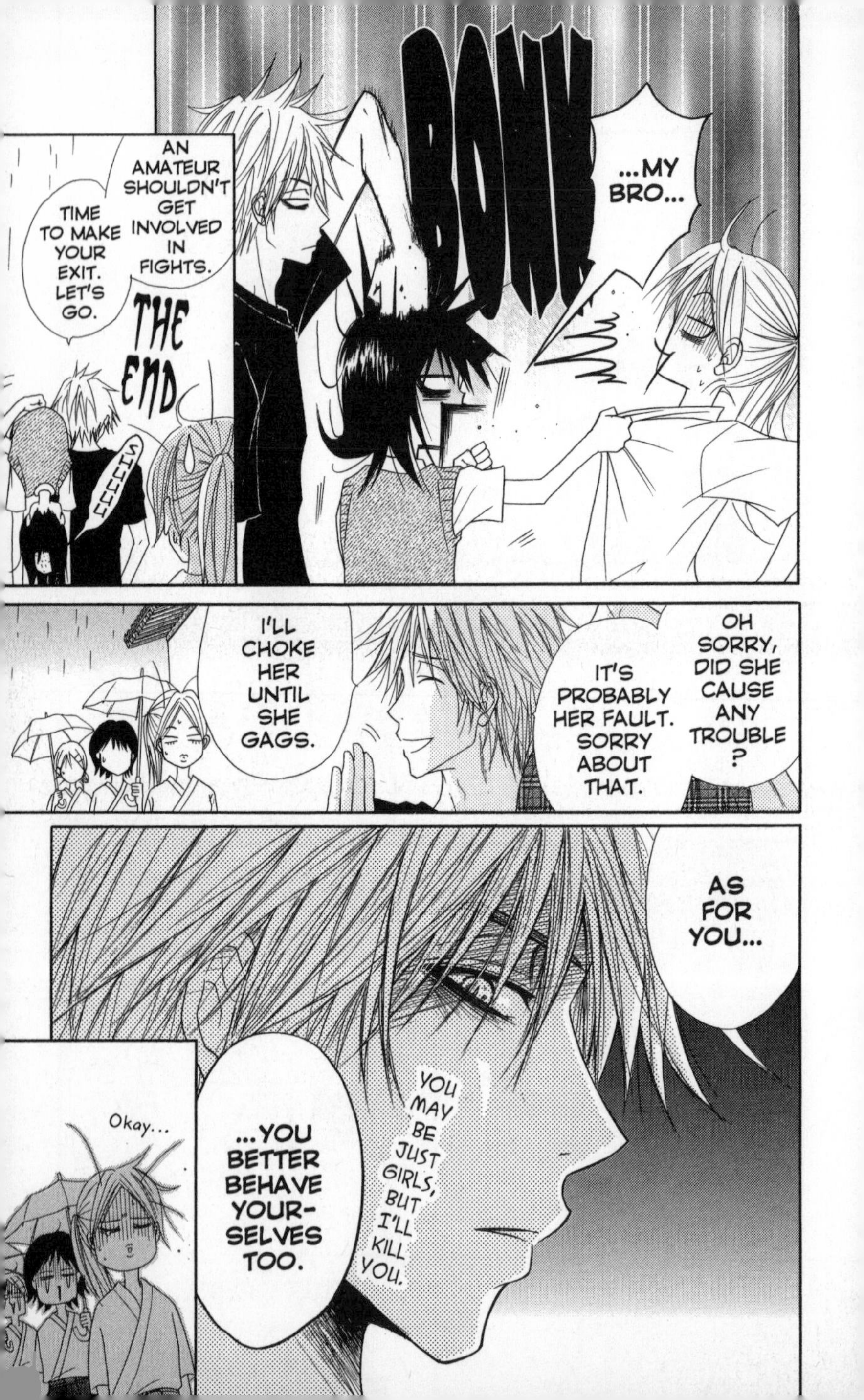
BONK
...MY BRO...
AN AMATEUR SHOULDN'T GET INVOLVED IN FIGHTS.
TIME TO MAKE YOUR EXIT. LET'S GO.
THE END
SHUUUU
OH SORRY, DID SHE CAUSE ANY TROUBLE?
IT'S PROBABLY HER FAULT. SORRY ABOUT THAT.
I'LL CHOKE HER UNTIL SHE GAGS.
AS FOR YOU...
...YOU BETTER BEHAVE YOURSELVES TOO.
YOU MAY BE JUST GIRLS, BUT I'LL KILL YOU.
Okay...

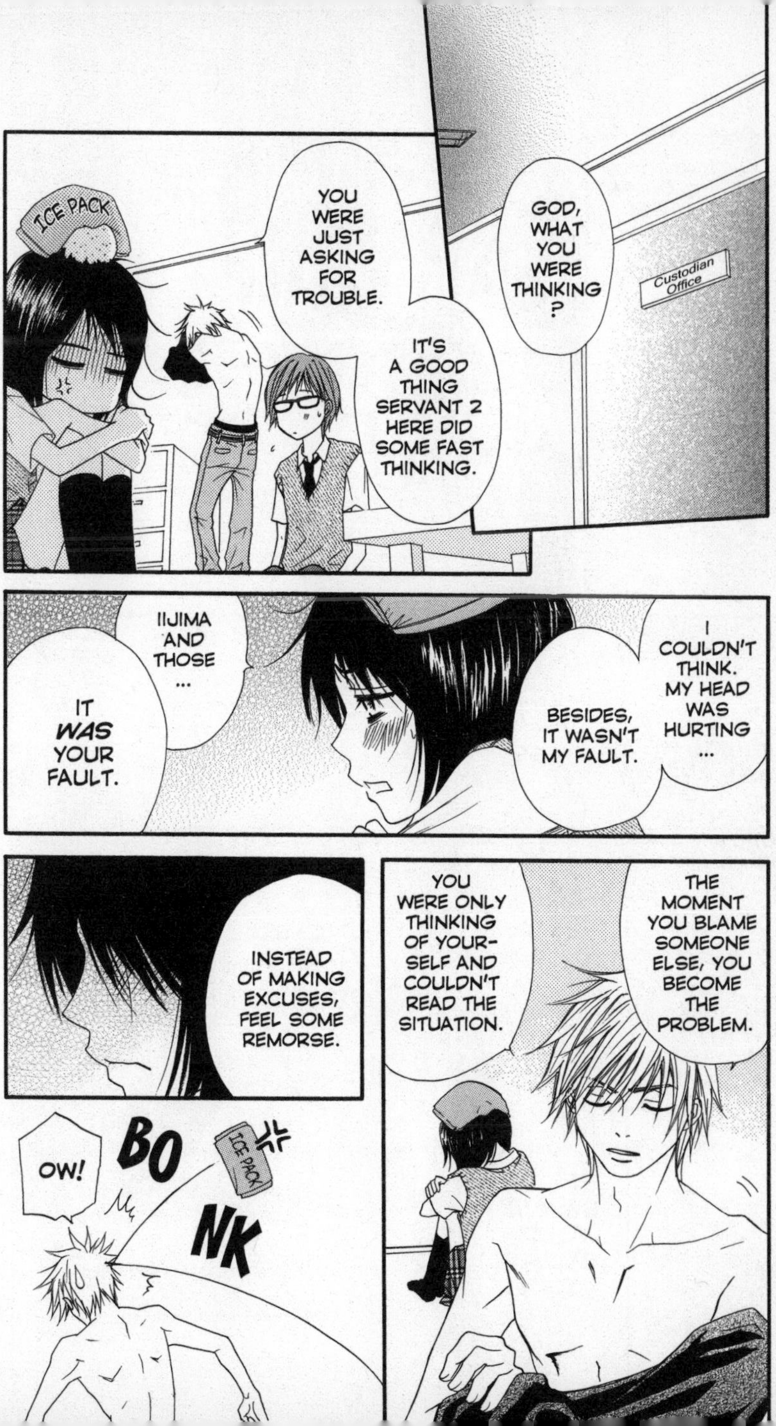
GOD, WHAT YOU WERE THINKING?
Custodian Office
YOU WERE JUST ASKING FOR TROUBLE.
ICE PACK
IT'S A GOOD THING SERVANT 2 HERE DID SOME FAST THINKING.
I COULDN'T THINK. MY HEAD WAS HURTING...
BESIDES, IT WASN'T MY FAULT.
IIJIMA AND THOSE...
IT *WAS* YOUR FAULT.
THE MOMENT YOU BLAME SOMEONE ELSE, YOU BECOME THE PROBLEM.
YOU WERE ONLY THINKING OF YOURSELF AND COULDN'T READ THE SITUATION.
INSTEAD OF MAKING EXCUSES, FEEL SOME REMORSE.
BONK
ICE PACK
OW!

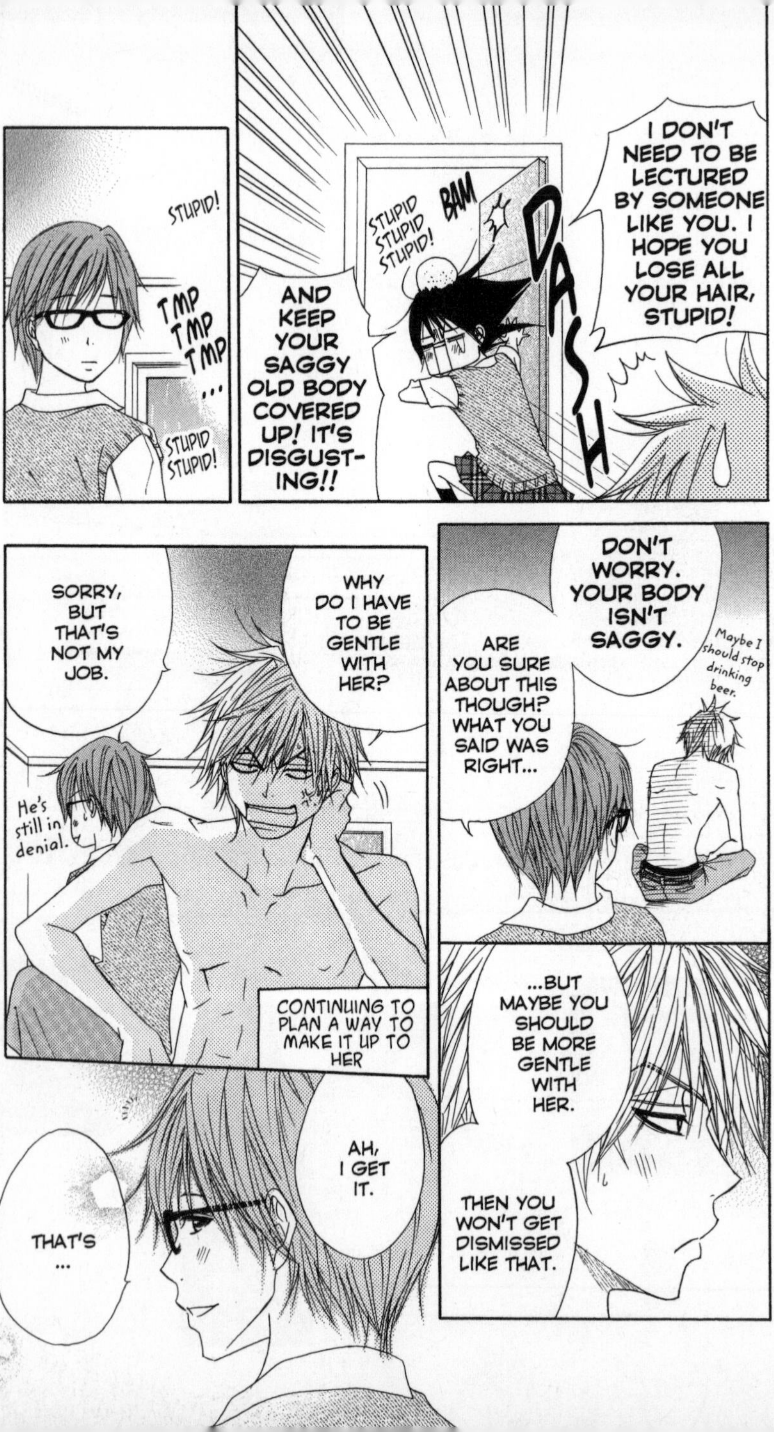
I DON'T NEED TO BE LECTURED BY SOMEONE LIKE YOU. I HOPE YOU LOSE ALL YOUR HAIR, STUPID!
DASH
BAM
STUPID STUPID STUPID!
AND KEEP YOUR SAGGY OLD BODY COVERED UP! IT'S DISGUST-ING!!
STUPID!
TMP TMP TMP
...
STUPID STUPID!
DON'T WORRY. YOUR BODY ISN'T SAGGY.
Maybe I should stop drinking beer.
ARE YOU SURE ABOUT THIS THOUGH? WHAT YOU SAID WAS RIGHT...
...BUT MAYBE YOU SHOULD BE MORE GENTLE WITH HER.
THEN YOU WON'T GET DISMISSED LIKE THAT.
WHY DO I HAVE TO BE GENTLE WITH HER?
SORRY, BUT THAT'S NOT MY JOB.
He's still in denial.
CONTINUING TO PLAN A WAY TO MAKE IT UP TO HER
AH, I GET IT.
THAT'S ...

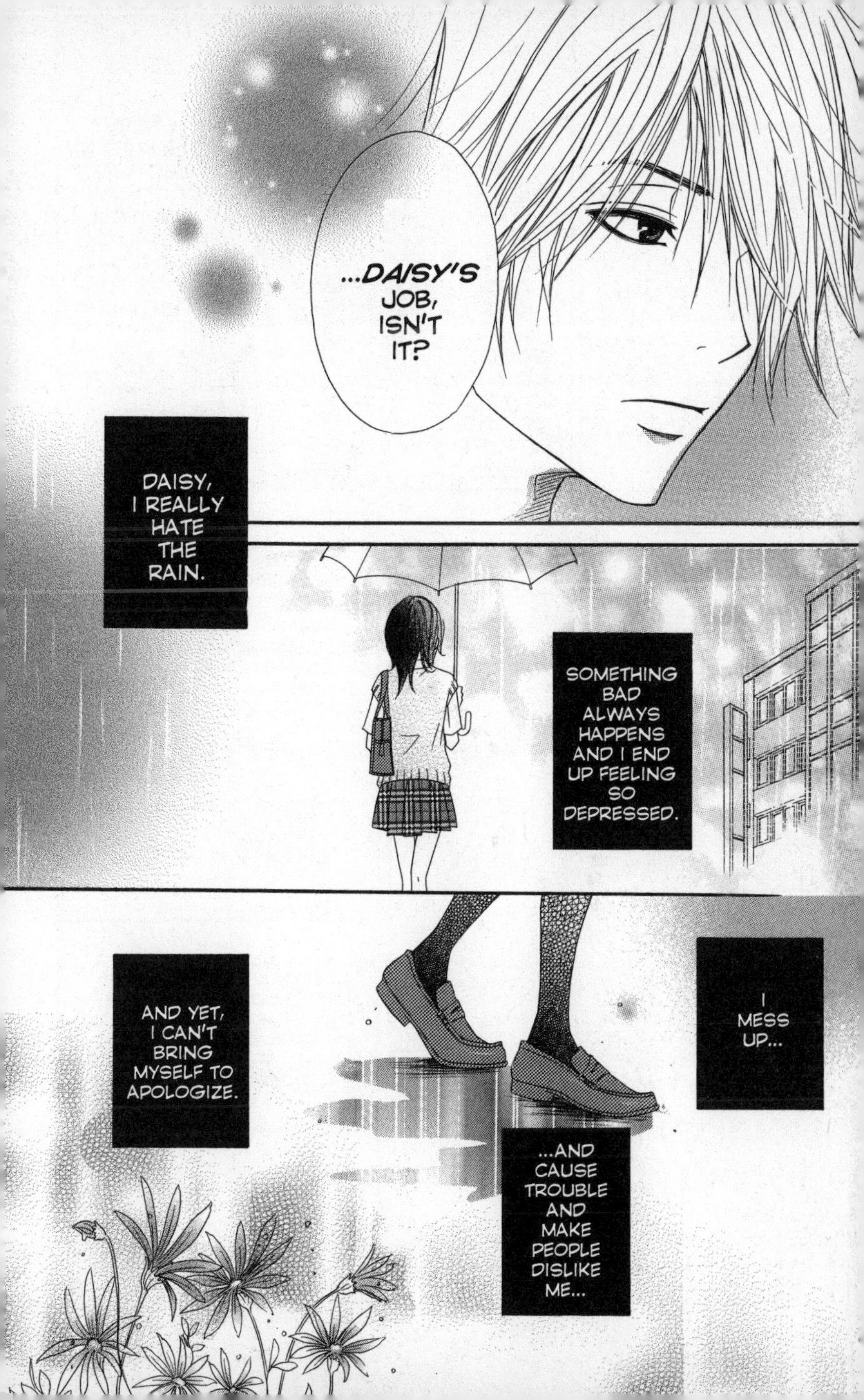
...DAISY'S JOB, ISN'T IT?
DAISY, I REALLY HATE THE RAIN.
SOMETHING BAD ALWAYS HAPPENS AND I END UP FEELING SO DEPRESSED.
I MESS UP...
...AND CAUSE TROUBLE AND MAKE PEOPLE DISLIKE ME...
AND YET, I CAN'T BRING MYSELF TO APOLOGIZE.

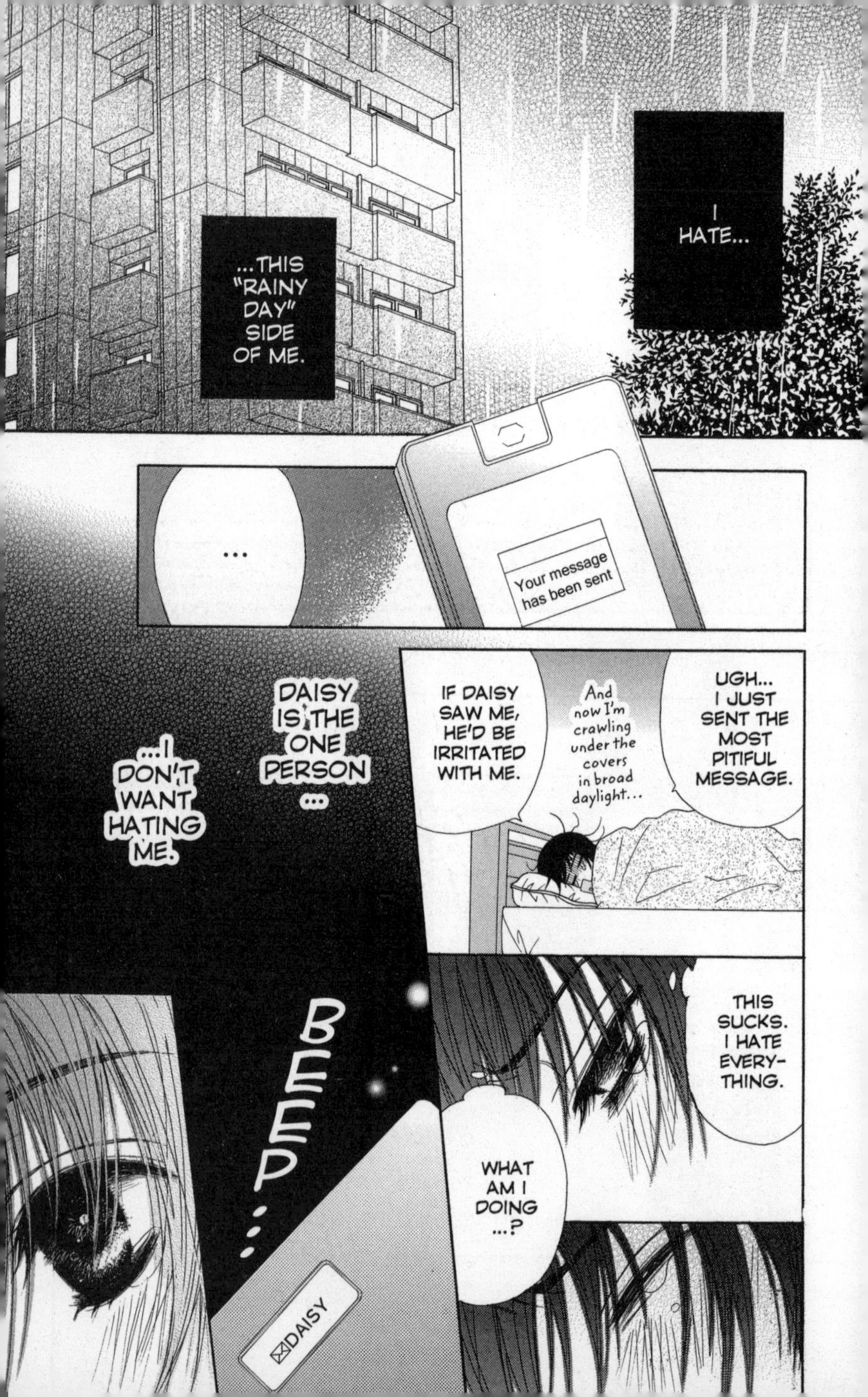
I HATE...
...THIS "RAINY DAY" SIDE OF ME.
Your message has been sent
...
UGH... I JUST SENT THE MOST PITIFUL MESSAGE.
And now I'm crawling under the covers in broad daylight...
IF DAISY SAW ME, HE'D BE IRRITATED WITH ME.
DAISY IS THE ONE PERSON...
...I DON'T WANT HATING ME.
THIS SUCKS. I HATE EVERYTHING.
WHAT AM I DOING...?
BEEP...
DAISY

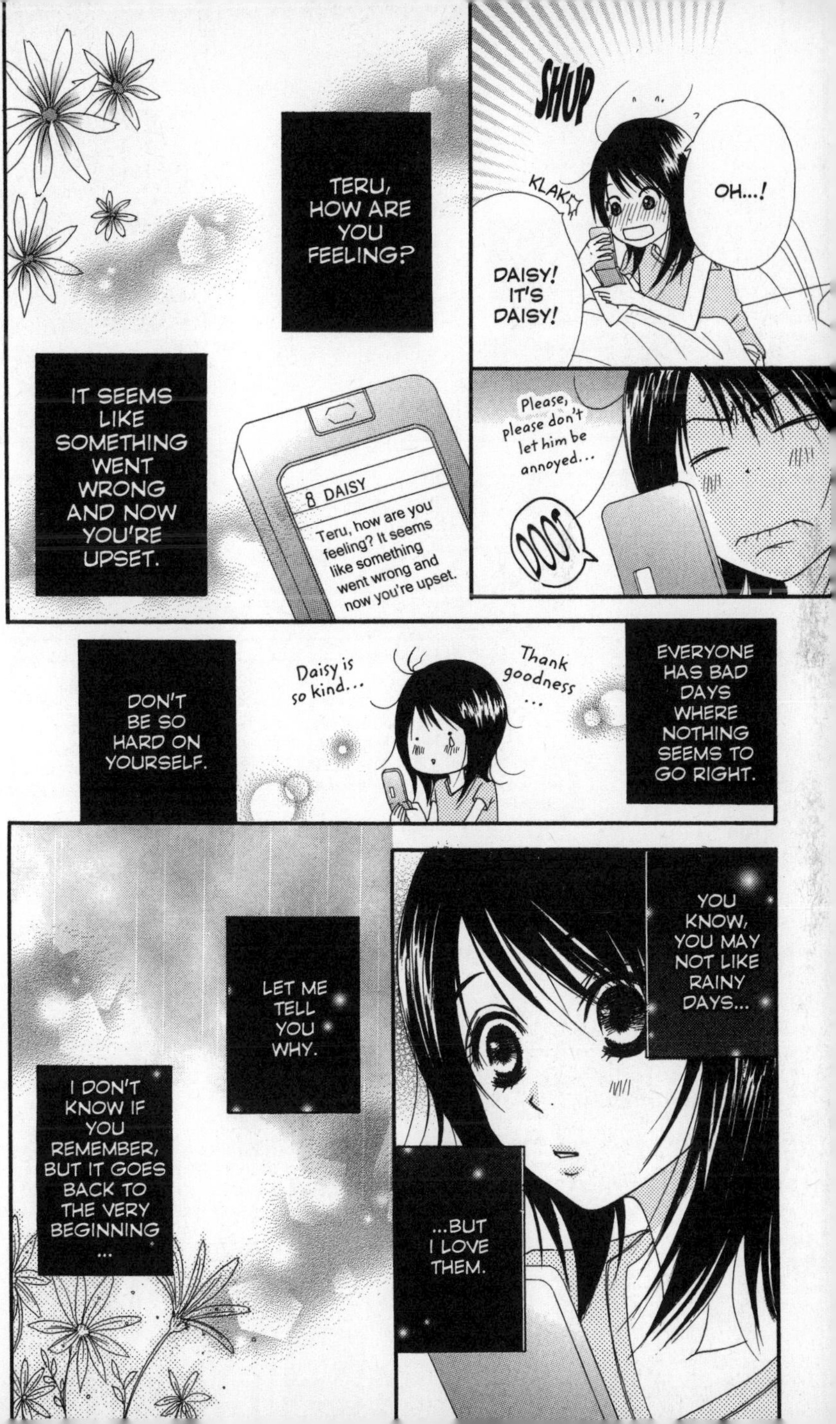
SHUP
OH...!
KLAK
DAISY! IT'S DAISY!
Please, please don't let him be annoyed...
DOOT
TERU, HOW ARE YOU FEELING?
IT SEEMS LIKE SOMETHING WENT WRONG AND NOW YOU'RE UPSET.
8 DAISY
Teru, how are you feeling? It seems like something went wrong and now you're upset.
EVERYONE HAS BAD DAYS WHERE NOTHING SEEMS TO GO RIGHT.
Thank goodness...
Daisy is so kind...
DON'T BE SO HARD ON YOURSELF.
YOU KNOW, YOU MAY NOT LIKE RAINY DAYS...
...BUT I LOVE THEM.
LET ME TELL YOU WHY.
I DON'T KNOW IF YOU REMEMBER, BUT IT GOES BACK TO THE VERY BEGINNING...

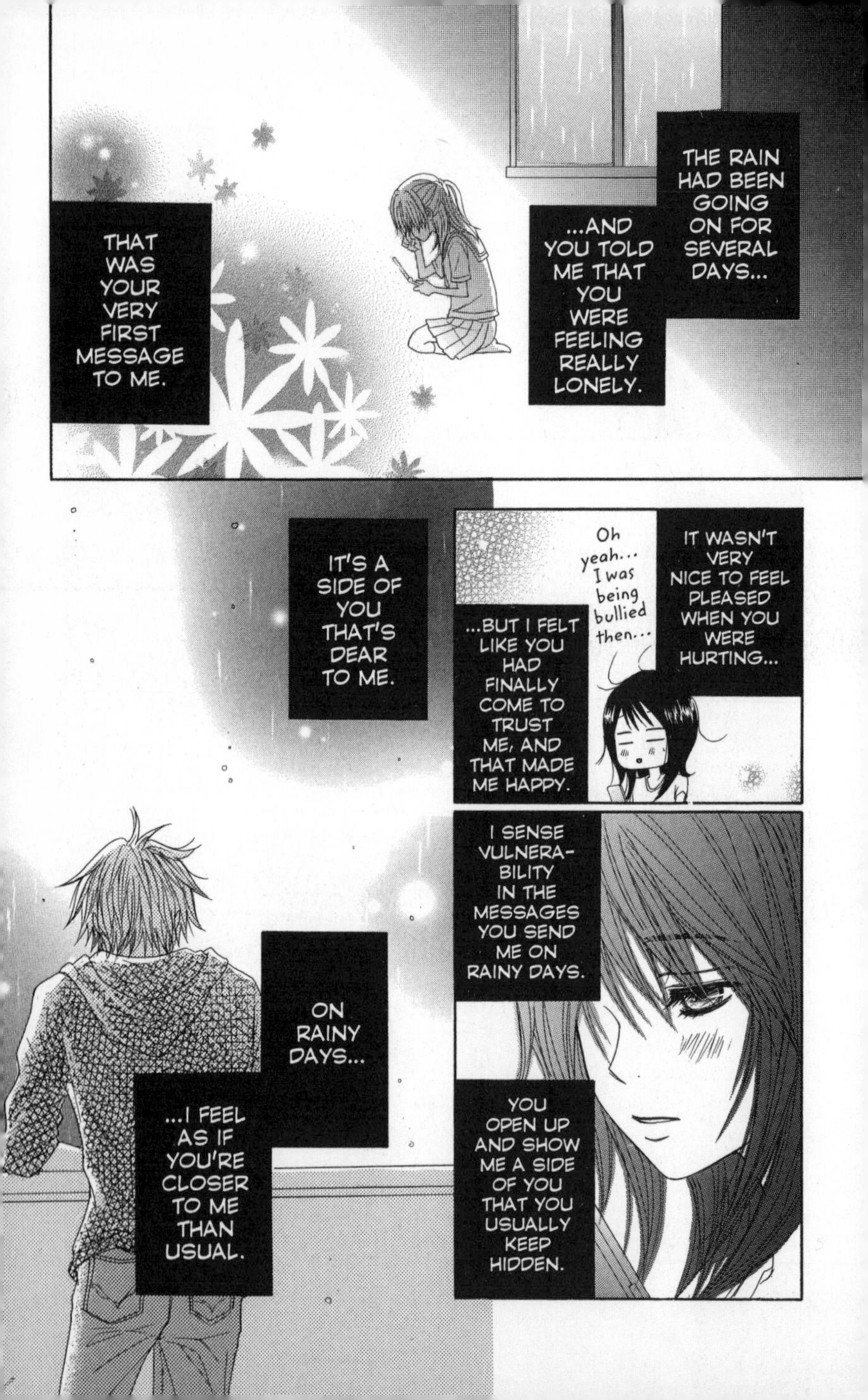
THE RAIN HAD BEEN GOING ON FOR SEVERAL DAYS...
...AND YOU TOLD ME THAT YOU WERE FEELING REALLY LONELY.
THAT WAS YOUR VERY FIRST MESSAGE TO ME.
IT WASN'T VERY NICE TO FEEL PLEASED WHEN YOU WERE HURTING...
Oh yeah... I was being bullied then...
...BUT I FELT LIKE YOU HAD FINALLY COME TO TRUST ME, AND THAT MADE ME HAPPY.
I SENSE VULNERA-BILITY IN THE MESSAGES YOU SEND ME ON RAINY DAYS.
YOU OPEN UP AND SHOW ME A SIDE OF YOU THAT YOU USUALLY KEEP HIDDEN.
IT'S A SIDE OF YOU THAT'S DEAR TO ME.
ON RAINY DAYS...
...I FEEL AS IF YOU'RE CLOSER TO ME THAN USUAL.

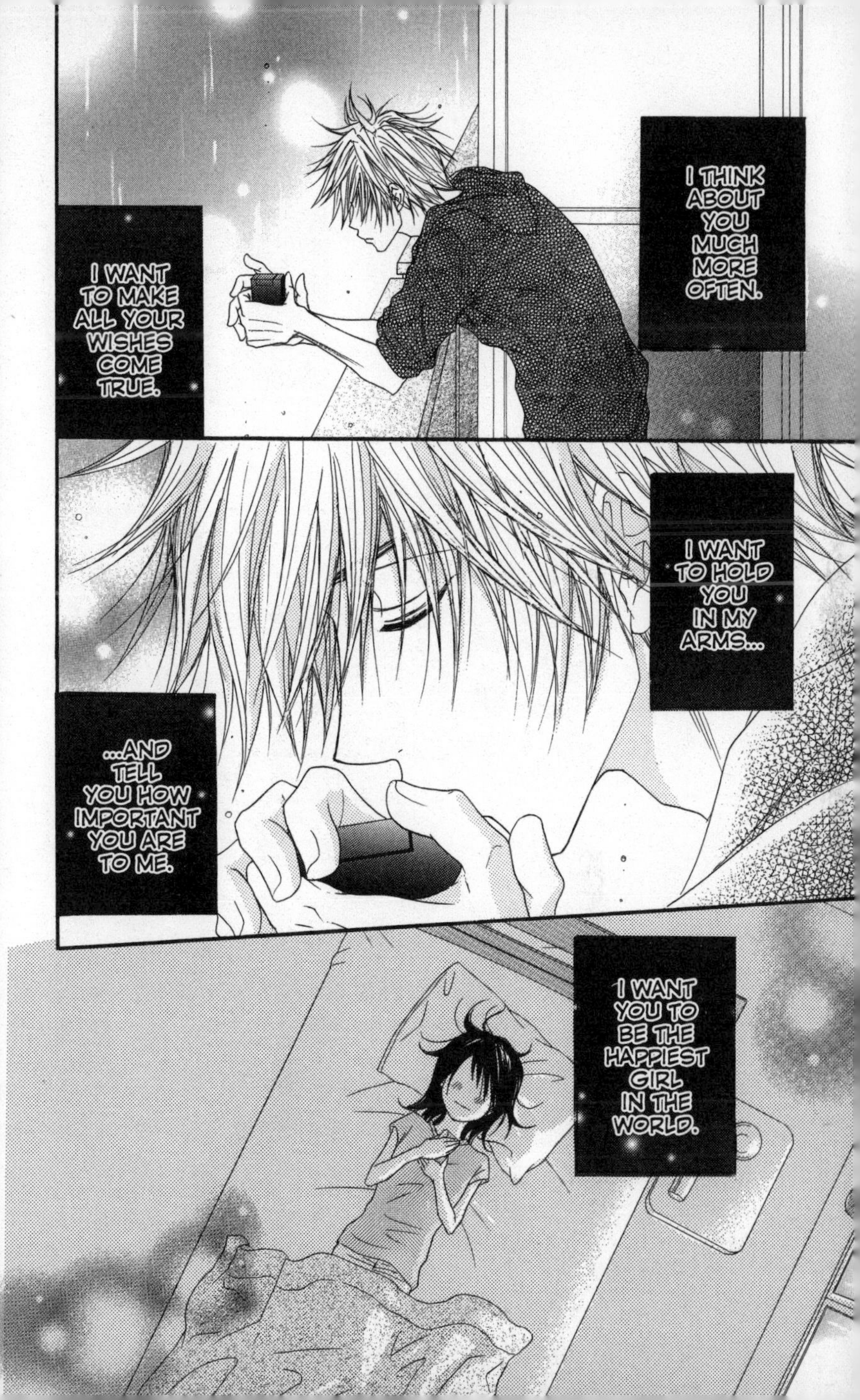
I THINK ABOUT YOU MUCH MORE OFTEN.
I WANT TO MAKE ALL YOUR WISHES COME TRUE.
I WANT TO HOLD YOU IN MY ARMS...
...AND TELL YOU HOW IMPORTANT YOU ARE TO ME.
I WANT YOU TO BE THE HAPPIEST GIRL IN THE WORLD.

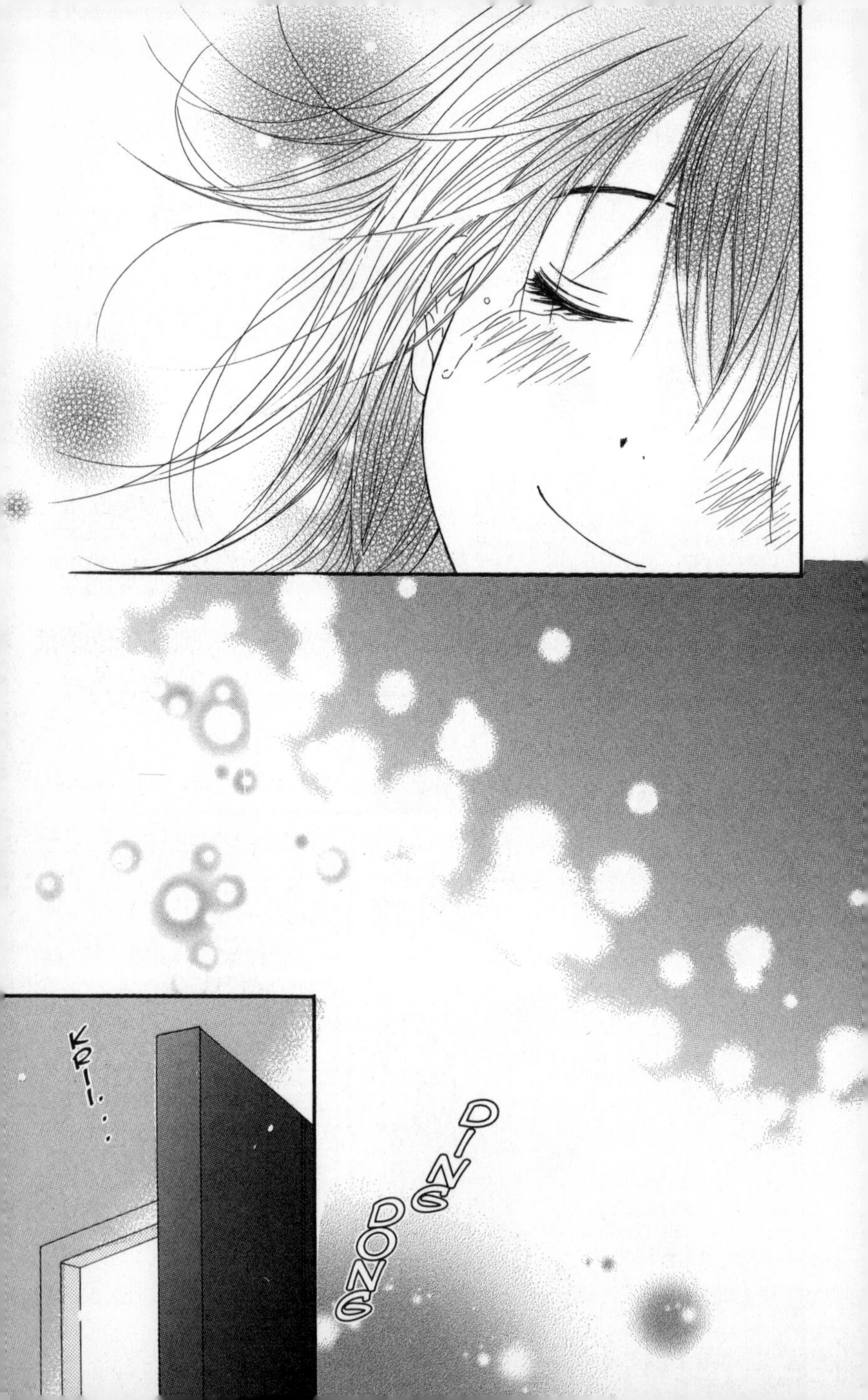
DING DONG
KRI...

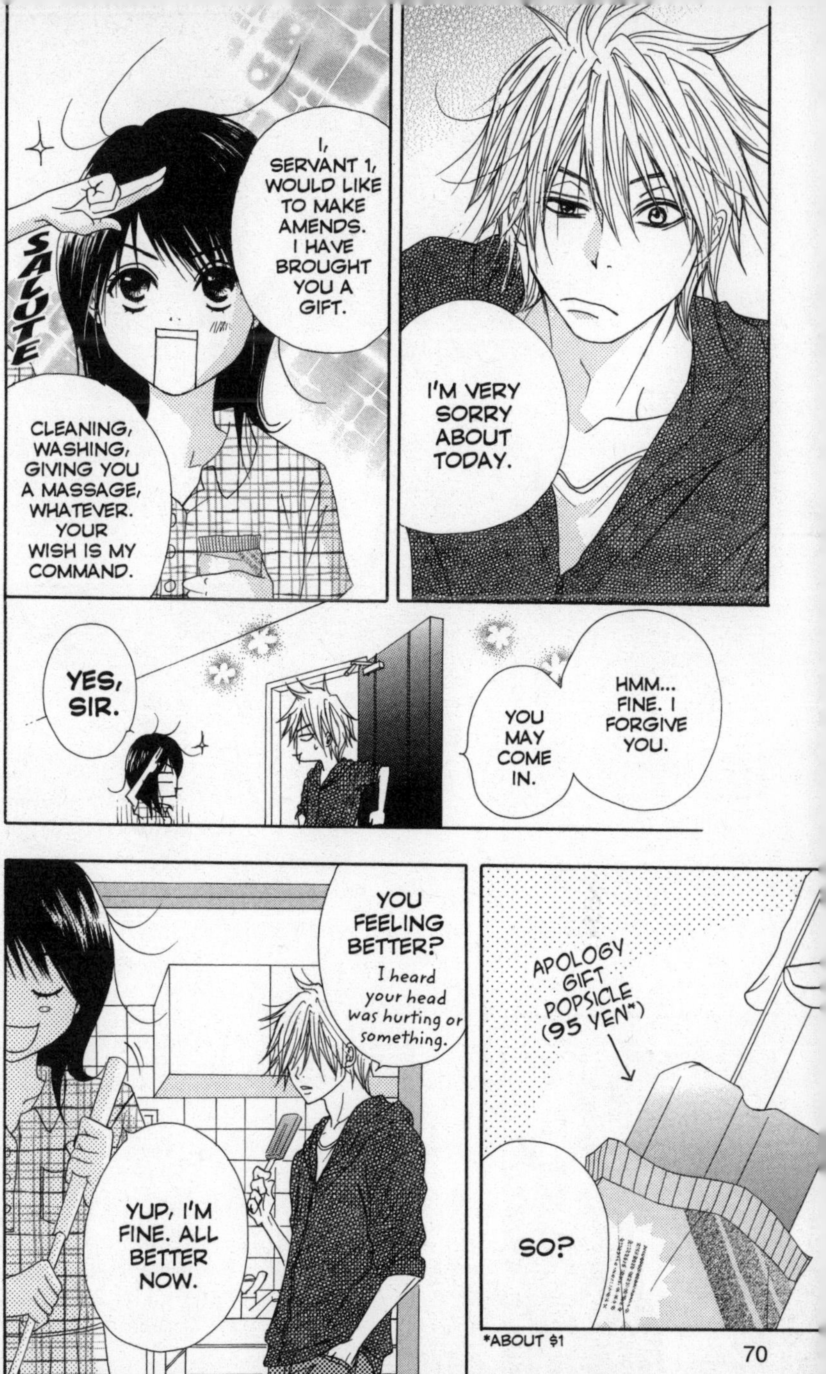
I'M VERY SORRY ABOUT TODAY.
I, SERVANT 1, WOULD LIKE TO MAKE AMENDS. I HAVE BROUGHT YOU A GIFT.
SALUTE
CLEANING, WASHING, GIVING YOU A MASSAGE, WHATEVER. YOUR WISH IS MY COMMAND.
HMM... FINE. I FORGIVE YOU.
YOU MAY COME IN.
YES, SIR.
APOLOGY GIFT POPSICLE (95 YEN*)
SO?
YOU FEELING BETTER?
I heard your head was hurting or something.
YUP, I'M FINE. ALL BETTER NOW.

*ABOUT $1

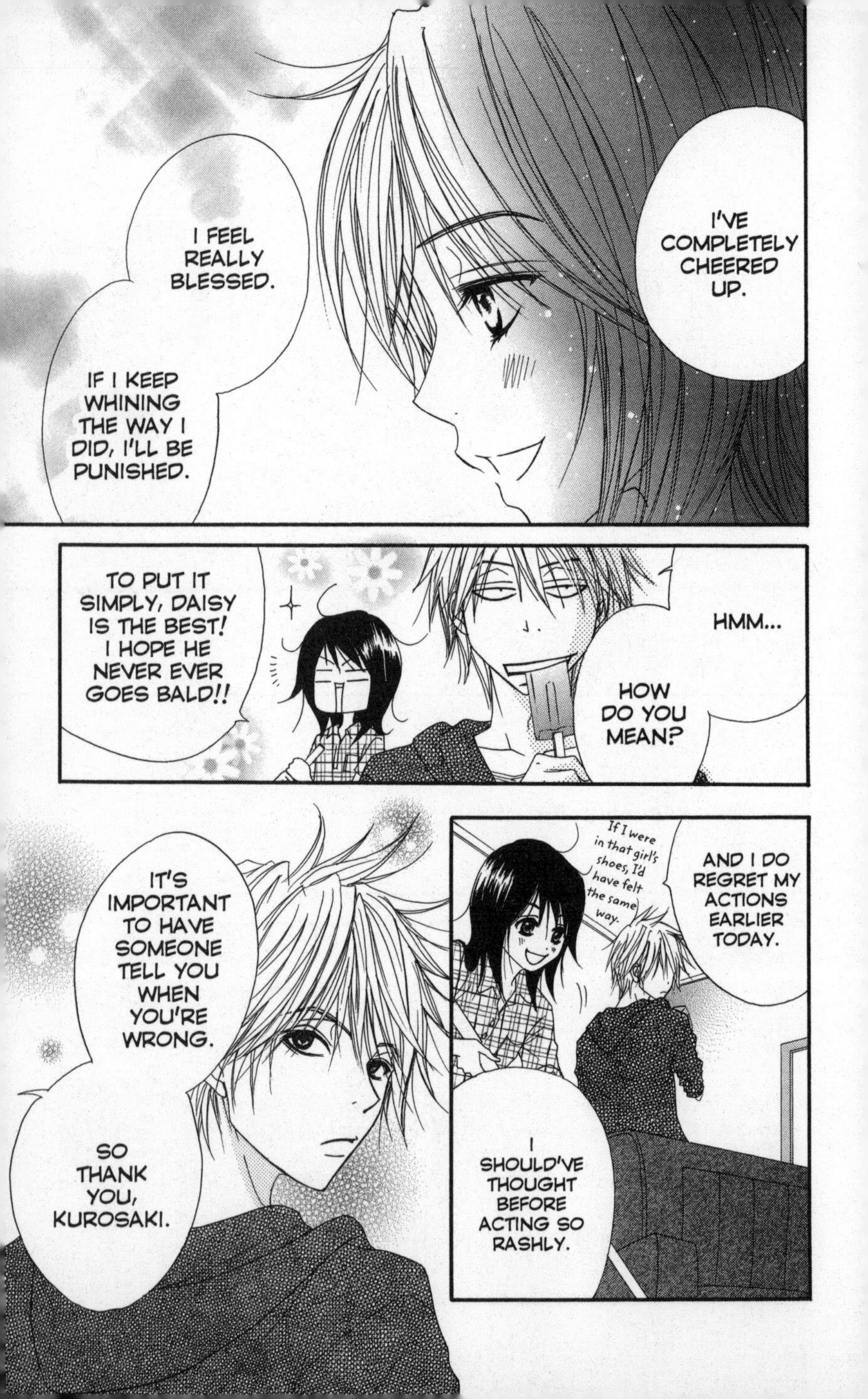
I'VE COMPLETELY CHEERED UP.
I FEEL REALLY BLESSED.
IF I KEEP WHINING THE WAY I DID, I'LL BE PUNISHED.
HMM...
HOW DO YOU MEAN?
TO PUT IT SIMPLY, DAISY IS THE BEST! I HOPE HE NEVER EVER GOES BALD!!
AND I DO REGRET MY ACTIONS EARLIER TODAY.
If I were in that girl's shoes, I'd have felt the same way.
I SHOULD'VE THOUGHT BEFORE ACTING SO RASHLY.
IT'S IMPORTANT TO HAVE SOMEONE TELL YOU WHEN YOU'RE WRONG.
SO THANK YOU, KUROSAKI.

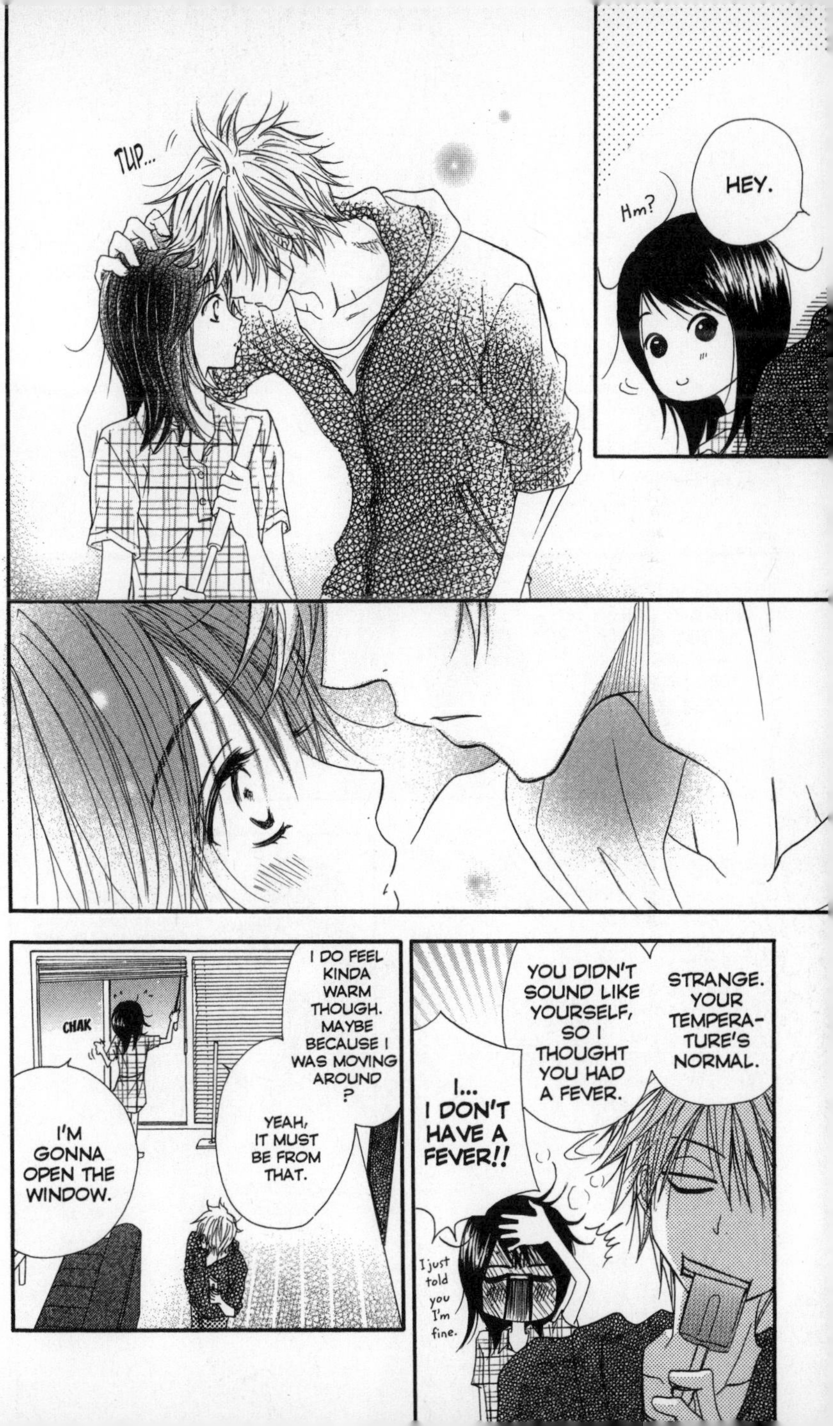
HEY.
Hm?
TUP...
STRANGE. YOUR TEMPERA-TURE'S NORMAL.
YOU DIDN'T SOUND LIKE YOURSELF, SO I THOUGHT YOU HAD A FEVER.
I... I DON'T HAVE A FEVER!!
I just told you I'm fine.
I DO FEEL KINDA WARM THOUGH. MAYBE BECAUSE I WAS MOVING AROUND?
CHAK
YEAH, IT MUST BE FROM THAT.
I'M GONNA OPEN THE WINDOW.

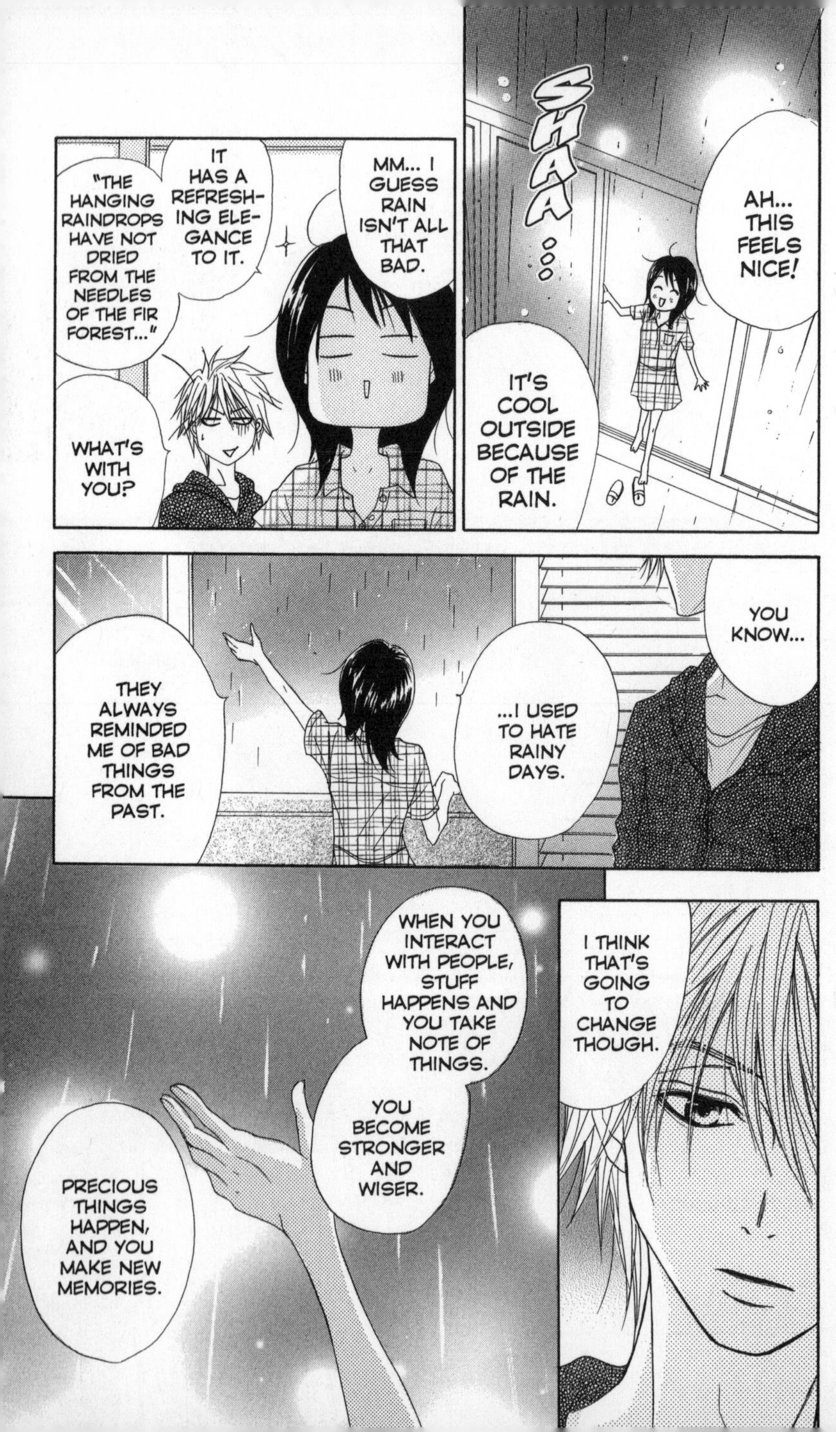
SHAA...
AH... THIS FEELS NICE!
IT'S COOL OUTSIDE BECAUSE OF THE RAIN.
MM... I GUESS RAIN ISN'T ALL THAT BAD.
IT HAS A REFRESHING ELEGANCE TO IT.
"THE HANGING RAINDROPS HAVE NOT DRIED FROM THE NEEDLES OF THE FIR FOREST..."
WHAT'S WITH YOU?
YOU KNOW...
...I USED TO HATE RAINY DAYS.
THEY ALWAYS REMINDED ME OF BAD THINGS FROM THE PAST.
I THINK THAT'S GOING TO CHANGE THOUGH.
WHEN YOU INTERACT WITH PEOPLE, STUFF HAPPENS AND YOU TAKE NOTE OF THINGS.
YOU BECOME STRONGER AND WISER.
PRECIOUS THINGS HAPPEN, AND YOU MAKE NEW MEMORIES.

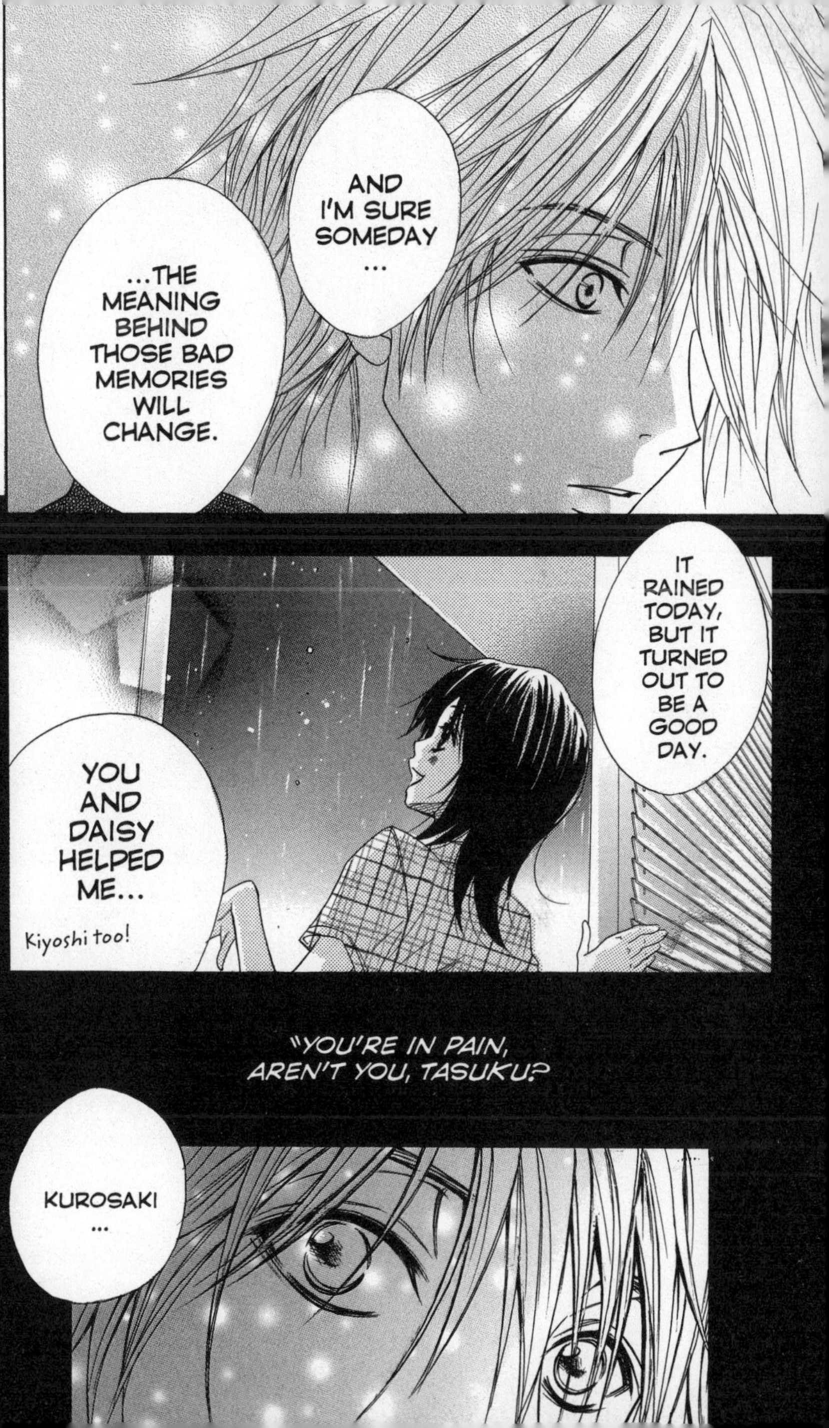
AND I'M SURE SOMEDAY ...
...THE MEANING BEHIND THOSE BAD MEMORIES WILL CHANGE.
IT RAINED TODAY, BUT IT TURNED OUT TO BE A GOOD DAY.
YOU AND DAISY HELPED ME...
Kiyoshi too!
"YOU'RE IN PAIN, AREN'T YOU, TASUKU?
KUROSAKI ...

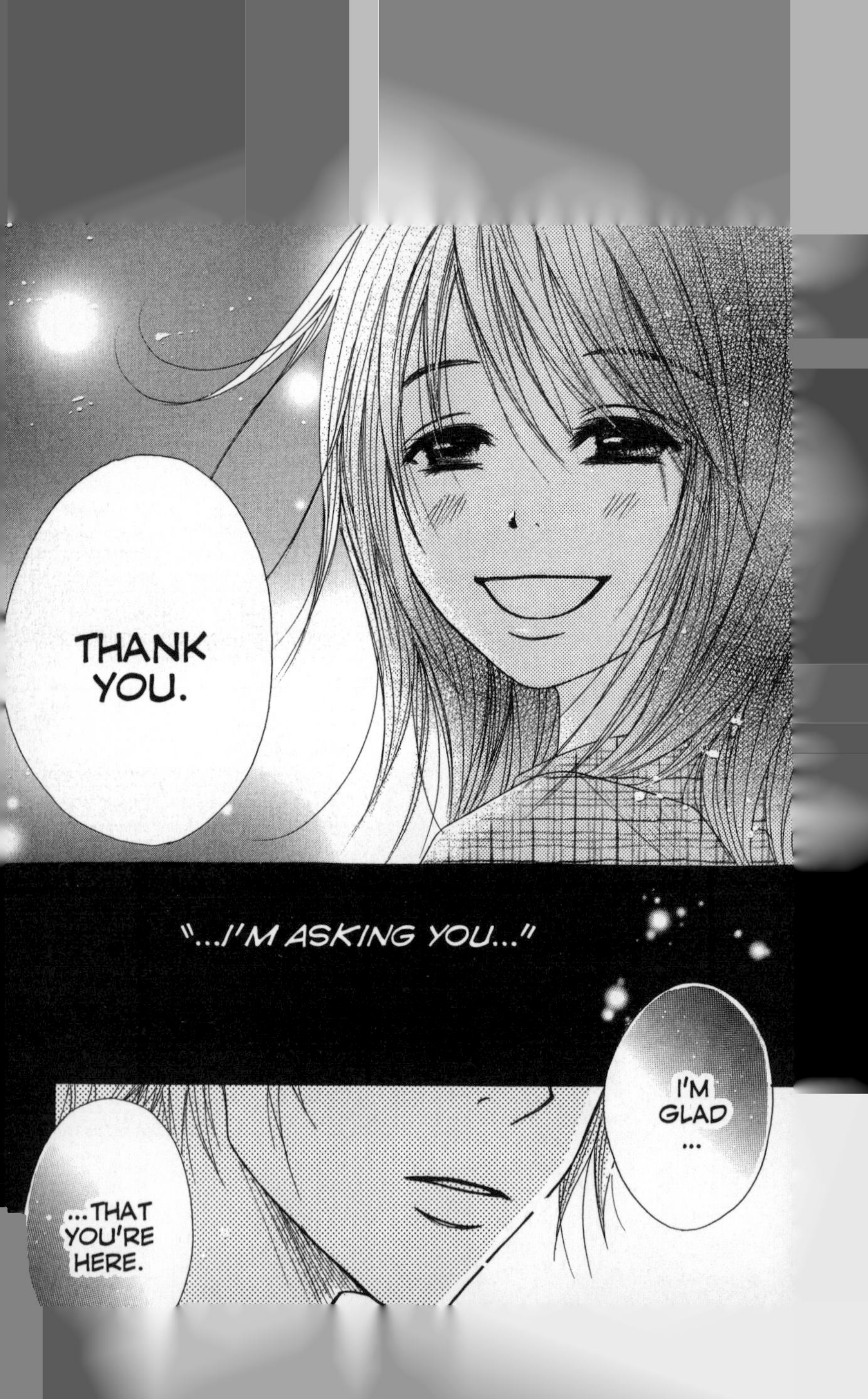
THANK YOU.
"...I'M ASKING YOU..."
I'M GLAD...
...THAT YOU'RE HERE.

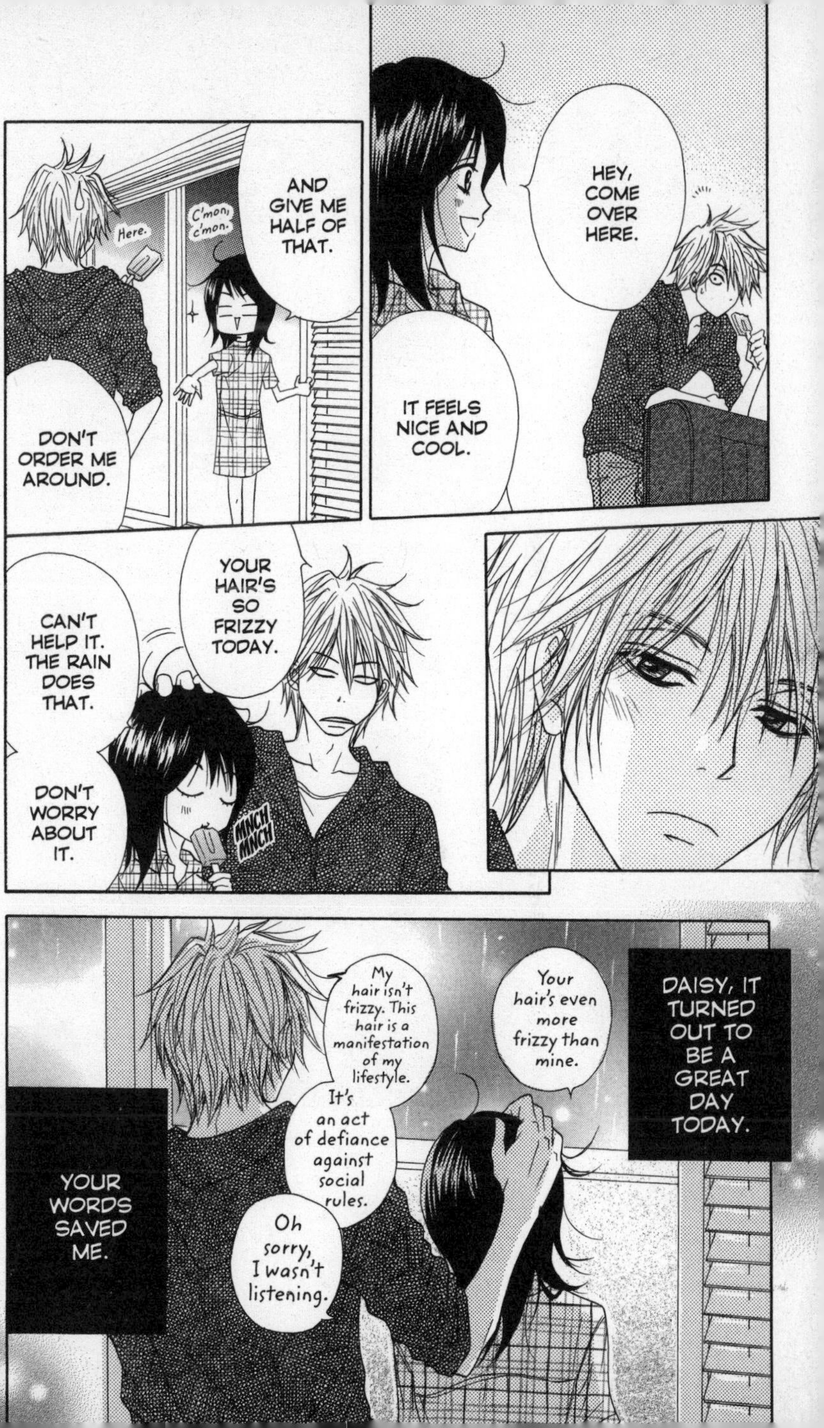
HEY, COME OVER HERE.
IT FEELS NICE AND COOL.
AND GIVE ME HALF OF THAT.
C'mon, c'mon.
Here.
DON'T ORDER ME AROUND.
YOUR HAIR'S SO FRIZZY TODAY.
CAN'T HELP IT. THE RAIN DOES THAT.
MNCH MNCH
DON'T WORRY ABOUT IT.
DAISY, IT TURNED OUT TO BE A GREAT DAY TODAY.
Your hair's even more frizzy than mine.
My hair isn't frizzy. This hair is a manifestation of my lifestyle.
It's an act of defiance against social rules.
Oh sorry, I wasn't listening.
YOUR WORDS SAVED ME.

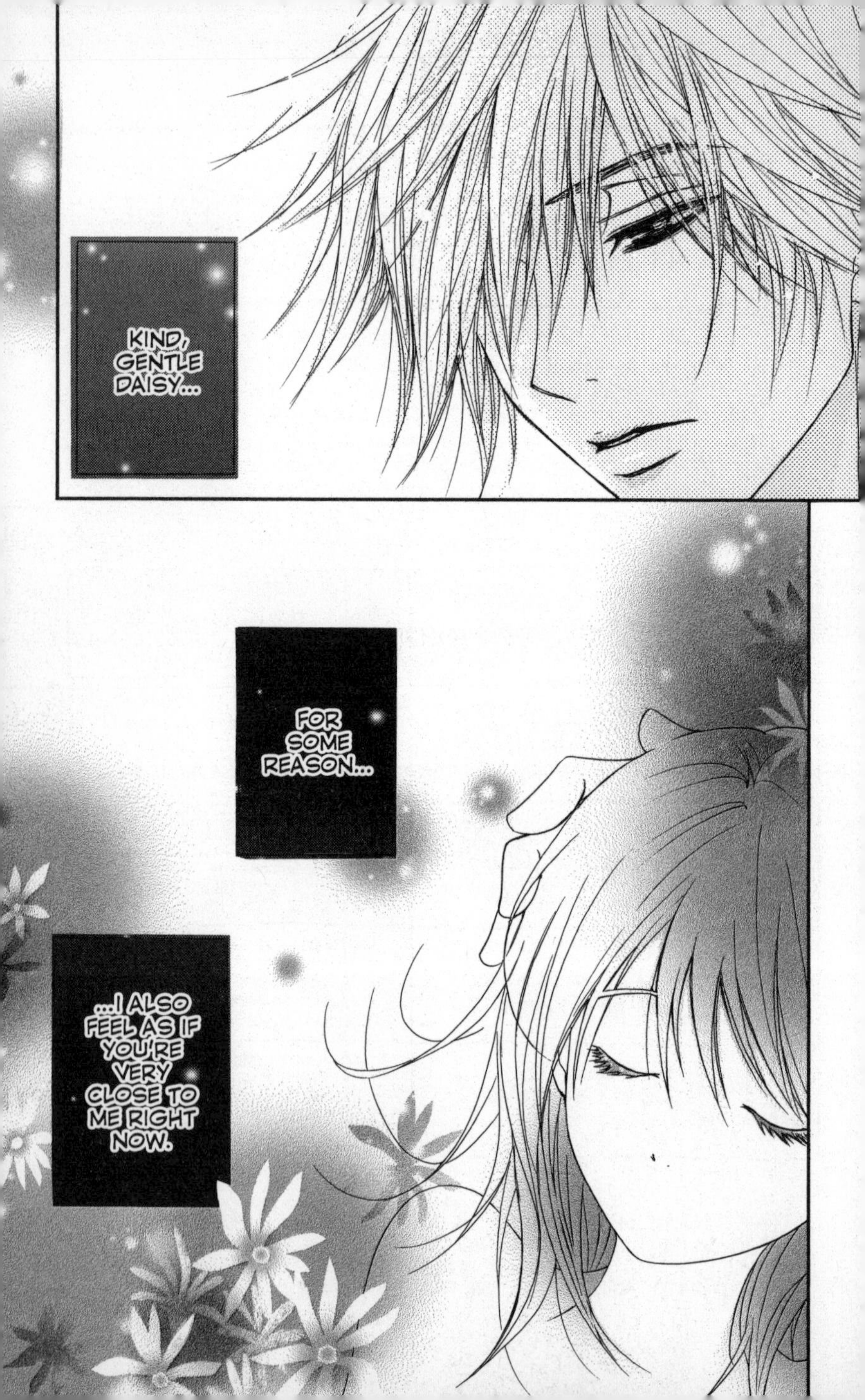
KIND, GENTLE DAISY...
FOR SOME REASON...
...I ALSO FEEL AS IF YOU'RE VERY CLOSE TO ME RIGHT NOW.

DENGEKI DAISY
COMMENTS FROM THE LAST PAGE
THAT CANNOT BE MISSED

ON THE LAST PAGE OF THE CHAPTER SERIALIZATIONS IN *BETSUCOMI*, THE BRILLIANT EDITOR K-TANI USUALLY ADDS A FEW INTERESTING CAPTIONS NEXT TO THE "TO BE CONTINUED IN... " LINE. (GENERALLY, THEY'RE RELATED TO THE CONTENTS OF THE MANGA ITSELF) HOWEVER, SINCE *DENGEKI DAISY* IS A SHOJO MANGA, SOME REALLY GREAT CAPTIONS WERE REJECTED DURING THE FINAL CHECK SINCE PRIORITY IS PLACED ON COMMON SENSE RATHER THAN SILLINESS. NOW I'D LIKE TO INTRODUCE THE CONTENTS OF K-TANI'S WORK HERE—THOSE THAT SAW THE LIGHT OF DAY AND THOSE THAT DIDN'T.

CH. 10	KUROSAKI'S WORN OUT FROM CONSTANTLY FALLING FOR WOMEN'S TRAPS. ♡		I AGREE.
CH. 11	CAN'T CONTROL THE FRIZZINESS OF HIS HAIR. THE MANIFESTATION OF LOVE ♡ AND FLIRTING ARE ON THE RISE. NEW DANGER AWAITS THE DUO?!		THE SENSE OF IMMINENT DANGER IS KEPT AT AN UNNECESSARILY HIGH LEVEL. IT'S A PRO'S JOB.
CH. 12	IS THE DAY WHERE TERU LEARNS THE TRUTH FAST APPROACHING? AND WILL KUROSAKI BE ABLE TO RETURN THE PEN TO THE PUBLIC PHONE?! THE NEXT ISSUE IS A MUST-SEE!!	REJECTED	BECAUSE THE FOLLOWING ISSUE HAD A FEATURE COVER FOR THE FIRST TIME, THE LATTER HALF HAD TO CHANGE, UNFORTUNATELY. THUS, IT BECAME "IN THE NEXT ISSUE, THE COVER AND COLOR OPENING PAGE ARE THE ONES I'VE BEEN DREAMING OF. " IT'S THE AUTHOR'S DREAM—DON'T REVEAL IT.
CH. 13	FINALLY, THE SECRET IS—?!! THE NEXT ISSUE'S OPENING PAGE WILL BE IN COLOR!!		WELL, IT *IS* THE OPENING PAGE, WHICH MAY NEVER HAPPEN AGAIN. THE INITIAL PLAN WAS TO USE THE CAPTION "WIND-STRONG!!" (THIS ISN'T J◯MP!)
CH. 14	TERU'S SAD WISH... PLUS! WHAT COMES AFTER THE DECISION?		K-TANI SOMETIMES SHOWS COMMON SENSE. NOW IF HE DIDN'T GRASP THE MOOD AND WROTE, "THE SECOND KISS!" HE'D HAVE BEEN INGENIOUS.

"THIS IS THE BRILLIANT WORK THAT THE GENIUS (LIKE IN *BA◯◯BON*) K-TANI PRODUCES EVERY MONTH AT *BETSUCOMI*. THERE'S ALSO AN EDGY CORRESPONDENCE CORNER CALLED "DENGEKI DAISY FAN PAGE-THE SECRET SCHOOL CUSTODIAN OFFICE." BE SURE TO CHECK IT OUT.

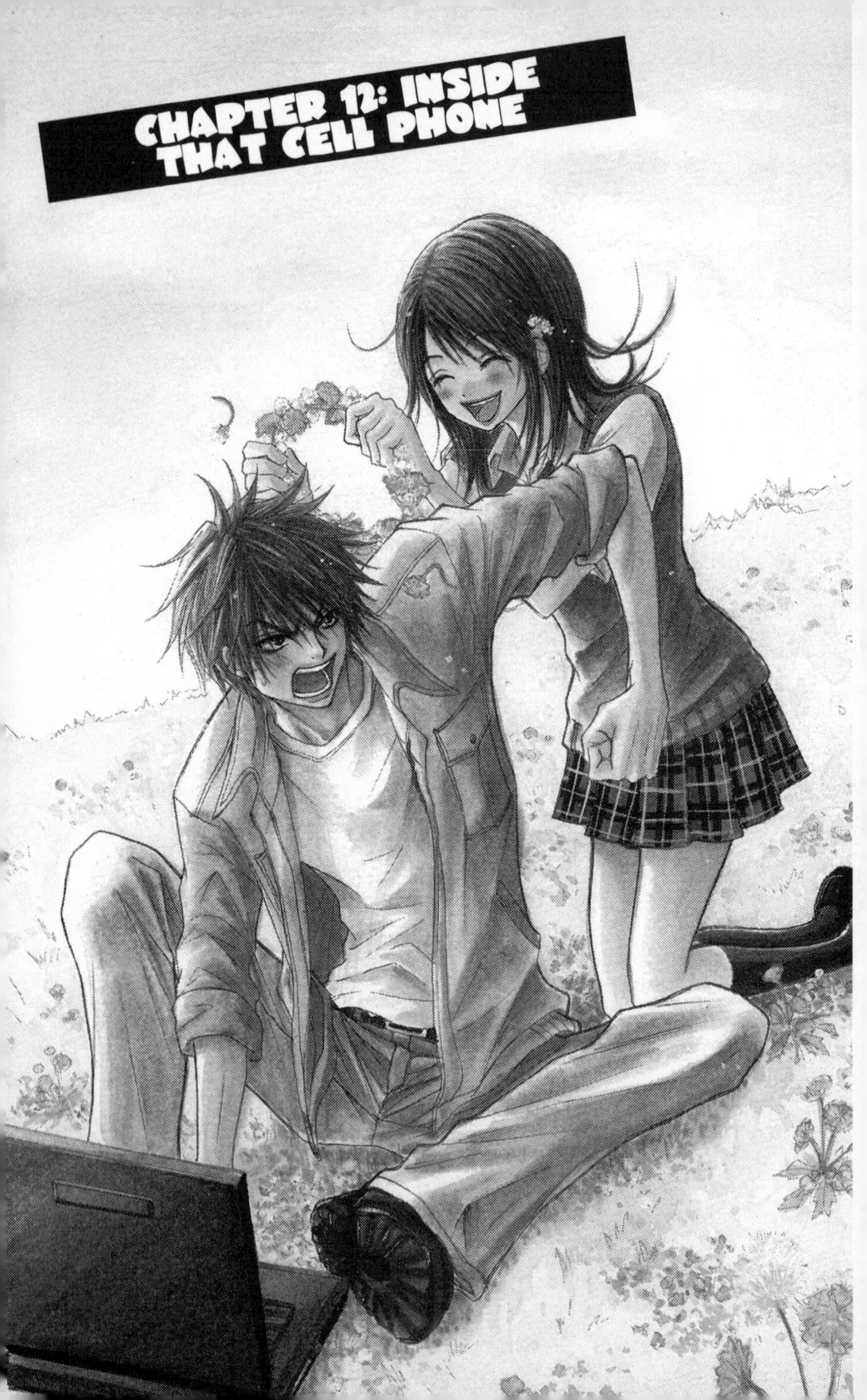
CHAPTER 12: INSIDE THAT CELL PHONE

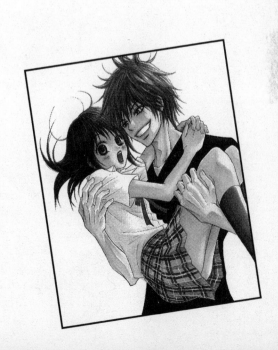

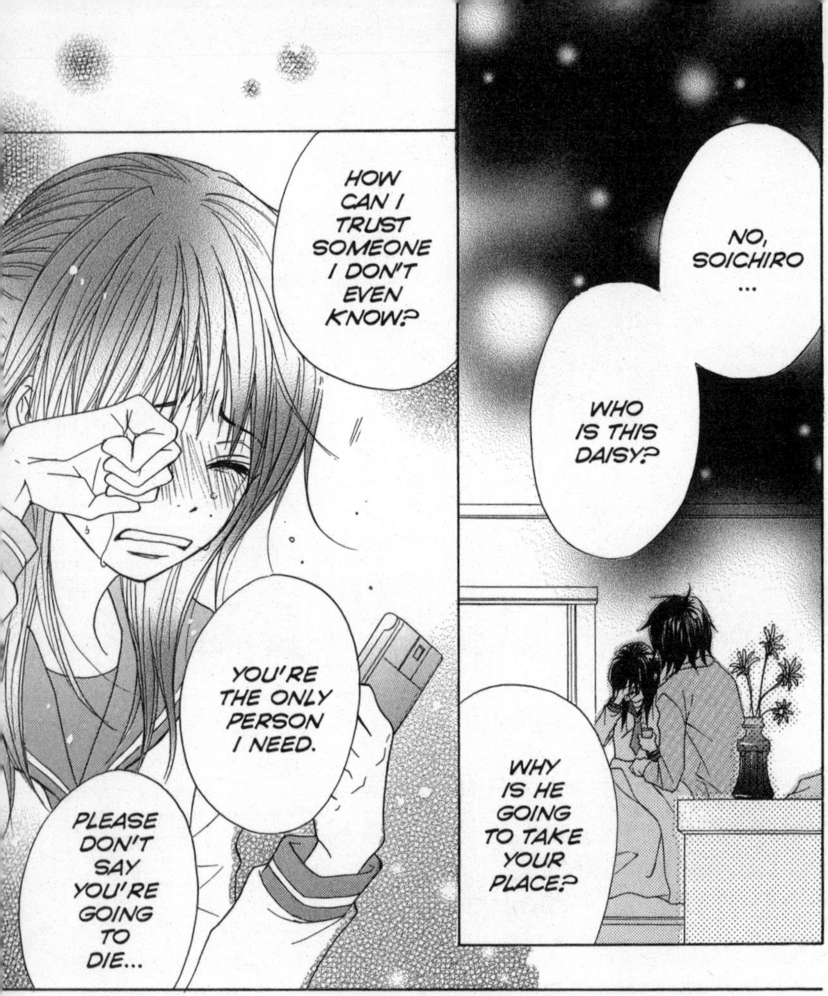
NO, SOICHIRO ...
WHO IS THIS DAISY?
WHY IS HE GOING TO TAKE YOUR PLACE?
HOW CAN I TRUST SOMEONE I DON'T EVEN KNOW?
YOU'RE THE ONLY PERSON I NEED.
PLEASE DON'T SAY YOU'RE GOING TO DIE...

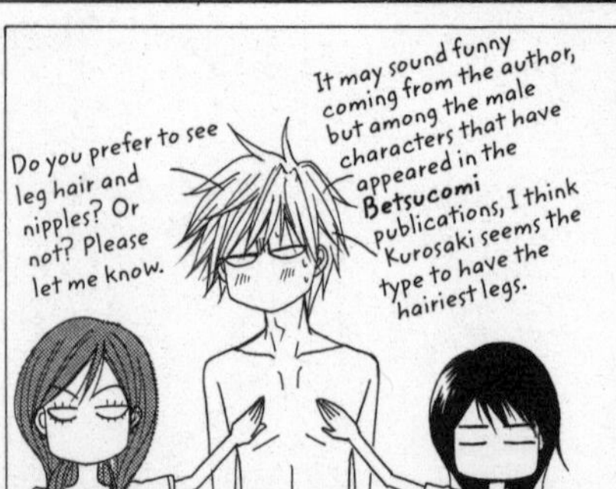
Do you prefer to see leg hair and nipples? Or not? Please let me know.
It may sound funny coming from the author, but among the male characters that have appeared in the Betsucomi publications, I think Kurosaki seems the type to have the hairiest legs.

IN CHAPTER 11, KUROSAKI IS SHIRTLESS. I ASKED MY EDITOR, "IS IT OKAY TO DRAW NIPPLES?" AND SHE REPLIED, "WHY NOT? IT'S PART OF THE BODY." SO I THOUGHT IT WAS OKAY. WHEN I LATER ASKED, "SO LEG HAIR AND UNDERARM HAIR ARE OKAY TOO, RIGHT? SINCE IT'S NATURAL," SHE (EDITOR J-KO) CAME BACK WITH, "I'M OVERRULING YOU, IT'S NOT OKAY." ...HMM, IT'S SO COMPLICATED. BUT NOW THAT I THINK ABOUT IT, YOU DON'T SEE UNDERARM HAIR IN SHONEN MANGA. POOR THINGS... EVEN ONE'S UNDERARMS DESERVE SOME CREDIT.

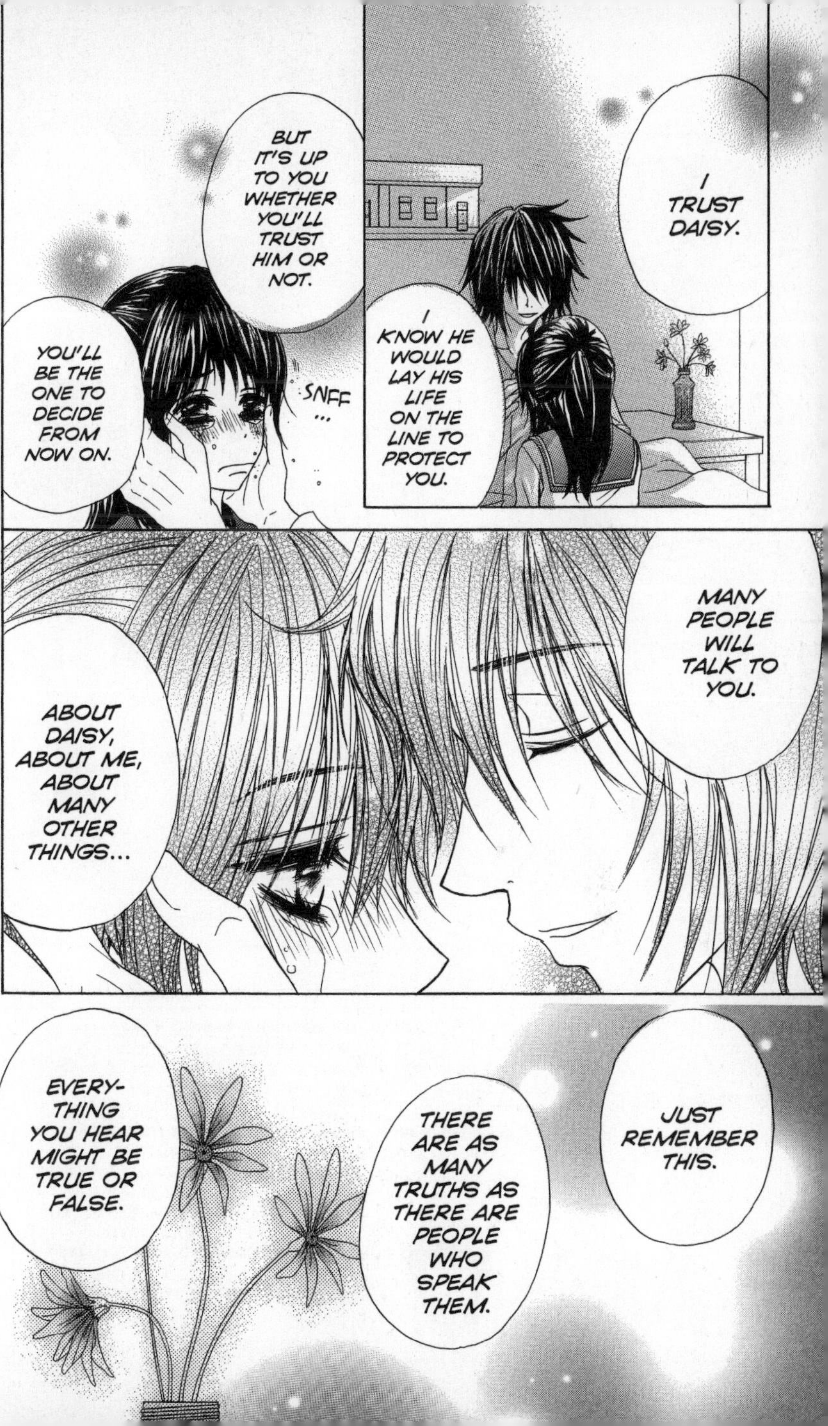
I TRUST DAISY.
I KNOW HE WOULD LAY HIS LIFE ON THE LINE TO PROTECT YOU.
BUT IT'S UP TO YOU WHETHER YOU'LL TRUST HIM OR NOT.
SNFF...
YOU'LL BE THE ONE TO DECIDE FROM NOW ON.
MANY PEOPLE WILL TALK TO YOU.
ABOUT DAISY, ABOUT ME, ABOUT MANY OTHER THINGS...
JUST REMEMBER THIS.
THERE ARE AS MANY TRUTHS AS THERE ARE PEOPLE WHO SPEAK THEM.
EVERY-THING YOU HEAR MIGHT BE TRUE OR FALSE.

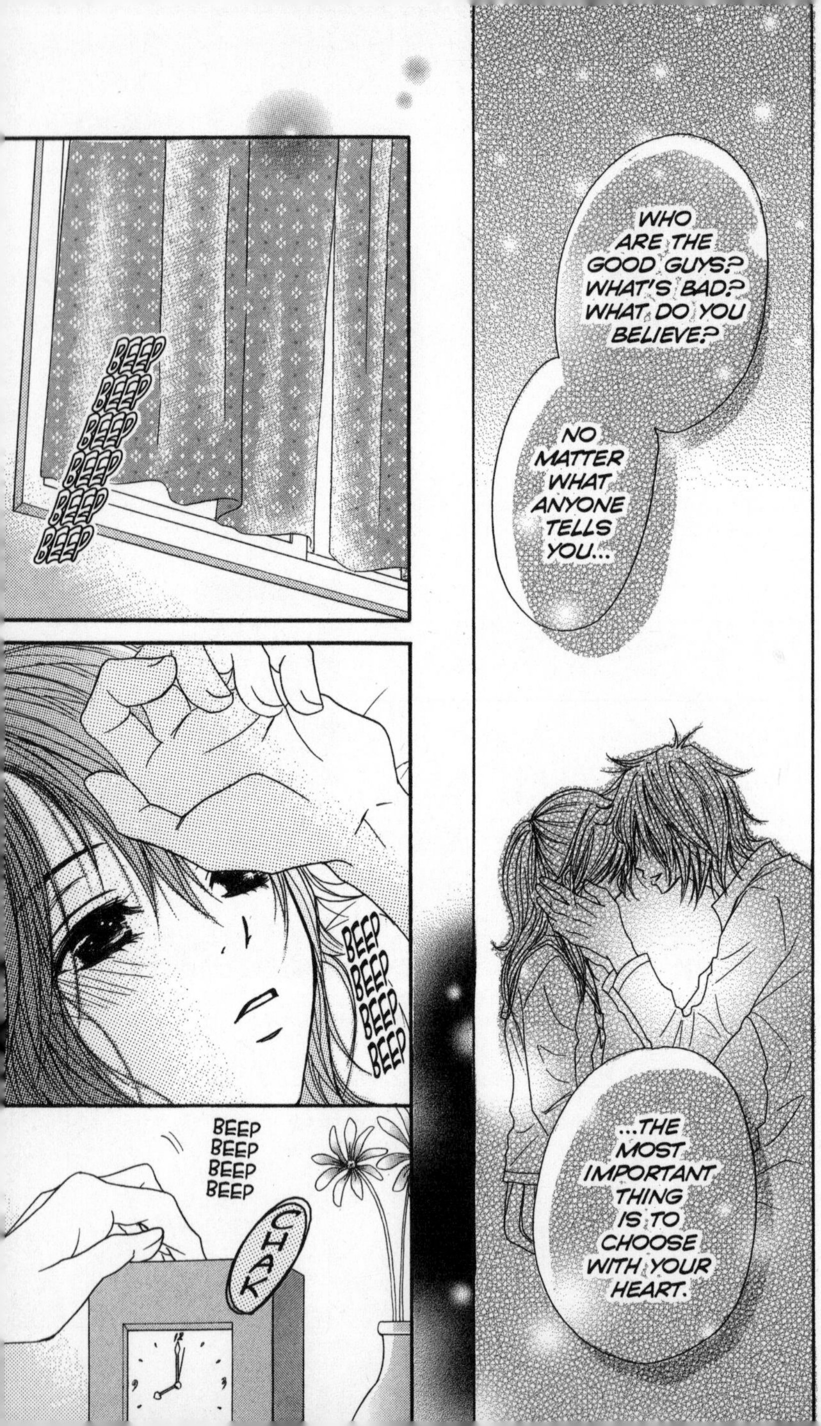
WHO ARE THE GOOD GUYS? WHAT'S BAD? WHAT DO YOU BELIEVE?
NO MATTER WHAT ANYONE TELLS YOU...
...THE MOST IMPORTANT THING IS TO CHOOSE WITH YOUR HEART.
BEEP BEEP BEEP BEEP BEEP BEEP
BEEP BEEP BEEP BEEP
BEEP BEEP BEEP BEEP
CHAK

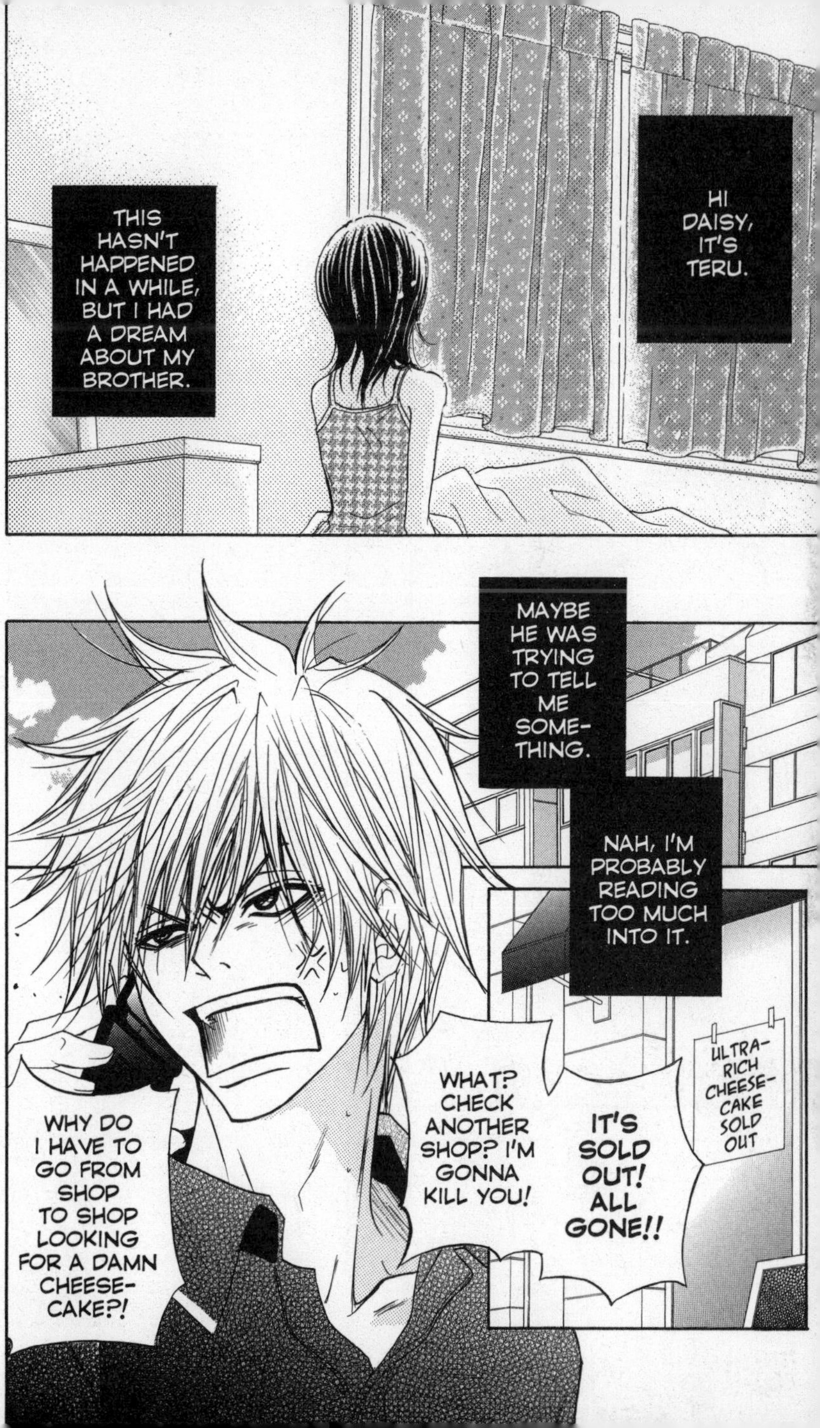
HI DAISY, IT'S TERU.
THIS HASN'T HAPPENED IN A WHILE, BUT I HAD A DREAM ABOUT MY BROTHER.
MAYBE HE WAS TRYING TO TELL ME SOME-THING.
NAH, I'M PROBABLY READING TOO MUCH INTO IT.
ULTRA-RICH CHEESE-CAKE SOLD OUT
IT'S SOLD OUT! ALL GONE!!
WHAT? CHECK ANOTHER SHOP? I'M GONNA KILL YOU!
WHY DO I HAVE TO GO FROM SHOP TO SHOP LOOKING FOR A DAMN CHEESE-CAKE?!

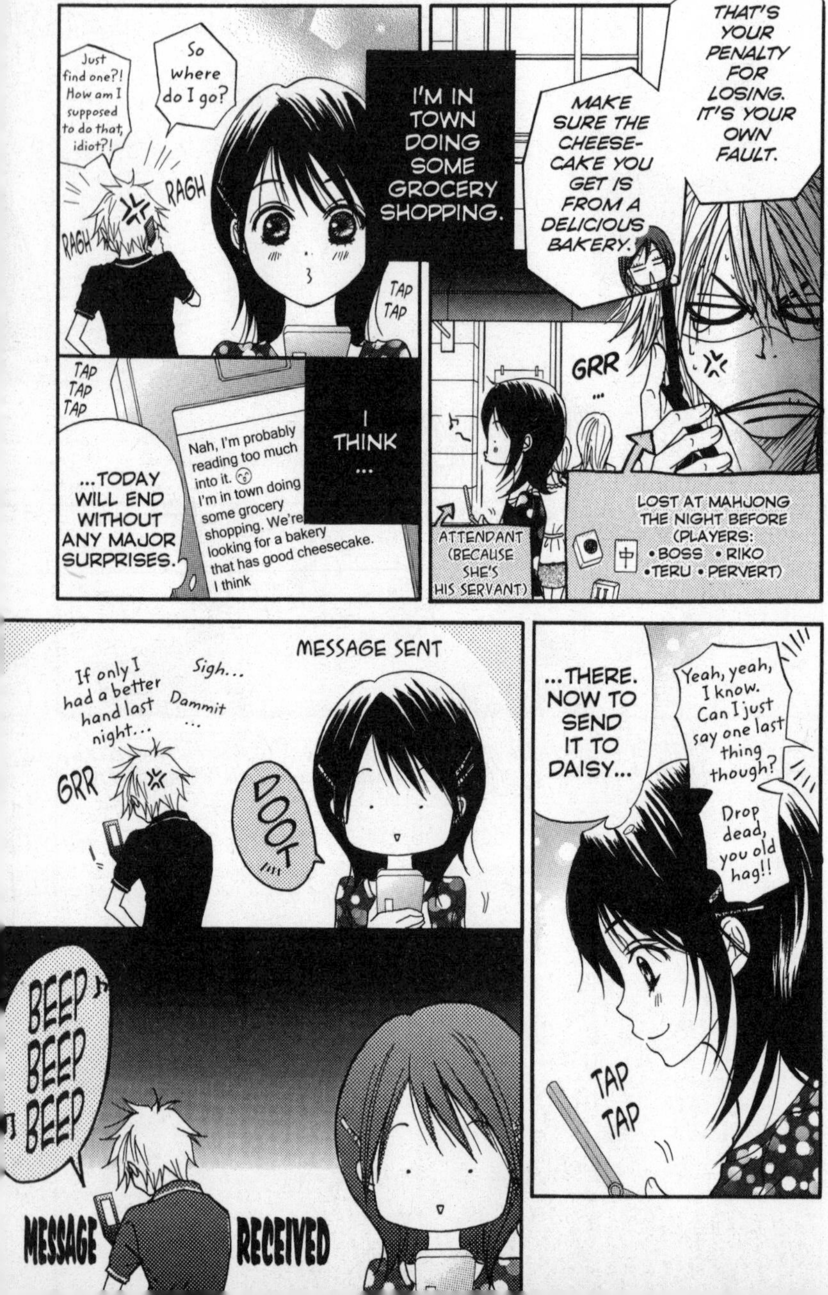
Excuse me?
THAT'S YOUR PENALTY FOR LOSING. IT'S YOUR OWN FAULT.
MAKE SURE THE CHEESE-CAKE YOU GET IS FROM A DELICIOUS BAKERY.
GRR
LOST AT MAHJONG THE NIGHT BEFORE (PLAYERS: •BOSS •RIKO •TERU •PERVERT)
ATTENDANT (BECAUSE SHE'S HIS SERVANT)
I'M IN TOWN DOING SOME GROCERY SHOPPING.
So where do I go?
Just find one?! How am I supposed to do that, idiot?!
RAGH
RAGH
TAP TAP
I THINK ...
Nah, I'm probably reading too much into it. I'm in town doing some grocery shopping. We're looking for a bakery that has good cheesecake. I think
...TODAY WILL END WITHOUT ANY MAJOR SURPRISES.
TAP TAP TAP
...THERE. NOW TO SEND IT TO DAISY...
Yeah, yeah, I know. Can I just say one last thing though?
Drop dead, you old hag!!
TAP TAP
MESSAGE SENT
Sigh... Dammit...
If only I had a better hand last night...
GRR
DOOT
BEEP BEEP BEEP
MESSAGE RECEIVED

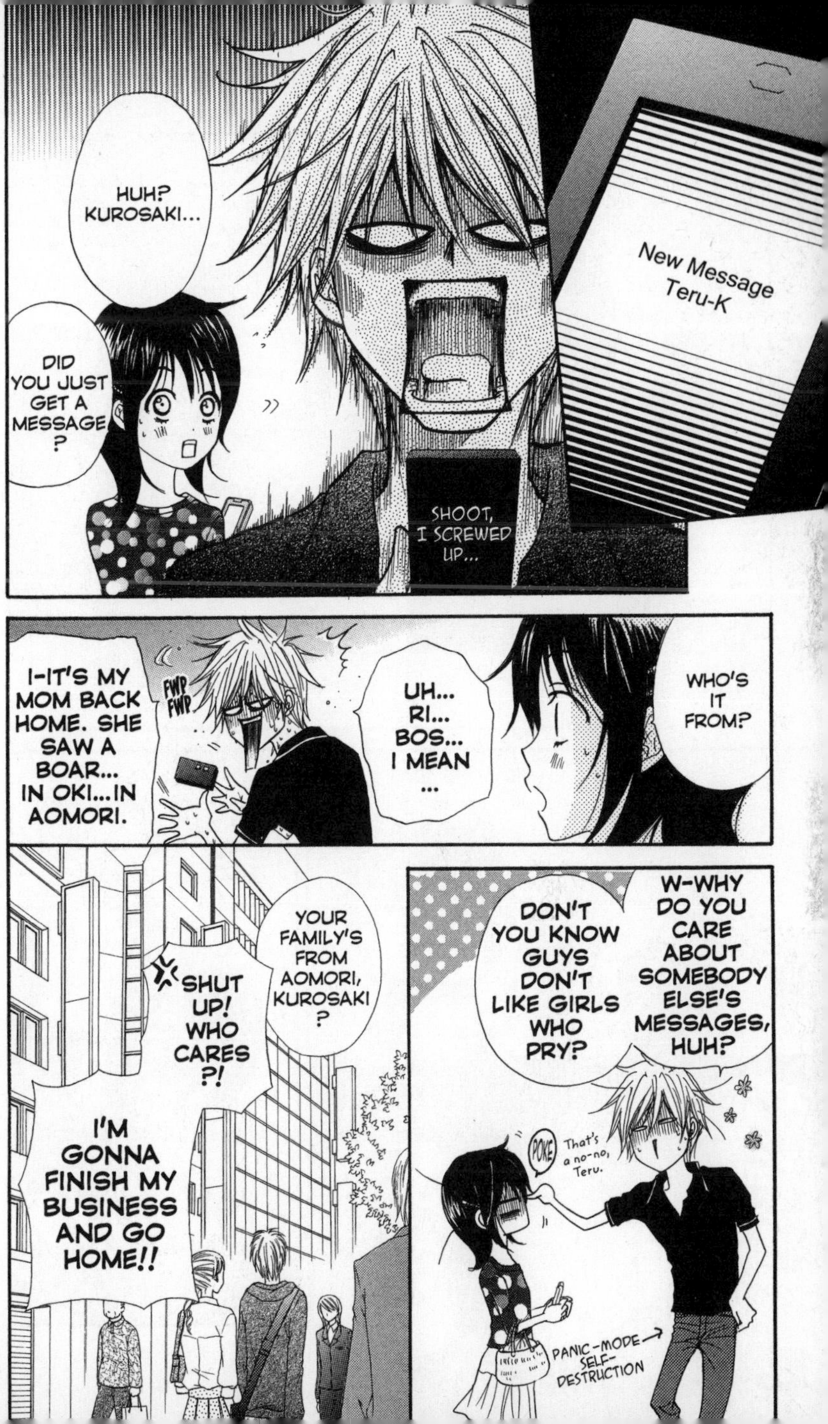
New Message
Teru-K
HUH? KUROSAKI...
DID YOU JUST GET A MESSAGE?
SHOOT, I SCREWED UP...
WHO'S IT FROM?
UH... RI... BOS... I MEAN...
FWP FWP
I-IT'S MY MOM BACK HOME. SHE SAW A BOAR... IN OKI...IN AOMORI.
W-WHY DO YOU CARE ABOUT SOMEBODY ELSE'S MESSAGES, HUH?
DON'T YOU KNOW GUYS DON'T LIKE GIRLS WHO PRY?
POKE
That's a no-no, Teru.
PANIC-MODE SELF-DESTRUCTION
YOUR FAMILY'S FROM AOMORI, KUROSAKI?
SHUT UP! WHO CARES?!
I'M GONNA FINISH MY BUSINESS AND GO HOME!!

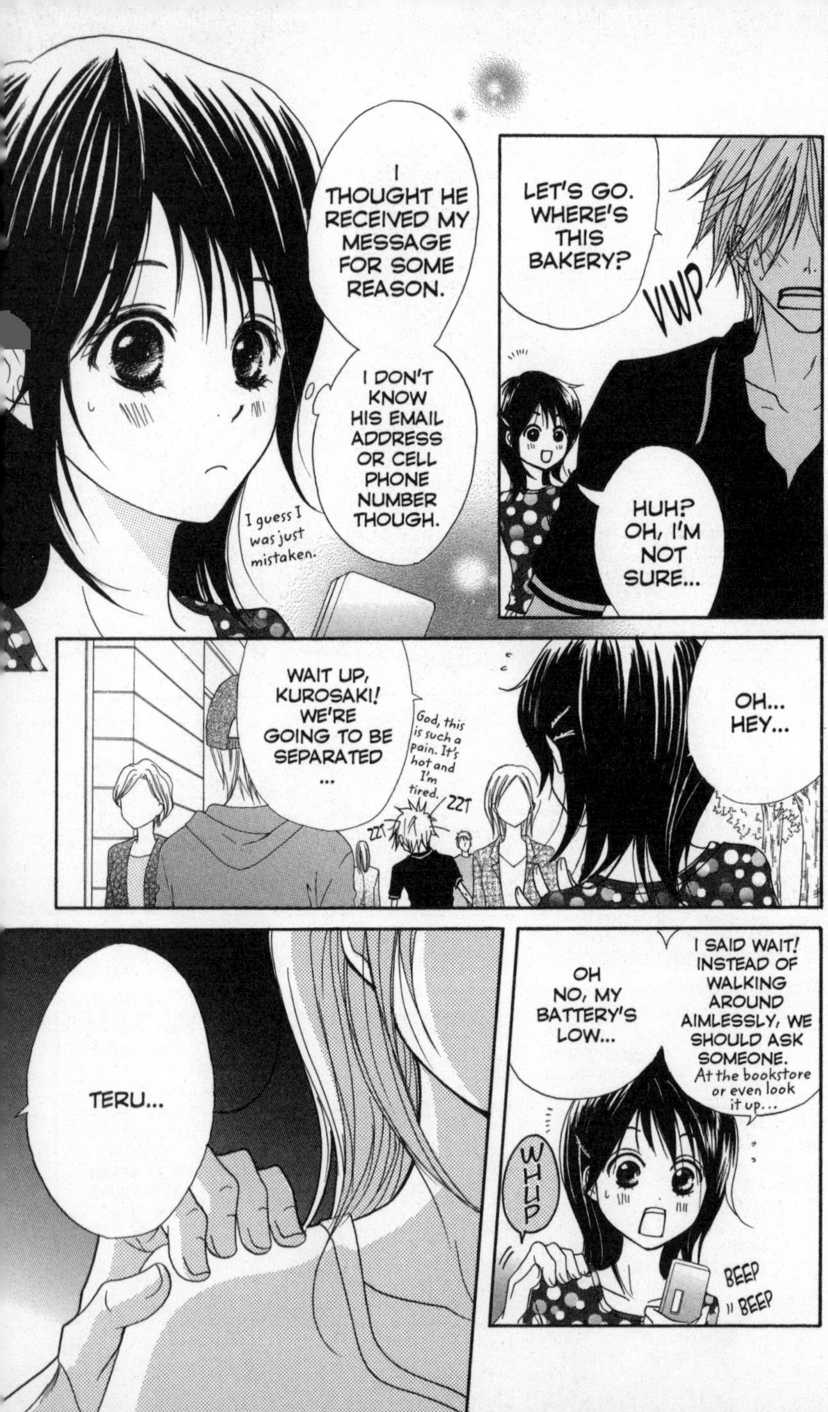
LET'S GO. WHERE'S THIS BAKERY?
VWP
HUH? OH, I'M NOT SURE...
I THOUGHT HE RECEIVED MY MESSAGE FOR SOME REASON.
I DON'T KNOW HIS EMAIL ADDRESS OR CELL PHONE NUMBER THOUGH.
I guess I was just mistaken.
OH... HEY...
WAIT UP, KUROSAKI! WE'RE GOING TO BE SEPARATED...
God, this is such a pain. It's hot and I'm tired.
ZZT
ZZT
I SAID WAIT! INSTEAD OF WALKING AROUND AIMLESSLY, WE SHOULD ASK SOMEONE. At the bookstore or even look it up...
OH NO, MY BATTERY'S LOW...
WHUP
BEEP BEEP
TERU...

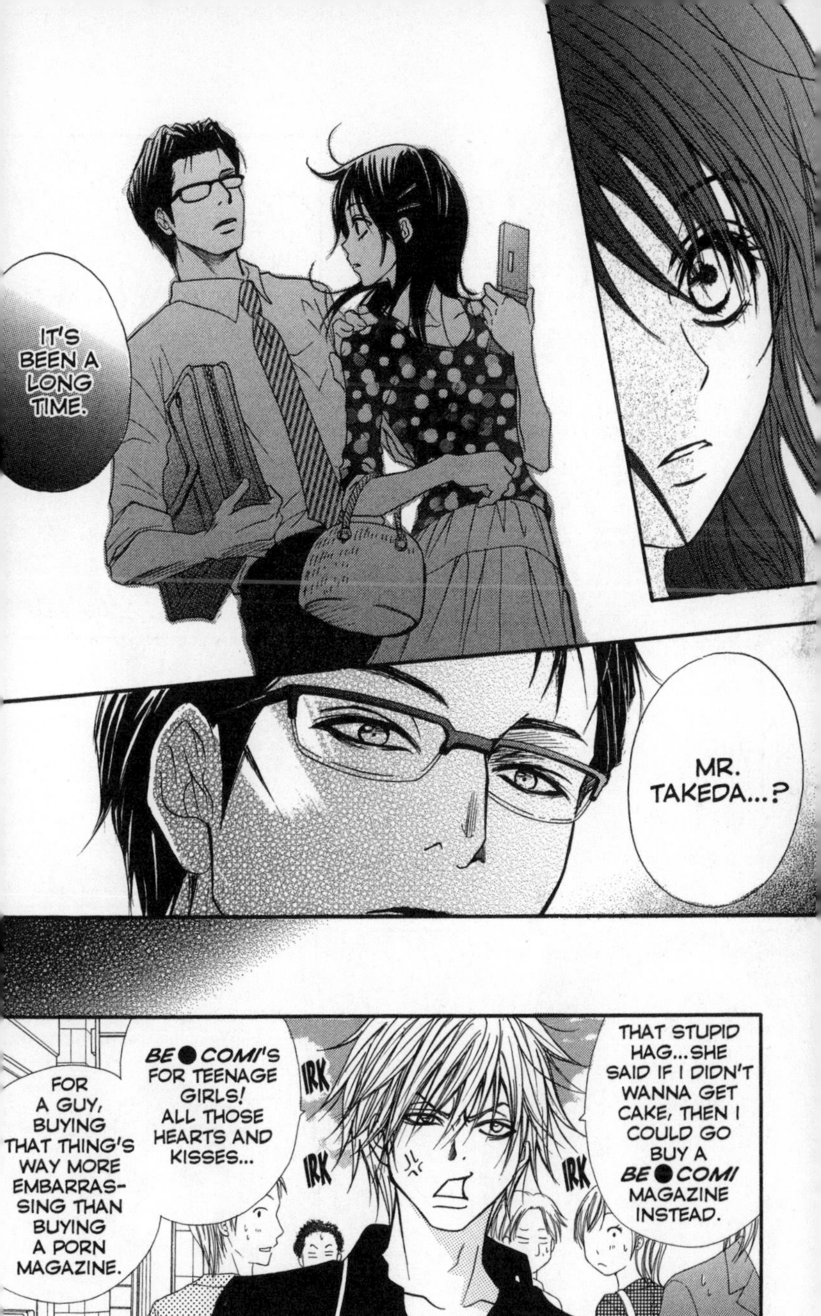
IT'S BEEN A LONG TIME.
MR. TAKEDA...?
THAT STUPID HAG...SHE SAID IF I DIDN'T WANNA GET CAKE, THEN I COULD GO BUY A BE●COMI MAGAZINE INSTEAD.
IRK
IRK
IRK
BE●COMI'S FOR TEENAGE GIRLS! ALL THOSE HEARTS AND KISSES...
FOR A GUY, BUYING THAT THING'S WAY MORE EMBARRAS-SING THAN BUYING A PORN MAGAZINE.

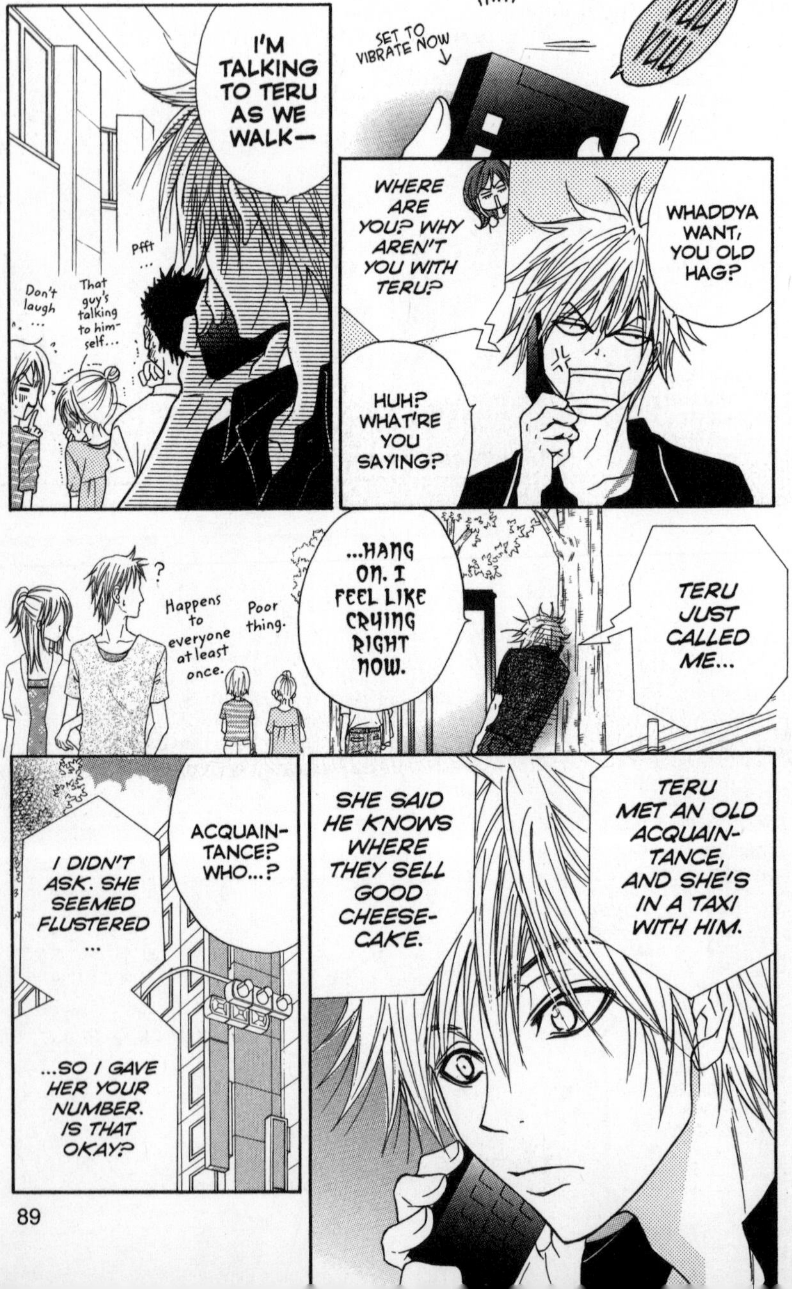
VUU VUU
SET TO VIBRATE NOW
WHADDYA WANT, YOU OLD HAG?
WHERE ARE YOU? WHY AREN'T YOU WITH TERU?
HUH? WHAT'RE YOU SAYING?
I'M TALKING TO TERU AS WE WALK—
Pfft...
That guy's talking to himself...
Don't laugh...
TERU JUST CALLED ME...
...HANG ON. I FEEL LIKE CRYING RIGHT NOW.
Poor thing.
Happens to everyone at least once.
TERU MET AN OLD ACQUAINTANCE, AND SHE'S IN A TAXI WITH HIM.
SHE SAID HE KNOWS WHERE THEY SELL GOOD CHEESECAKE.
ACQUAINTANCE? WHO...?
I DIDN'T ASK. SHE SEEMED FLUSTERED...
...SO I GAVE HER YOUR NUMBER. IS THAT OKAY?

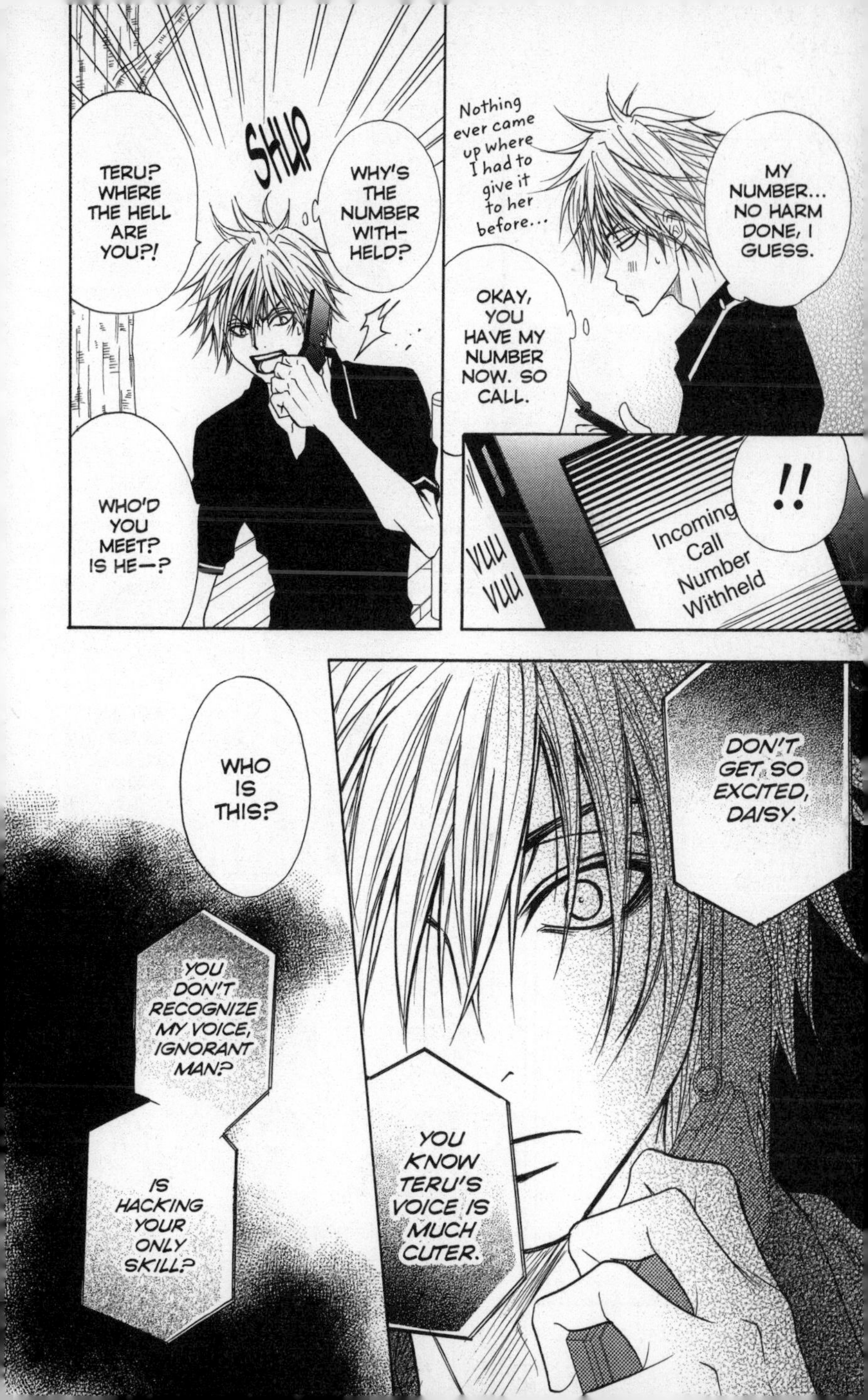
MY NUMBER... NO HARM DONE, I GUESS.
Nothing ever came up where I had to give it to her before...
OKAY, YOU HAVE MY NUMBER NOW. SO CALL.
!!
Incoming Call Number Withheld
VUU VUU
WHY'S THE NUMBER WITHHELD?
SHUP
TERU? WHERE THE HELL ARE YOU?!
WHO'D YOU MEET? IS HE—?
DON'T GET SO EXCITED, DAISY.
WHO IS THIS?
YOU DON'T RECOGNIZE MY VOICE, IGNORANT MAN?
YOU KNOW TERU'S VOICE IS MUCH CUTER.
IS HACKING YOUR ONLY SKILL?

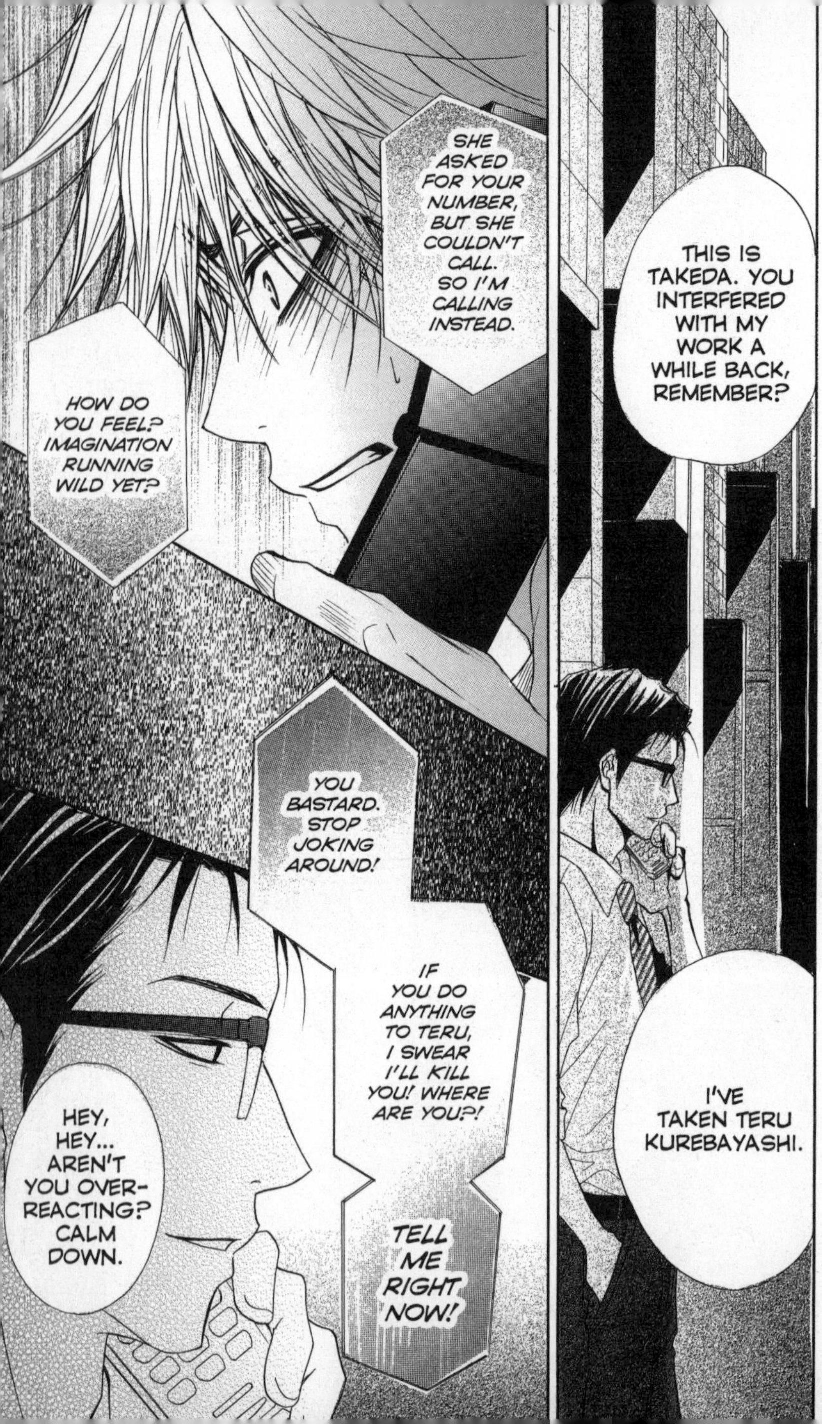
THIS IS TAKEDA. YOU INTERFERED WITH MY WORK A WHILE BACK, REMEMBER?
I'VE TAKEN TERU KUREBAYASHI.
SHE ASKED FOR YOUR NUMBER, BUT SHE COULDN'T CALL. SO I'M CALLING INSTEAD.
HOW DO YOU FEEL? IMAGINATION RUNNING WILD YET?
YOU BASTARD. STOP JOKING AROUND!
IF YOU DO ANYTHING TO TERU, I SWEAR I'LL KILL YOU! WHERE ARE YOU?!
TELL ME RIGHT NOW!
HEY, HEY... AREN'T YOU OVER-REACTING? CALM DOWN.

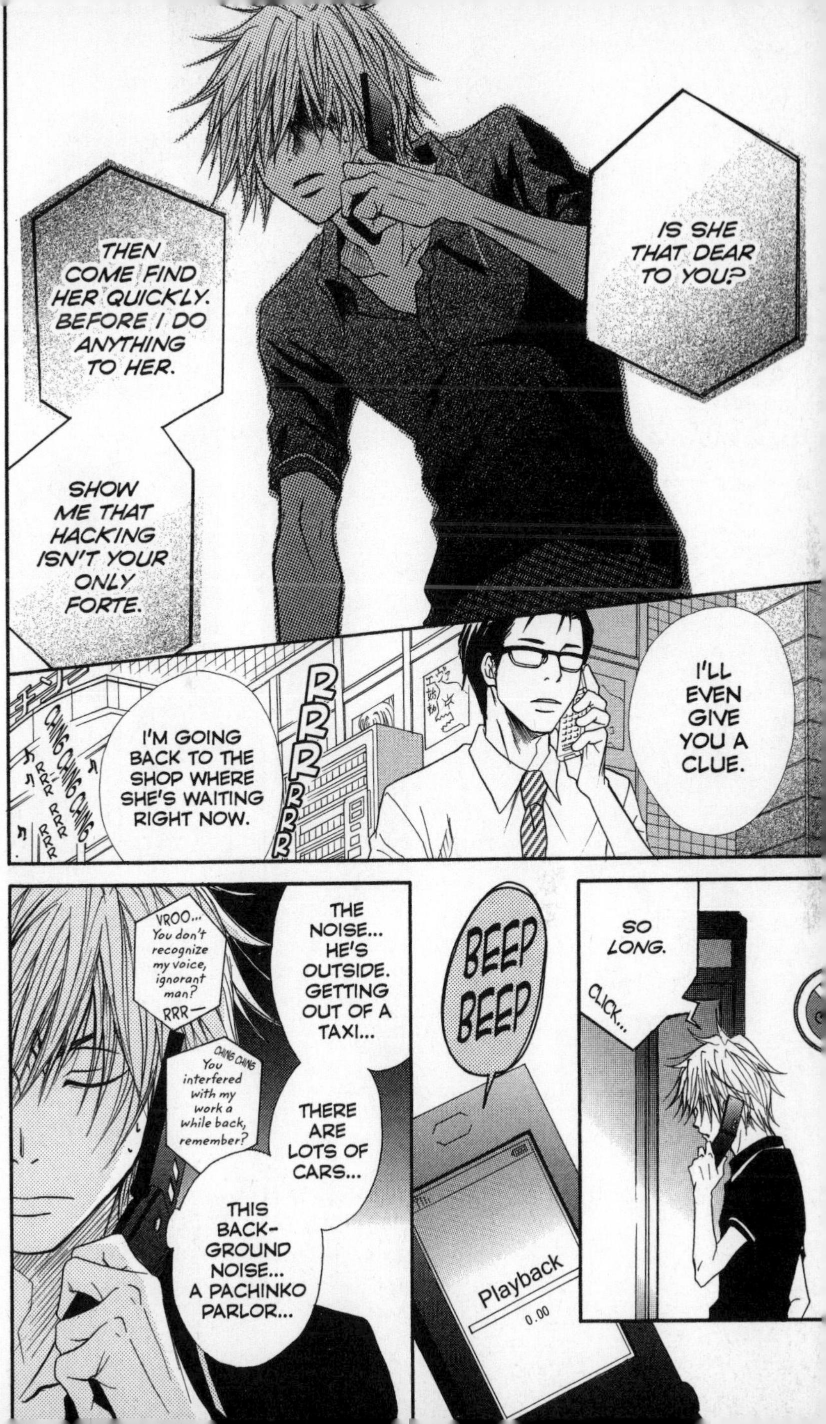
IS SHE THAT DEAR TO YOU?
THEN COME FIND HER QUICKLY. BEFORE I DO ANYTHING TO HER.
SHOW ME THAT HACKING ISN'T YOUR ONLY FORTE.
I'LL EVEN GIVE YOU A CLUE.
RRRRRRR
I'M GOING BACK TO THE SHOP WHERE SHE'S WAITING RIGHT NOW.
CHING CHING CHING
RRR RRR RRR
SO LONG.
CLICK...
BEEP BEEP
Playback
0.00
THE NOISE... HE'S OUTSIDE. GETTING OUT OF A TAXI...
VROO... You don't recognize my voice, ignorant man? RRR—
THERE ARE LOTS OF CARS...
CHING CHING You interfered with my work a while back, remember?
THIS BACK-GROUND NOISE... A PACHINKO PARLOR...

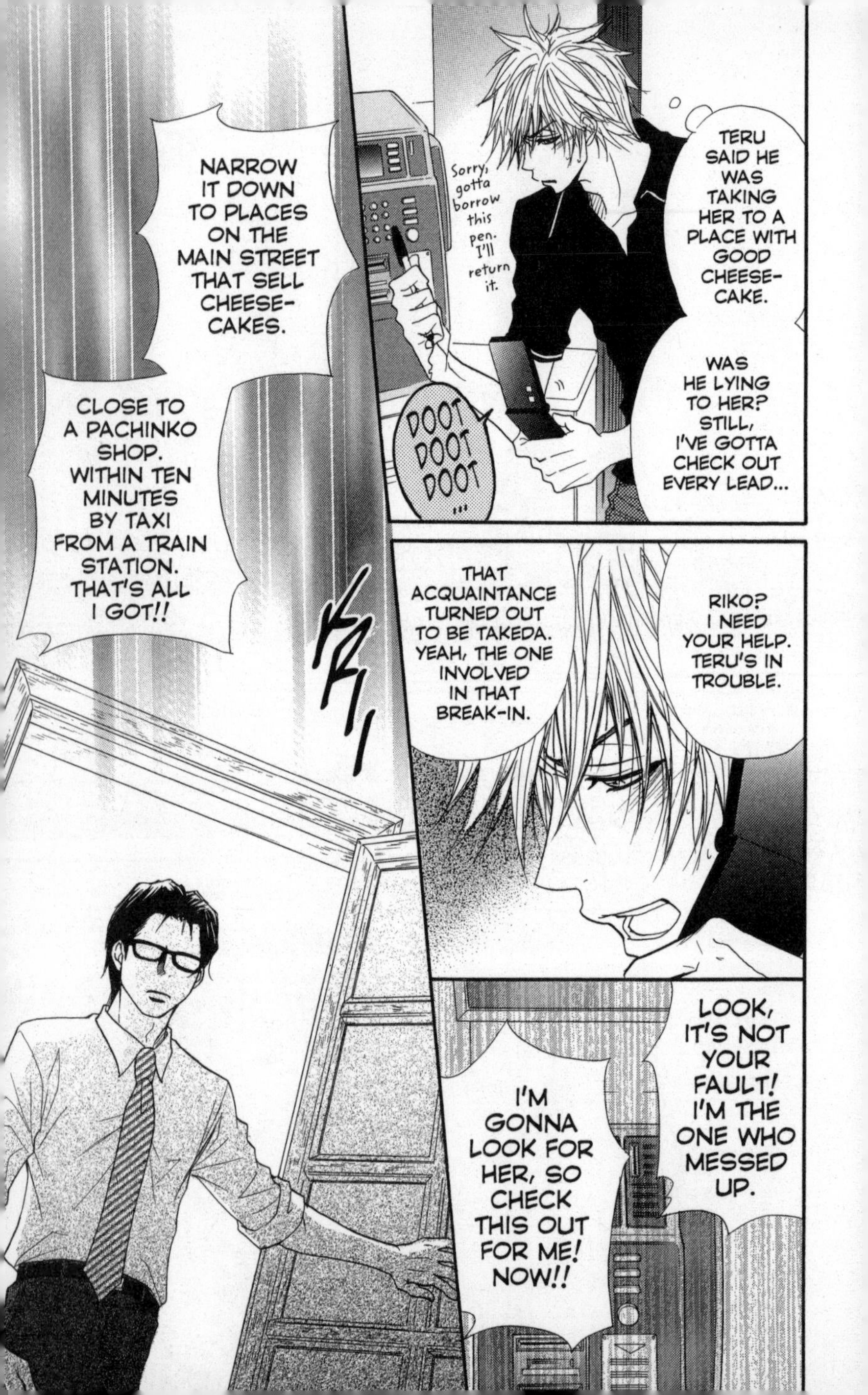
TERU SAID HE WAS TAKING HER TO A PLACE WITH GOOD CHEESE-CAKE.
WAS HE LYING TO HER? STILL, I'VE GOTTA CHECK OUT EVERY LEAD...
Sorry, gotta borrow this pen. I'll return it.
DOOT DOOT DOOT ...
RIKO? I NEED YOUR HELP. TERU'S IN TROUBLE.
THAT ACQUAINTANCE TURNED OUT TO BE TAKEDA. YEAH, THE ONE INVOLVED IN THAT BREAK-IN.
LOOK, IT'S NOT YOUR FAULT! I'M THE ONE WHO MESSED UP.
I'M GONNA LOOK FOR HER, SO CHECK THIS OUT FOR ME! NOW!!
NARROW IT DOWN TO PLACES ON THE MAIN STREET THAT SELL CHEESE-CAKES.
CLOSE TO A PACHINKO SHOP. WITHIN TEN MINUTES BY TAXI FROM A TRAIN STATION. THAT'S ALL I GOT!!
KRII

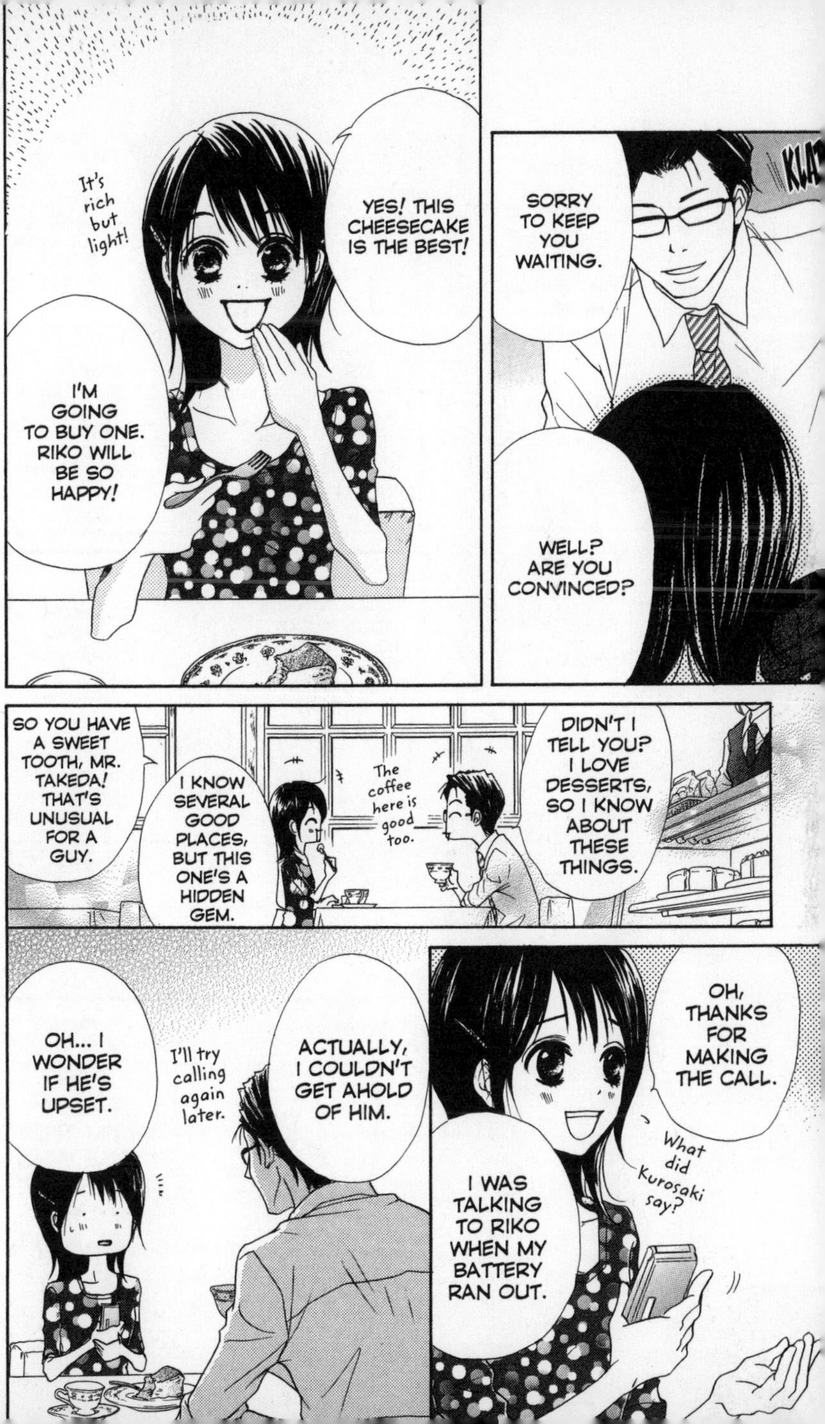
SORRY TO KEEP YOU WAITING.
WELL? ARE YOU CONVINCED?
YES! THIS CHEESECAKE IS THE BEST!
It's rich but light!
I'M GOING TO BUY ONE. RIKO WILL BE SO HAPPY!
DIDN'T I TELL YOU? I LOVE DESSERTS, SO I KNOW ABOUT THESE THINGS.
The coffee here is good too.
I KNOW SEVERAL GOOD PLACES, BUT THIS ONE'S A HIDDEN GEM.
SO YOU HAVE A SWEET TOOTH, MR. TAKEDA! THAT'S UNUSUAL FOR A GUY.
OH, THANKS FOR MAKING THE CALL.
What did Kurosaki say?
I WAS TALKING TO RIKO WHEN MY BATTERY RAN OUT.
ACTUALLY, I COULDN'T GET AHOLD OF HIM.
I'll try calling again later.
OH... I WONDER IF HE'S UPSET.

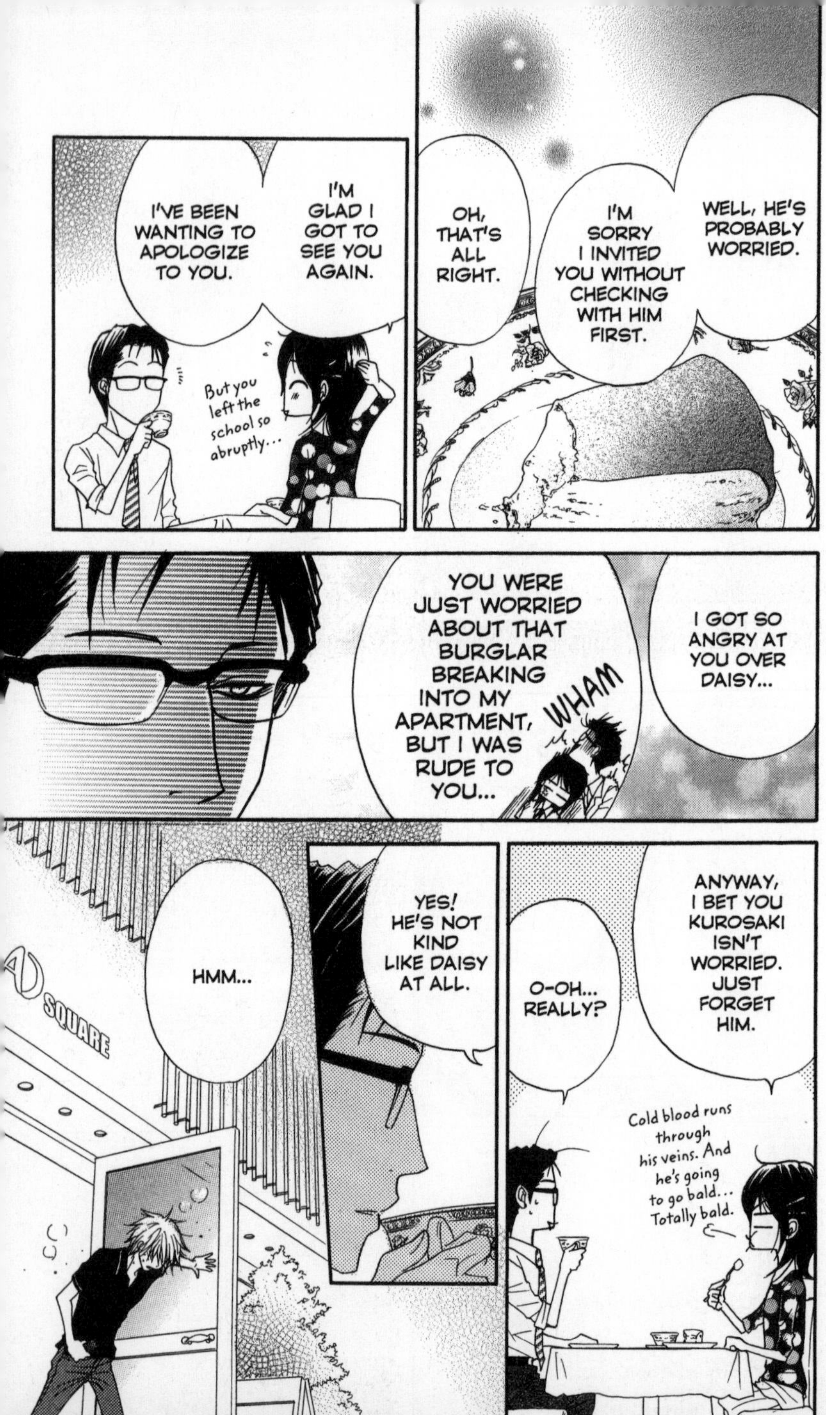
WELL, HE'S PROBABLY WORRIED.
I'M SORRY I INVITED YOU WITHOUT CHECKING WITH HIM FIRST.
OH, THAT'S ALL RIGHT.
I'M GLAD I GOT TO SEE YOU AGAIN.
I'VE BEEN WANTING TO APOLOGIZE TO YOU.
But you left the school so abruptly...
I GOT SO ANGRY AT YOU OVER DAISY...
YOU WERE JUST WORRIED ABOUT THAT BURGLAR BREAKING INTO MY APARTMENT, BUT I WAS RUDE TO YOU...
WHAM
ANYWAY, I BET YOU KUROSAKI ISN'T WORRIED. JUST FORGET HIM.
O-OH... REALLY?
Cold blood runs through his veins. And he's going to go bald... Totally bald.
YES! HE'S NOT KIND LIKE DAISY AT ALL.
HMM...
SQUARE

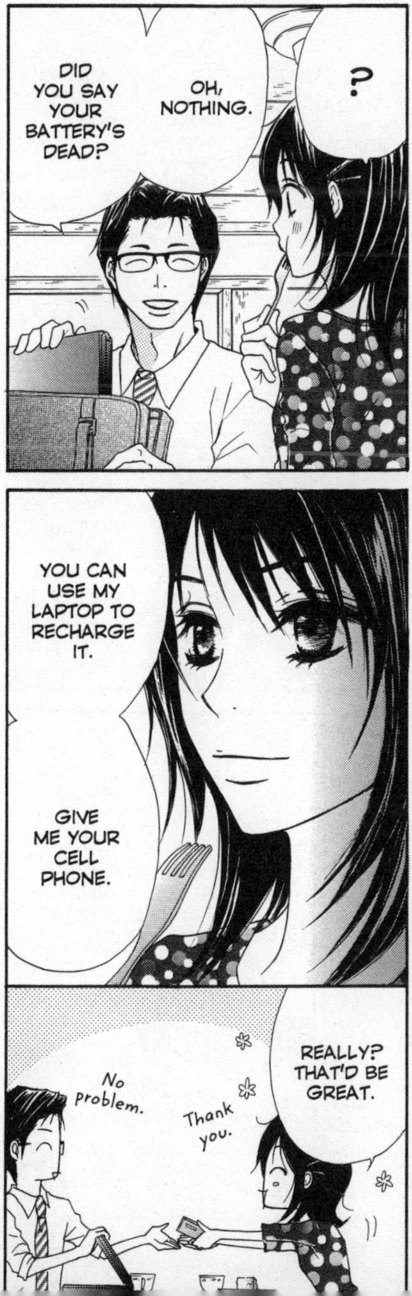
DID YOU SAY YOUR BATTERY'S DEAD?
OH, NOTHING.
?
YOU CAN USE MY LAPTOP TO RECHARGE IT.
GIVE ME YOUR CELL PHONE.
No problem.
Thank you.
REALLY? THAT'D BE GREAT.
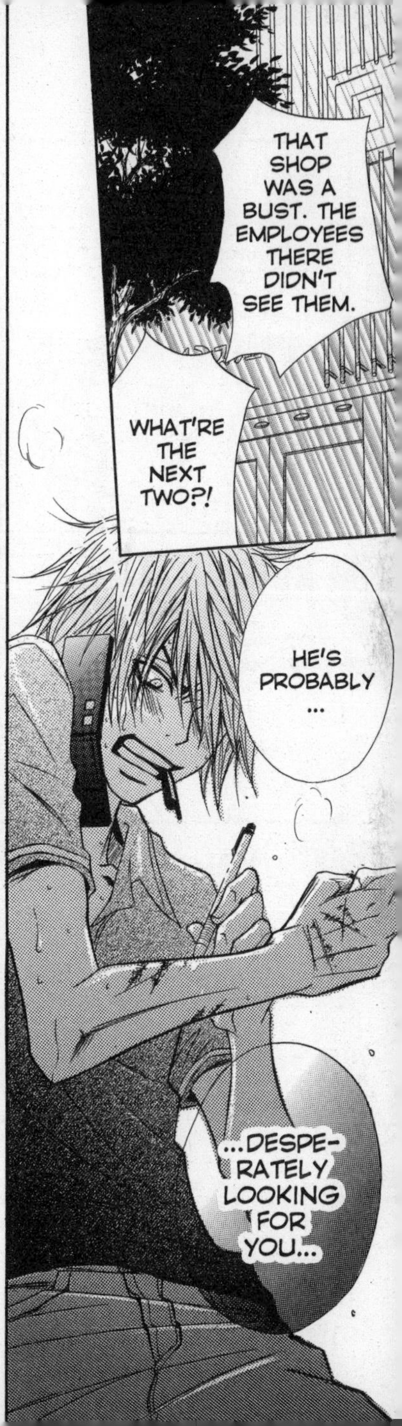
THAT SHOP WAS A BUST. THE EMPLOYEES THERE DIDN'T SEE THEM.
WHAT'RE THE NEXT TWO?!
HE'S PROBABLY ...
...DESPE-RATELY LOOKING FOR YOU...

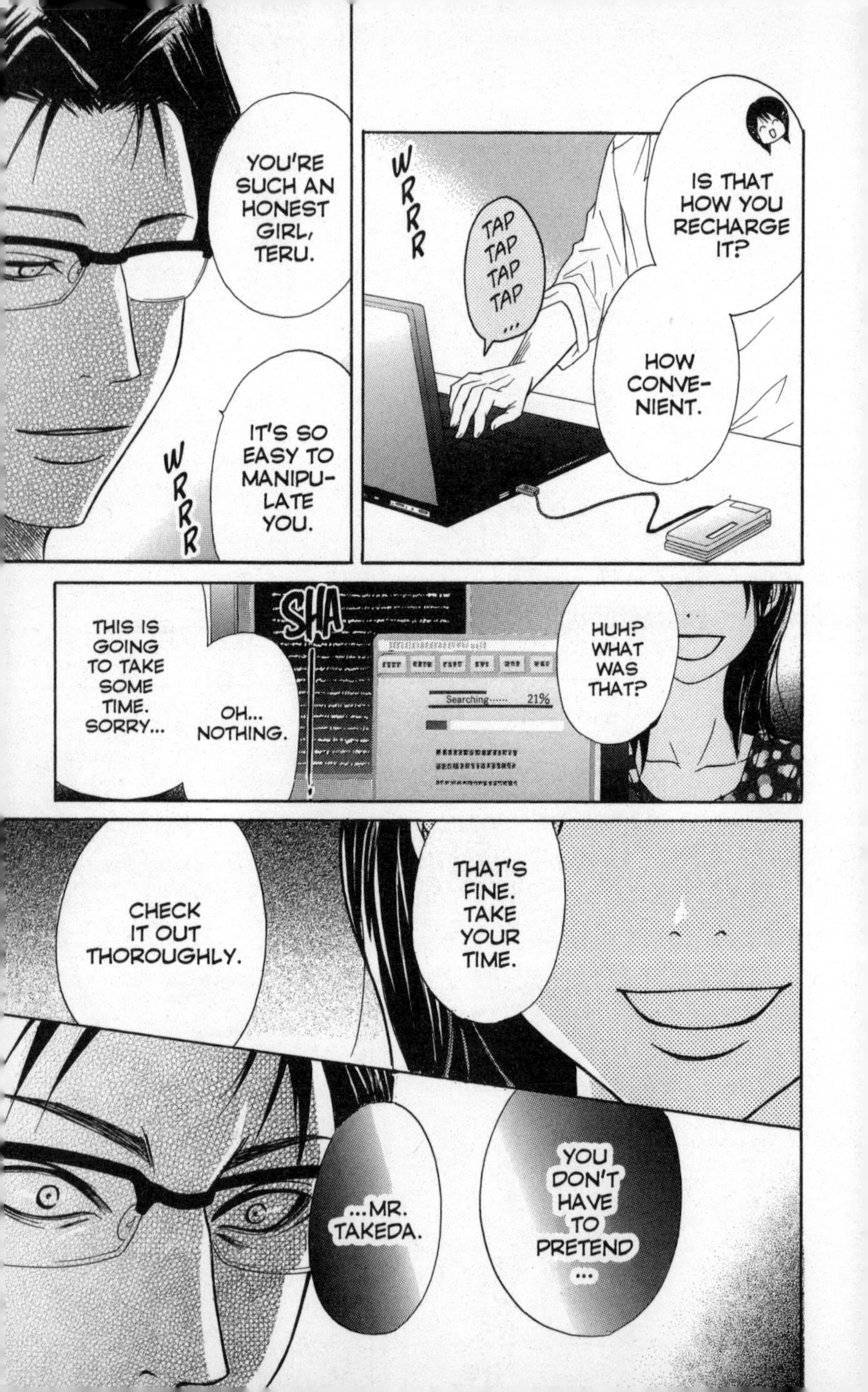
IS THAT HOW YOU RECHARGE IT?
WRRR
TAP TAP TAP TAP ...
HOW CONVE-NIENT.
YOU'RE SUCH AN HONEST GIRL, TERU.
IT'S SO EASY TO MANIPU-LATE YOU.
WRRR
HUH? WHAT WAS THAT?
SHA
Searching...... 21%
OH... NOTHING.
THIS IS GOING TO TAKE SOME TIME. SORRY...
THAT'S FINE. TAKE YOUR TIME.
CHECK IT OUT THOROUGHLY.
YOU DON'T HAVE TO PRETEND ...
...MR. TAKEDA.

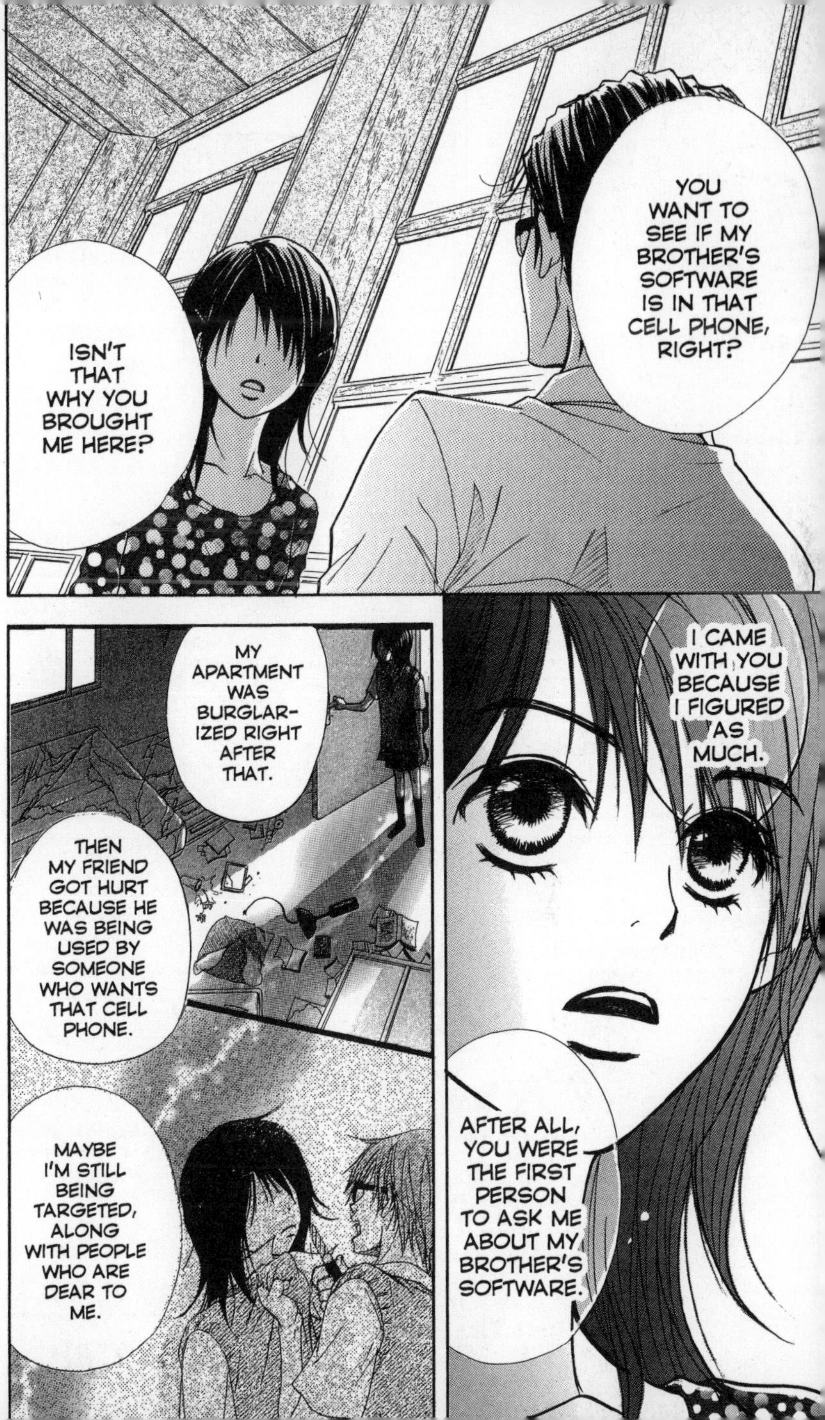
YOU WANT TO SEE IF MY BROTHER'S SOFTWARE IS IN THAT CELL PHONE, RIGHT?
ISN'T THAT WHY YOU BROUGHT ME HERE?
I CAME WITH YOU BECAUSE I FIGURED AS MUCH.
AFTER ALL, YOU WERE THE FIRST PERSON TO ASK ME ABOUT MY BROTHER'S SOFTWARE.
MY APARTMENT WAS BURGLAR-IZED RIGHT AFTER THAT.
THEN MY FRIEND GOT HURT BECAUSE HE WAS BEING USED BY SOMEONE WHO WANTS THAT CELL PHONE.
MAYBE I'M STILL BEING TARGETED, ALONG WITH PEOPLE WHO ARE DEAR TO ME.

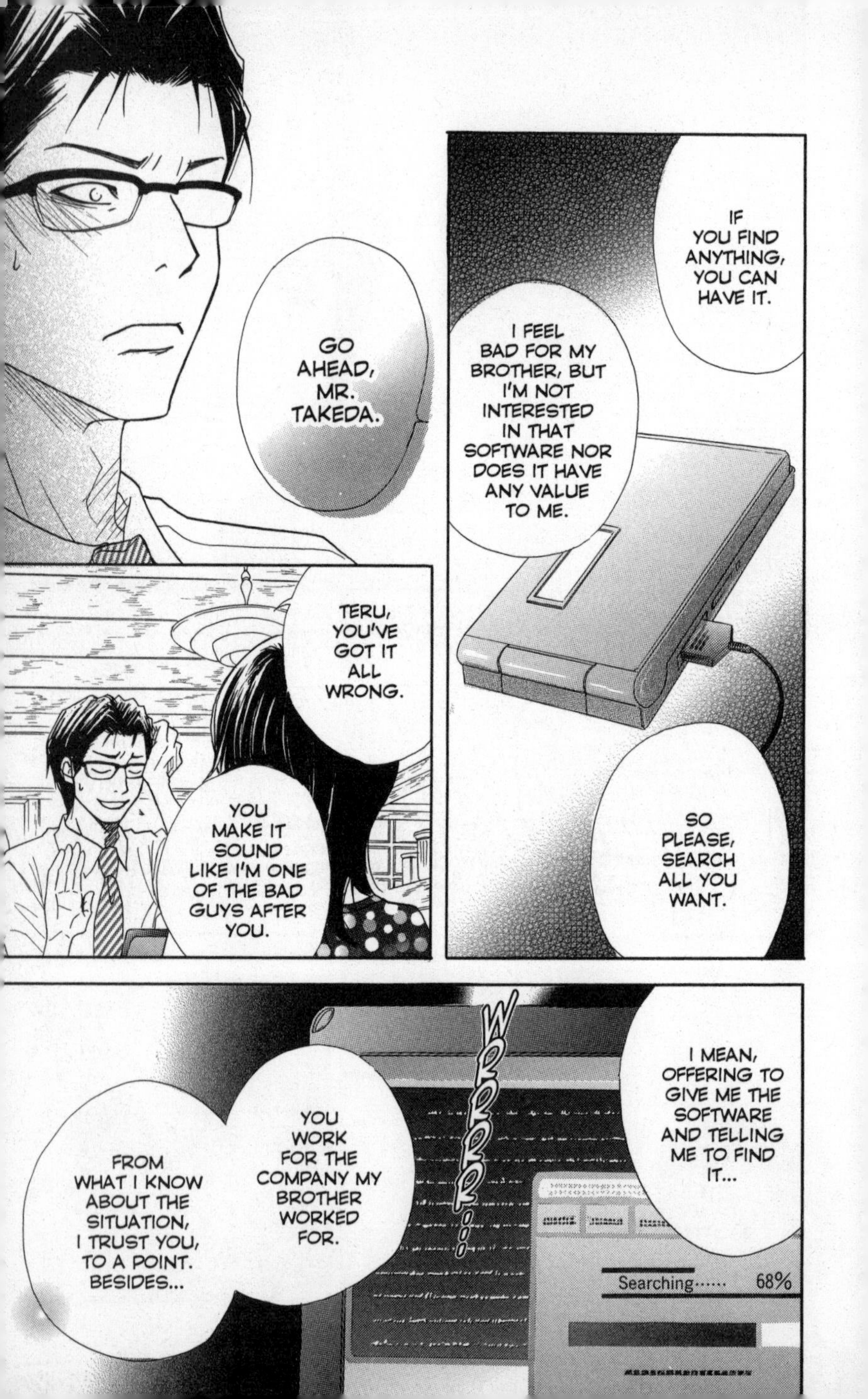
IF YOU FIND ANYTHING, YOU CAN HAVE IT.
I FEEL BAD FOR MY BROTHER, BUT I'M NOT INTERESTED IN THAT SOFTWARE NOR DOES IT HAVE ANY VALUE TO ME.
SO PLEASE, SEARCH ALL YOU WANT.
GO AHEAD, MR. TAKEDA.
TERU, YOU'VE GOT IT ALL WRONG.
YOU MAKE IT SOUND LIKE I'M ONE OF THE BAD GUYS AFTER YOU.
I MEAN, OFFERING TO GIVE ME THE SOFTWARE AND TELLING ME TO FIND IT...
WORRRR...
Searching······ 68%
YOU WORK FOR THE COMPANY MY BROTHER WORKED FOR.
FROM WHAT I KNOW ABOUT THE SITUATION, I TRUST YOU, TO A POINT. BESIDES...

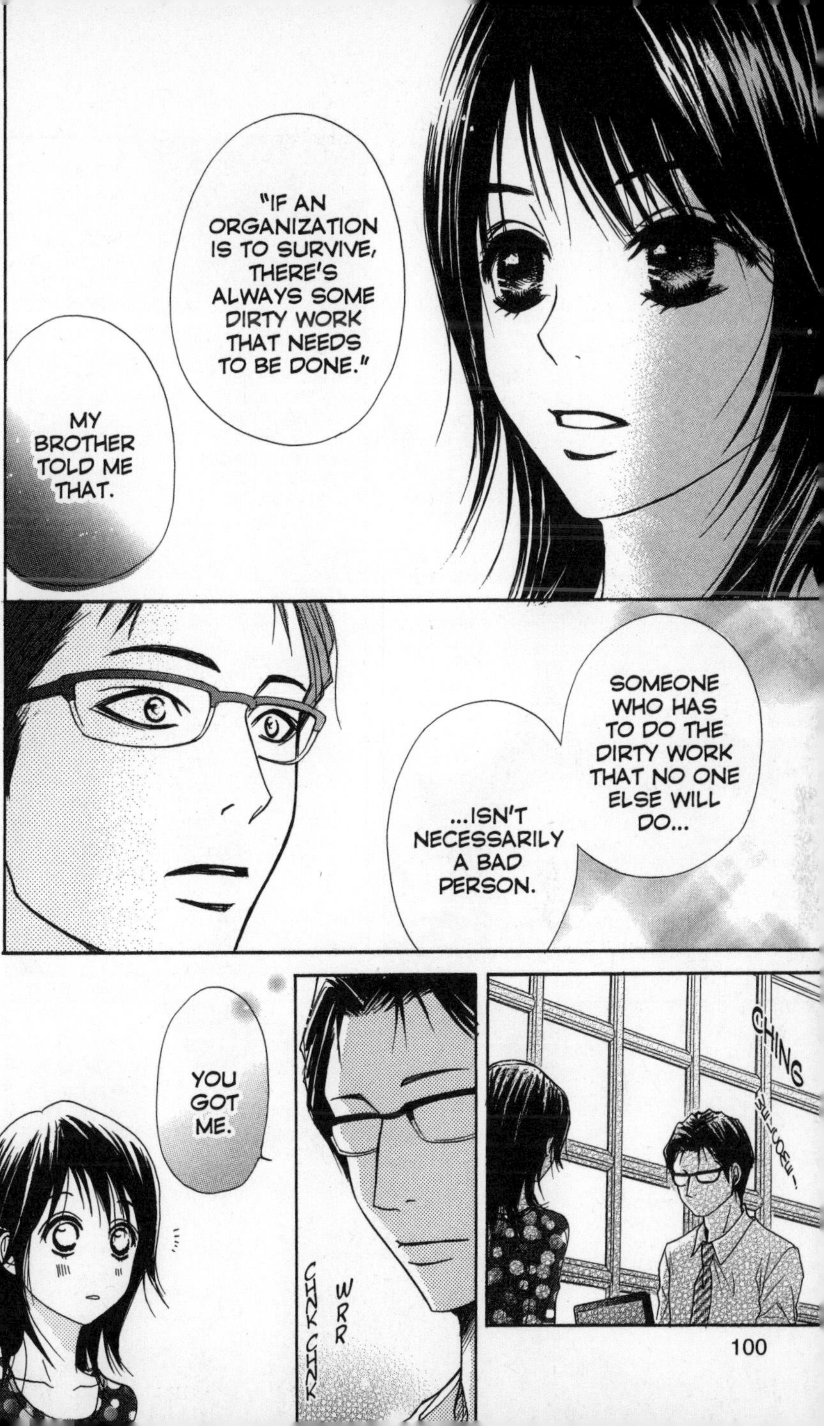
"IF AN ORGANIZATION IS TO SURVIVE, THERE'S ALWAYS SOME DIRTY WORK THAT NEEDS TO BE DONE."
MY BROTHER TOLD ME THAT.
SOMEONE WHO HAS TO DO THE DIRTY WORK THAT NO ONE ELSE WILL DO...
...ISN'T NECESSARILY A BAD PERSON.
CHING
WRR
CHNK CHNK
YOU GOT ME.

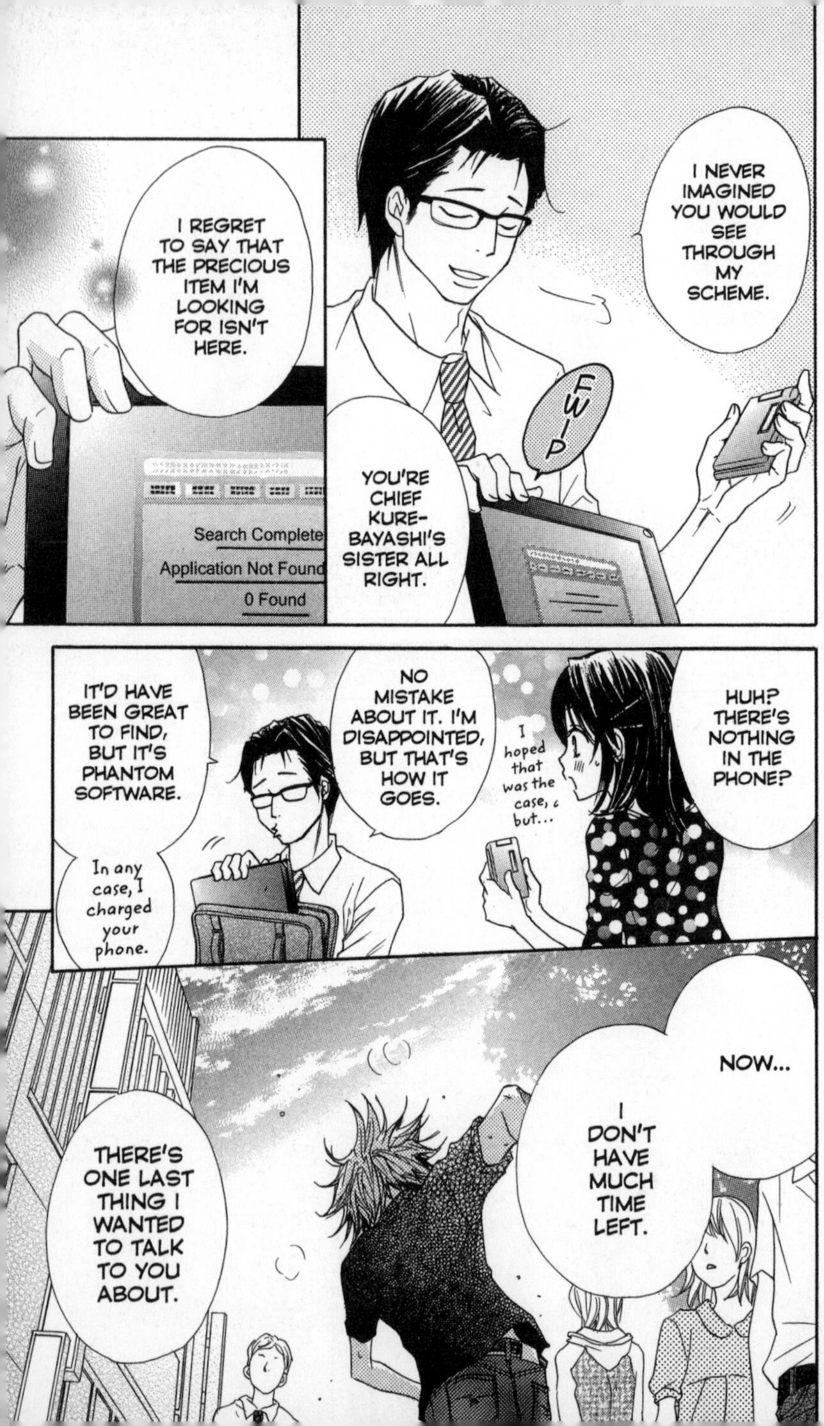
I NEVER IMAGINED YOU WOULD SEE THROUGH MY SCHEME.
FWIP
YOU'RE CHIEF KURE-BAYASHI'S SISTER ALL RIGHT.
I REGRET TO SAY THAT THE PRECIOUS ITEM I'M LOOKING FOR ISN'T HERE.
Search Complete
Application Not Found
0 Found
HUH? THERE'S NOTHING IN THE PHONE?
I hoped that was the case, but...
NO MISTAKE ABOUT IT. I'M DISAPPOINTED, BUT THAT'S HOW IT GOES.
IT'D HAVE BEEN GREAT TO FIND, BUT IT'S PHANTOM SOFTWARE.
In any case, I charged your phone.
NOW...
I DON'T HAVE MUCH TIME LEFT.
THERE'S ONE LAST THING I WANTED TO TALK TO YOU ABOUT.

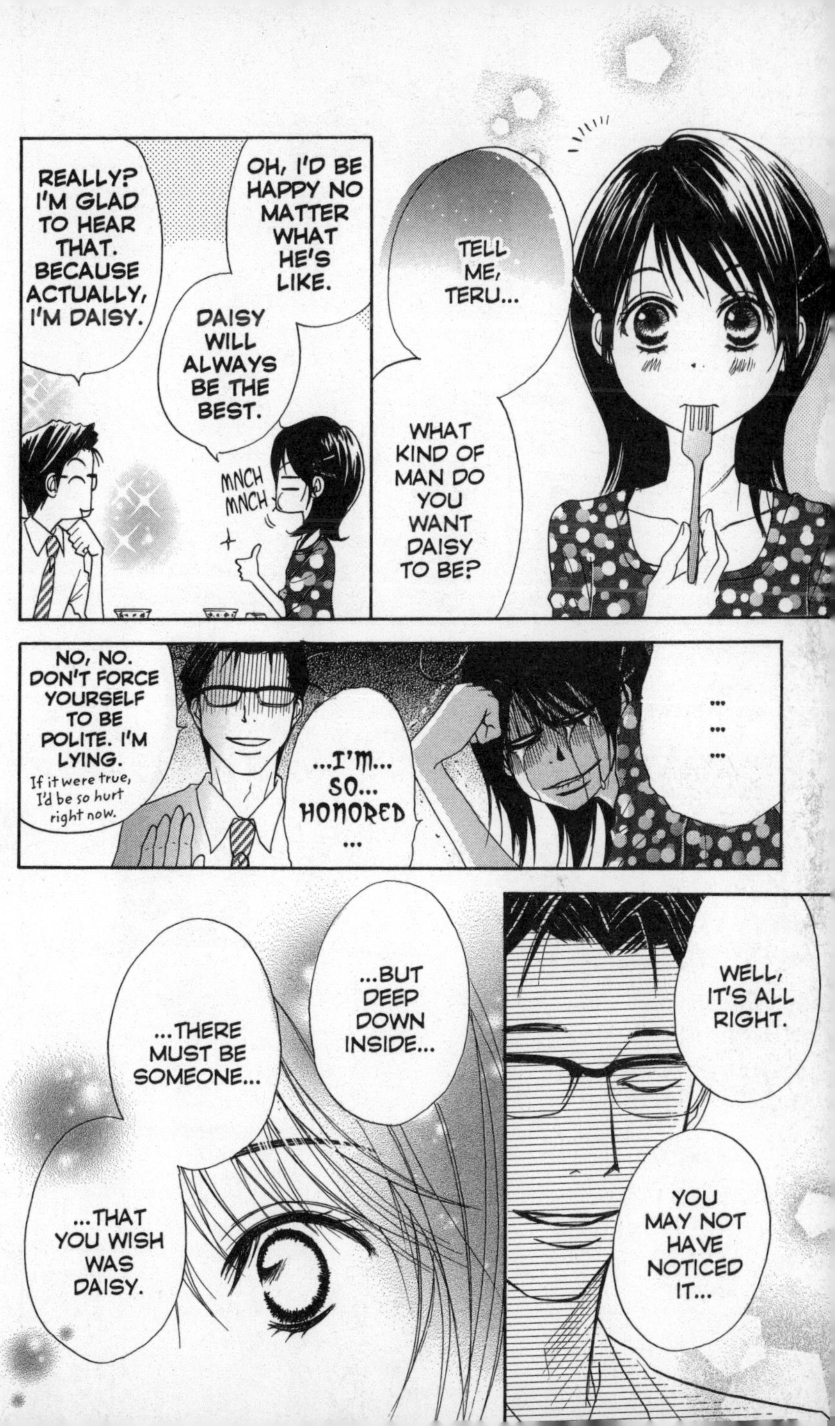
TELL ME, TERU...
WHAT KIND OF MAN DO YOU WANT DAISY TO BE?
OH, I'D BE HAPPY NO MATTER WHAT HE'S LIKE.
DAISY WILL ALWAYS BE THE BEST.
MNCH MNCH
REALLY? I'M GLAD TO HEAR THAT. BECAUSE ACTUALLY, I'M DAISY.
... ...
...I'M... SO... HONORED...
NO, NO. DON'T FORCE YOURSELF TO BE POLITE. I'M LYING.
If it were true, I'd be so hurt right now.
WELL, IT'S ALL RIGHT.
YOU MAY NOT HAVE NOTICED IT...
...BUT DEEP DOWN INSIDE...
...THERE MUST BE SOMEONE...
...THAT YOU WISH WAS DAISY.

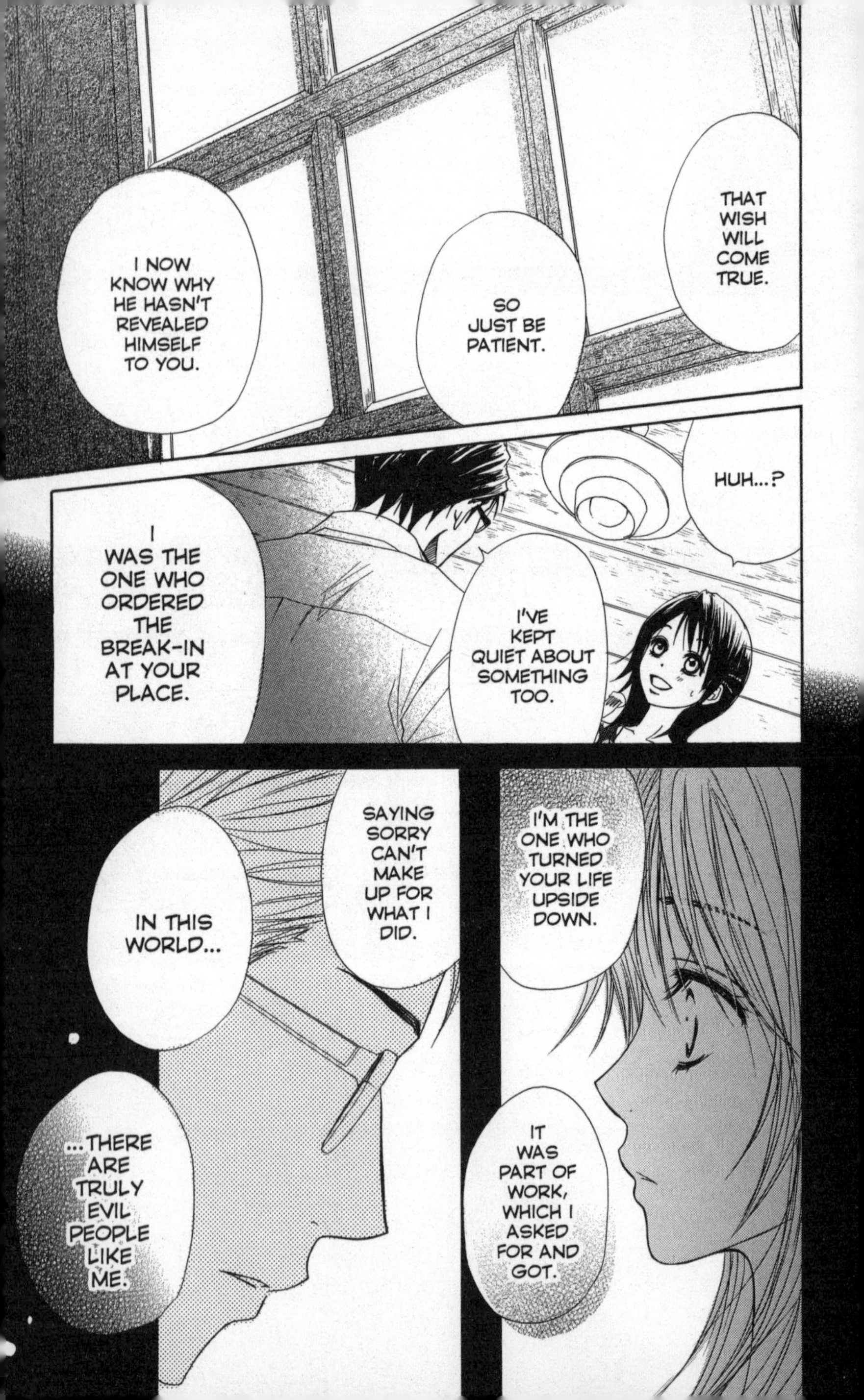
THAT WISH WILL COME TRUE.
SO JUST BE PATIENT.
I NOW KNOW WHY HE HASN'T REVEALED HIMSELF TO YOU.
HUH...?
I'VE KEPT QUIET ABOUT SOMETHING TOO.
I WAS THE ONE WHO ORDERED THE BREAK-IN AT YOUR PLACE.
I'M THE ONE WHO TURNED YOUR LIFE UPSIDE DOWN.
IT WAS PART OF WORK, WHICH I ASKED FOR AND GOT.
SAYING SORRY CAN'T MAKE UP FOR WHAT I DID.
IN THIS WORLD...
...THERE ARE TRULY EVIL PEOPLE LIKE ME.

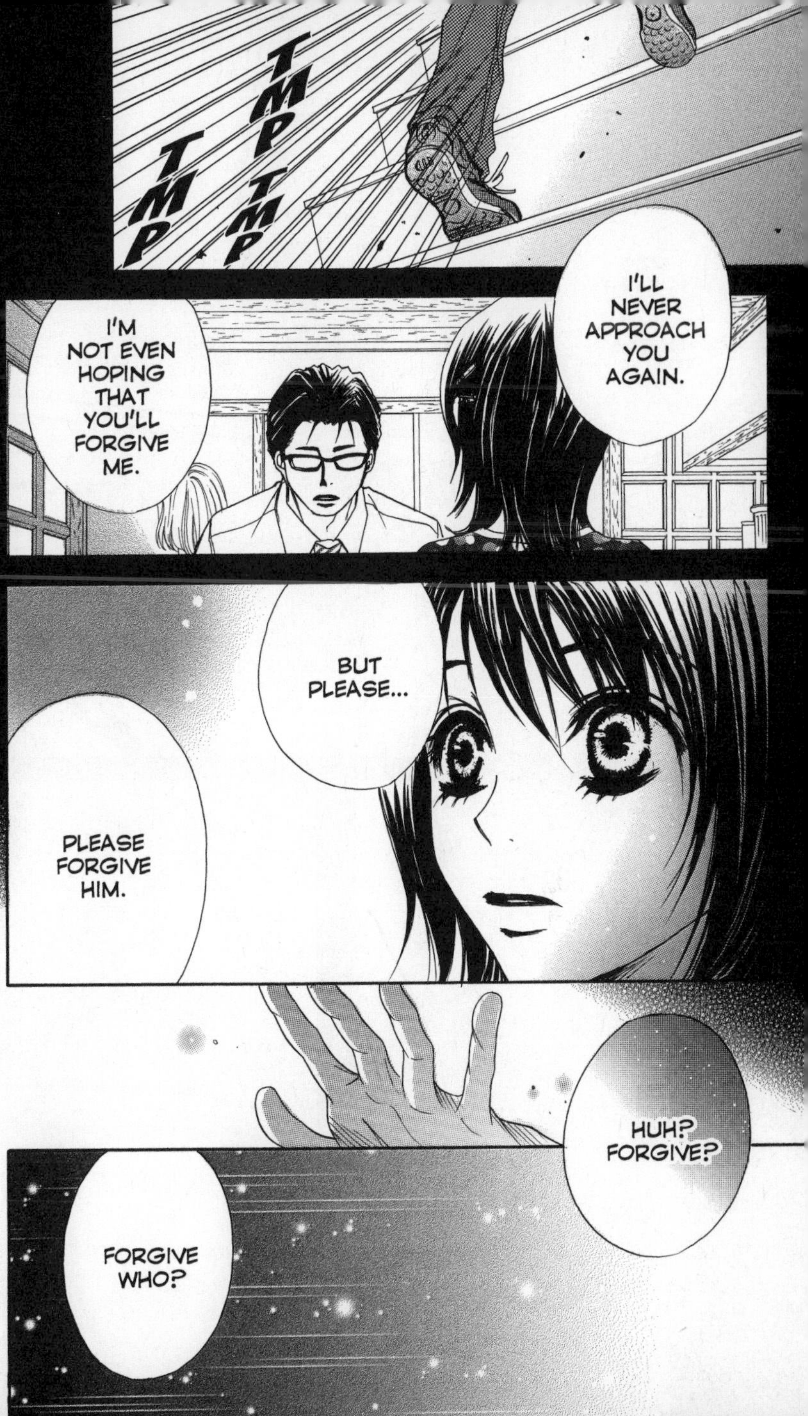
TMP TMP
TMP
I'LL NEVER APPROACH YOU AGAIN.
I'M NOT EVEN HOPING THAT YOU'LL FORGIVE ME.
BUT PLEASE...
PLEASE FORGIVE HIM.
HUH? FORGIVE?
FORGIVE WHO?

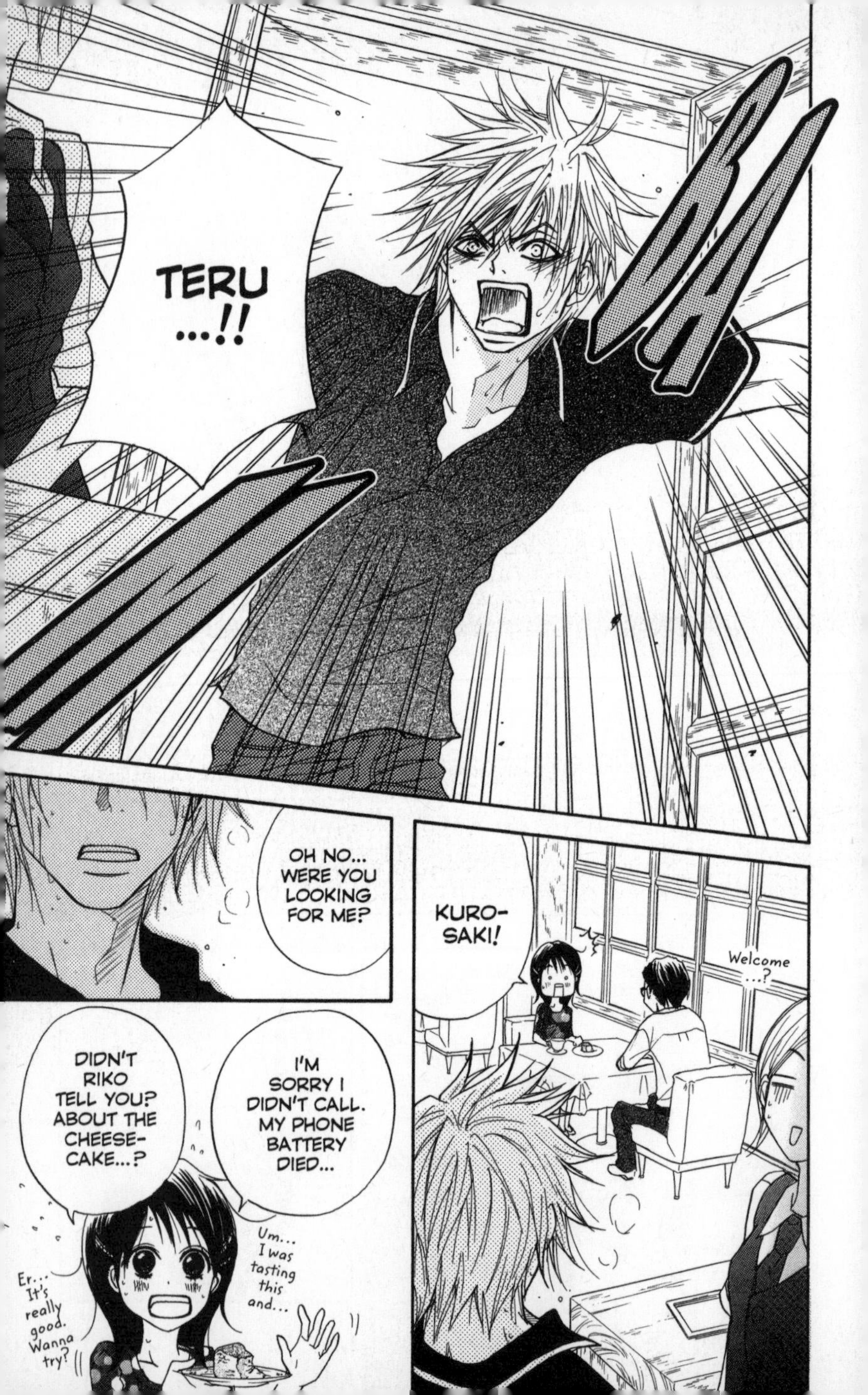
TERU ...!!
KURO-SAKI!
Welcome ...?
OH NO... WERE YOU LOOKING FOR ME?
I'M SORRY I DIDN'T CALL. MY PHONE BATTERY DIED...
DIDN'T RIKO TELL YOU? ABOUT THE CHEESE-CAKE...?
Um... I was tasting this and...
Er... It's really good. Wanna try?

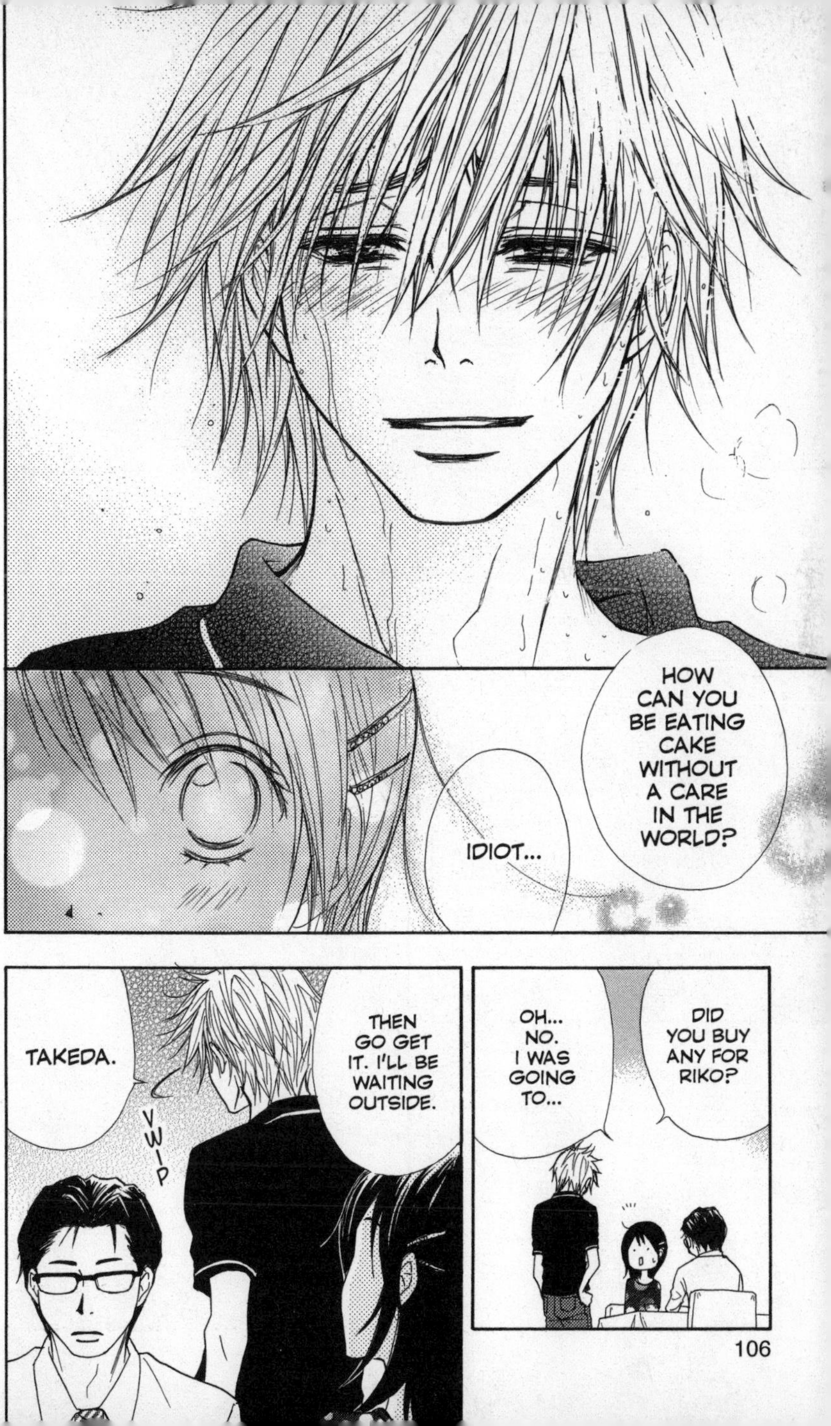
HOW CAN YOU BE EATING CAKE WITHOUT A CARE IN THE WORLD?
IDIOT...
DID YOU BUY ANY FOR RIKO?
OH... NO. I WAS GOING TO...
THEN GO GET IT. I'LL BE WAITING OUTSIDE.
VWIP
TAKEDA.

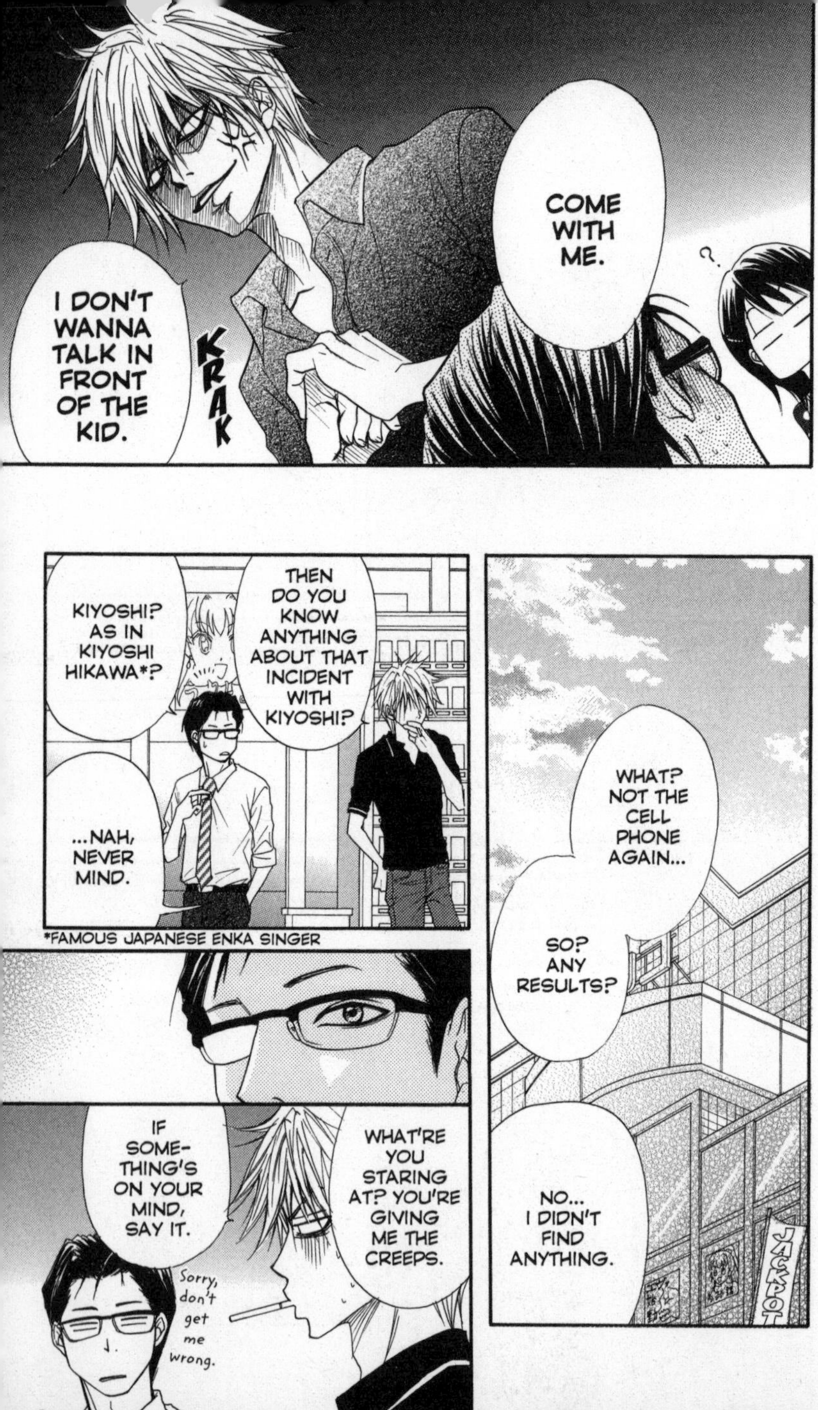
COME WITH ME.
?
I DON'T WANNA TALK IN FRONT OF THE KID.
KRAK
WHAT? NOT THE CELL PHONE AGAIN...
SO? ANY RESULTS?
NO... I DIDN'T FIND ANYTHING.
JACKPOT
THEN DO YOU KNOW ANYTHING ABOUT THAT INCIDENT WITH KIYOSHI?
KIYOSHI? AS IN KIYOSHI HIKAWA*?
...NAH, NEVER MIND.
WHAT'RE YOU STARING AT? YOU'RE GIVING ME THE CREEPS.
IF SOMETHING'S ON YOUR MIND, SAY IT.
Sorry, don't get me wrong.

*FAMOUS JAPANESE ENKA SINGER

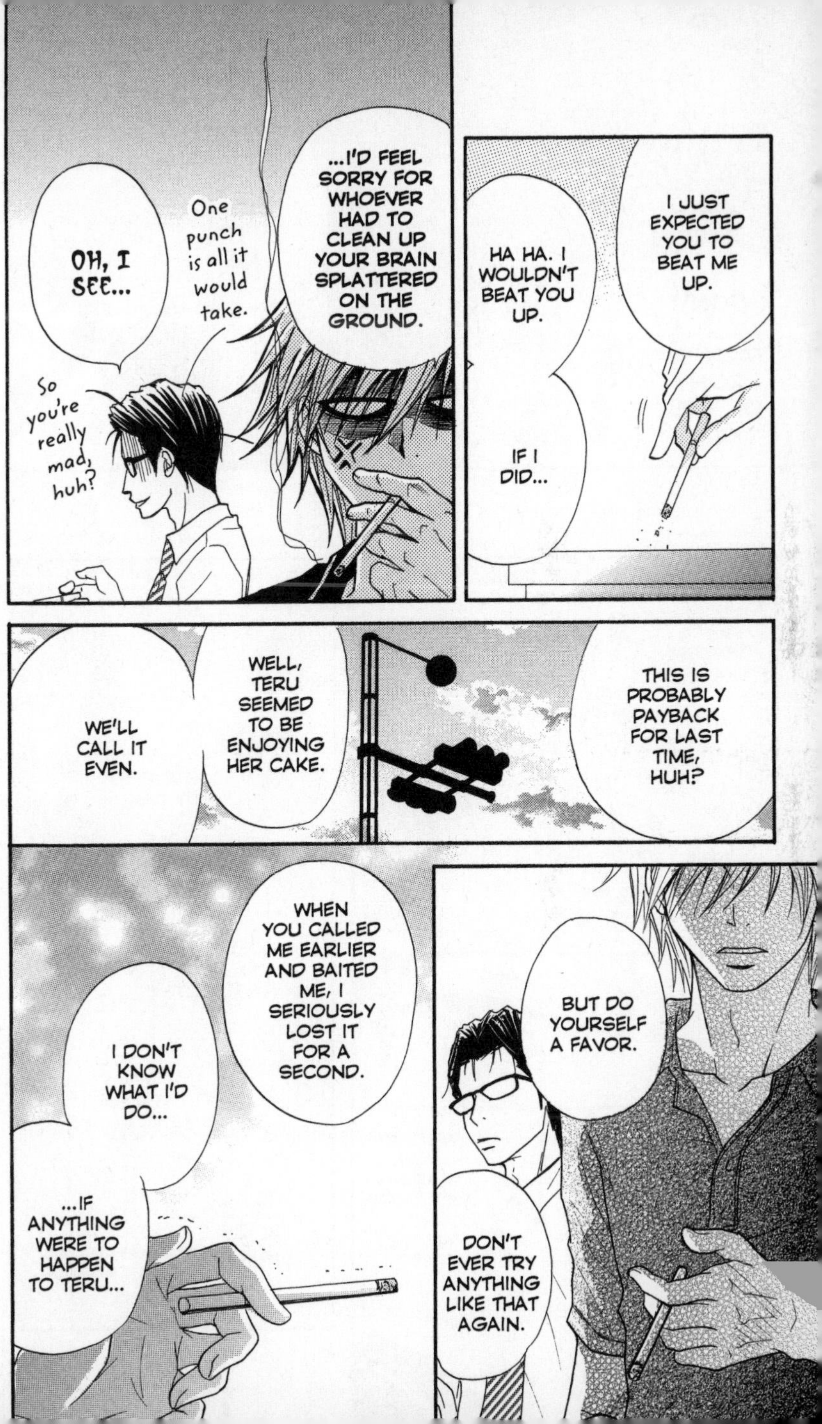
I JUST EXPECTED YOU TO BEAT ME UP.
HA HA. I WOULDN'T BEAT YOU UP.
IF I DID...
...I'D FEEL SORRY FOR WHOEVER HAD TO CLEAN UP YOUR BRAIN SPLATTERED ON THE GROUND.
One punch is all it would take.
OH, I SEE...
So you're really mad, huh?
THIS IS PROBABLY PAYBACK FOR LAST TIME, HUH?
WELL, TERU SEEMED TO BE ENJOYING HER CAKE.
WE'LL CALL IT EVEN.
BUT DO YOURSELF A FAVOR.
DON'T EVER TRY ANYTHING LIKE THAT AGAIN.
WHEN YOU CALLED ME EARLIER AND BAITED ME, I SERIOUSLY LOST IT FOR A SECOND.
I DON'T KNOW WHAT I'D DO...
...IF ANYTHING WERE TO HAPPEN TO TERU...

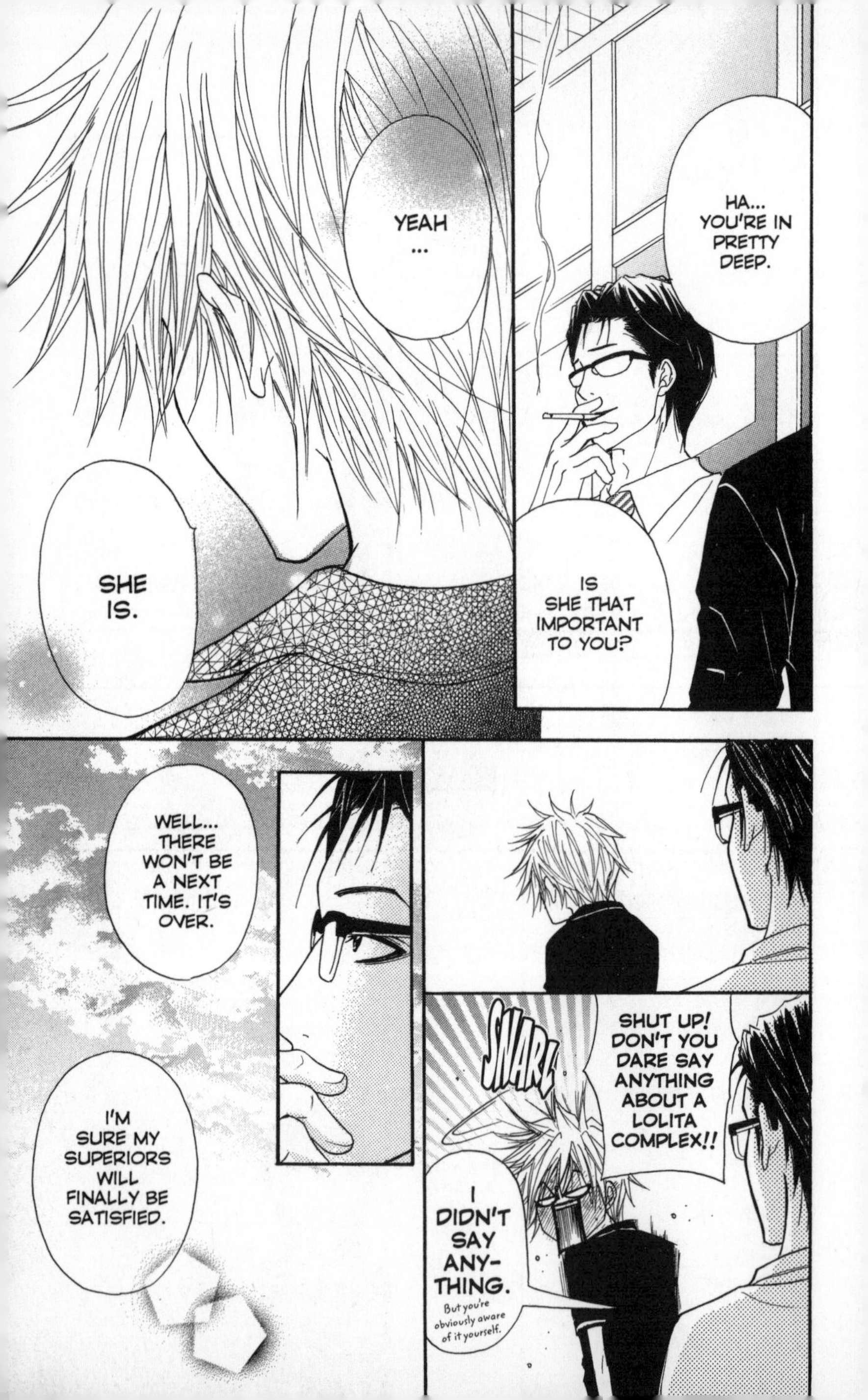
HA... YOU'RE IN PRETTY DEEP.
IS SHE THAT IMPORTANT TO YOU?
YEAH ...
SHE IS.
SNARL
SHUT UP! DON'T YOU DARE SAY ANYTHING ABOUT A LOLITA COMPLEX!!
I DIDN'T SAY ANY-THING.
But you're obviously aware of it yourself.
WELL... THERE WON'T BE A NEXT TIME. IT'S OVER.
I'M SURE MY SUPERIORS WILL FINALLY BE SATISFIED.

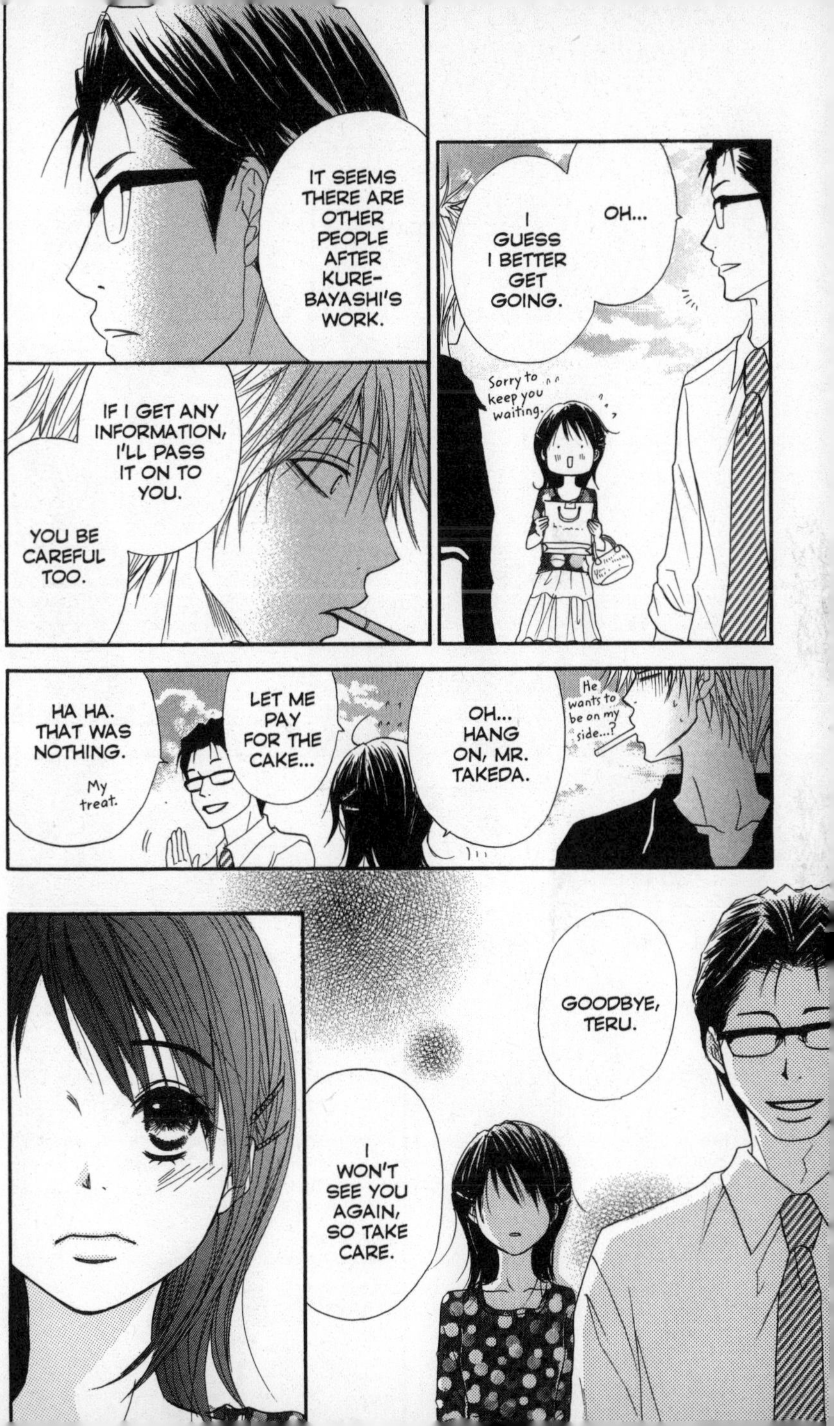
IT SEEMS THERE ARE OTHER PEOPLE AFTER KURE-BAYASHI'S WORK.
IF I GET ANY INFORMATION, I'LL PASS IT ON TO YOU.
YOU BE CAREFUL TOO.
OH...
I GUESS I BETTER GET GOING.
Sorry to keep you waiting.
He wants to be on my side...?
OH... HANG ON, MR. TAKEDA.
LET ME PAY FOR THE CAKE...
HA HA. THAT WAS NOTHING.
My treat.
GOODBYE, TERU.
I WON'T SEE YOU AGAIN, SO TAKE CARE.

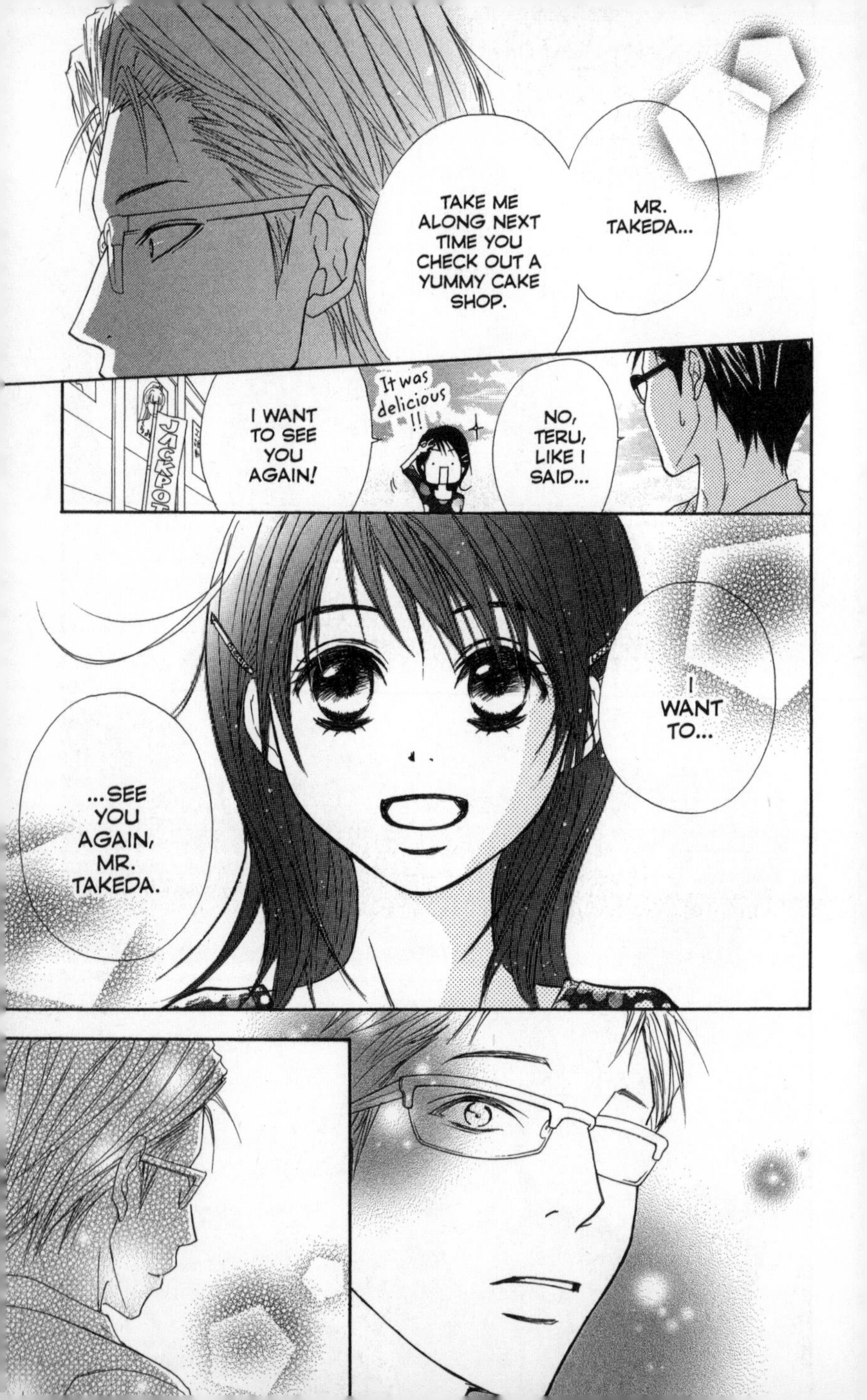
MR. TAKEDA...
TAKE ME ALONG NEXT TIME YOU CHECK OUT A YUMMY CAKE SHOP.
NO, TERU, LIKE I SAID...
It was delicious !!
I WANT TO SEE YOU AGAIN!
I WANT TO...
...SEE YOU AGAIN, MR. TAKEDA.

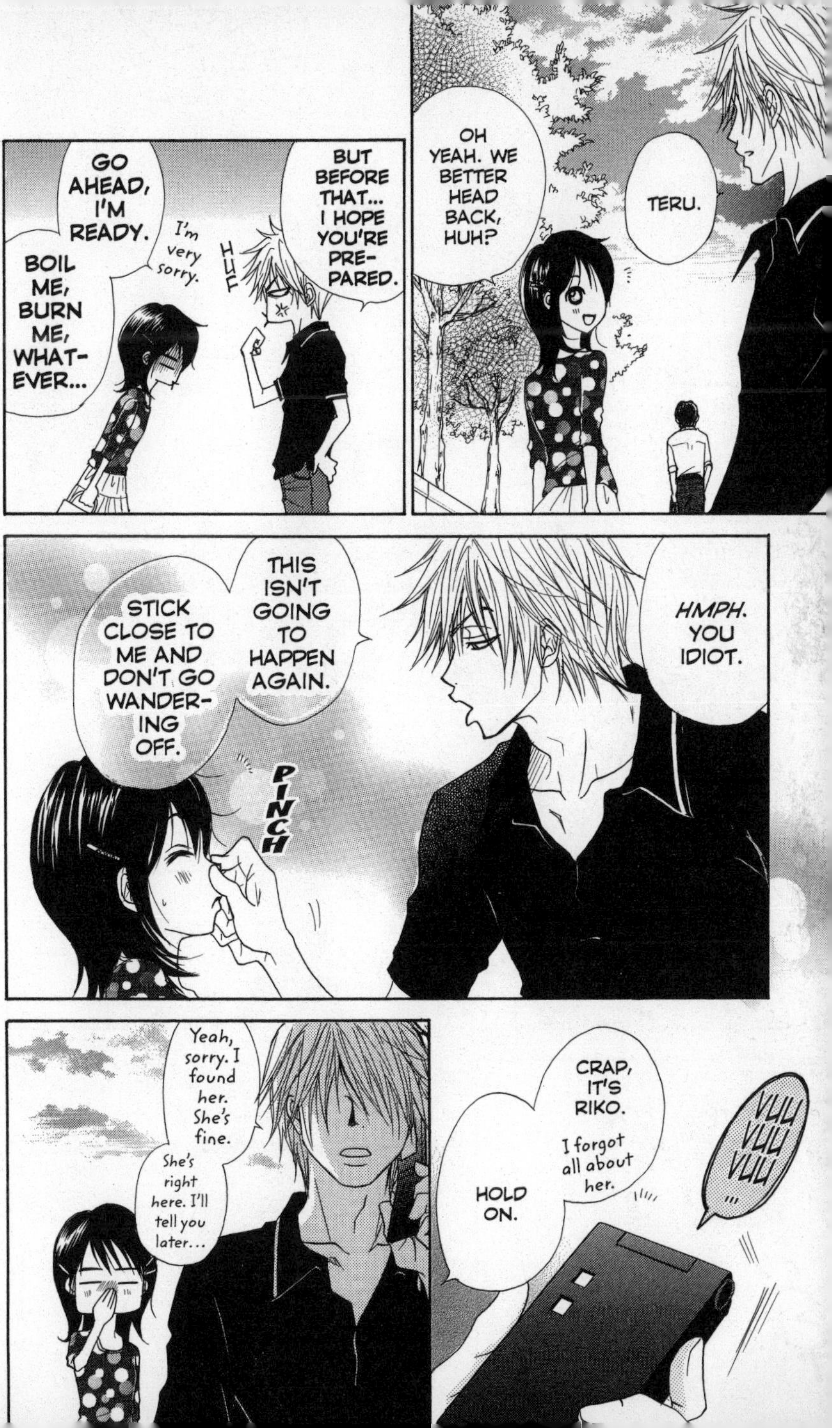
TERU.
OH YEAH. WE BETTER HEAD BACK, HUH?
BUT BEFORE THAT... I HOPE YOU'RE PREPARED.
HUF
GO AHEAD, I'M READY.
I'm very sorry.
BOIL ME, BURN ME, WHATEVER...
HMPH. YOU IDIOT.
THIS ISN'T GOING TO HAPPEN AGAIN.
STICK CLOSE TO ME AND DON'T GO WANDERING OFF.
PINCH
VUU VUU VUU...
CRAP, IT'S RIKO.
I forgot all about her.
HOLD ON.
Yeah, sorry. I found her. She's fine.
She's right here. I'll tell you later...

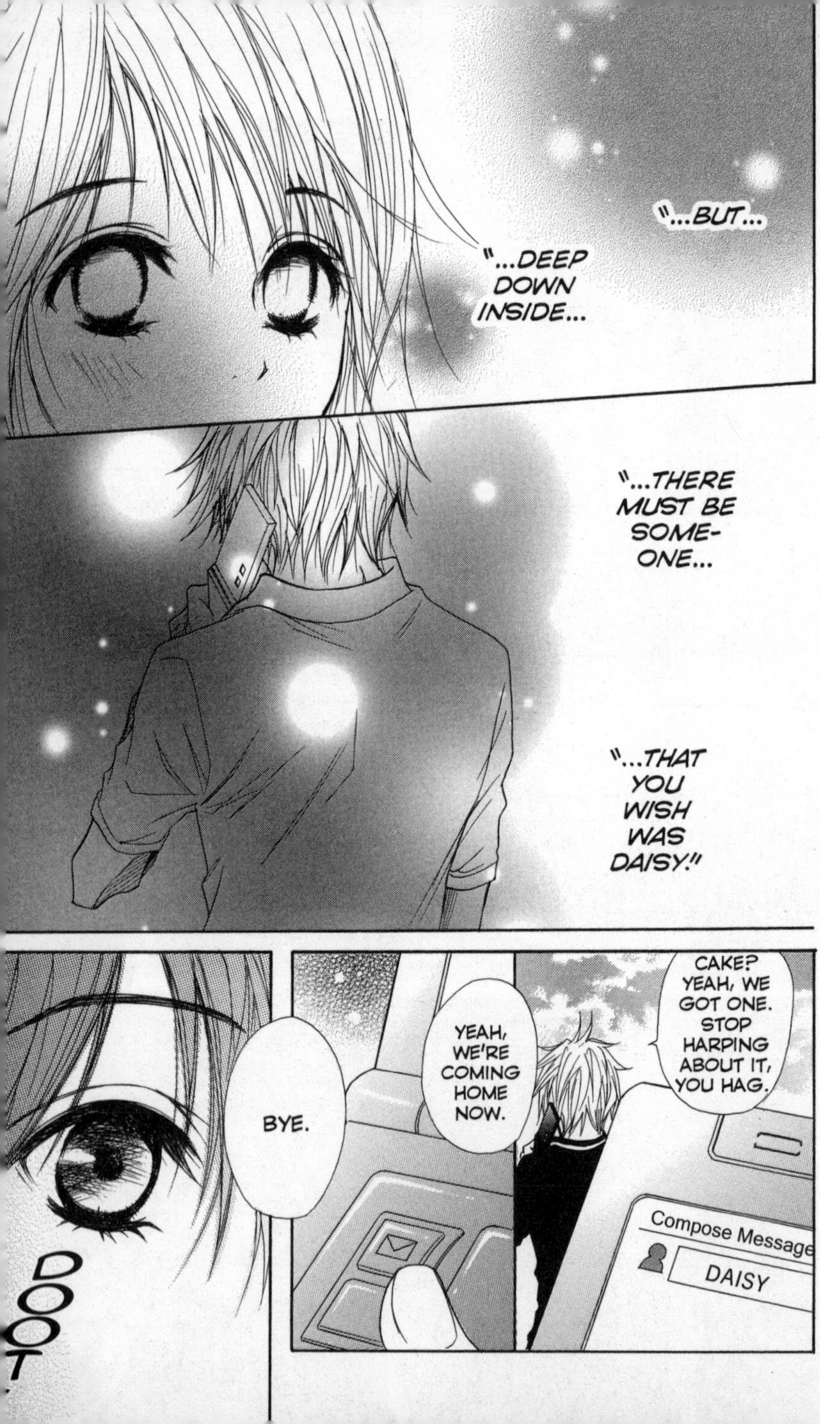
"...BUT...
"...DEEP DOWN INSIDE...
"...THERE MUST BE SOME-ONE...
"...THAT YOU WISH WAS DAISY!"
CAKE? YEAH, WE GOT ONE. STOP HARPING ABOUT IT, YOU HAG.
YEAH, WE'RE COMING HOME NOW.
BYE.
Compose Message
DAISY
DOOT

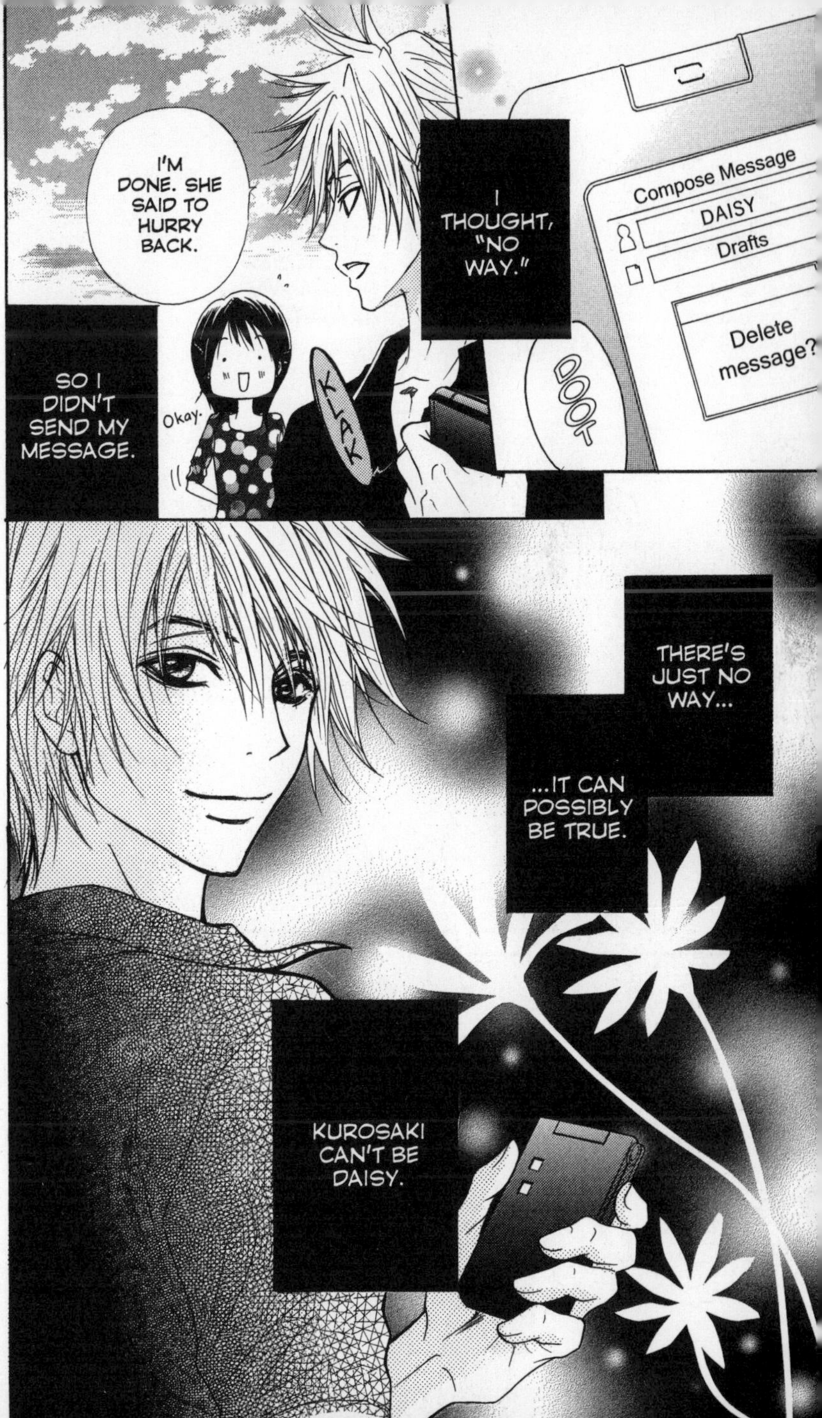
Compose Message
DAISY
Drafts
Delete message?
DOOT
I THOUGHT, "NO WAY."
I'M DONE. SHE SAID TO HURRY BACK.
KLAK
Okay.
SO I DIDN'T SEND MY MESSAGE.
THERE'S JUST NO WAY...
...IT CAN POSSIBLY BE TRUE.
KUROSAKI CAN'T BE DAISY.

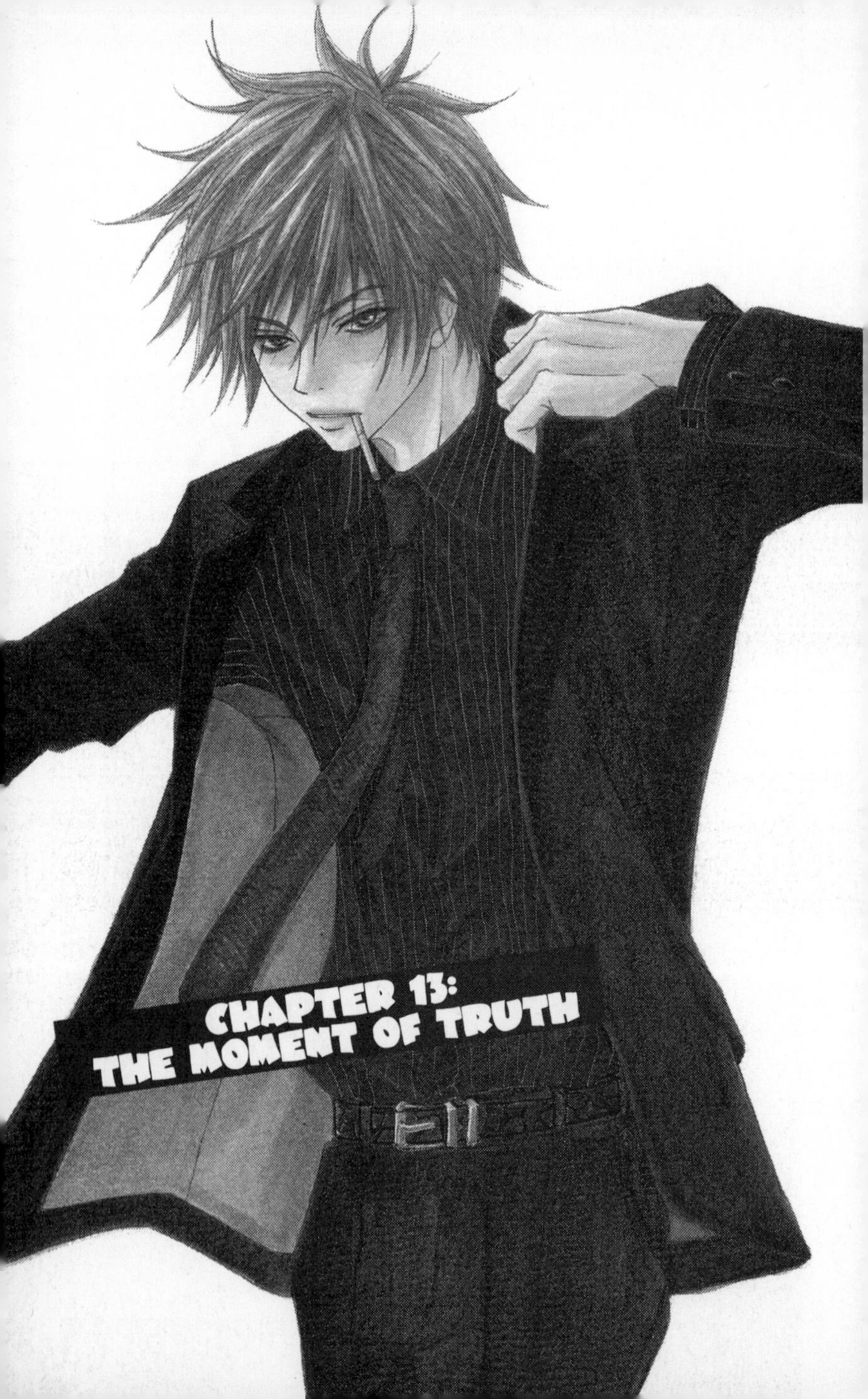
CHAPTER 13:
THE MOMENT OF TRUTH

A NUMBER OF PEOPLE INVOLVED
WITH THIS TITLE BURST OUT LAUGHING...

KYOUSUKE MOTOMI'S
MAJOR MESS-UP (CHAPTER 14)

LIGHTNING
(WRATH OF GOD LEVEL)

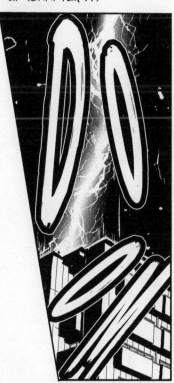

I DID IT RATHER POORLY. AND I'M REGRETTING IT.

*THIS "GODLY SCENE" CAN BE SEEN ON PAGE 180. ♥

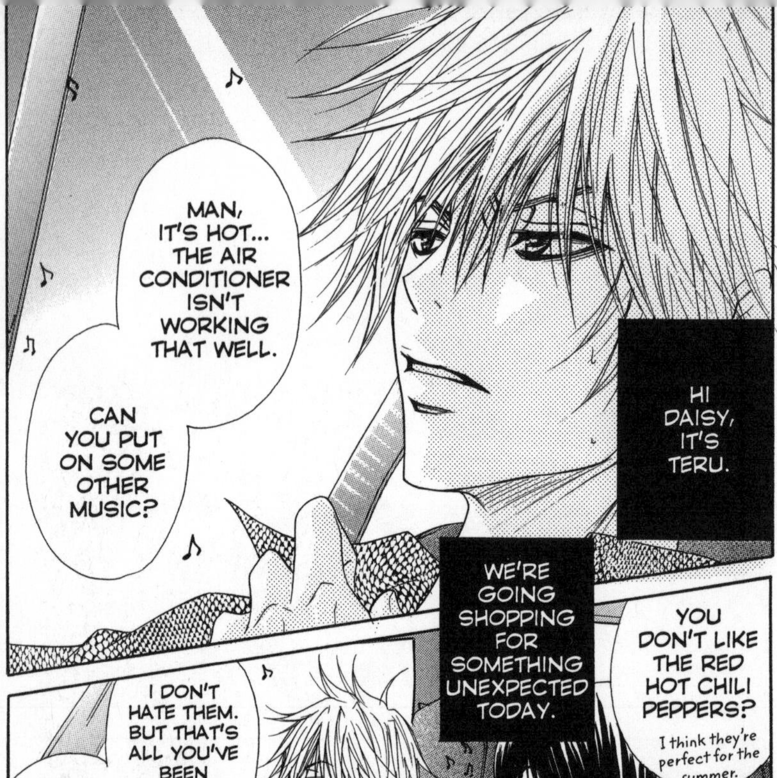
HI DAISY, IT'S TERU.
MAN, IT'S HOT... THE AIR CONDITIONER ISN'T WORKING THAT WELL.
CAN YOU PUT ON SOME OTHER MUSIC?
WE'RE GOING SHOPPING FOR SOMETHING UNEXPECTED TODAY.
YOU DON'T LIKE THE RED HOT CHILI PEPPERS?
I think they're perfect for the summer.
I DON'T HATE THEM. BUT THAT'S ALL YOU'VE BEEN LISTENING TO LATELY.
You like them that much?
PICK SOMETHING WE HAVEN'T LISTENED TO YET AND PUT THAT ON.

I DON'T THINK THERE ARE THAT MANY READERS WHO WERE HAPPY TO SEE TAKEDA RETURN. I (THE AUTHOR) ACTUALLY LIKE TAKEDA.
HE'S EASY TO DRAW (OTHER THAN HIS GLASSES). I THINK THERE ARE PEOPLE LIKE HIM IN REAL LIFE. HIS NARROW-MINDEDNESS, THE LIKELIHOOD THAT HE HAS LOLICON TENDENCIES, THE FACT THAT HE'S THE TYPE TO SHINE WHEN HE'S UNDER EXTREME PRESSURE... HE HAS A LOT IN COMMON WITH KUROSAKI.

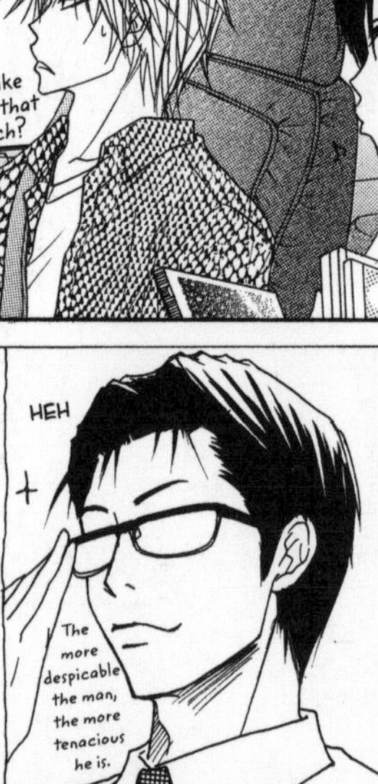
HEH
The more despicable the man, the more tenacious he is.

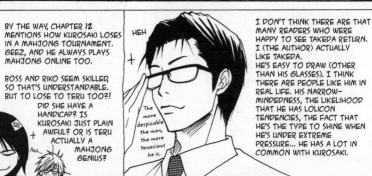

BY THE WAY, CHAPTER 12 MENTIONS HOW KUROSAKI LOSES IN A MAHJONG TOURNAMENT. GEEZ, AND HE ALWAYS PLAYS MAHJONG ONLINE TOO.

BOSS AND RIKO SEEM SKILLED, SO THAT'S UNDERSTANDABLE. BUT TO LOSE TO TERU TOO?! DID SHE HAVE A HANDICAP? IS KUROSAKI JUST PLAIN AWFUL? OR IS TERU ACTUALLY A MAHJONG GENIUS?

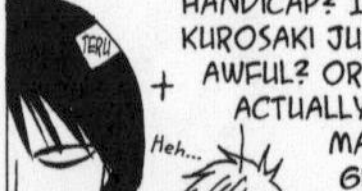
TERU
Heh...

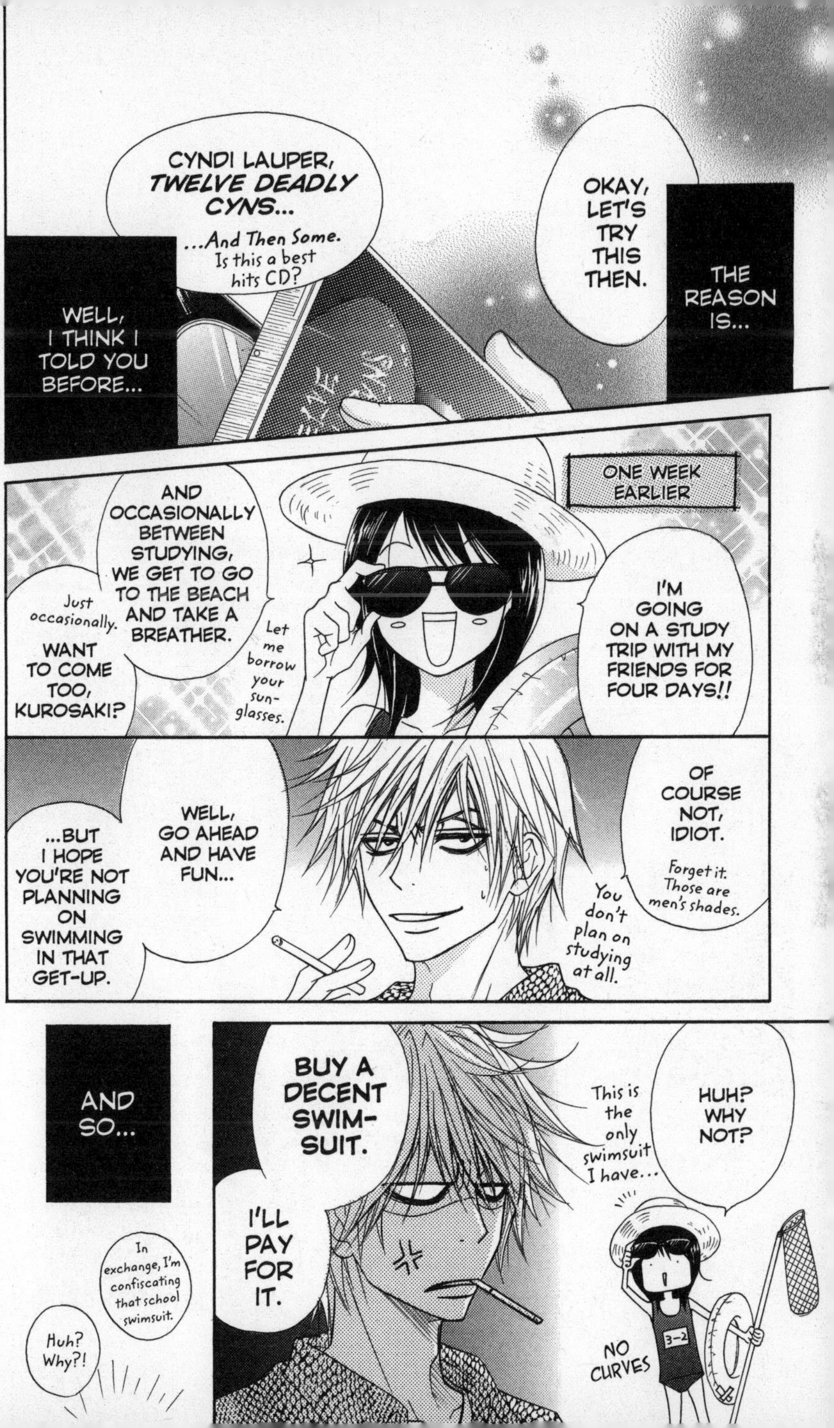
OKAY, LET'S TRY THIS THEN.
THE REASON IS...
CYNDI LAUPER, *TWELVE DEADLY CYNS*...
...And Then Some. Is this a best hits CD?
WELL, I THINK I TOLD YOU BEFORE...
ONE WEEK EARLIER
I'M GOING ON A STUDY TRIP WITH MY FRIENDS FOR FOUR DAYS!!
Let me borrow your sun-glasses.
AND OCCASIONALLY BETWEEN STUDYING, WE GET TO GO TO THE BEACH AND TAKE A BREATHER.
Just occasionally.
WANT TO COME TOO, KUROSAKI?
OF COURSE NOT, IDIOT.
Forget it. Those are men's shades.
You don't plan on studying at all.
WELL, GO AHEAD AND HAVE FUN...
...BUT I HOPE YOU'RE NOT PLANNING ON SWIMMING IN THAT GET-UP.
HUH? WHY NOT?
This is the only swimsuit I have...
3-2
NO CURVES
BUY A DECENT SWIM-SUIT.
I'LL PAY FOR IT.
In exchange, I'm confiscating that school swimsuit.
Huh? Why?!
AND SO...

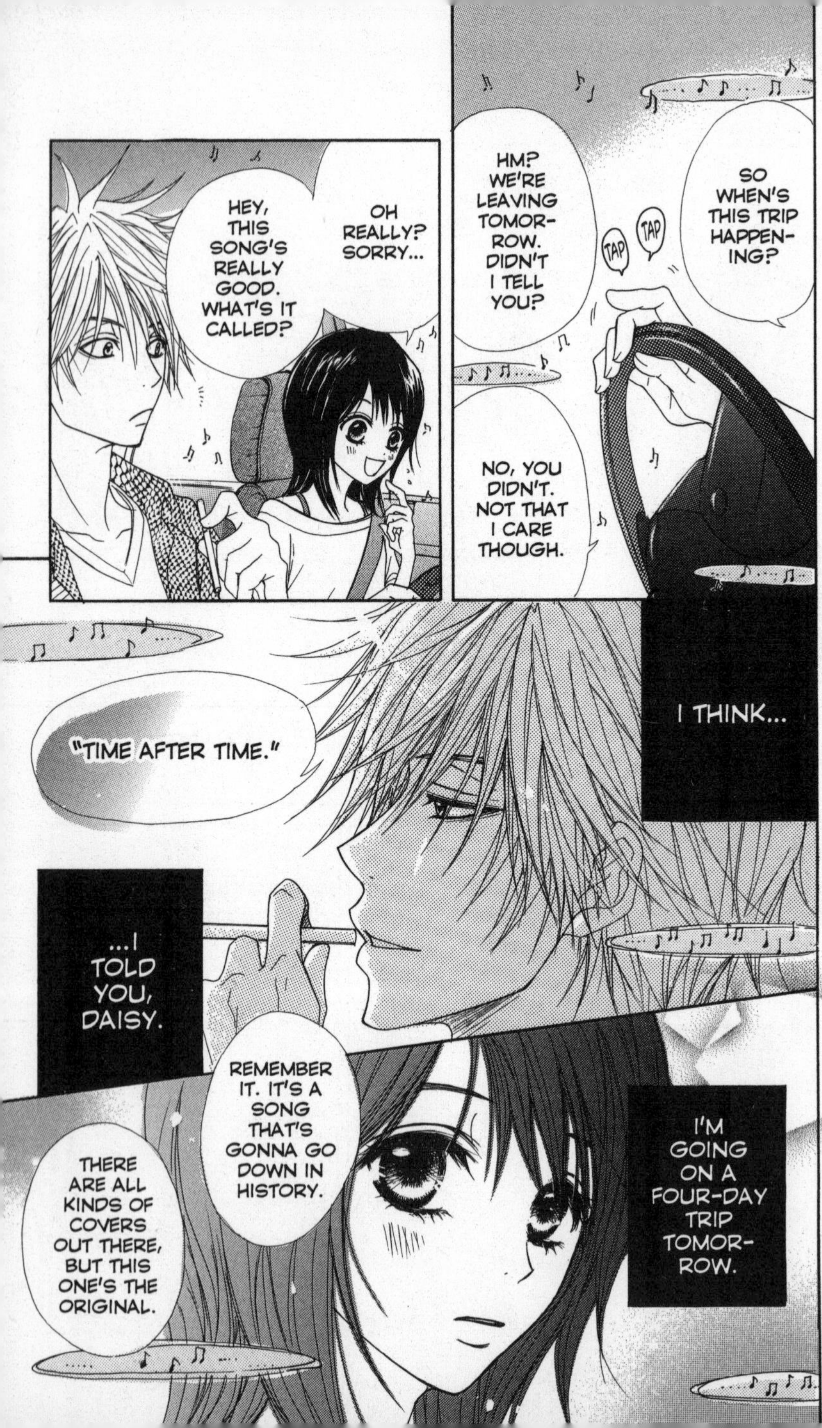
SO WHEN'S THIS TRIP HAPPENING?
TAP
TAP
HM? WE'RE LEAVING TOMORROW. DIDN'T I TELL YOU?
NO, YOU DIDN'T. NOT THAT I CARE THOUGH.
OH REALLY? SORRY...
HEY, THIS SONG'S REALLY GOOD. WHAT'S IT CALLED?
I THINK...
"TIME AFTER TIME."
...I TOLD YOU, DAISY.
I'M GOING ON A FOUR-DAY TRIP TOMORROW.
REMEMBER IT. IT'S A SONG THAT'S GONNA GO DOWN IN HISTORY.
THERE ARE ALL KINDS OF COVERS OUT THERE, BUT THIS ONE'S THE ORIGINAL.

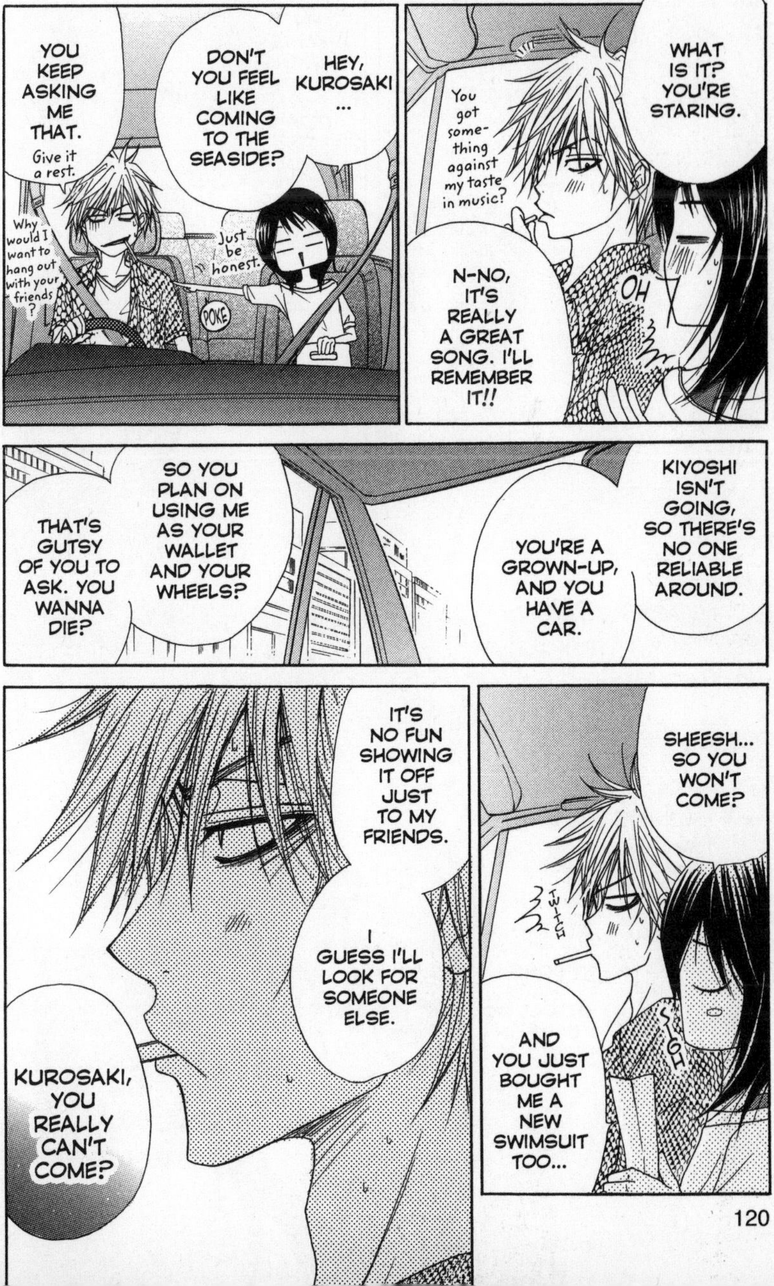
WHAT IS IT? YOU'RE STARING.
You got something against my taste in music?
OH
N-NO, IT'S REALLY A GREAT SONG. I'LL REMEMBER IT!!
HEY, KUROSAKI...
DON'T YOU FEEL LIKE COMING TO THE SEASIDE?
Just be honest.
POKE
YOU KEEP ASKING ME THAT.
Give it a rest.
Why would I want to hang out with your friends?
KIYOSHI ISN'T GOING, SO THERE'S NO ONE RELIABLE AROUND.
YOU'RE A GROWN-UP, AND YOU HAVE A CAR.
SO YOU PLAN ON USING ME AS YOUR WALLET AND YOUR WHEELS?
THAT'S GUTSY OF YOU TO ASK. YOU WANNA DIE?
SHEESH... SO YOU WON'T COME?
TWITCH
SIGH
AND YOU JUST BOUGHT ME A NEW SWIMSUIT TOO...
IT'S NO FUN SHOWING IT OFF JUST TO MY FRIENDS.
I GUESS I'LL LOOK FOR SOMEONE ELSE.
KUROSAKI, YOU REALLY CAN'T COME?

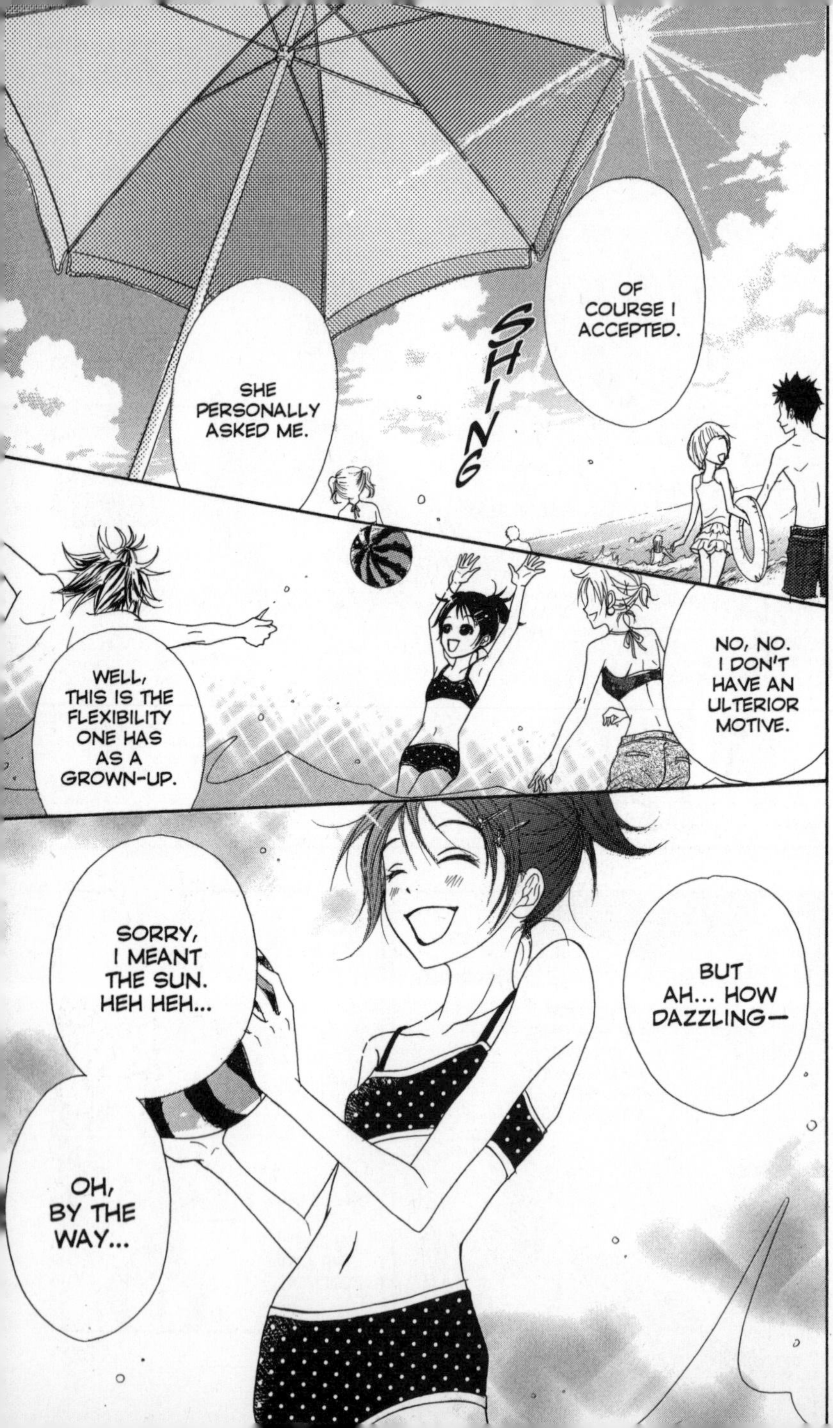
OF COURSE I ACCEPTED.
SHING
SHE PERSONALLY ASKED ME.
NO, NO. I DON'T HAVE AN ULTERIOR MOTIVE.
WELL, THIS IS THE FLEXIBILITY ONE HAS AS A GROWN-UP.
BUT AH... HOW DAZZLING—
SORRY, I MEANT THE SUN. HEH HEH...
OH, BY THE WAY...

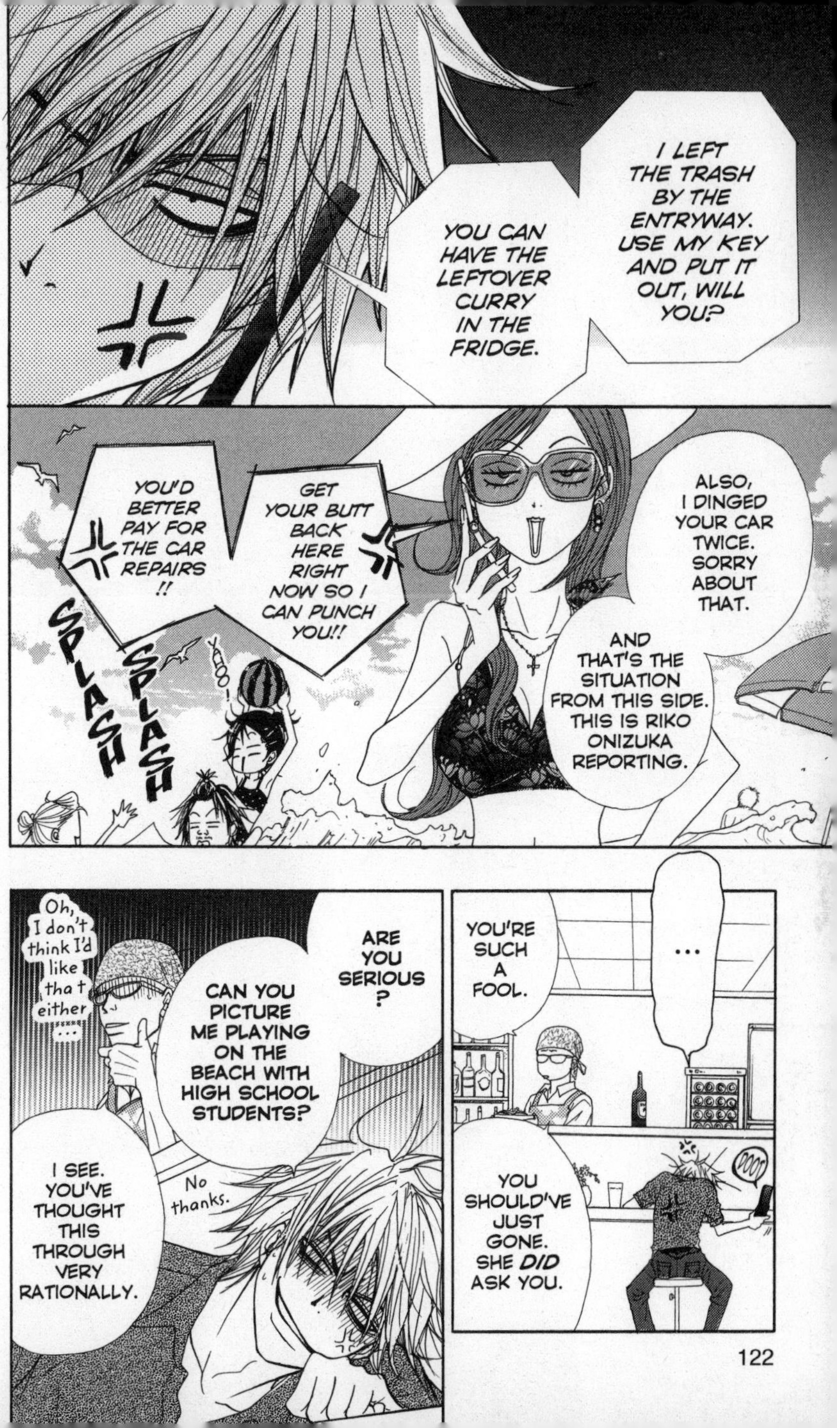
I LEFT THE TRASH BY THE ENTRYWAY. USE MY KEY AND PUT IT OUT, WILL YOU?
YOU CAN HAVE THE LEFTOVER CURRY IN THE FRIDGE.
ALSO, I DINGED YOUR CAR TWICE. SORRY ABOUT THAT.
AND THAT'S THE SITUATION FROM THIS SIDE. THIS IS RIKO ONIZUKA REPORTING.
GET YOUR BUTT BACK HERE RIGHT NOW SO I CAN PUNCH YOU!!
YOU'D BETTER PAY FOR THE CAR REPAIRS!!
YAOO!
SPLASH
SPLASH
...
YOU'RE SUCH A FOOL.
YOU SHOULD'VE JUST GONE. SHE *DID* ASK YOU.
DOOT
ARE YOU SERIOUS?
CAN YOU PICTURE ME PLAYING ON THE BEACH WITH HIGH SCHOOL STUDENTS?
Oh, I don't think I'd like that either...
No thanks.
I SEE. YOU'VE THOUGHT THIS THROUGH VERY RATIONALLY.

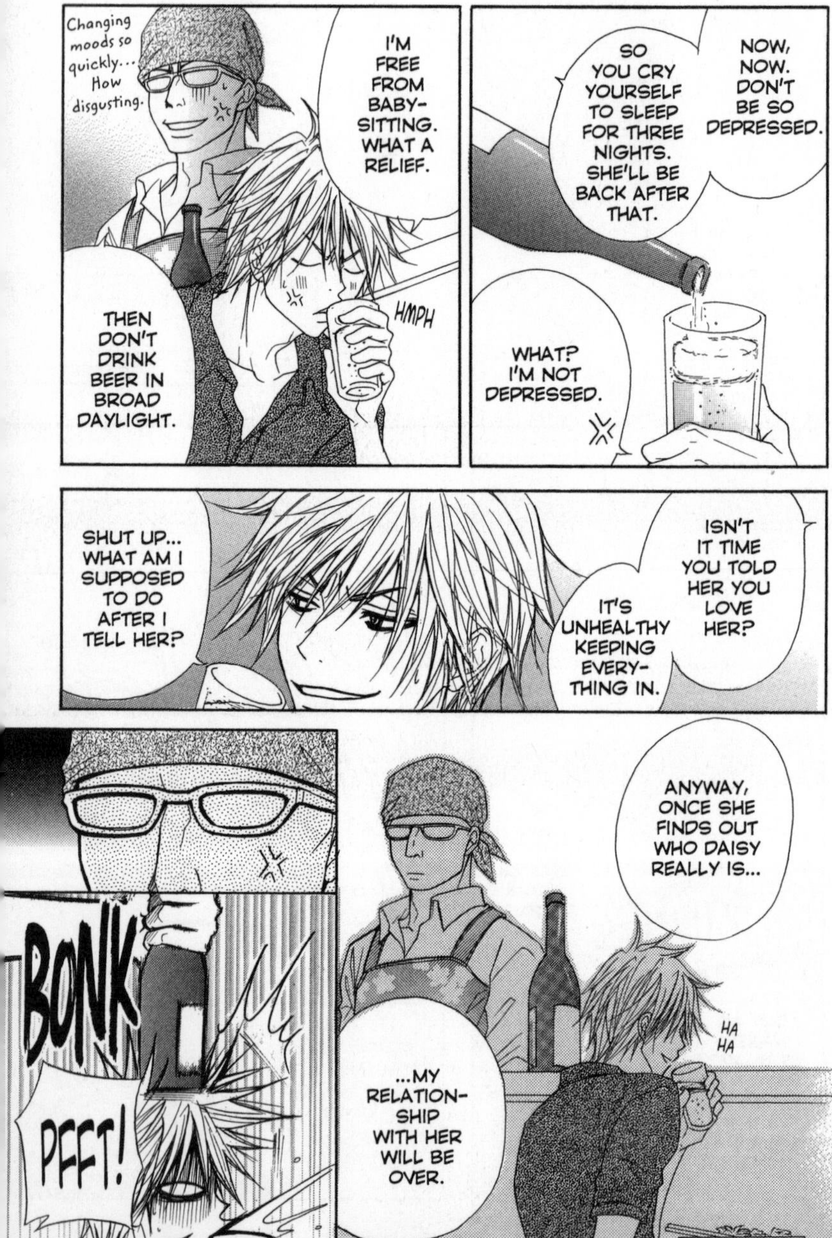
NOW, NOW. DON'T BE SO DEPRESSED.
SO YOU CRY YOURSELF TO SLEEP FOR THREE NIGHTS. SHE'LL BE BACK AFTER THAT.
WHAT? I'M NOT DEPRESSED.
I'M FREE FROM BABY-SITTING. WHAT A RELIEF.
Changing moods so quickly... How disgusting.
HMPH
THEN DON'T DRINK BEER IN BROAD DAYLIGHT.
ISN'T IT TIME YOU TOLD HER YOU LOVE HER?
IT'S UNHEALTHY KEEPING EVERY-THING IN.
SHUT UP... WHAT AM I SUPPOSED TO DO AFTER I TELL HER?
ANYWAY, ONCE SHE FINDS OUT WHO DAISY REALLY IS...
HA HA
...MY RELATION-SHIP WITH HER WILL BE OVER.
BONK
PFFT!

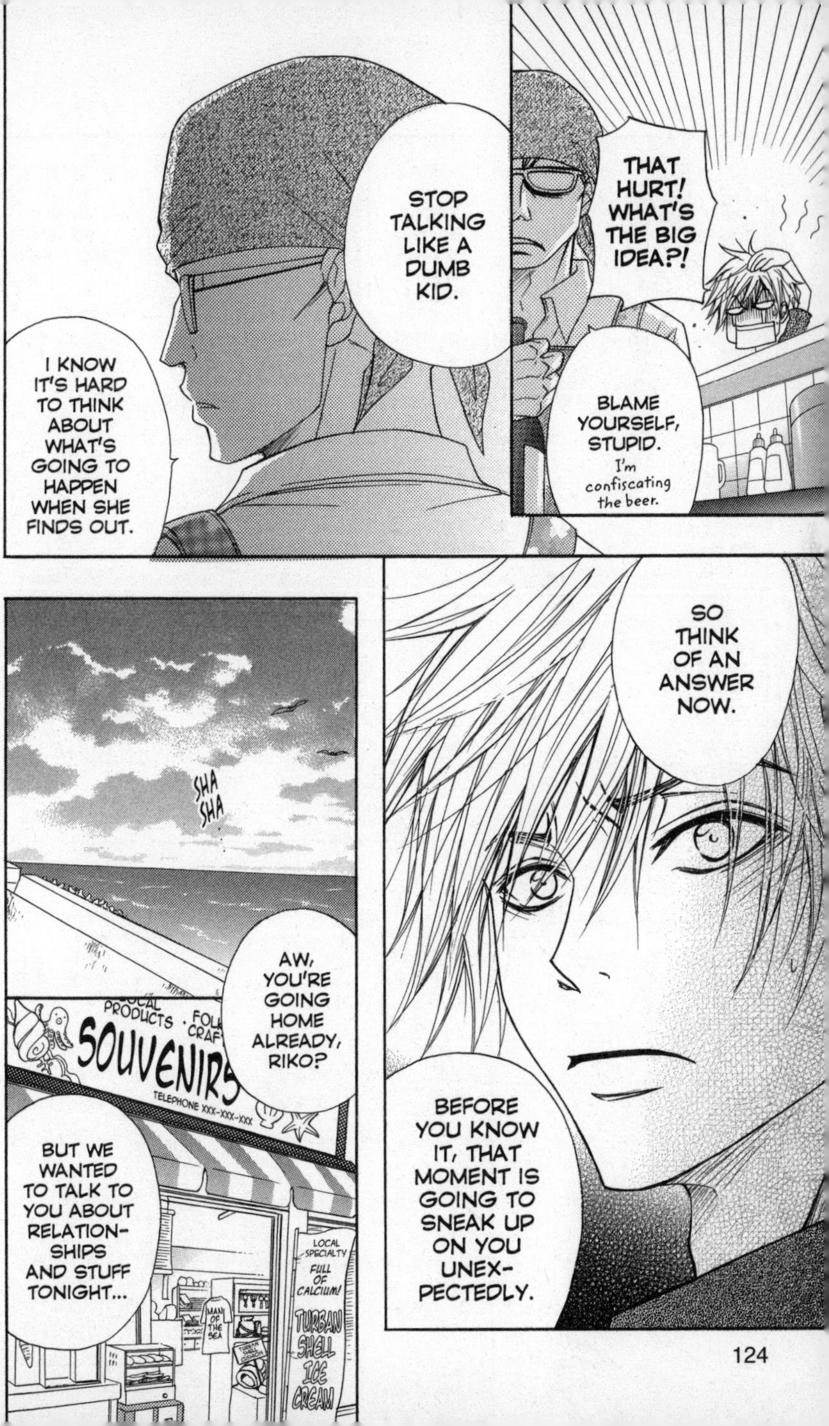
THAT HURT! WHAT'S THE BIG IDEA?!
BLAME YOURSELF, STUPID.
I'm confiscating the beer.
STOP TALKING LIKE A DUMB KID.
I KNOW IT'S HARD TO THINK ABOUT WHAT'S GOING TO HAPPEN WHEN SHE FINDS OUT.
SO THINK OF AN ANSWER NOW.
BEFORE YOU KNOW IT, THAT MOMENT IS GOING TO SNEAK UP ON YOU UNEXPECTEDLY.
SHA SHA
AW, YOU'RE GOING HOME ALREADY, RIKO?
PRODUCTS · FOLK
SOUVENIRS
TELEPHONE XXX-XXX-XXX
LOCAL SPECIALTY
FULL OF CALCIUM!
TURBAN SHELL ICE CREAM
MAN OF THE SEA
BUT WE WANTED TO TALK TO YOU ABOUT RELATIONSHIPS AND STUFF TONIGHT...

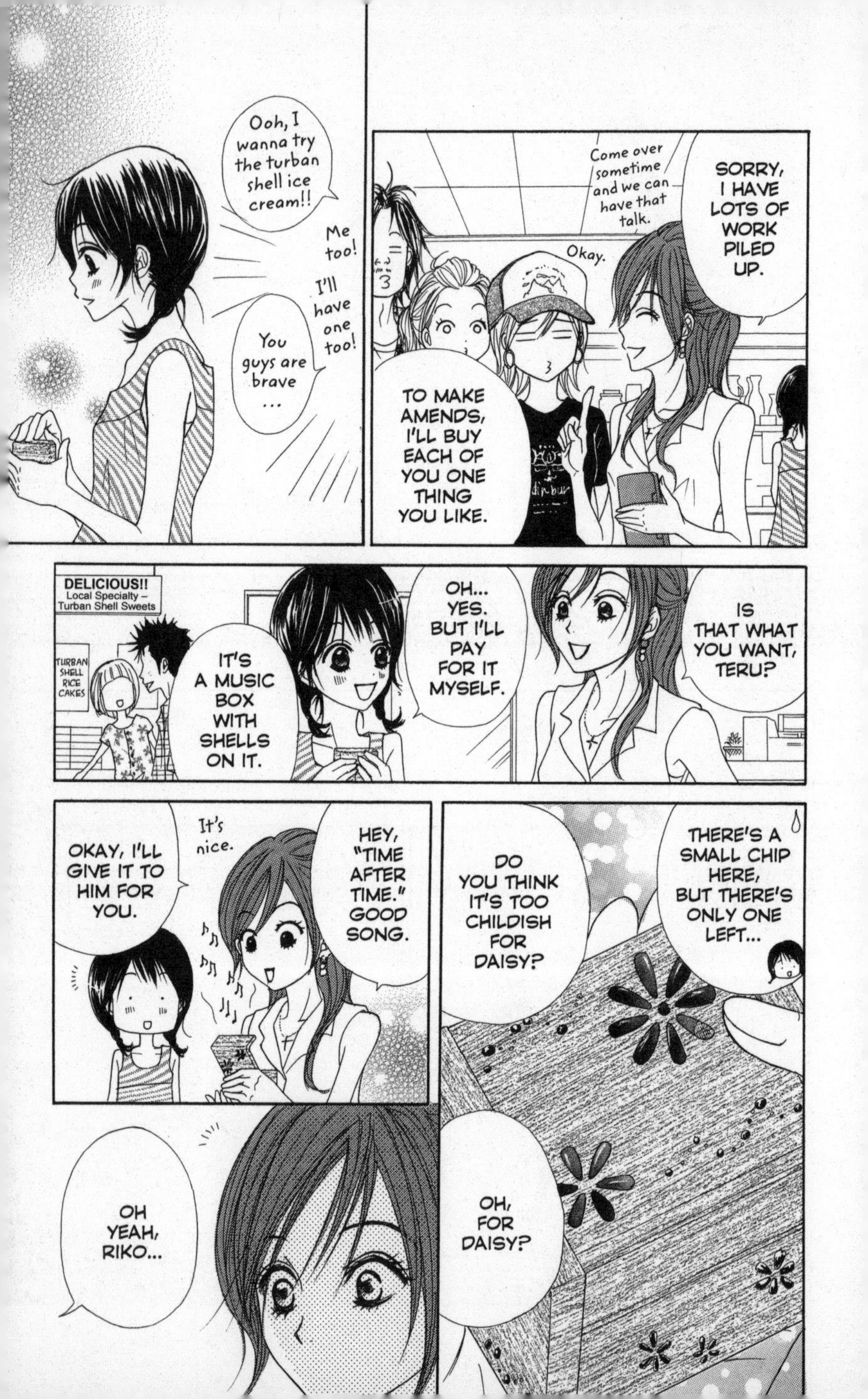
SORRY, I HAVE LOTS OF WORK PILED UP.
Come over sometime and we can have that talk.
Okay.
TO MAKE AMENDS, I'LL BUY EACH OF YOU ONE THING YOU LIKE.
Ooh, I wanna try the turban shell ice cream!!
Me too!
I'll have one too!
You guys are brave...
IS THAT WHAT YOU WANT, TERU?
OH... YES. BUT I'LL PAY FOR IT MYSELF.
IT'S A MUSIC BOX WITH SHELLS ON IT.
DELICIOUS!! Local Specialty – Turban Shell Sweets
TURBAN SHELL RICE CAKES
THERE'S A SMALL CHIP HERE, BUT THERE'S ONLY ONE LEFT...
DO YOU THINK IT'S TOO CHILDISH FOR DAISY?
OH, FOR DAISY?
HEY, "TIME AFTER TIME." GOOD SONG.
It's nice.
OKAY, I'LL GIVE IT TO HIM FOR YOU.
OH YEAH, RIKO...

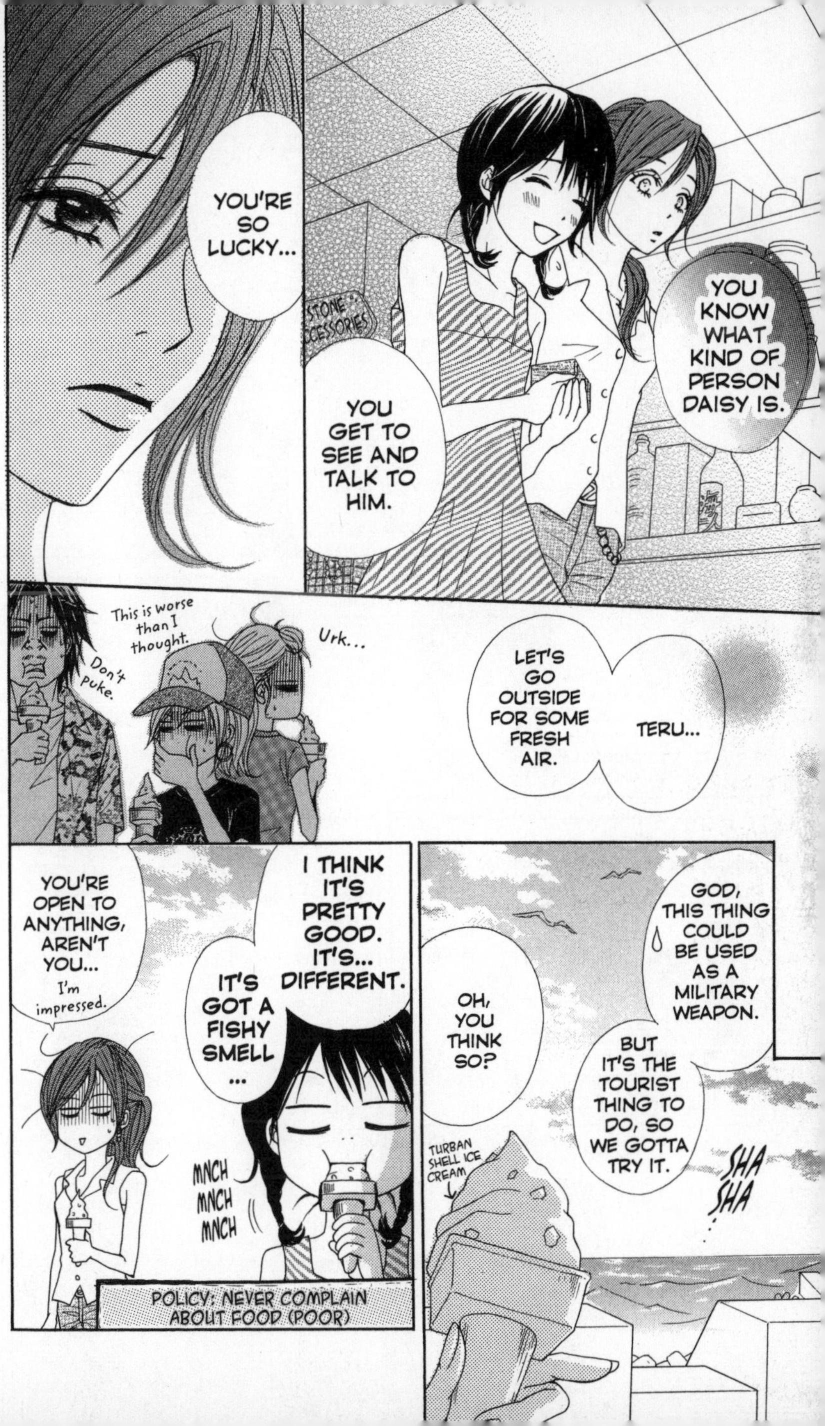
YOU KNOW WHAT KIND OF PERSON DAISY IS.
STONE ACCESSORIES
YOU GET TO SEE AND TALK TO HIM.
YOU'RE SO LUCKY...
TERU...
LET'S GO OUTSIDE FOR SOME FRESH AIR.
Urk...
This is worse than I thought.
Don't puke.
GOD, THIS THING COULD BE USED AS A MILITARY WEAPON.
OH, YOU THINK SO?
BUT IT'S THE TOURIST THING TO DO, SO WE GOTTA TRY IT.
SHA SHA
TURBAN SHELL ICE CREAM
I THINK IT'S PRETTY GOOD. IT'S... DIFFERENT.
IT'S GOT A FISHY SMELL ...
YOU'RE OPEN TO ANYTHING, AREN'T YOU...
I'm impressed.
MNCH MNCH MNCH
POLICY: NEVER COMPLAIN ABOUT FOOD (POOR)

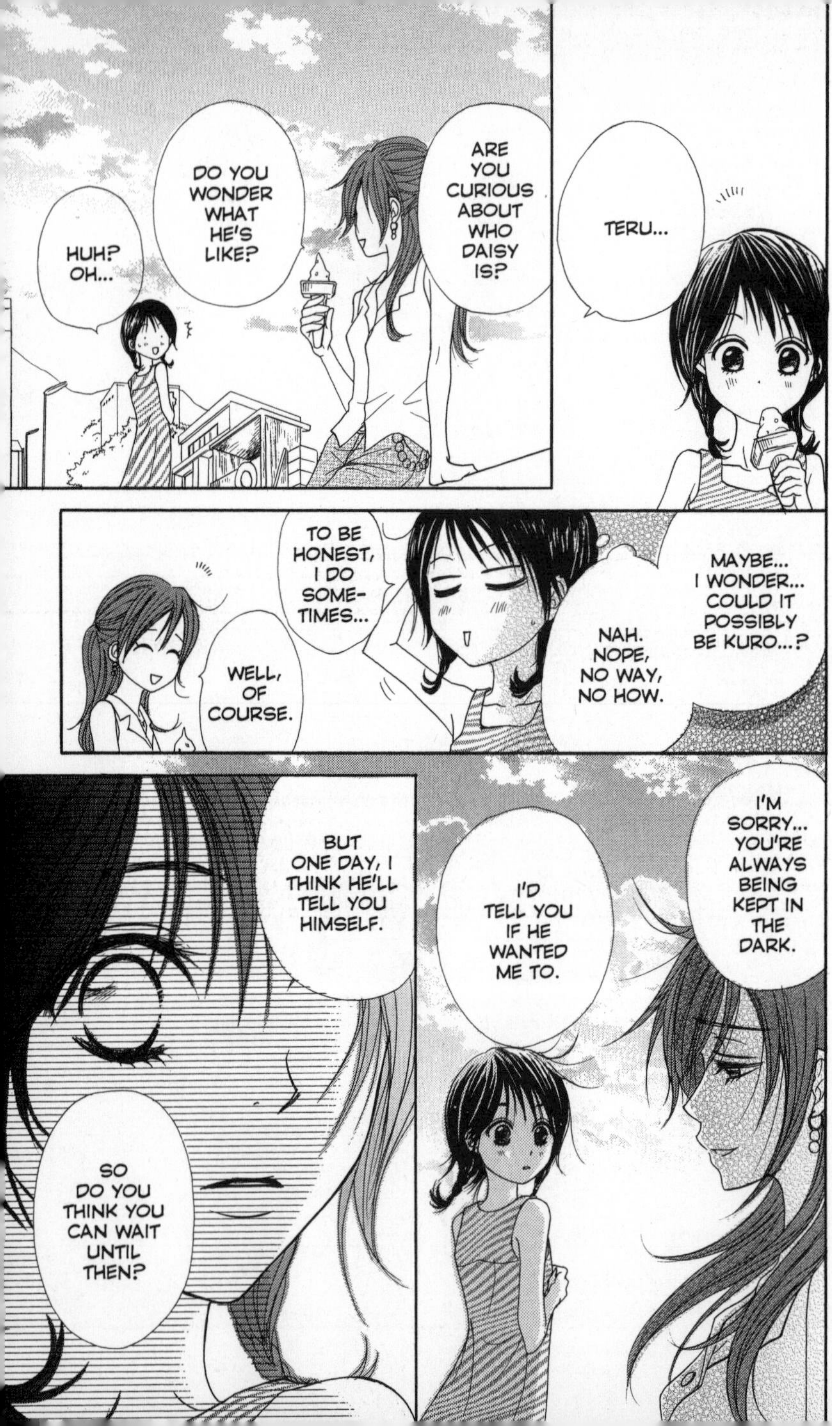
TERU...
ARE YOU CURIOUS ABOUT WHO DAISY IS?
DO YOU WONDER WHAT HE'S LIKE?
HUH? OH...
MAYBE... I WONDER... COULD IT POSSIBLY BE KURO...?
NAH. NOPE, NO WAY, NO HOW.
TO BE HONEST, I DO SOME-TIMES...
WELL, OF COURSE.
I'M SORRY... YOU'RE ALWAYS BEING KEPT IN THE DARK.
I'D TELL YOU IF HE WANTED ME TO.
BUT ONE DAY, I THINK HE'LL TELL YOU HIMSELF.
SO DO YOU THINK YOU CAN WAIT UNTIL THEN?

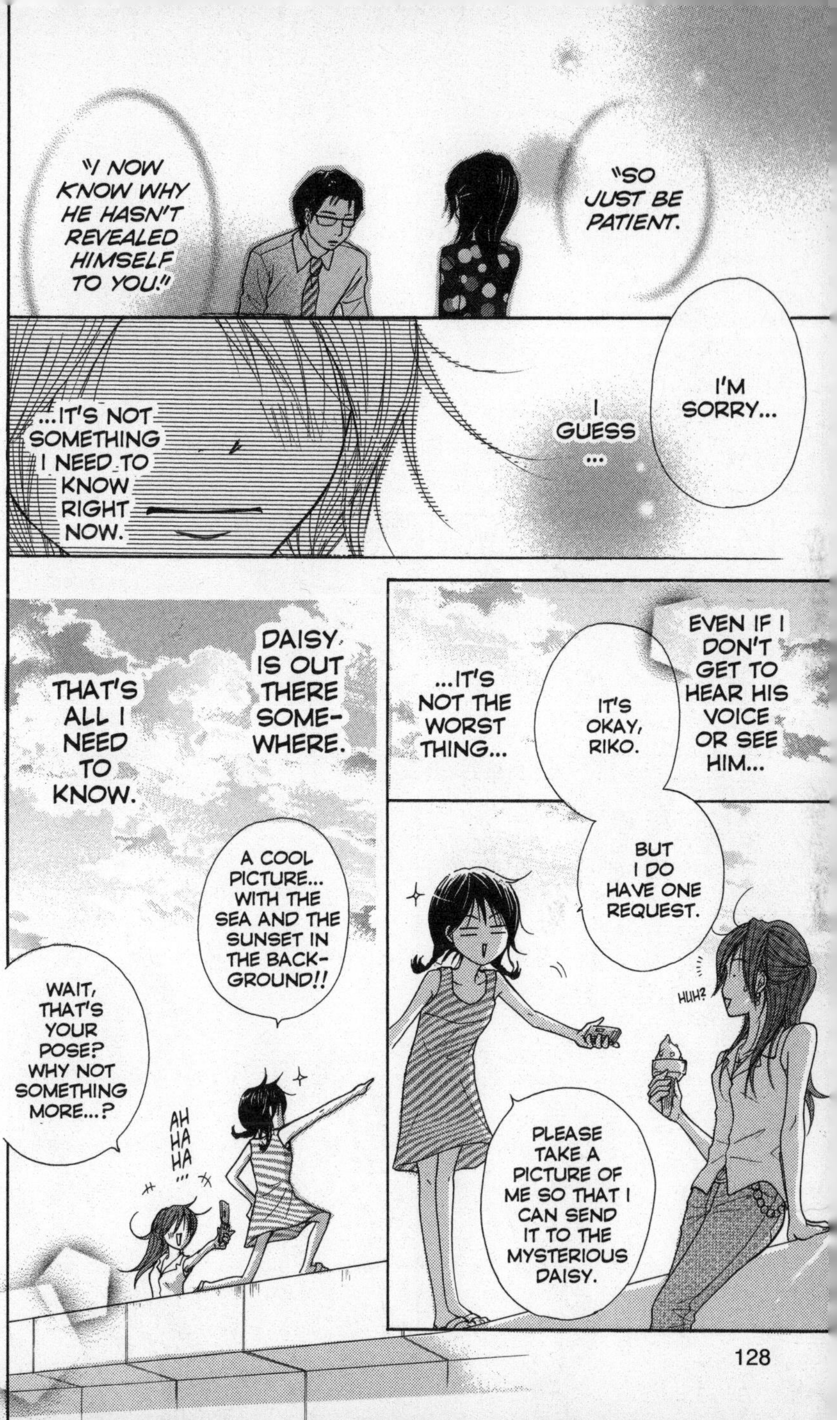
"SO JUST BE PATIENT.
"I NOW KNOW WHY HE HASN'T REVEALED HIMSELF TO YOU!"
I'M SORRY...
I GUESS...
...IT'S NOT SOMETHING I NEED TO KNOW RIGHT NOW.
EVEN IF I DON'T GET TO HEAR HIS VOICE OR SEE HIM...
IT'S OKAY, RIKO.
...IT'S NOT THE WORST THING...
BUT I DO HAVE ONE REQUEST.
HUH?
PLEASE TAKE A PICTURE OF ME SO THAT I CAN SEND IT TO THE MYSTERIOUS DAISY.
DAISY IS OUT THERE SOME-WHERE.
THAT'S ALL I NEED TO KNOW.
A COOL PICTURE... WITH THE SEA AND THE SUNSET IN THE BACK-GROUND!!
WAIT, THAT'S YOUR POSE? WHY NOT SOMETHING MORE...?
AH HA HA...

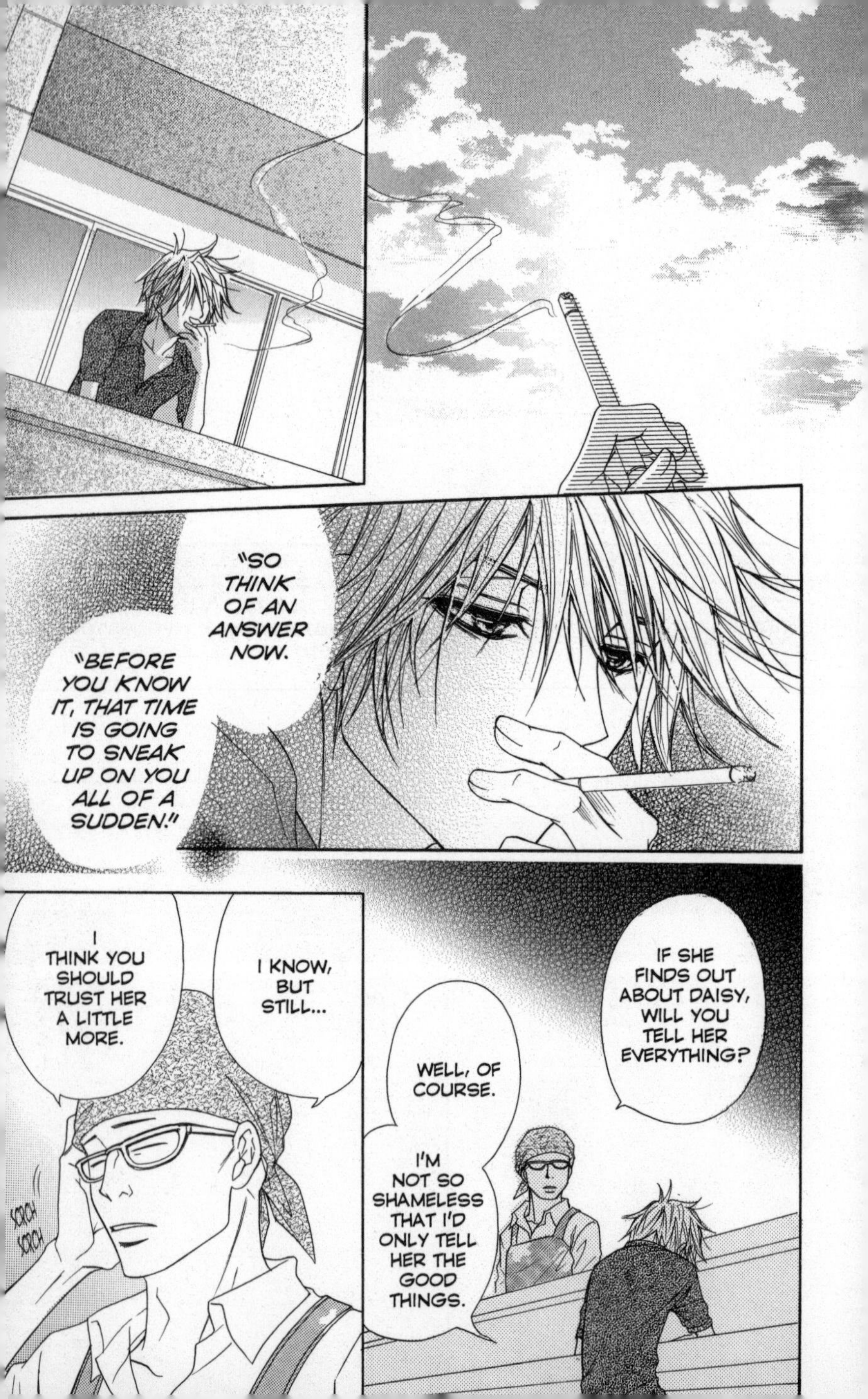
"SO THINK OF AN ANSWER NOW.
"BEFORE YOU KNOW IT, THAT TIME IS GOING TO SNEAK UP ON YOU ALL OF A SUDDEN."
IF SHE FINDS OUT ABOUT DAISY, WILL YOU TELL HER EVERYTHING?
WELL, OF COURSE.
I'M NOT SO SHAMELESS THAT I'D ONLY TELL HER THE GOOD THINGS.
I KNOW, BUT STILL...
I THINK YOU SHOULD TRUST HER A LITTLE MORE.
SCRCH SCRCH

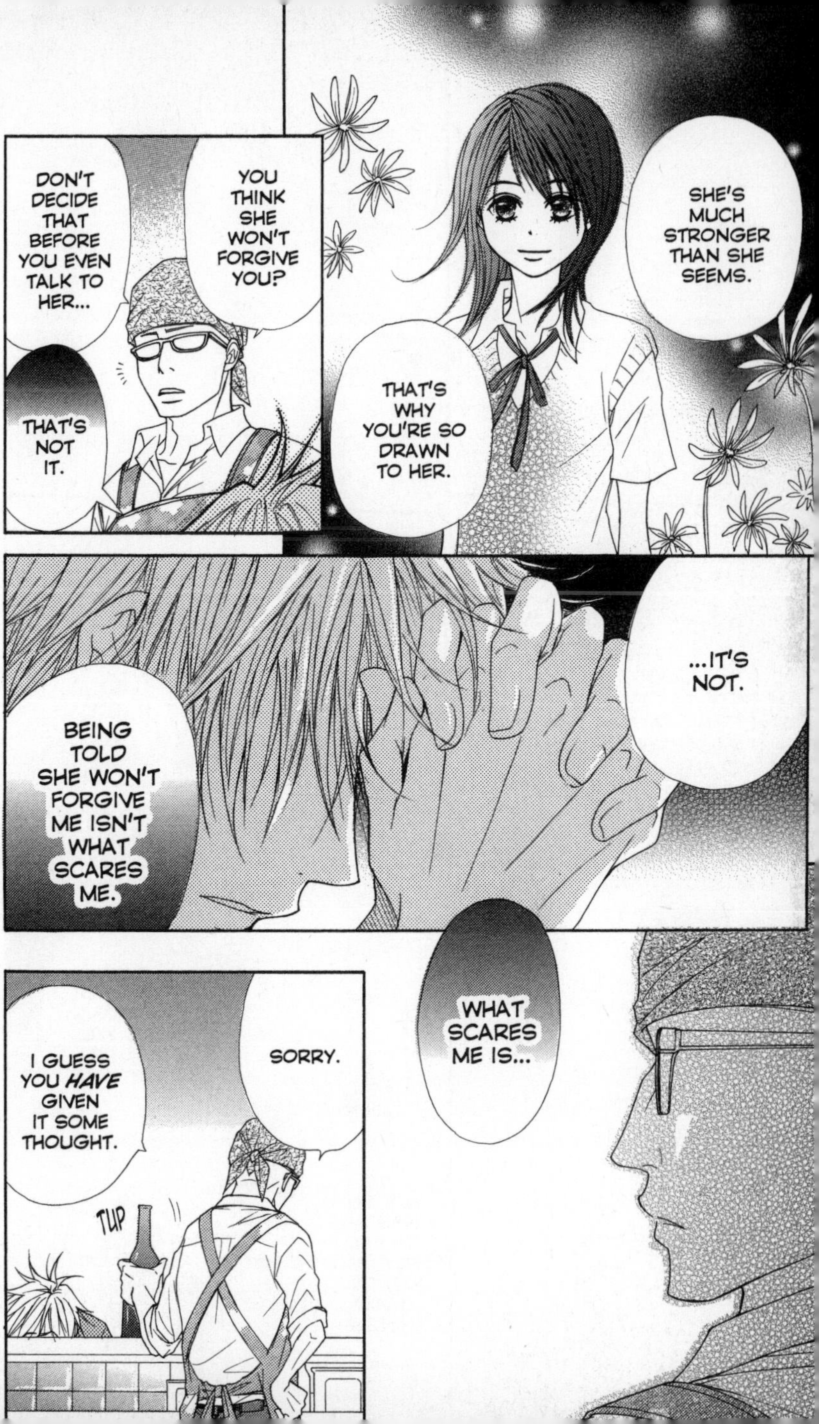
SHE'S MUCH STRONGER THAN SHE SEEMS.
THAT'S WHY YOU'RE SO DRAWN TO HER.
YOU THINK SHE WON'T FORGIVE YOU?
DON'T DECIDE THAT BEFORE YOU EVEN TALK TO HER...
THAT'S NOT IT.
...IT'S NOT.
BEING TOLD SHE WON'T FORGIVE ME ISN'T WHAT SCARES ME.
WHAT SCARES ME IS...
SORRY.
TUP
I GUESS YOU *HAVE* GIVEN IT SOME THOUGHT.

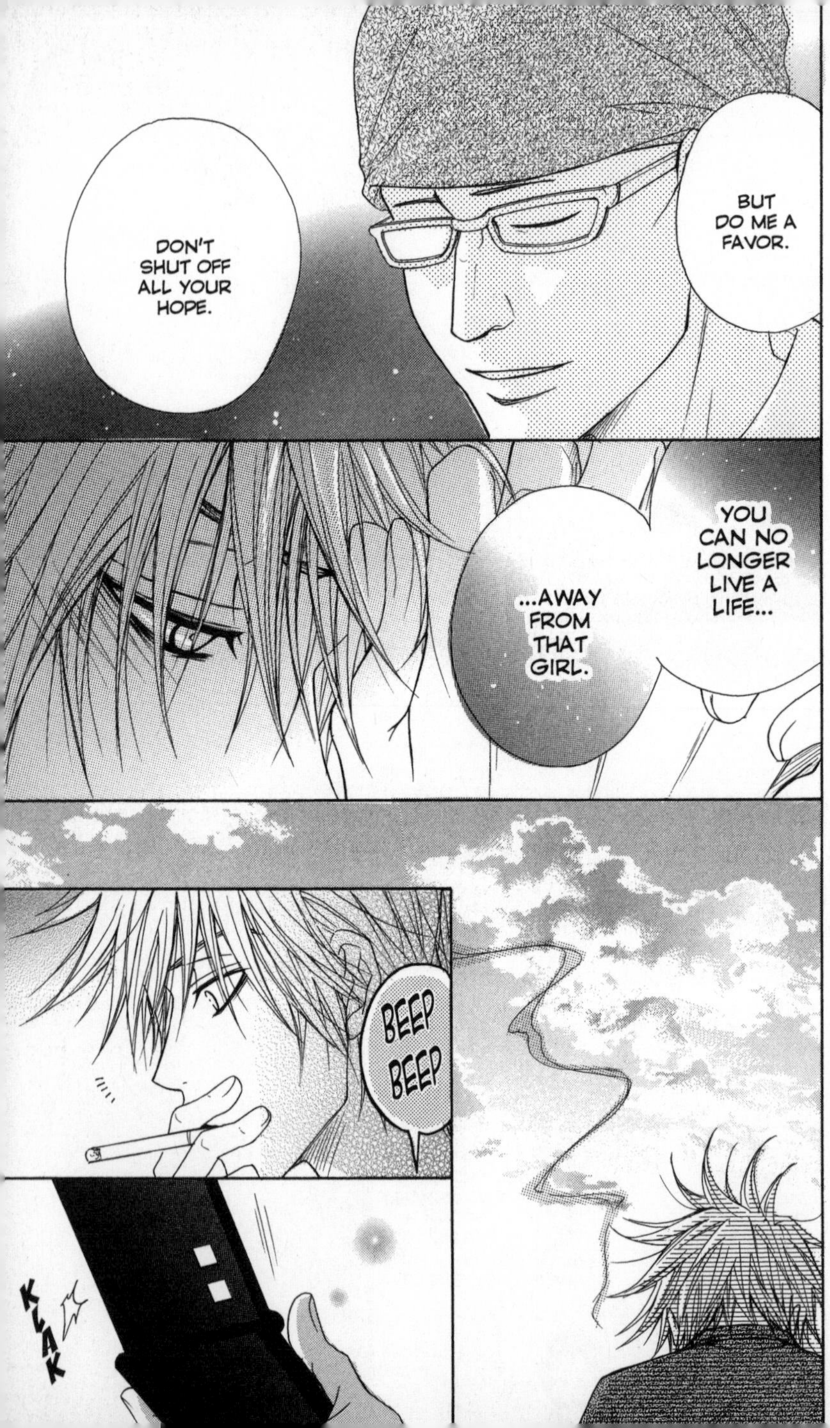
BUT DO ME A FAVOR.
DON'T SHUT OFF ALL YOUR HOPE.
YOU CAN NO LONGER LIVE A LIFE...
...AWAY FROM THAT GIRL.
BEEP BEEP
KLAK

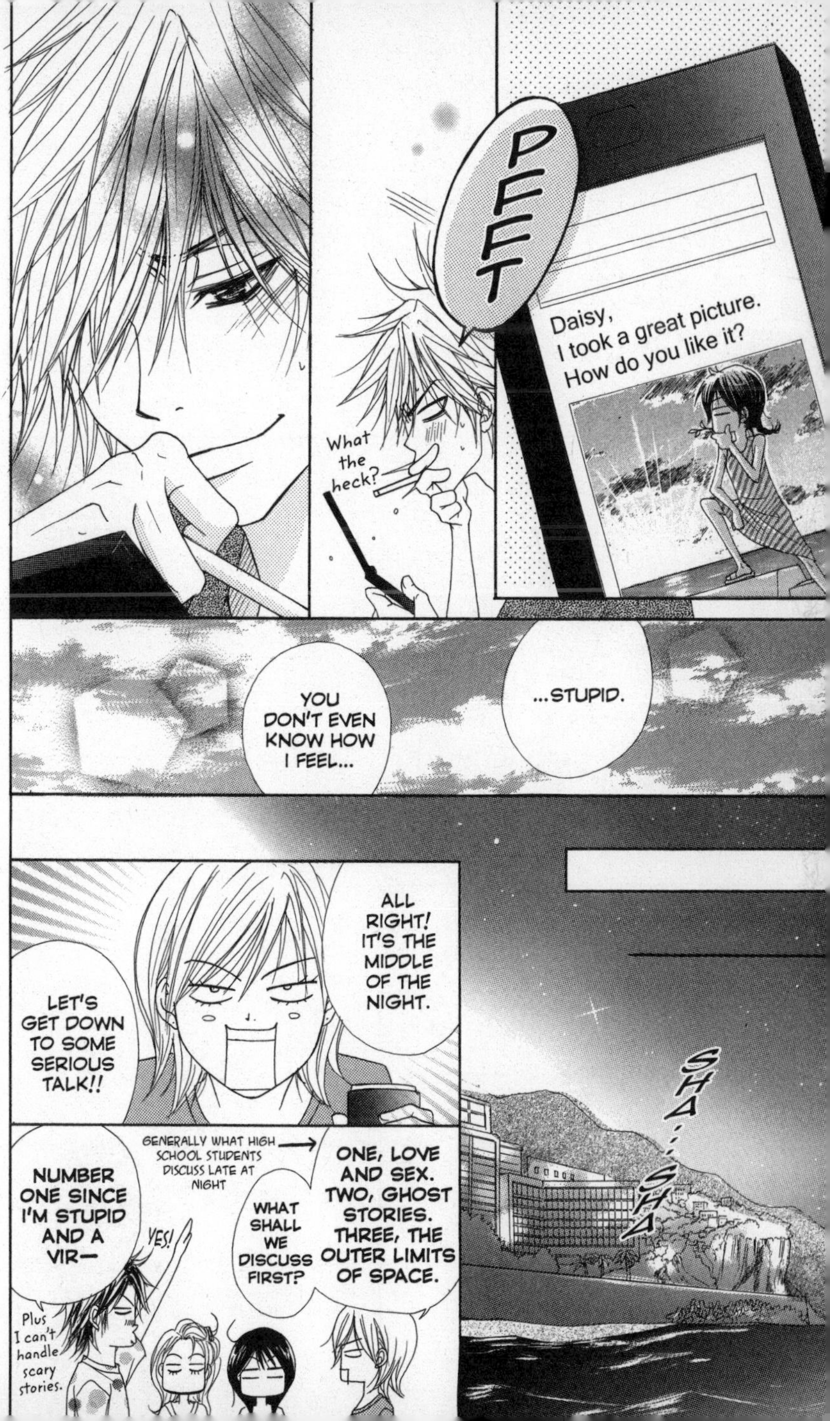

Daisy,
I took a great picture.
How do you like it?
PFFT
What the heck?
...STUPID.
YOU DON'T EVEN KNOW HOW I FEEL...
SHA...SHA
ALL RIGHT! IT'S THE MIDDLE OF THE NIGHT.
LET'S GET DOWN TO SOME SERIOUS TALK!!
ONE, LOVE AND SEX. TWO, GHOST STORIES. THREE, THE OUTER LIMITS OF SPACE.
GENERALLY WHAT HIGH SCHOOL STUDENTS DISCUSS LATE AT NIGHT
WHAT SHALL WE DISCUSS FIRST?
YES!
NUMBER ONE SINCE I'M STUPID AND A VIR—
Plus I can't handle scary stories.

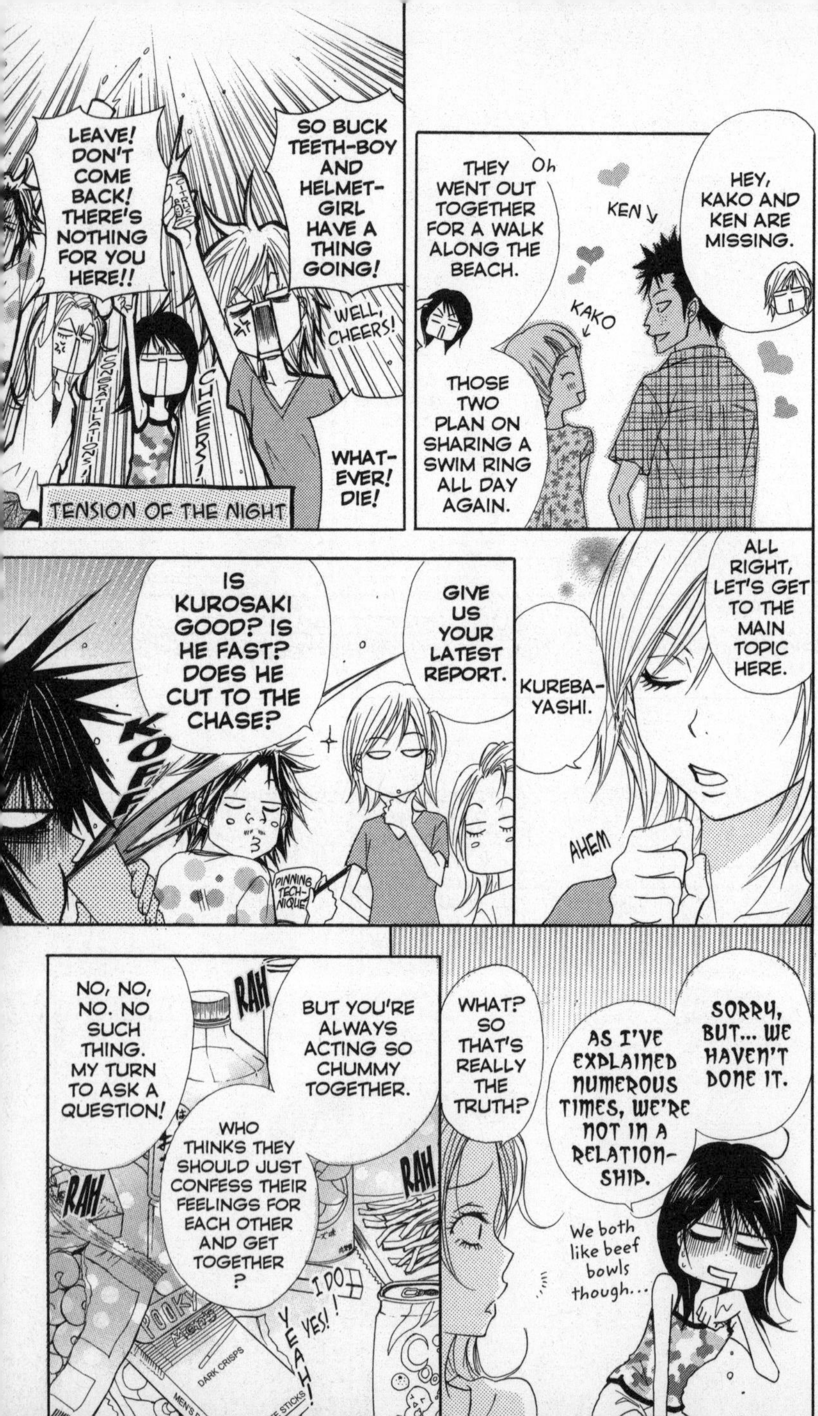
HEY, KAKO AND KEN ARE MISSING.
THEY WENT OUT TOGETHER FOR A WALK ALONG THE BEACH.
Oh
KEN
KAKO
THOSE TWO PLAN ON SHARING A SWIM RING ALL DAY AGAIN.
SO BUCK TEETH-BOY AND HELMET-GIRL HAVE A THING GOING!
LEAVE! DON'T COME BACK! THERE'S NOTHING FOR YOU HERE!!
CITRUS
WELL, CHEERS!
CHEERS!
CONGRATULATIONS!
WHAT-EVER! DIE!
TENSION OF THE NIGHT
ALL RIGHT, LET'S GET TO THE MAIN TOPIC HERE.
KUREBA-YASHI.
AHEM
GIVE US YOUR LATEST REPORT.
IS KUROSAKI GOOD? IS HE FAST? DOES HE CUT TO THE CHASE?
KOFF
PINNING TECH-NIQUE!
SORRY, BUT... WE HAVEN'T DONE IT.
AS I'VE EXPLAINED NUMEROUS TIMES, WE'RE NOT IN A RELATION-SHIP.
We both like beef bowls though...
WHAT? SO THAT'S REALLY THE TRUTH?
BUT YOU'RE ALWAYS ACTING SO CHUMMY TOGETHER.
RAH
NO, NO, NO. NO SUCH THING. MY TURN TO ASK A QUESTION!
WHO THINKS THEY SHOULD JUST CONFESS THEIR FEELINGS FOR EACH OTHER AND GET TOGETHER?
RAH
RAH
I DO!
YES!
YEAH!
POOKY
DARK CRISPS

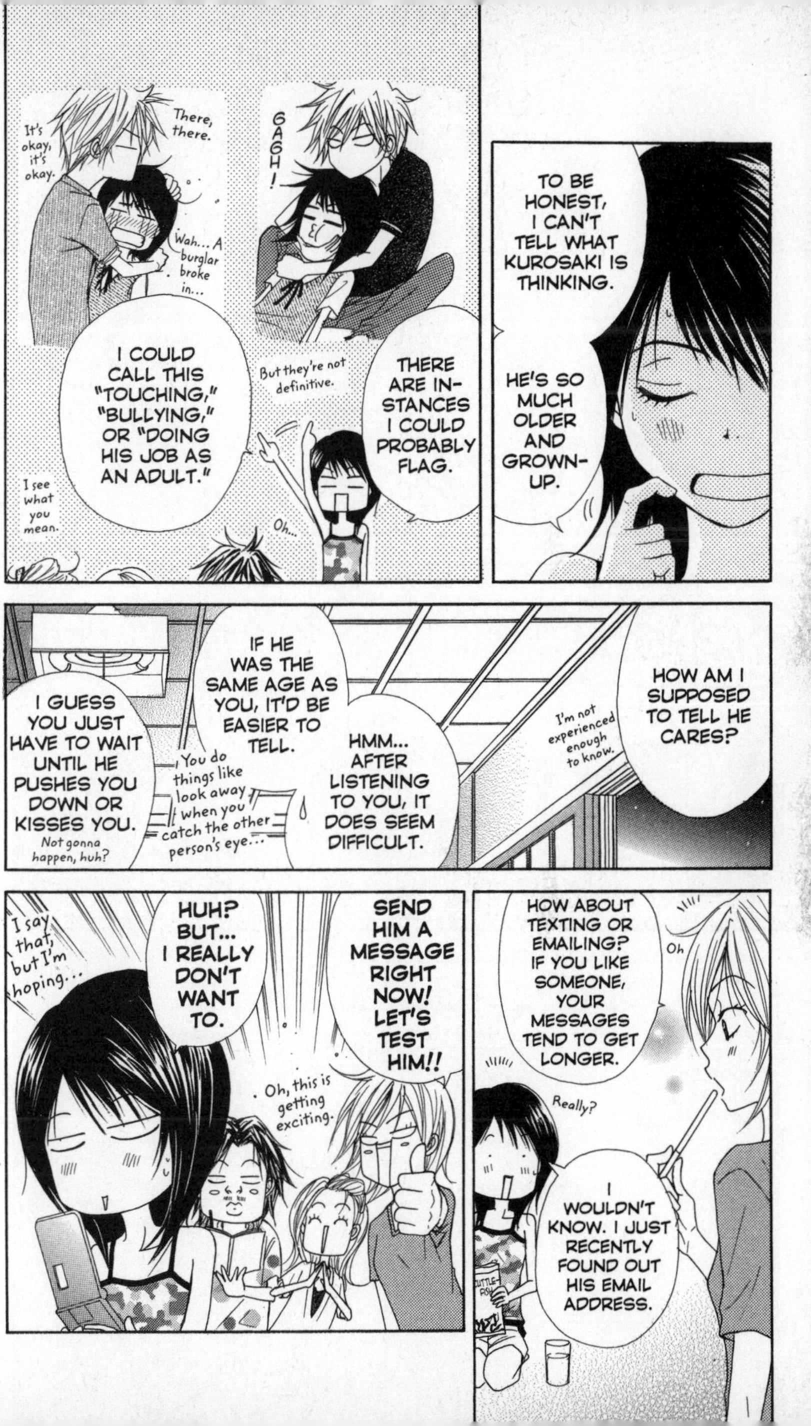
TO BE HONEST, I CAN'T TELL WHAT KUROSAKI IS THINKING.
HE'S SO MUCH OLDER AND GROWN-UP.
There, there.
It's okay, it's okay.
Wah... A burglar broke in...
GAGH!
THERE ARE INSTANCES I COULD PROBABLY FLAG.
But they're not definitive.
I COULD CALL THIS "TOUCHING," "BULLYING," OR "DOING HIS JOB AS AN ADULT."
I see what you mean.
Oh...
HOW AM I SUPPOSED TO TELL HE CARES?
I'm not experienced enough to know.
HMM... AFTER LISTENING TO YOU, IT DOES SEEM DIFFICULT.
IF HE WAS THE SAME AGE AS YOU, IT'D BE EASIER TO TELL.
You do things like look away when you catch the other person's eye...
I GUESS YOU JUST HAVE TO WAIT UNTIL HE PUSHES YOU DOWN OR KISSES YOU.
Not gonna happen, huh?
Oh
HOW ABOUT TEXTING OR EMAILING? IF YOU LIKE SOMEONE, YOUR MESSAGES TEND TO GET LONGER.
Really?
I WOULDN'T KNOW. I JUST RECENTLY FOUND OUT HIS EMAIL ADDRESS.
SEND HIM A MESSAGE RIGHT NOW! LET'S TEST HIM!!
Oh, this is getting exciting.
HUH? BUT... I REALLY DON'T WANT TO.
I say that, but I'm hoping...

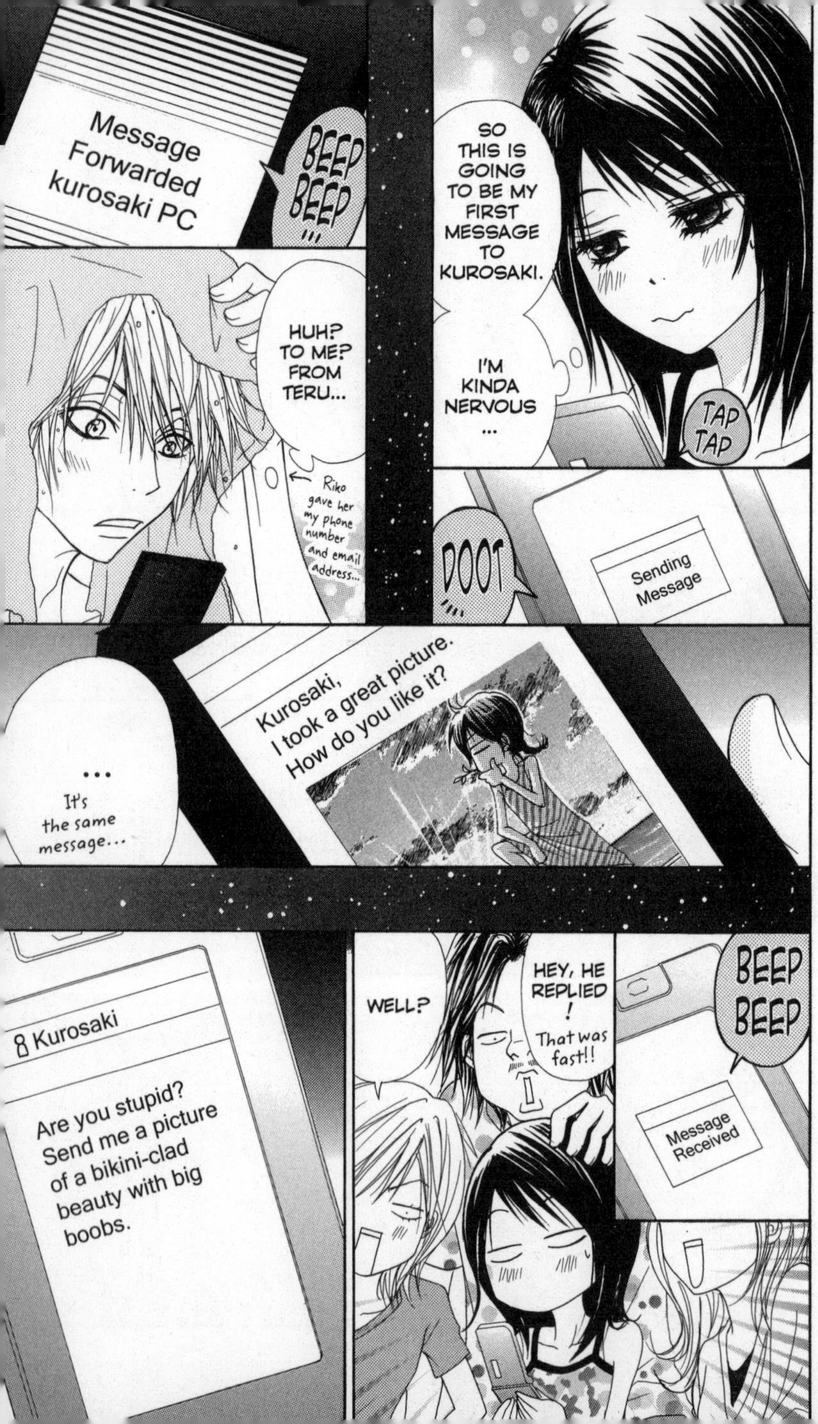
SO THIS IS GOING TO BE MY FIRST MESSAGE TO KUROSAKI.
I'M KINDA NERVOUS...
TAP TAP
Sending Message
DOOT...
Message Forwarded kurosaki PC
BEEP BEEP...
HUH? TO ME? FROM TERU...
Riko gave her my phone number and email address...
Kurosaki, I took a great picture. How do you like it?
... It's the same message...
BEEP BEEP
Message Received
HEY, HE REPLIED! That was fast!!
WELL?
Kurosaki
Are you stupid? Send me a picture of a bikini-clad beauty with big boobs.

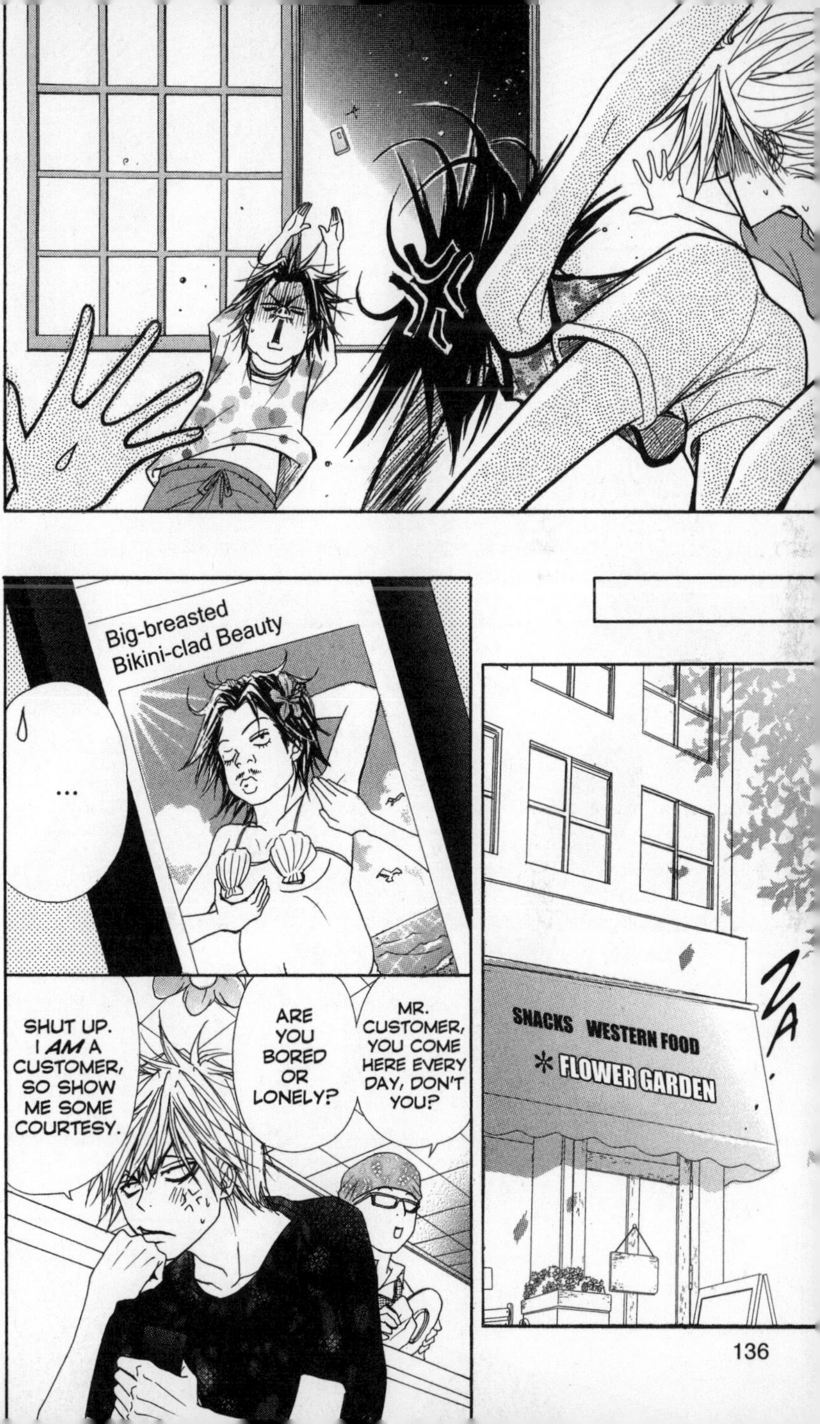
SNACKS WESTERN FOOD
* FLOWER GARDEN
ZA
Big-breasted Bikini-clad Beauty
...
MR. CUSTOMER, YOU COME HERE EVERY DAY, DON'T YOU?
ARE YOU BORED OR LONELY?
SHUT UP. I *AM* A CUSTOMER, SO SHOW ME SOME COURTESY.

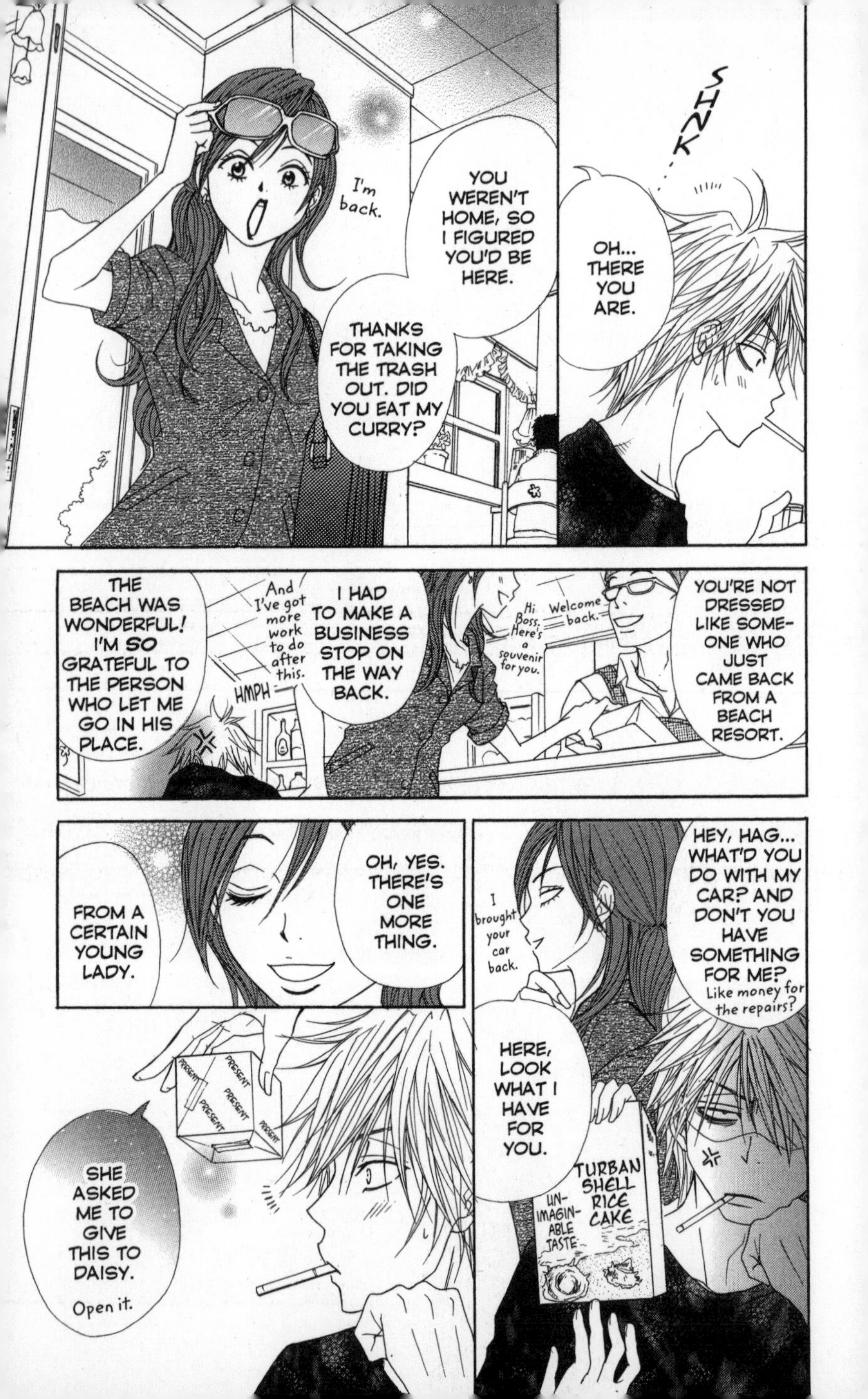SHNK...
OH... THERE YOU ARE.
I'm back.
YOU WEREN'T HOME, SO I FIGURED YOU'D BE HERE.
THANKS FOR TAKING THE TRASH OUT. DID YOU EAT MY CURRY?
YOU'RE NOT DRESSED LIKE SOMEONE WHO JUST CAME BACK FROM A BEACH RESORT.
Welcome back.
Hi Boss. Here's a souvenir for you.
I HAD TO MAKE A BUSINESS STOP ON THE WAY BACK.
And I've got more work to do after this.
HMPH
THE BEACH WAS WONDERFUL! I'M SO GRATEFUL TO THE PERSON WHO LET ME GO IN HIS PLACE.
HEY, HAG... WHAT'D YOU DO WITH MY CAR? AND DON'T YOU HAVE SOMETHING FOR ME?
Like money for the repairs?
I brought your car back.
HERE, LOOK WHAT I HAVE FOR YOU.
TURBAN SHELL RICE CAKE
UNIMAGINABLE TASTE
OH, YES. THERE'S ONE MORE THING.
FROM A CERTAIN YOUNG LADY.
PRESENT PRESENT PRESENT PRESENT PRESENT
SHE ASKED ME TO GIVE THIS TO DAISY.
Open it.

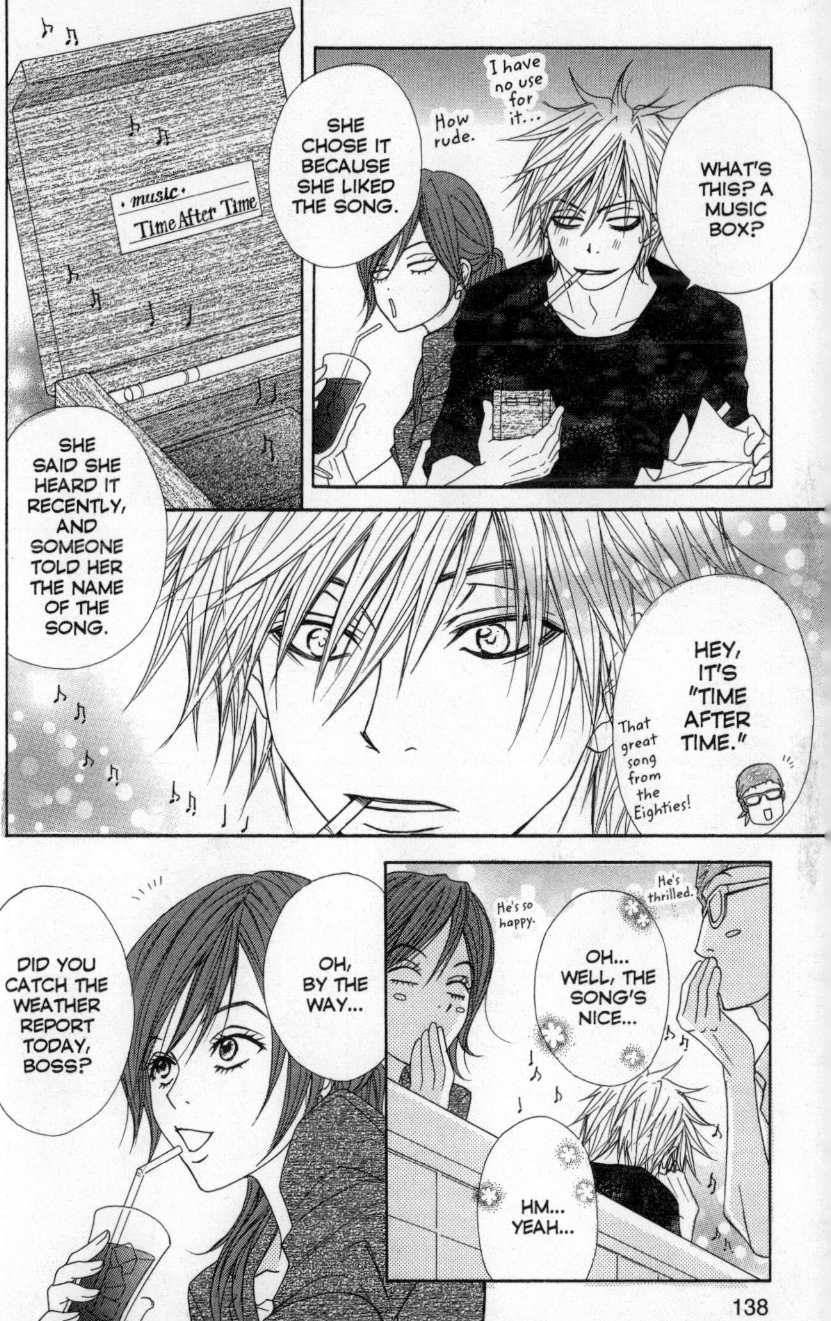
WHAT'S THIS? A MUSIC BOX?
I have no use for it...
How rude.
SHE CHOSE IT BECAUSE SHE LIKED THE SONG.
music
Time After Time
SHE SAID SHE HEARD IT RECENTLY, AND SOMEONE TOLD HER THE NAME OF THE SONG.
HEY, IT'S "TIME AFTER TIME."
That great song from the Eighties!
He's thrilled.
He's so happy.
OH... WELL, THE SONG'S NICE...
HM... YEAH...
OH, BY THE WAY...
DID YOU CATCH THE WEATHER REPORT TODAY, BOSS?

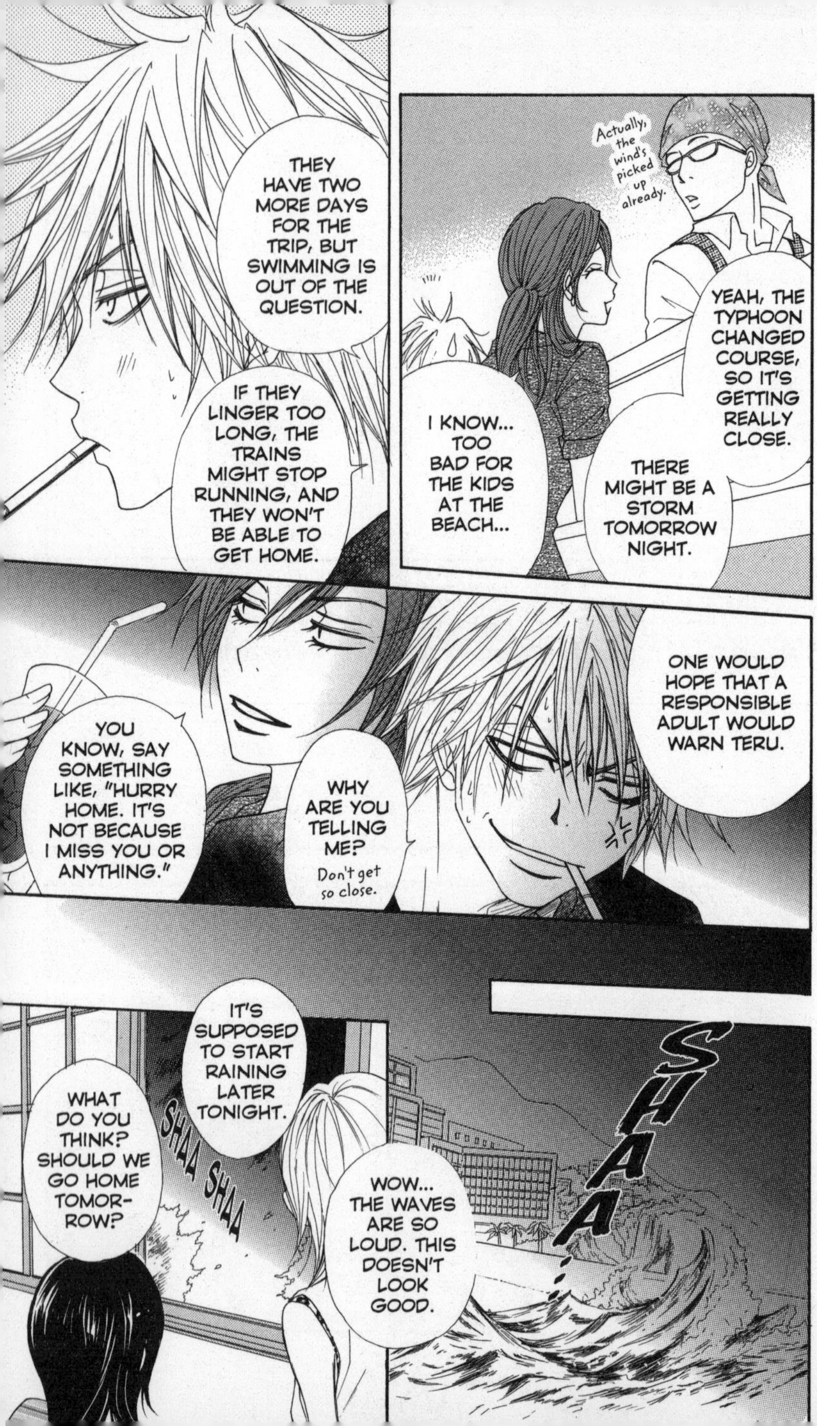
Actually, the wind's picked up already.
YEAH, THE TYPHOON CHANGED COURSE, SO IT'S GETTING REALLY CLOSE.
THERE MIGHT BE A STORM TOMORROW NIGHT.
I KNOW... TOO BAD FOR THE KIDS AT THE BEACH...
THEY HAVE TWO MORE DAYS FOR THE TRIP, BUT SWIMMING IS OUT OF THE QUESTION.
IF THEY LINGER TOO LONG, THE TRAINS MIGHT STOP RUNNING, AND THEY WON'T BE ABLE TO GET HOME.
ONE WOULD HOPE THAT A RESPONSIBLE ADULT WOULD WARN TERU.
WHY ARE YOU TELLING ME?
Don't get so close.
YOU KNOW, SAY SOMETHING LIKE, "HURRY HOME. IT'S NOT BECAUSE I MISS YOU OR ANYTHING."
SHAA...
WOW... THE WAVES ARE SO LOUD. THIS DOESN'T LOOK GOOD.
IT'S SUPPOSED TO START RAINING LATER TONIGHT.
WHAT DO YOU THINK? SHOULD WE GO HOME TOMOR-ROW?
SHAA SHAA

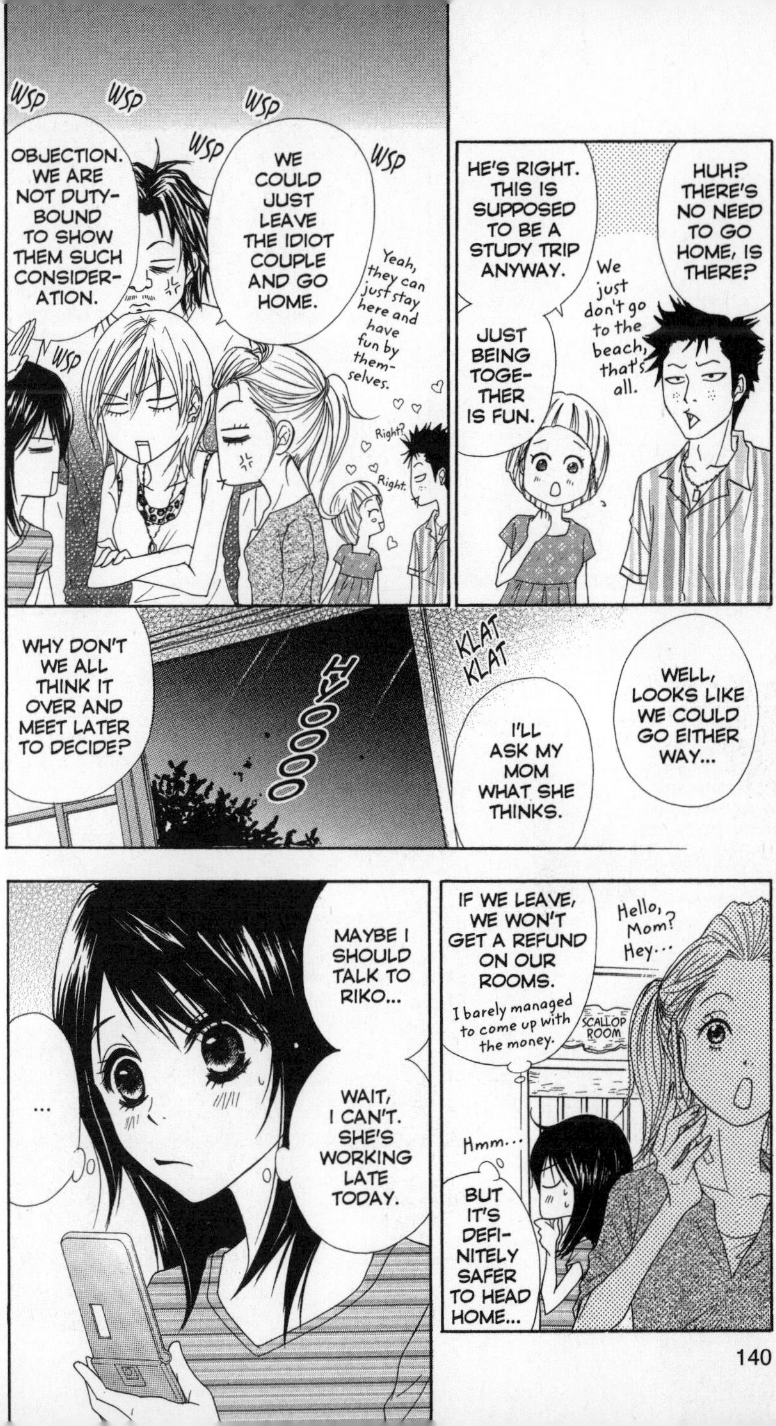
HUH? THERE'S NO NEED TO GO HOME, IS THERE?
HE'S RIGHT. THIS IS SUPPOSED TO BE A STUDY TRIP ANYWAY.
We just don't go to the beach, that's all.
JUST BEING TOGE-THER IS FUN.
WSP
WSP
WSP
WE COULD JUST LEAVE THE IDIOT COUPLE AND GO HOME.
Yeah, they can just stay here and have fun by them-selves.
WSP
WSP
OBJECTION. WE ARE NOT DUTY-BOUND TO SHOW THEM SUCH CONSIDER-ATION.
WSP
Right?
Right.
WELL, LOOKS LIKE WE COULD GO EITHER WAY...
KLAT KLAT
I'LL ASK MY MOM WHAT SHE THINKS.
HYOOOOO
WHY DON'T WE ALL THINK IT OVER AND MEET LATER TO DECIDE?
Hello, Mom? Hey...
IF WE LEAVE, WE WON'T GET A REFUND ON OUR ROOMS.
I barely managed to come up with the money.
SCALLOP ROOM
Hmm...
BUT IT'S DEFI-NITELY SAFER TO HEAD HOME...
MAYBE I SHOULD TALK TO RIKO...
WAIT, I CAN'T. SHE'S WORKING LATE TODAY.
...

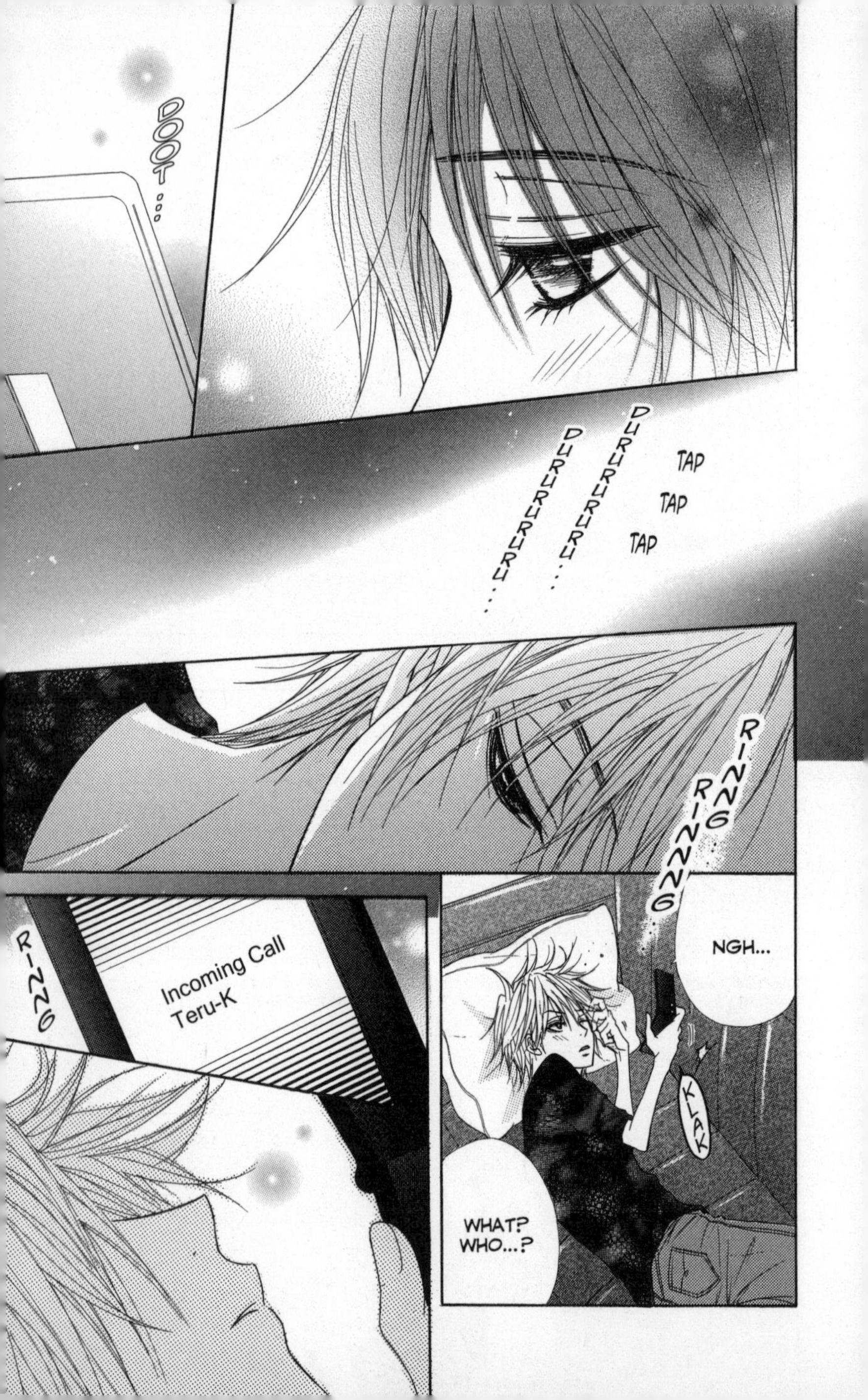
DOOT...
DURURURURU...
DURURURURU...
TAP
TAP
TAP
RINNG
RINNNG
NGH...
KLAK
WHAT? WHO...?
Incoming Call
Teru-K
RINNG

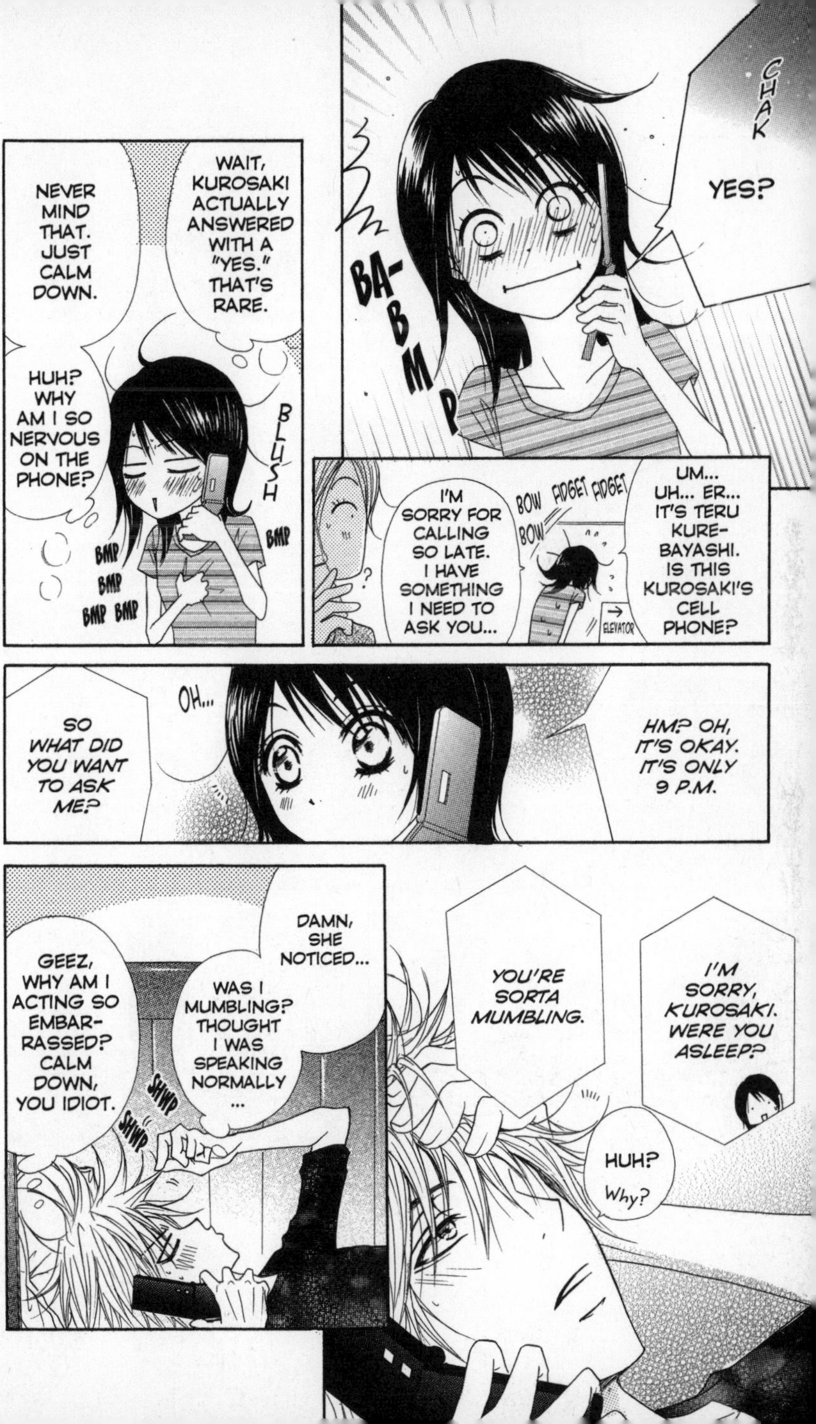
CHAK
YES?
BA-BMP
UM... UH... ER... IT'S TERU KURE-BAYASHI. IS THIS KUROSAKI'S CELL PHONE?
FIDGET FIDGET
BOW BOW
I'M SORRY FOR CALLING SO LATE. I HAVE SOMETHING I NEED TO ASK YOU...
→ ELEVATOR
WAIT, KUROSAKI ACTUALLY ANSWERED WITH A "YES." THAT'S RARE.
NEVER MIND THAT. JUST CALM DOWN.
BLUSH
HUH? WHY AM I SO NERVOUS ON THE PHONE?
BMP
BMP BMP BMP BMP
HM? OH, IT'S OKAY. IT'S ONLY 9 P.M.
OH...
SO WHAT DID YOU WANT TO ASK ME?
I'M SORRY, KUROSAKI. WERE YOU ASLEEP?
YOU'RE SORTA MUMBLING.
HUH? Why?
DAMN, SHE NOTICED...
WAS I MUMBLING? THOUGHT I WAS SPEAKING NORMALLY ...
GEEZ, WHY AM I ACTING SO EMBAR-RASSED? CALM DOWN, YOU IDIOT.
SHWP SHWP

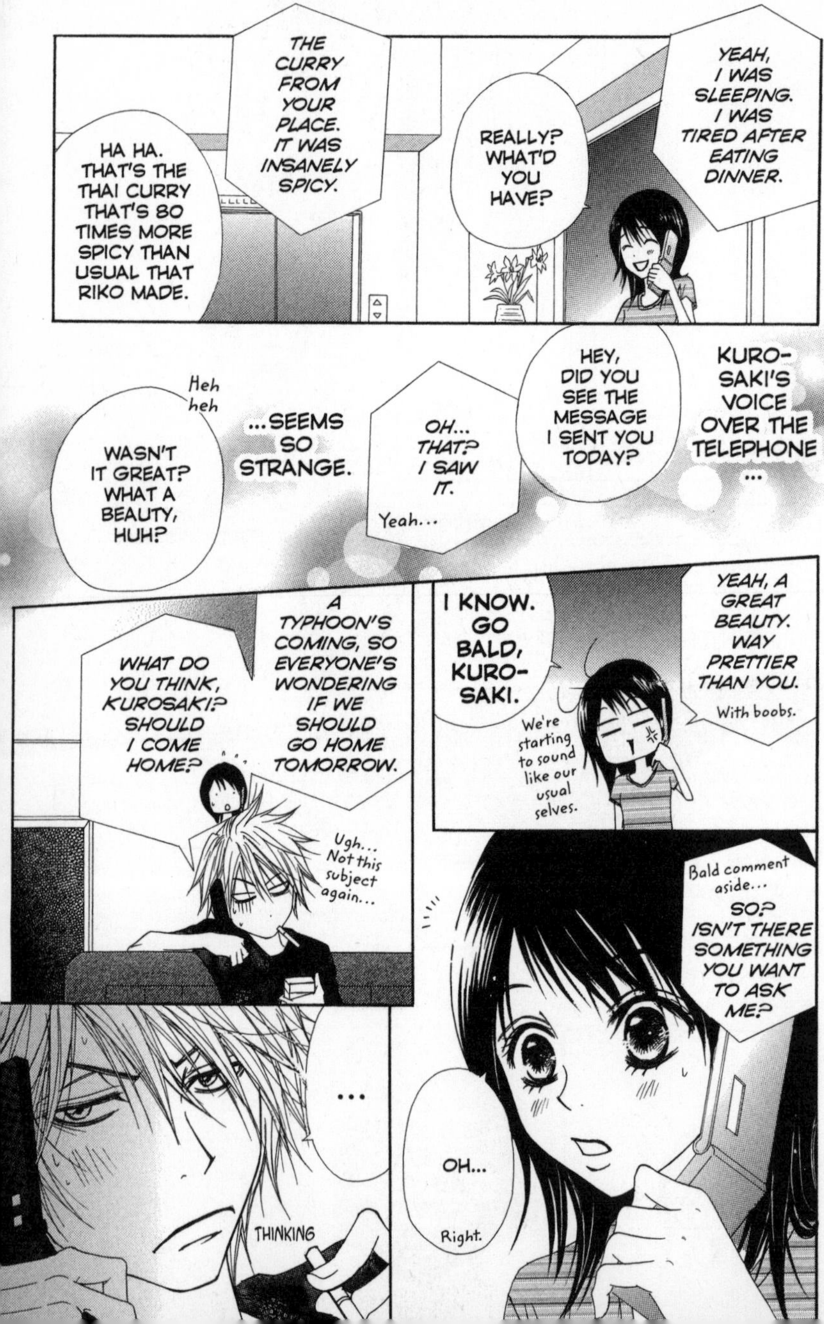
YEAH, I WAS SLEEPING. I WAS TIRED AFTER EATING DINNER.
REALLY? WHAT'D YOU HAVE?
THE CURRY FROM YOUR PLACE. IT WAS INSANELY SPICY.
HA HA. THAT'S THE THAI CURRY THAT'S 80 TIMES MORE SPICY THAN USUAL THAT RIKO MADE.
KURO-SAKI'S VOICE OVER THE TELEPHONE...
HEY, DID YOU SEE THE MESSAGE I SENT YOU TODAY?
OH... THAT? I SAW IT.
Yeah...
...SEEMS SO STRANGE.
WASN'T IT GREAT? WHAT A BEAUTY, HUH?
Heh heh
YEAH, A GREAT BEAUTY. WAY PRETTIER THAN YOU.
With boobs.
I KNOW. GO BALD, KURO-SAKI.
We're starting to sound like our usual selves.
A TYPHOON'S COMING, SO EVERYONE'S WONDERING IF WE SHOULD GO HOME TOMORROW.
WHAT DO YOU THINK, KUROSAKI? SHOULD I COME HOME?
Ugh... Not this subject again...
Bald comment aside...
SO? ISN'T THERE SOMETHING YOU WANT TO ASK ME?
OH...
Right.
...
THINKING

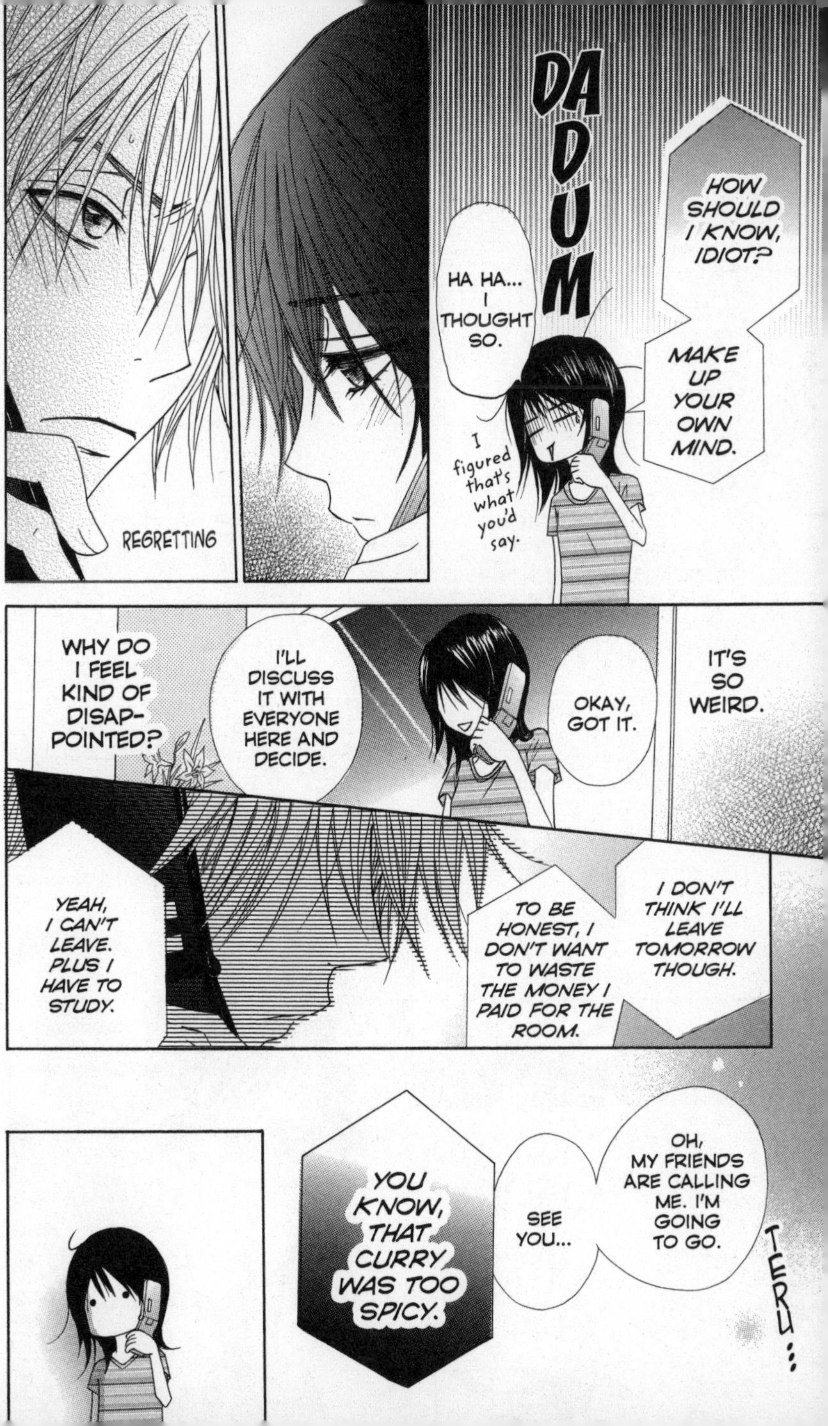
DA DUM
HOW SHOULD I KNOW, IDIOT?
MAKE UP YOUR OWN MIND.
HA HA... I THOUGHT SO.
I figured that's what you'd say.
REGRETTING
IT'S SO WEIRD.
OKAY, GOT IT.
I'LL DISCUSS IT WITH EVERYONE HERE AND DECIDE.
WHY DO I FEEL KIND OF DISAP-POINTED?
I DON'T THINK I'LL LEAVE TOMORROW THOUGH.
TO BE HONEST, I DON'T WANT TO WASTE THE MONEY I PAID FOR THE ROOM.
YEAH, I CAN'T LEAVE. PLUS I HAVE TO STUDY.
TERU...
OH, MY FRIENDS ARE CALLING ME. I'M GOING TO GO.
SEE YOU...
YOU KNOW, THAT CURRY WAS TOO SPICY.

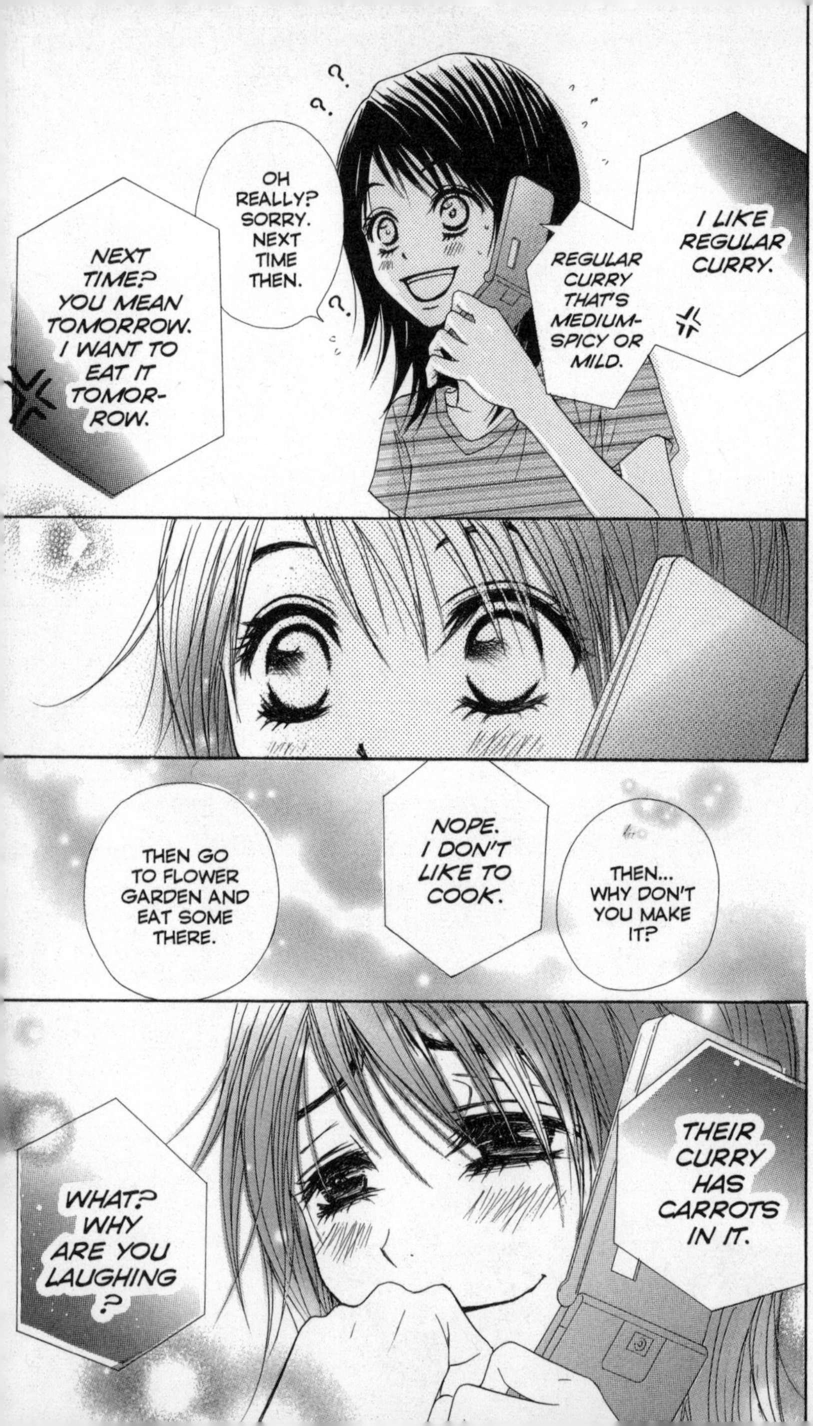
I LIKE REGULAR CURRY.
REGULAR CURRY THAT'S MEDIUM-SPICY OR MILD.
OH REALLY? SORRY. NEXT TIME THEN.
NEXT TIME? YOU MEAN TOMORROW. I WANT TO EAT IT TOMORROW.
THEN... WHY DON'T YOU MAKE IT?
NOPE. I DON'T LIKE TO COOK.
THEN GO TO FLOWER GARDEN AND EAT SOME THERE.
THEIR CURRY HAS CARROTS IN IT.
WHAT? WHY ARE YOU LAUGHING?

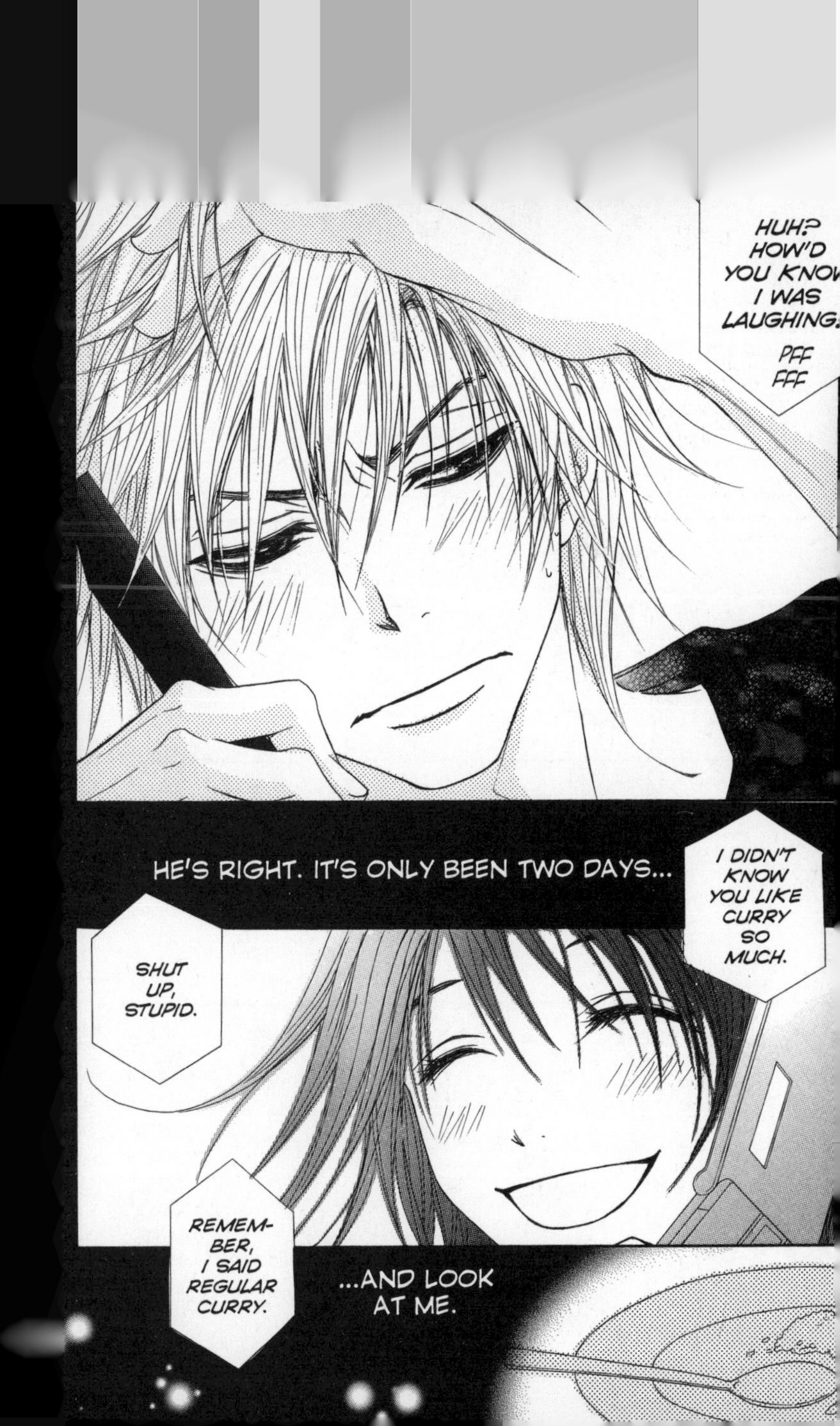
HUH? HOW'D YOU KNOW I WAS LAUGHING?
PFF FFF
I DIDN'T KNOW YOU LIKE CURRY SO MUCH.
HE'S RIGHT. IT'S ONLY BEEN TWO DAYS...
SHUT UP, STUPID.
REMEM-BER, I SAID REGULAR CURRY.
...AND LOOK AT ME.

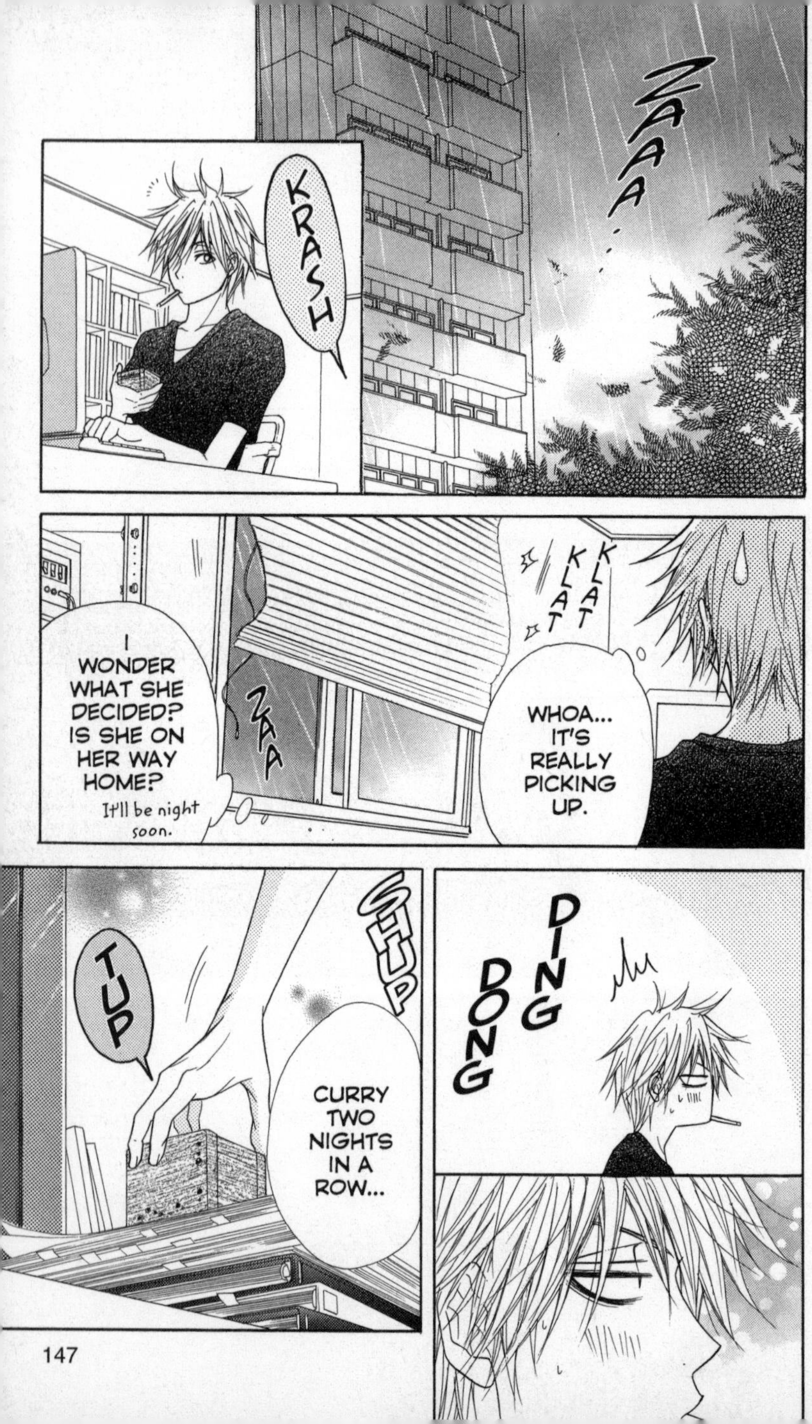
ZAAAA...
KRASH
KLAT KLAT
WHOA... IT'S REALLY PICKING UP.
ZAA
I WONDER WHAT SHE DECIDED? IS SHE ON HER WAY HOME?
It'll be night soon.
DING DONG
SHUP
CURRY TWO NIGHTS IN A ROW...
TUP

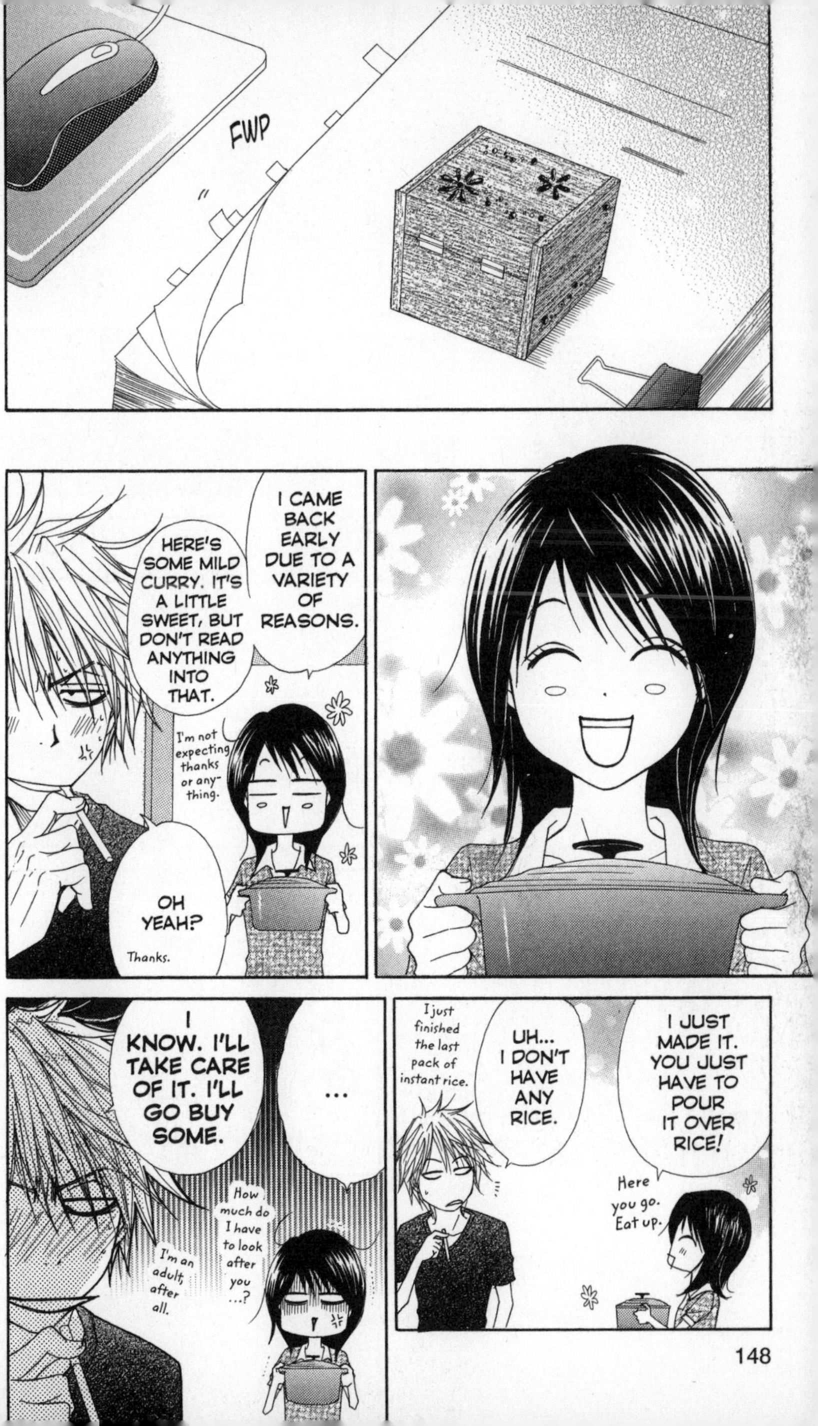
FWP
I CAME BACK EARLY DUE TO A VARIETY OF REASONS.
HERE'S SOME MILD CURRY. IT'S A LITTLE SWEET, BUT DON'T READ ANYTHING INTO THAT.
I'm not expecting thanks or any-thing.
OH YEAH?
Thanks.
I JUST MADE IT. YOU JUST HAVE TO POUR IT OVER RICE!
Here you go. Eat up.
UH... I DON'T HAVE ANY RICE.
I just finished the last pack of instant rice.
...
I KNOW. I'LL TAKE CARE OF IT. I'LL GO BUY SOME.
How much do I have to look after you ...?
I'm an adult, after all.

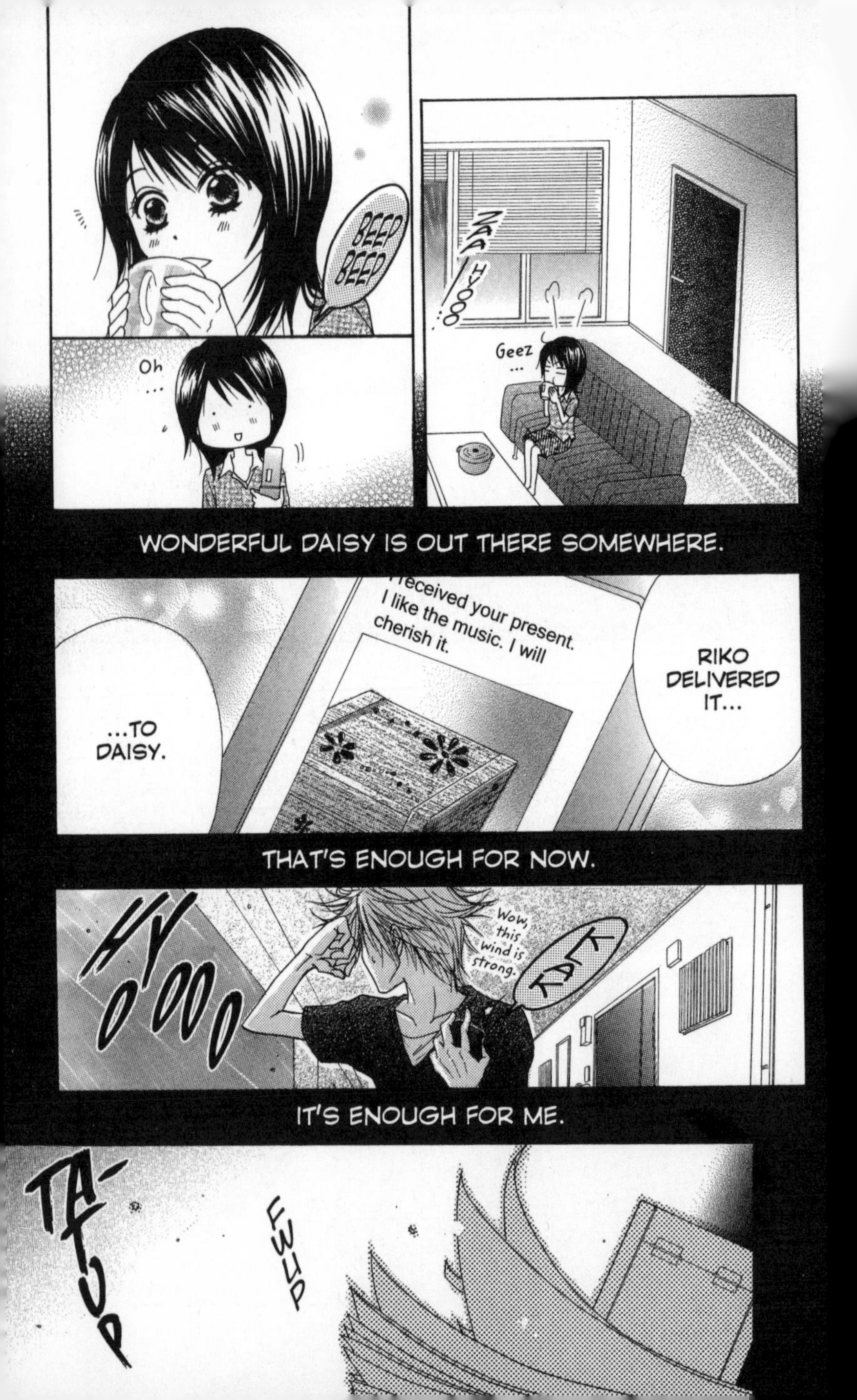
ZAA HYOOO
Geez ...
BEEP BEEP
Oh ...
WONDERFUL DAISY IS OUT THERE SOMEWHERE.
RIKO DELIVERED IT...
received your present.
I like the music. I will
cherish it.
...TO DAISY.
THAT'S ENOUGH FOR NOW.
KLAK
Wow, this wind is strong.
HYOOOO
IT'S ENOUGH FOR ME.
FWUP
TA-TUP

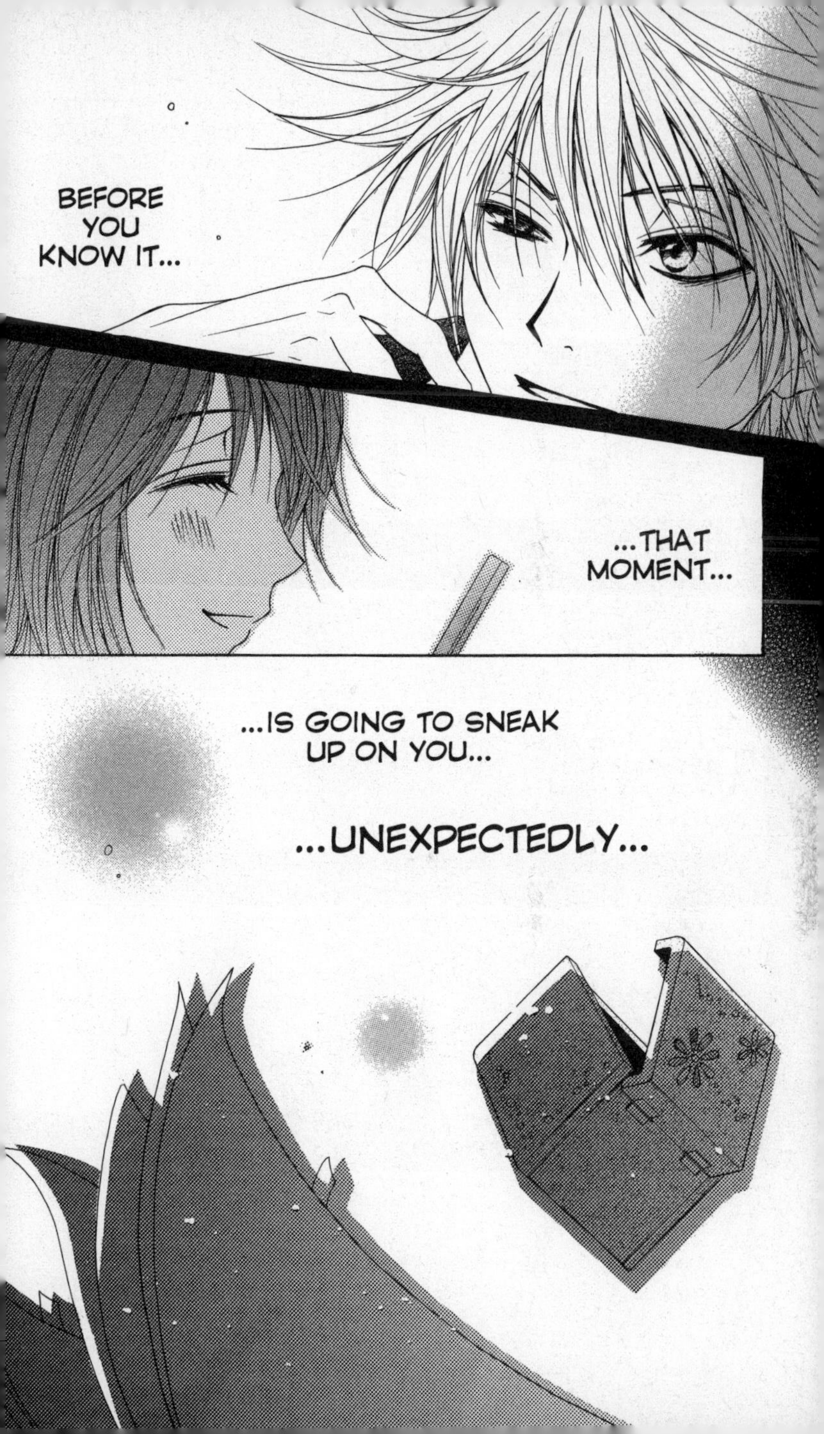
BEFORE YOU KNOW IT...
...THAT MOMENT...
...IS GOING TO SNEAK UP ON YOU...
...UNEXPECTEDLY...

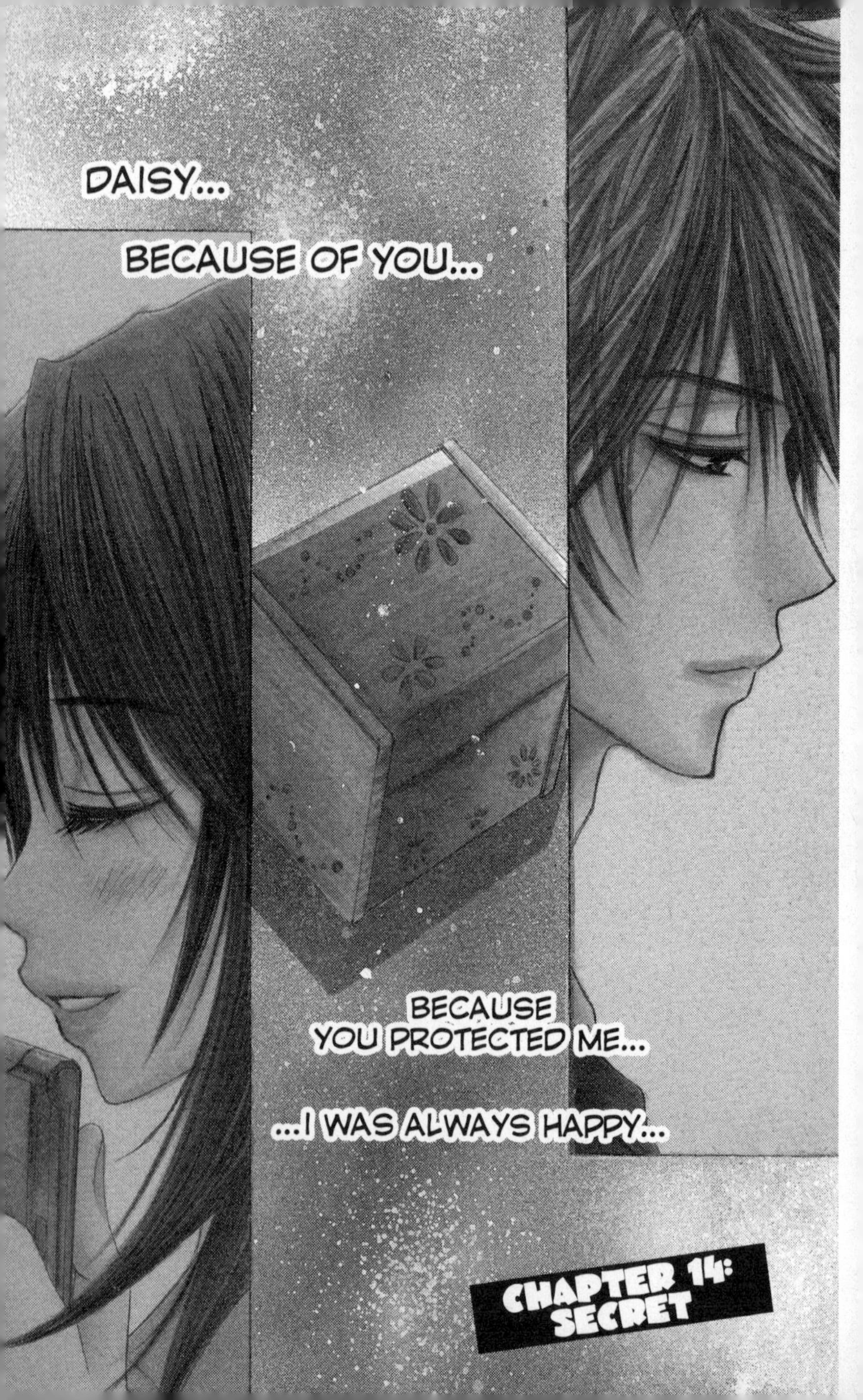
DAISY...
BECAUSE OF YOU...
BECAUSE YOU PROTECTED ME...
...I WAS ALWAYS HAPPY...
CHAPTER 14: SECRET

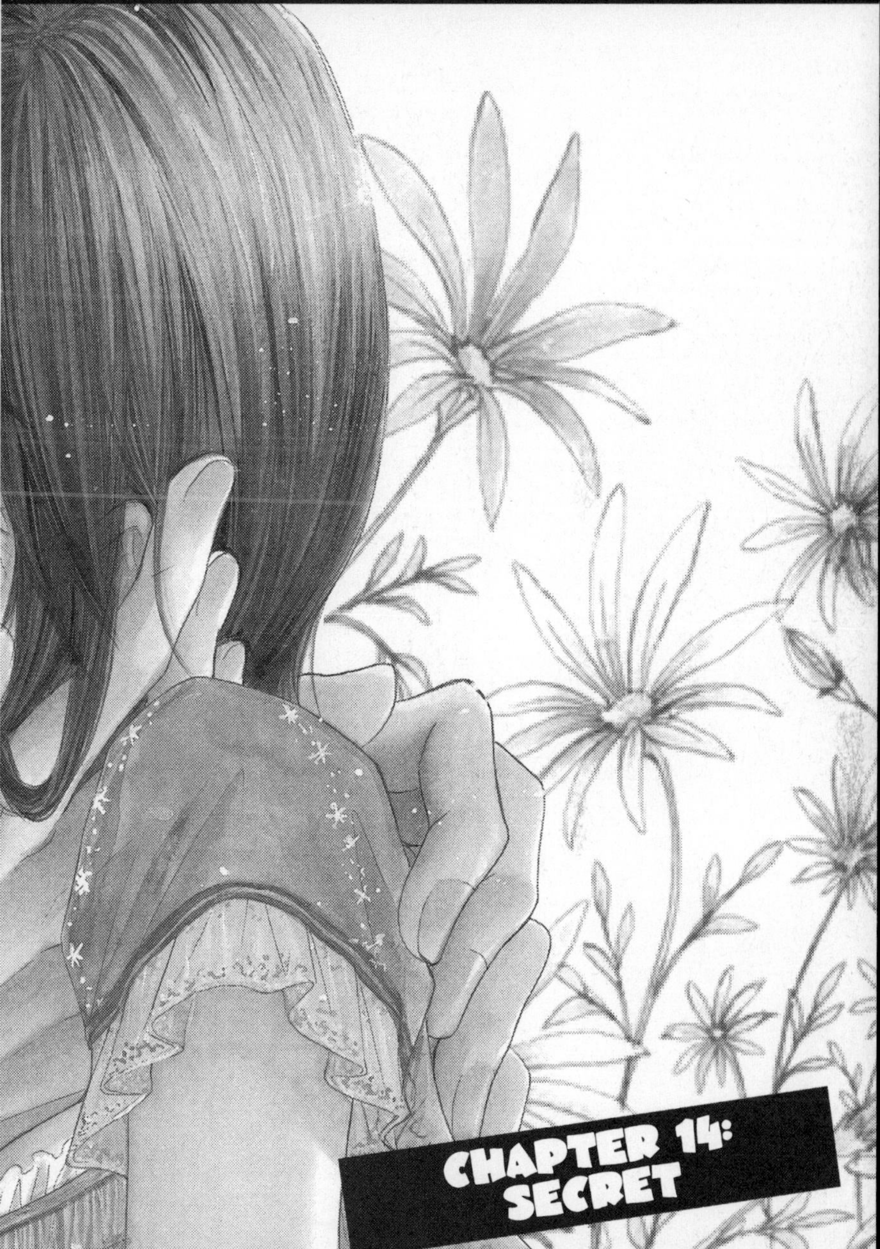
CHAPTER 14:
SECRET

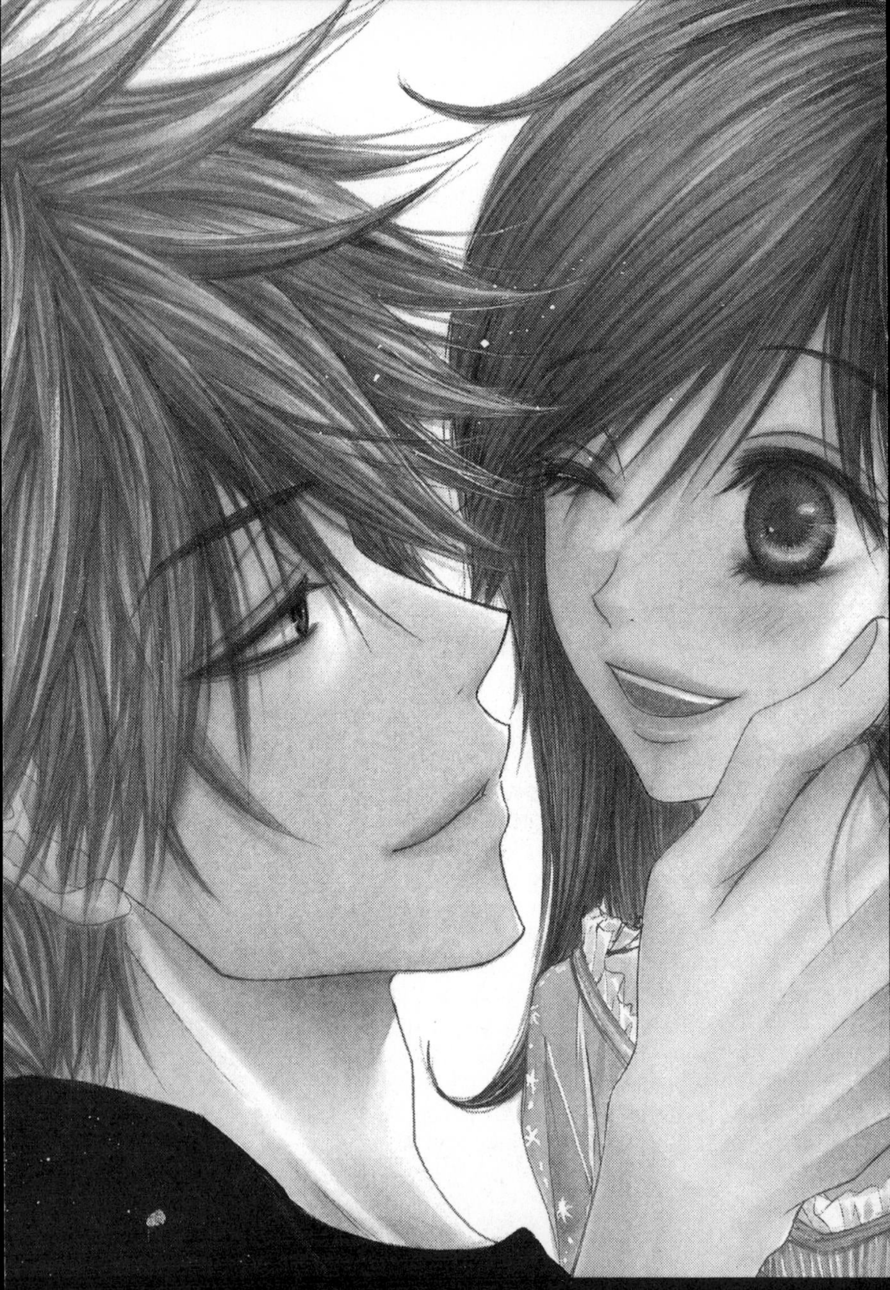

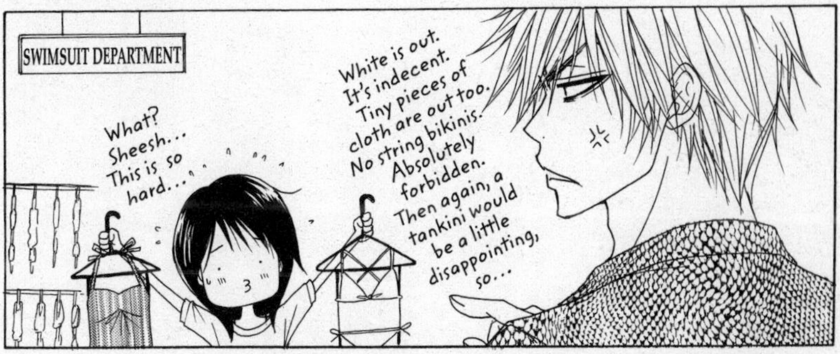
White is out. It's indecent. Tiny pieces of cloth are out too. No string bikinis. Absolutely forbidden. Then again, a tankini would be a little disappointing, so...
SWIMSUIT DEPARTMENT
What? Sheesh... This is so hard...

THANK YOU FOR READING ***DENGEKI DAISY*** 3.

(THERE'S A BLANK PAGE HERE, SO THIS IS THE AFTERWORD.)

SINCE I HAVE THE SPACE, I'M GOING TO BE FRANK. WHEN I FIRST BEGAN THIS SERIES,

***DENGEKI DAISY* WAS ONLY SUPPOSED TO BE THREE CHAPTERS. (IT'S TRUE.)**

THAT WAS ***DAISY*** THEN!! AND HERE WE ARE WITH THREE WHOLE VOLUMES. WHAT A SHOCK!! THREE CHAPTERS BECAME THREE VOLUMES. WHAT A MIRACLE.
I'M SO GRATEFUL. I CAN ONLY SAY THAT IT'S DUE TO ALL OF YOU WHO READ THIS SERIES. I, KYOUSUKE MOTOMI, AM A VERY FORTUNATE PERSON. I'M FILLED WITH GRATITUDE.
ANYWAY, FOR ME THE AUTHOR, THIS HAS GONE FAR BEYOND MY EXPECTATIONS, AND ***DENGEKI DAISY*** CONTINUES TO BE SERIALIZED. THE MIRACLE CONTINUES. IF THINGS GO WELL, THERE MAY EVEN BE A FOURTH VOLUME...NAH NAH NAH!! MY HAND'S STARTING TO SHAKE. I'D BETTER NOT BRAG SO MUCH.
IT'S A POOR PIECE OF WORK, BUT I PUT EVERYTHING INTO IT EACH AND EVERY TIME. SO IF PEOPLE WHO READ IT FIND SOME JOY IN IT, NEITHER I NOR KUROSAKI WILL HAVE ANY REGRETS. EVEN IF WE GO BALD (?). I'LL KEEP DOING MY BEST. TO ALL OF YOU WHO KINDLY WATCH OVER ME THE SAME WAY THAT ***DAISY*** WATCHES OVER TERU AND KUROSAKI, MY HEARTFELT THANKS.
SEE YOU AGAIN. HOPEFULLY, VERY SOON.

KYOUSUKE MOTOMI
最富 キョウスケ

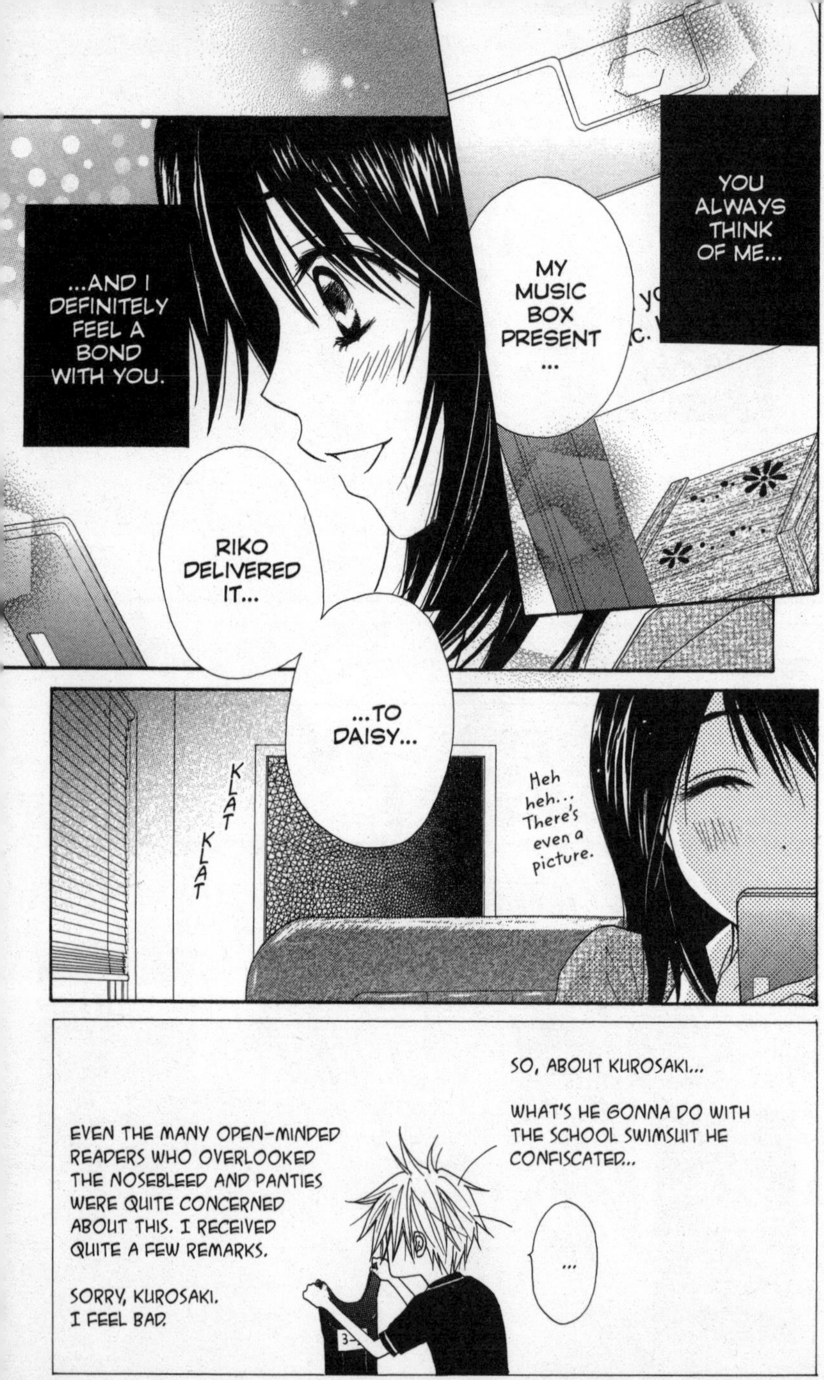
YOU ALWAYS THINK OF ME...
MY MUSIC BOX PRESENT...
...AND I DEFINITELY FEEL A BOND WITH YOU.
RIKO DELIVERED IT...
...TO DAISY...
Heh heh... There's even a picture.
KLAT KLAT
SO, ABOUT KUROSAKI...
WHAT'S HE GONNA DO WITH THE SCHOOL SWIMSUIT HE CONFISCATED...
...
EVEN THE MANY OPEN-MINDED READERS WHO OVERLOOKED THE NOSEBLEED AND PANTIES WERE QUITE CONCERNED ABOUT THIS. I RECEIVED QUITE A FEW REMARKS.
SORRY, KUROSAKI. I FEEL BAD.

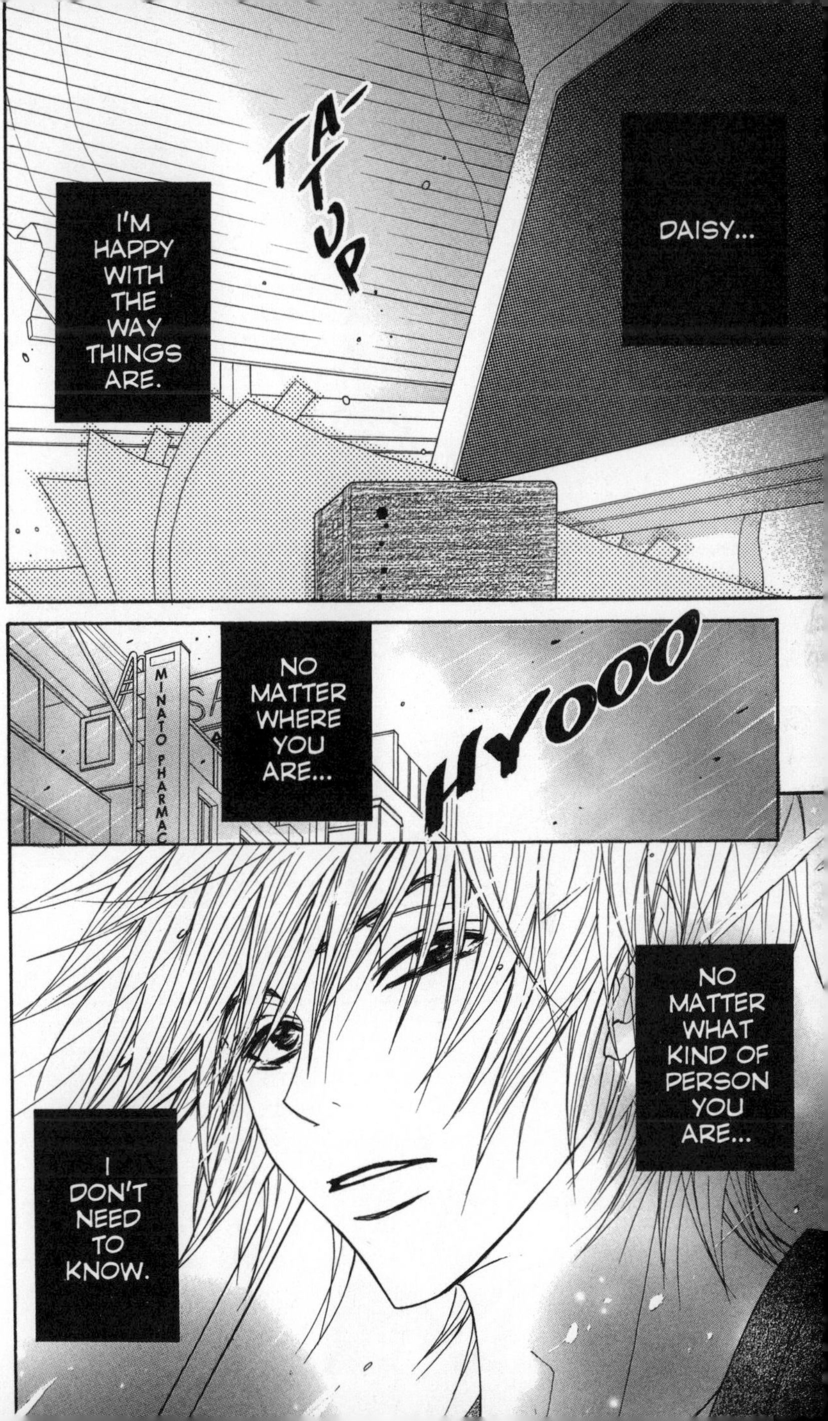
DAISY...
TA-TUP
I'M HAPPY WITH THE WAY THINGS ARE.
HYOOO
NO MATTER WHERE YOU ARE...
MINATO PHARMAC
NO MATTER WHAT KIND OF PERSON YOU ARE...
I DON'T NEED TO KNOW.

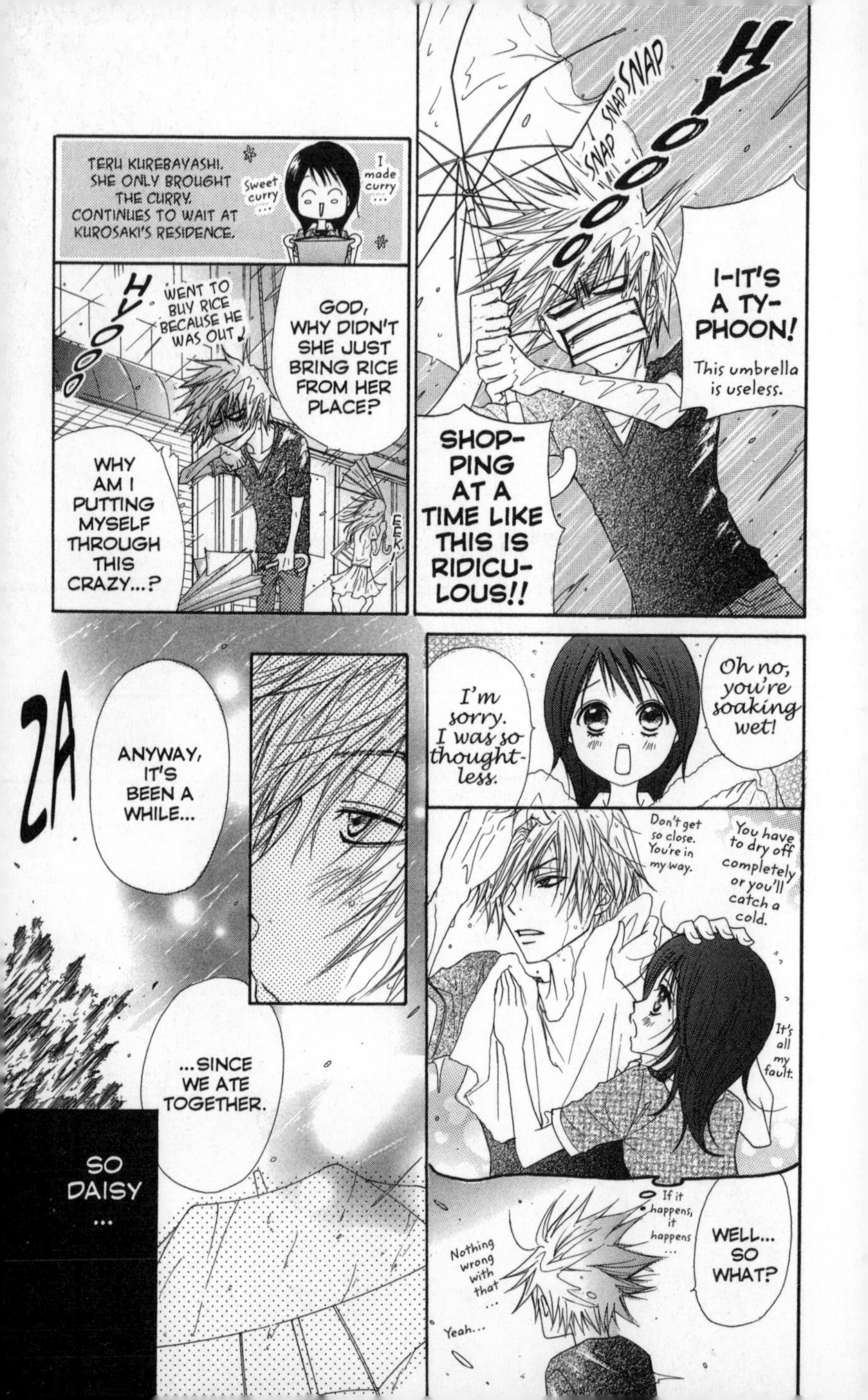
HYOOOOOOO
SNAP SNAP SNAP
I-IT'S A TY-PHOON!
This umbrella is useless.
SHOP-PING AT A TIME LIKE THIS IS RIDICU-LOUS!!
TERU KUREBAYASHI. SHE ONLY BROUGHT THE CURRY. CONTINUES TO WAIT AT KUROSAKI'S RESIDENCE.
I made curry...
Sweet curry...
HYOOOO
GOD, WHY DIDN'T SHE JUST BRING RICE FROM HER PLACE?
WENT TO BUY RICE BECAUSE HE WAS OUT ♪
WHY AM I PUTTING MYSELF THROUGH THIS CRAZY...?
EEK!
Oh no, you're soaking wet!
I'm sorry. I was so thought-less.
You have to dry off completely or you'll catch a cold.
Don't get so close. You're in my way.
It's all my fault.
WELL... SO WHAT?
If it happens, it happens...
Nothing wrong with that...
Yeah...
ZA
ANYWAY, IT'S BEEN A WHILE...
...SINCE WE ATE TOGETHER.
SO DAISY...

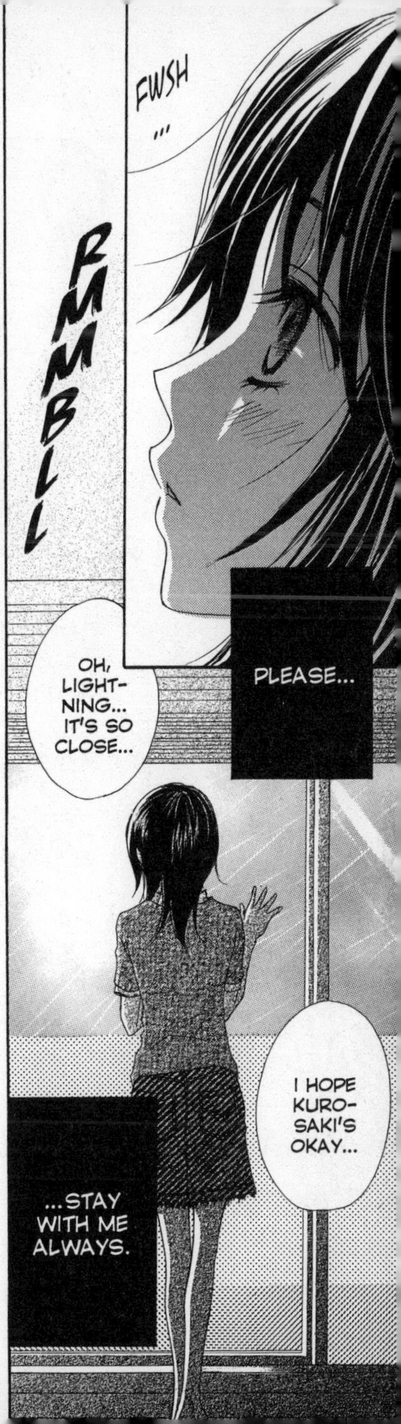
FWSH...
RMMBLL
PLEASE...
OH, LIGHTNING... IT'S SO CLOSE...
I HOPE KUROSAKI'S OKAY...
...STAY WITH ME ALWAYS.
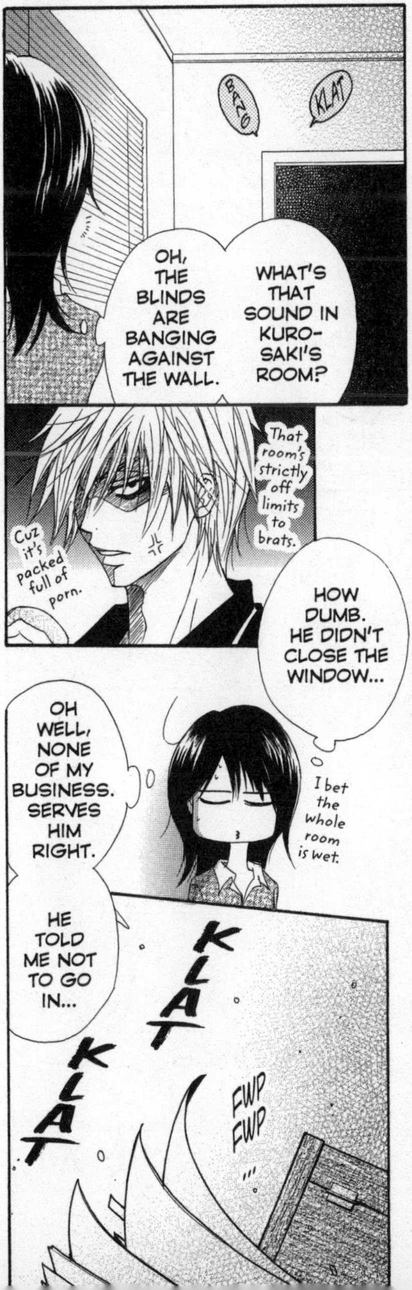
KLAT
BRZO
WHAT'S THAT SOUND IN KUROSAKI'S ROOM?
OH, THE BLINDS ARE BANGING AGAINST THE WALL.
That room's strictly off limits to brats.
Cuz it's packed full of porn.
HOW DUMB. HE DIDN'T CLOSE THE WINDOW...
I bet the whole room is wet.
OH WELL, NONE OF MY BUSINESS. SERVES HIM RIGHT.
HE TOLD ME NOT TO GO IN...
KLAT
KLAT
FWP FWP...

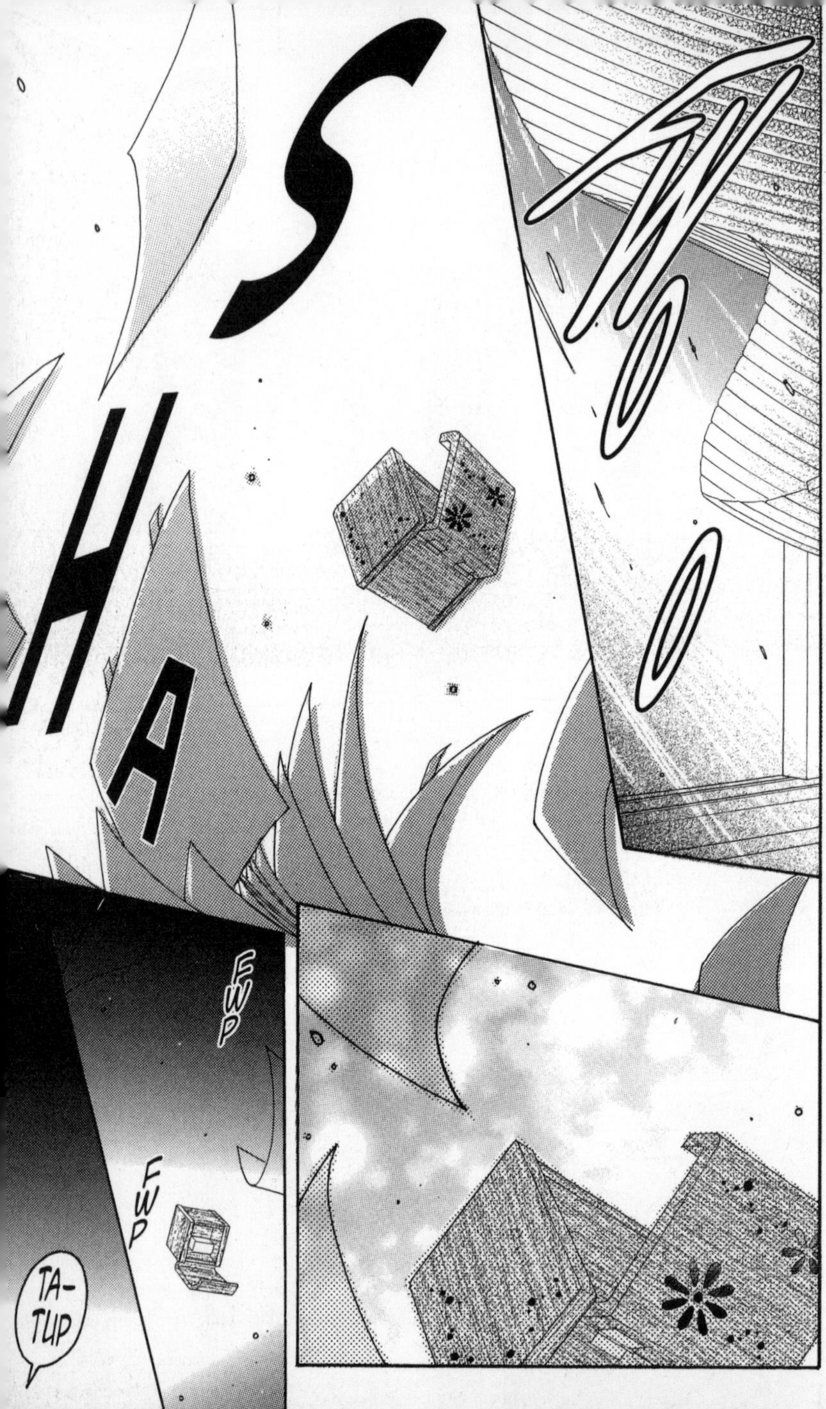
SHA
FWP
FWP
TA-TUP

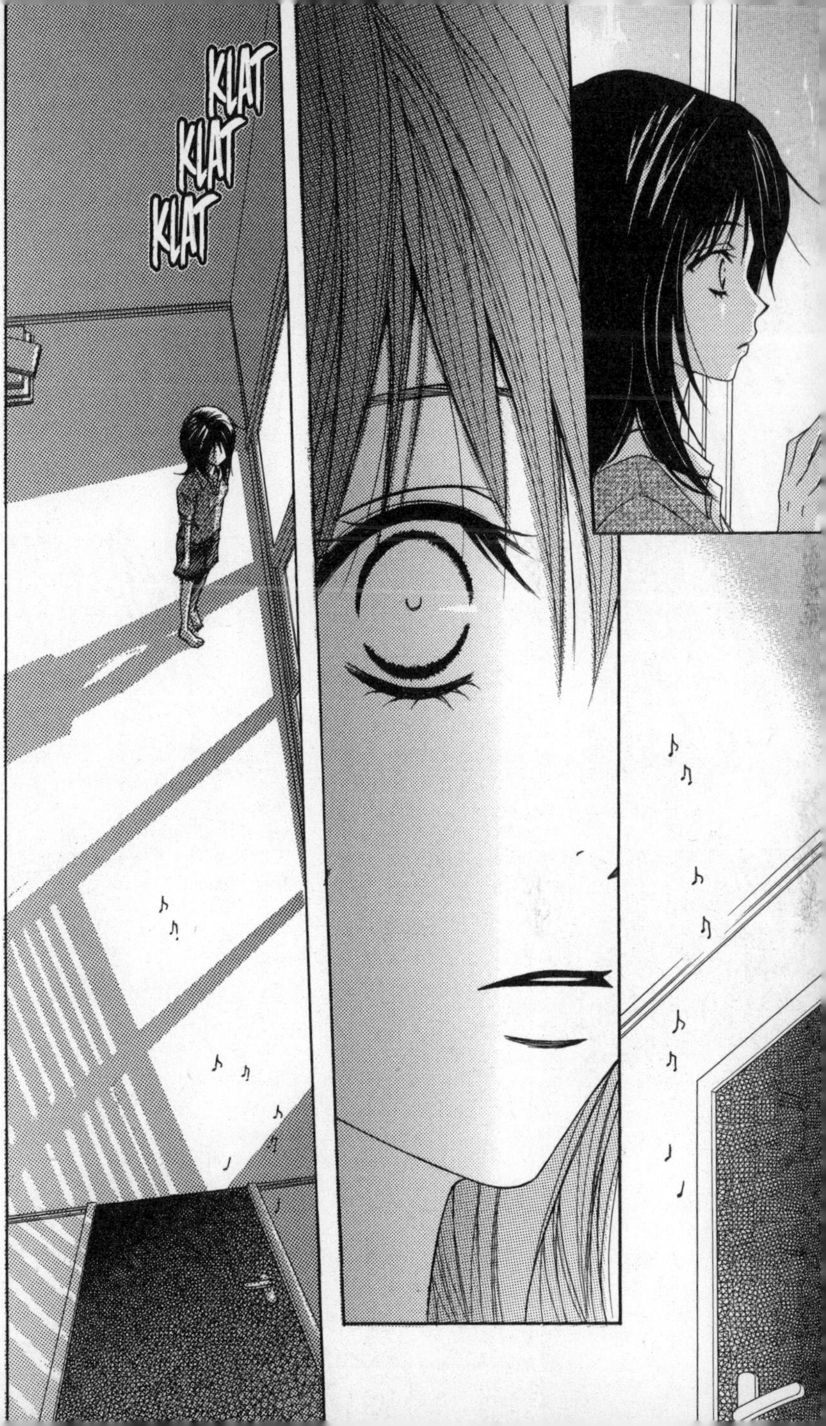
KLAT
KLAT
KLAT

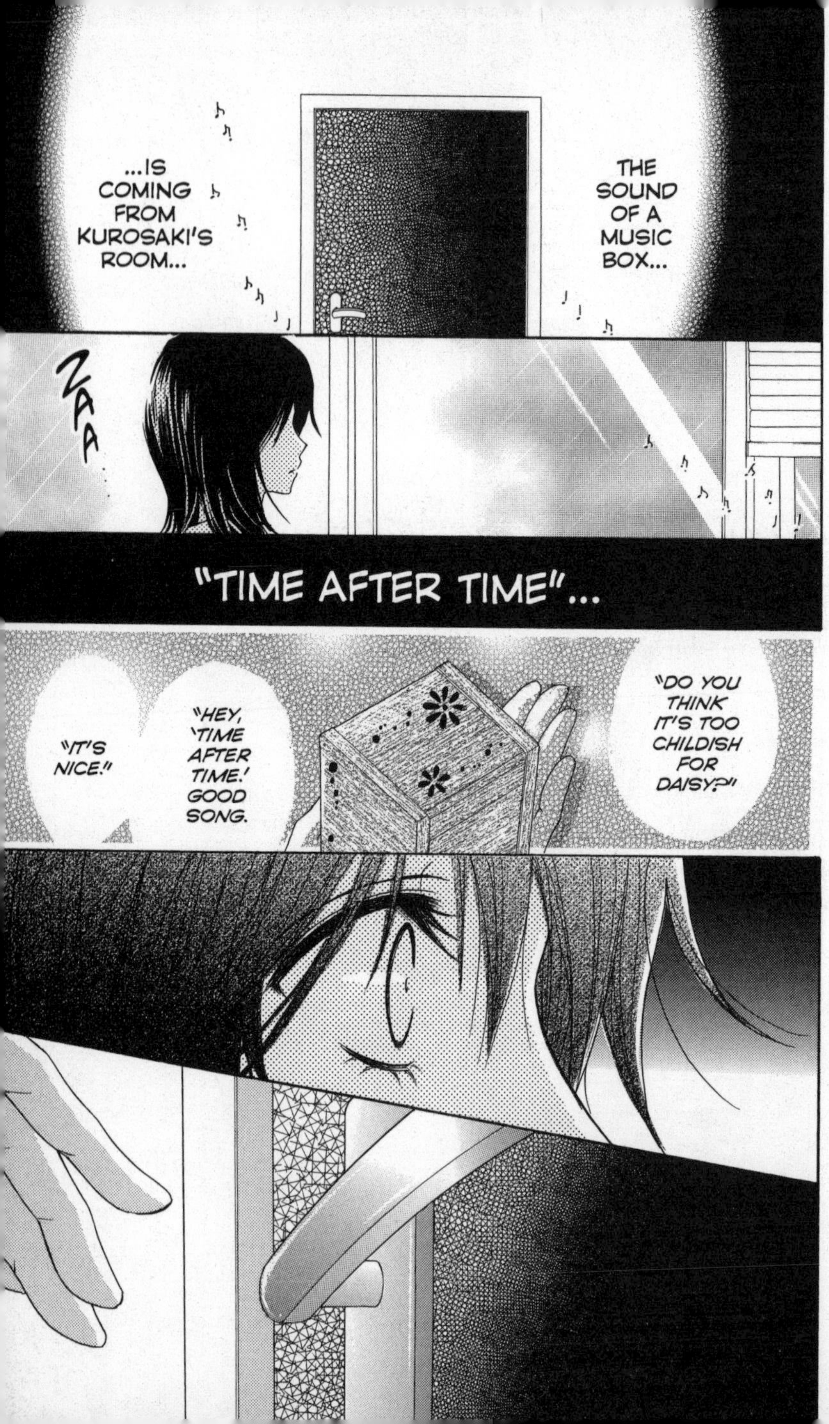
THE SOUND OF A MUSIC BOX...
...IS COMING FROM KUROSAKI'S ROOM...
ZAA
"TIME AFTER TIME"...
"DO YOU THINK IT'S TOO CHILDISH FOR DAISY?"
"HEY, 'TIME AFTER TIME.' GOOD SONG.
"IT'S NICE."

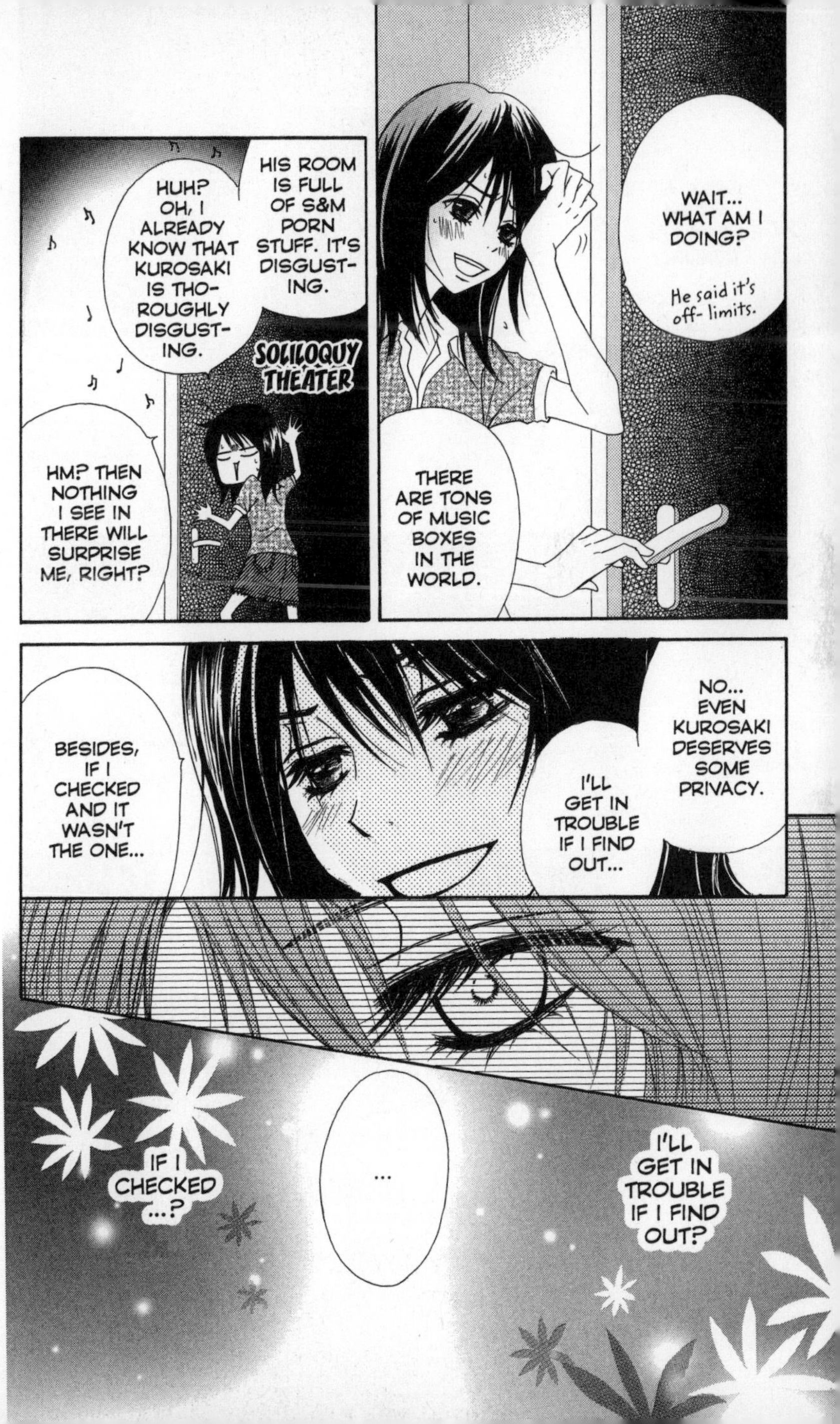
WAIT... WHAT AM I DOING?
He said it's off-limits.
THERE ARE TONS OF MUSIC BOXES IN THE WORLD.
HIS ROOM IS FULL OF S&M PORN STUFF. IT'S DISGUSTING.
HUH? OH, I ALREADY KNOW THAT KUROSAKI IS THOROUGHLY DISGUSTING.
SOLILOQUY THEATER
HM? THEN NOTHING I SEE IN THERE WILL SURPRISE ME, RIGHT?
NO... EVEN KUROSAKI DESERVES SOME PRIVACY.
I'LL GET IN TROUBLE IF I FIND OUT...
BESIDES, IF I CHECKED AND IT WASN'T THE ONE...
I'LL GET IN TROUBLE IF I FIND OUT?
...
IF I CHECKED ...?

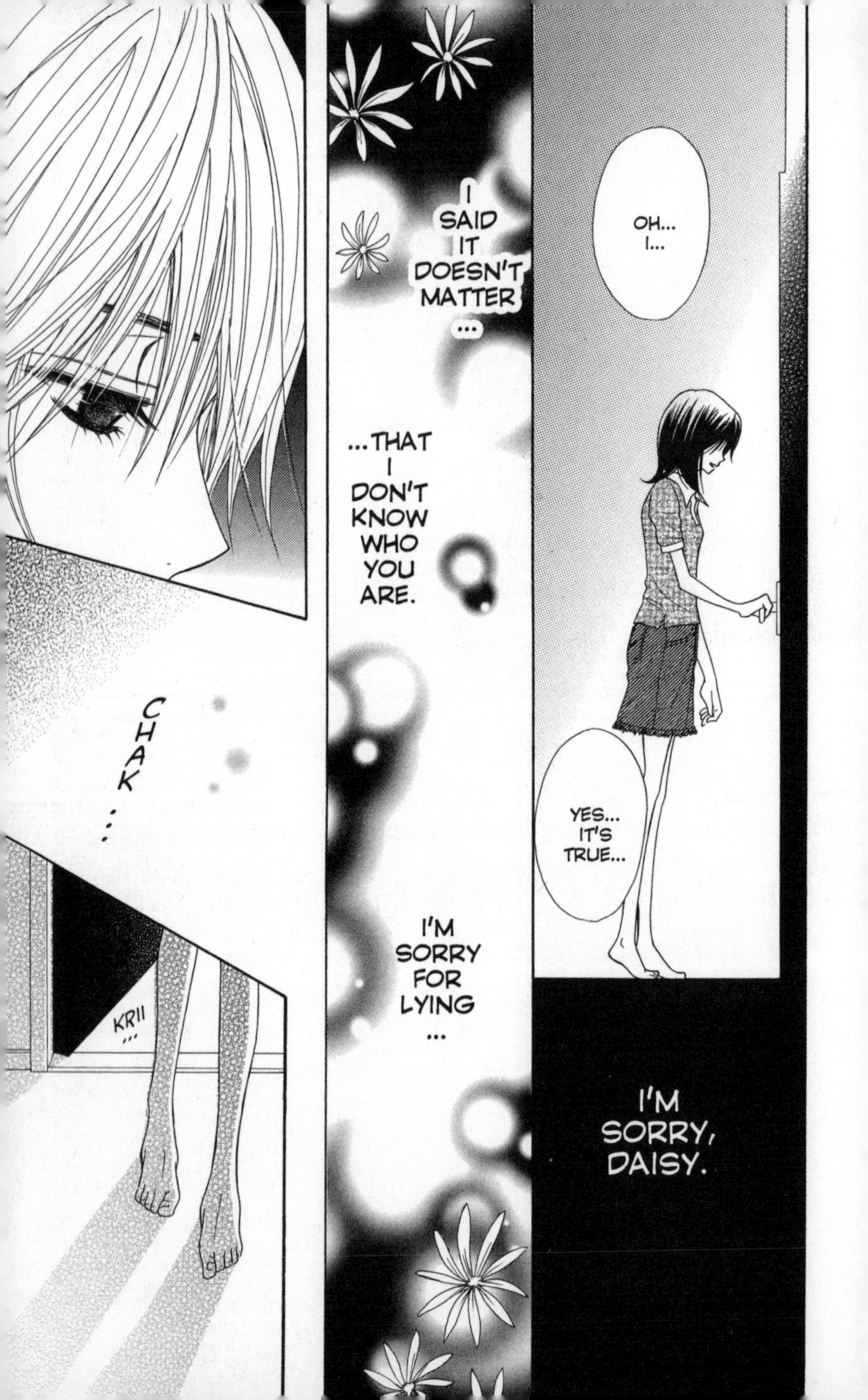
OH... I...
YES... IT'S TRUE...
I'M SORRY, DAISY.
I SAID IT DOESN'T MATTER...
...THAT I DON'T KNOW WHO YOU ARE.
I'M SORRY FOR LYING...
CHAK...
KRII...

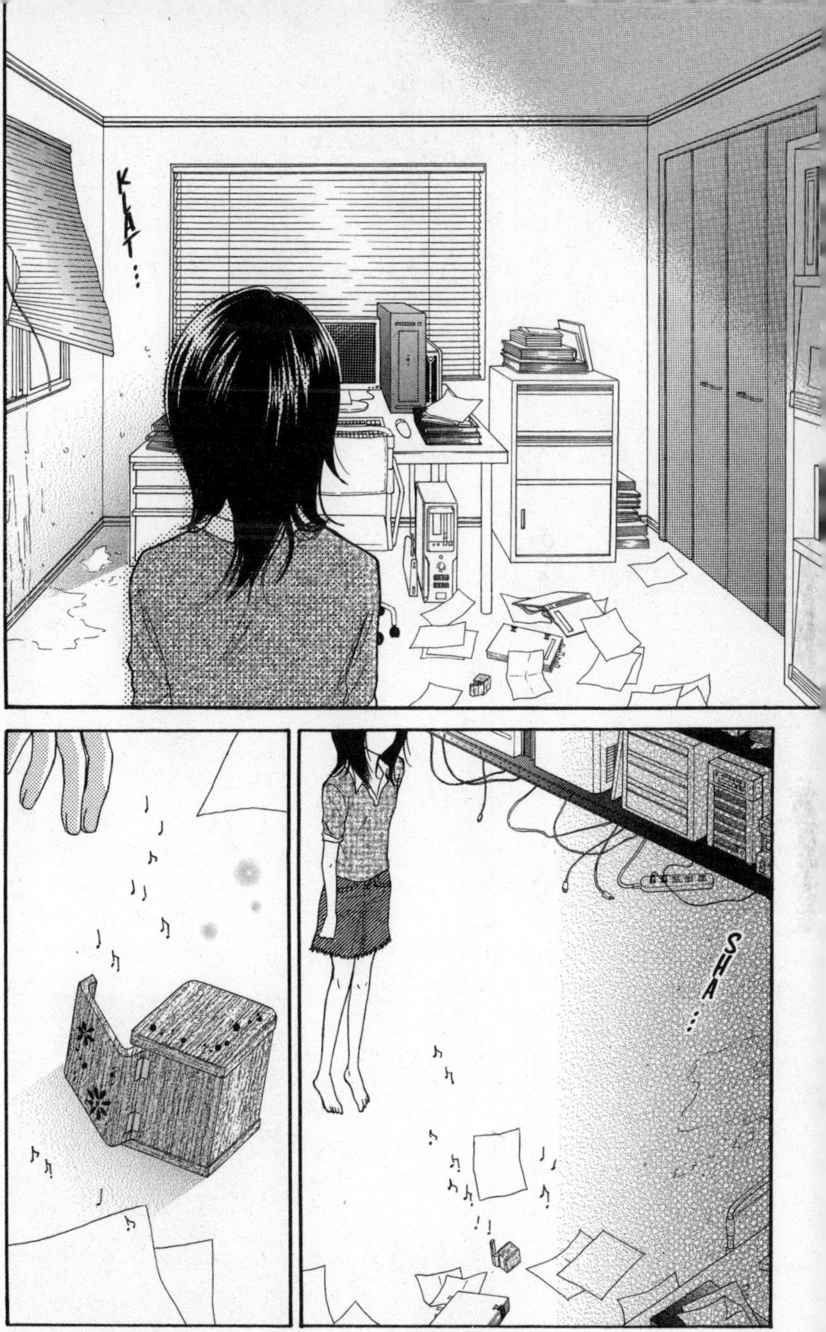
KLAT...
SHA...

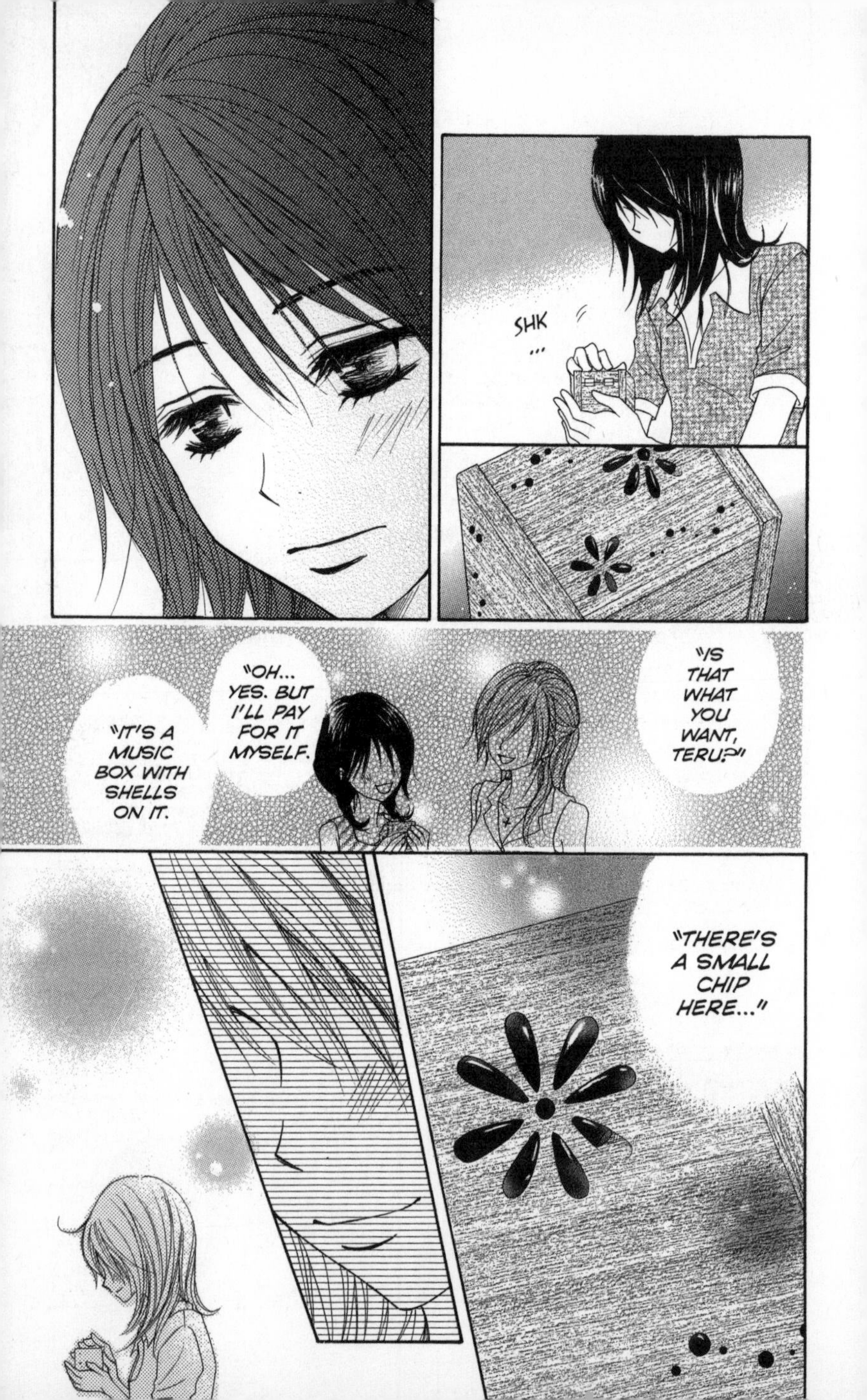
SHK
...
"IS THAT WHAT YOU WANT, TERU?"
"OH... YES. BUT I'LL PAY FOR IT MYSELF.
"IT'S A MUSIC BOX WITH SHELLS ON IT.
"THERE'S A SMALL CHIP HERE..."

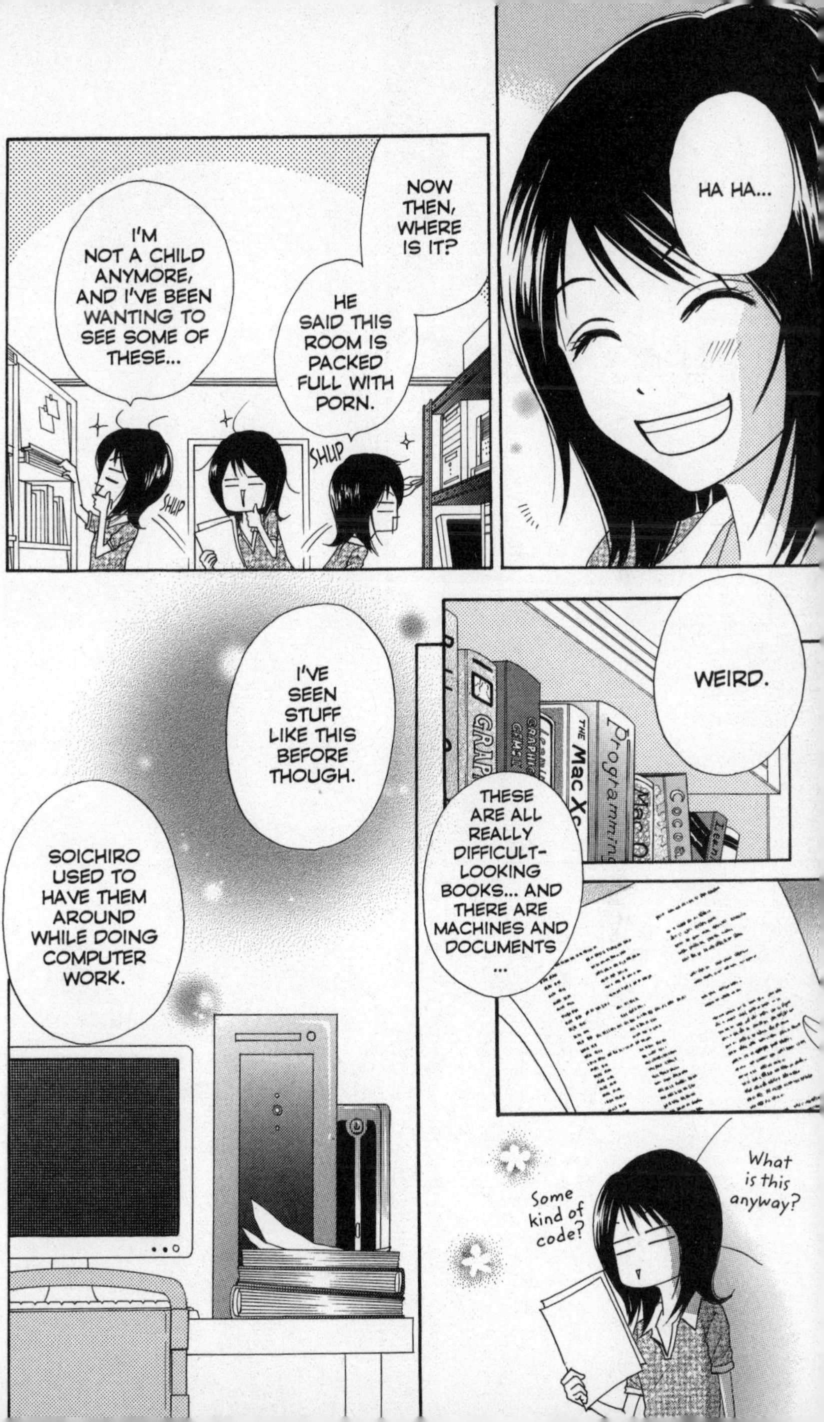
HA HA...
NOW THEN, WHERE IS IT?
HE SAID THIS ROOM IS PACKED FULL WITH PORN.
I'M NOT A CHILD ANYMORE, AND I'VE BEEN WANTING TO SEE SOME OF THESE...
SHUP
SHUP
WEIRD.
THESE ARE ALL REALLY DIFFICULT-LOOKING BOOKS... AND THERE ARE MACHINES AND DOCUMENTS ...
What is this anyway?
Some kind of code?
I'VE SEEN STUFF LIKE THIS BEFORE THOUGH.
SOICHIRO USED TO HAVE THEM AROUND WHILE DOING COMPUTER WORK.

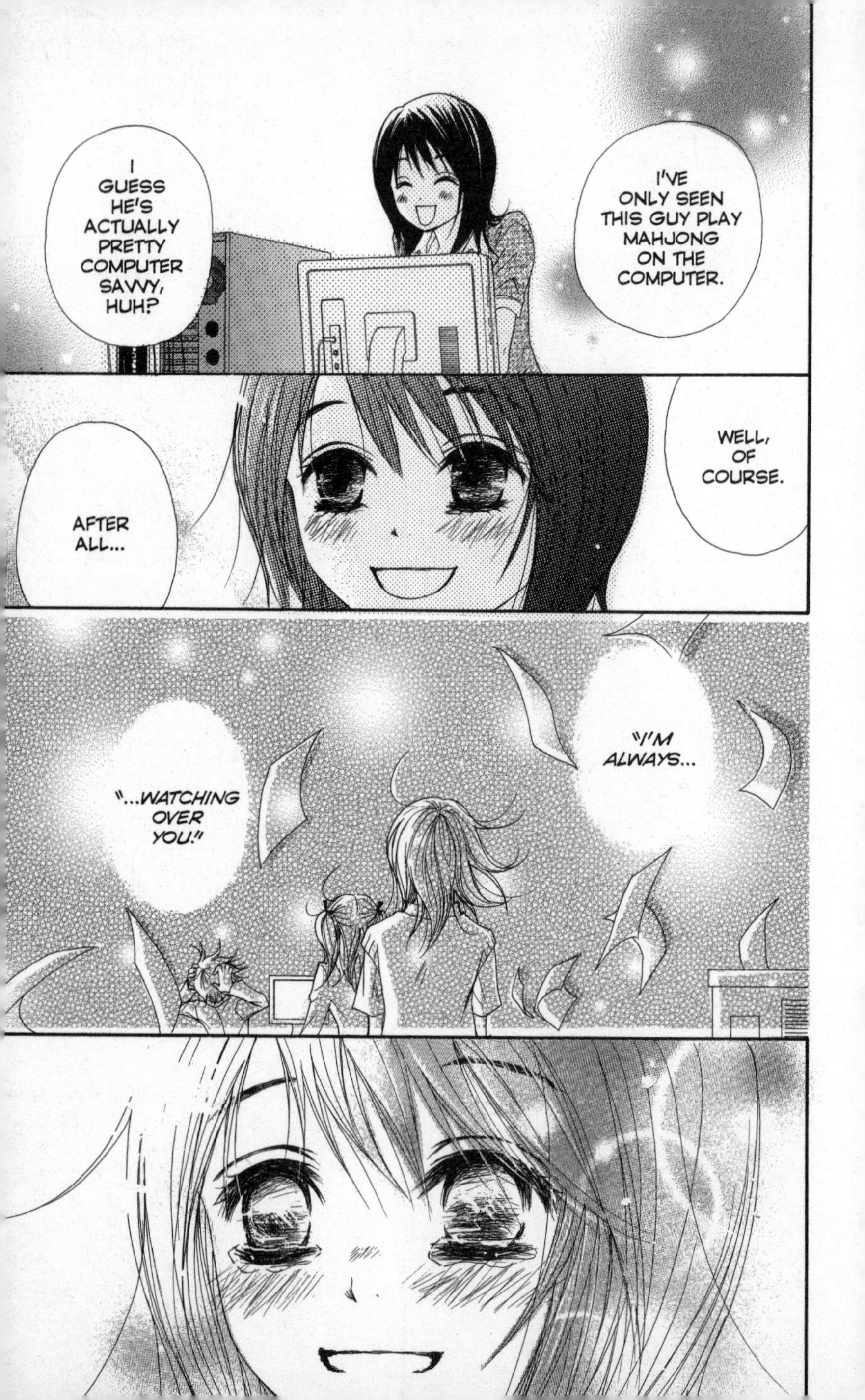
I'VE ONLY SEEN THIS GUY PLAY MAHJONG ON THE COMPUTER.
I GUESS HE'S ACTUALLY PRETTY COMPUTER SAVVY, HUH?
WELL, OF COURSE.
AFTER ALL...
"I'M ALWAYS...
"...WATCHING OVER YOU."

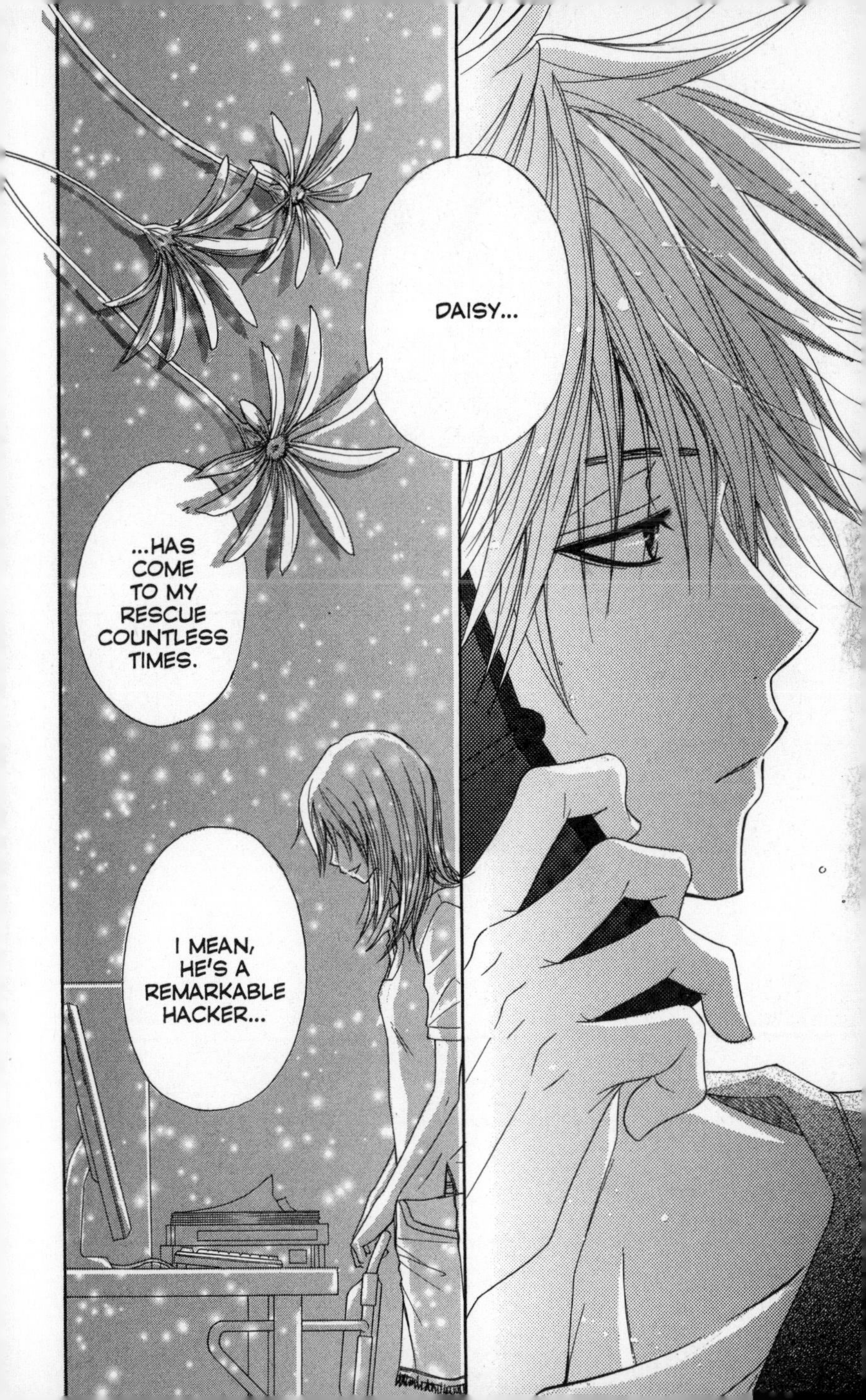
DAISY...
...HAS COME TO MY RESCUE COUNTLESS TIMES.
I MEAN, HE'S A REMARKABLE HACKER...

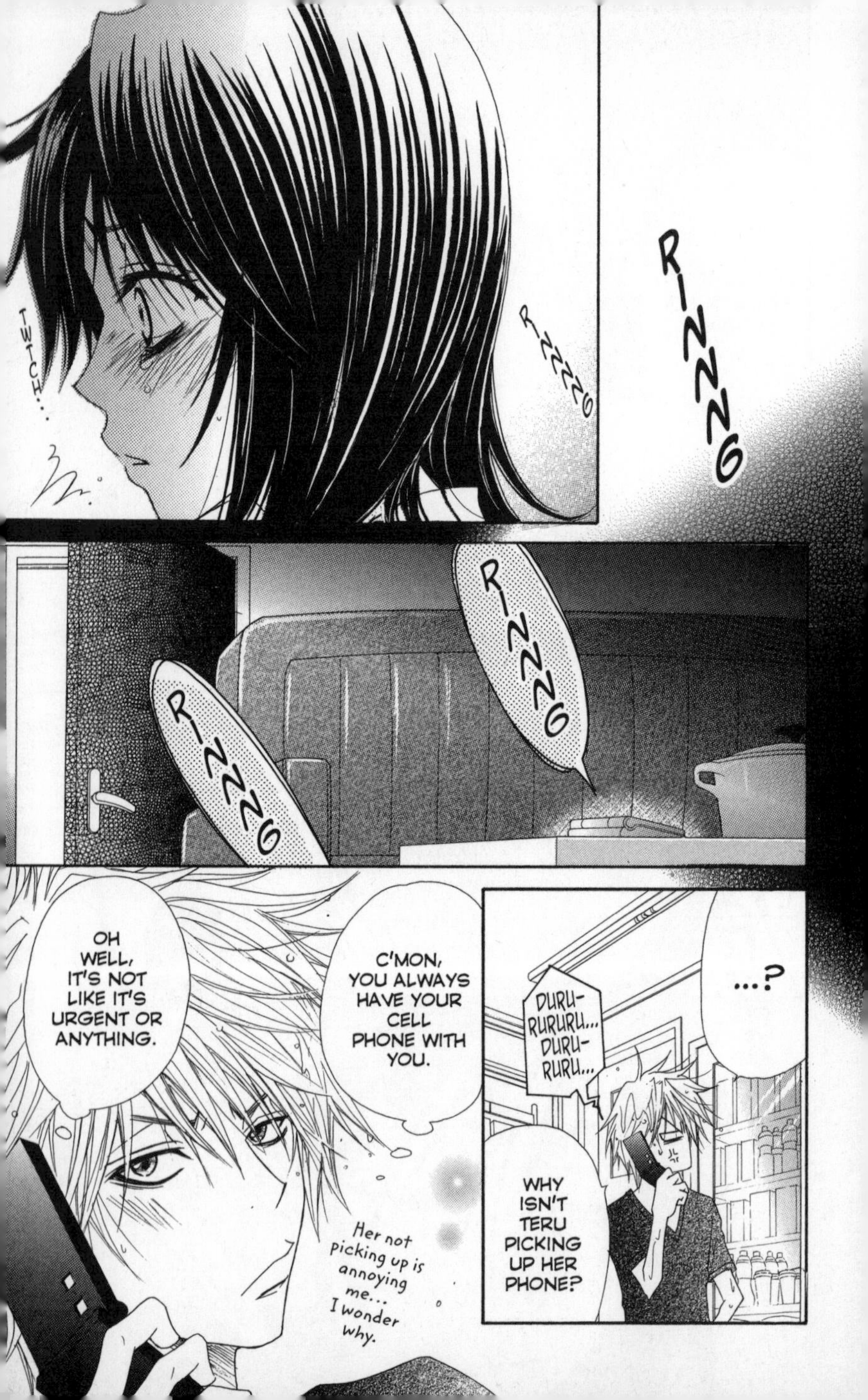

RINNNG
RIZZZZZG
TWITCH...
RINNNG
RINNNG
...?
DURU-RURURU... DURU-RURU...
WHY ISN'T TERU PICKING UP HER PHONE?
C'MON, YOU ALWAYS HAVE YOUR CELL PHONE WITH YOU.
OH WELL, IT'S NOT LIKE IT'S URGENT OR ANYTHING.
Her not picking up is annoying me... I wonder why.

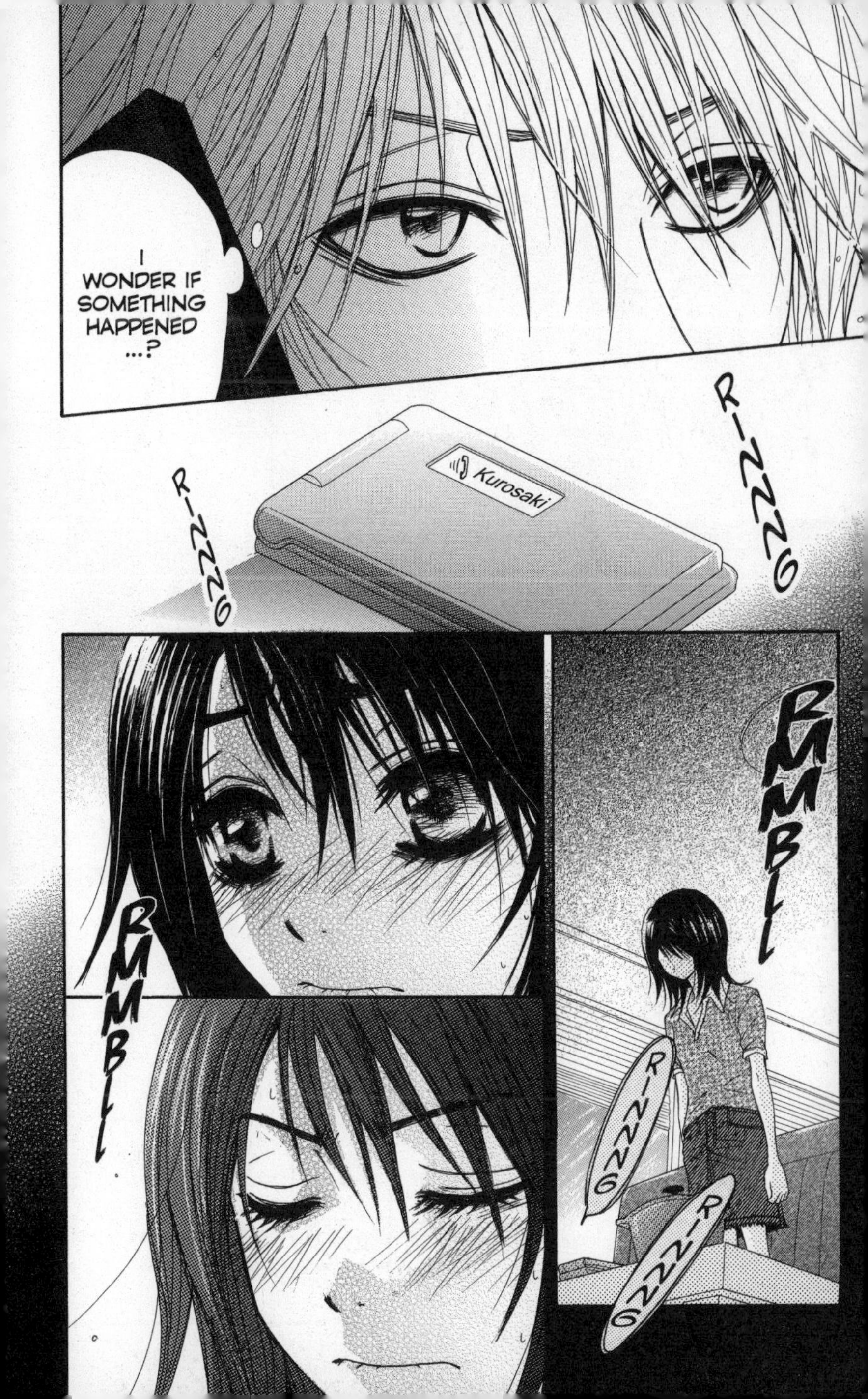
I WONDER IF SOMETHING HAPPENED ...?
RINNNG
Kurosaki
RINNNG
RUMBLL
RINNNG
RINNNG
RUMBLL

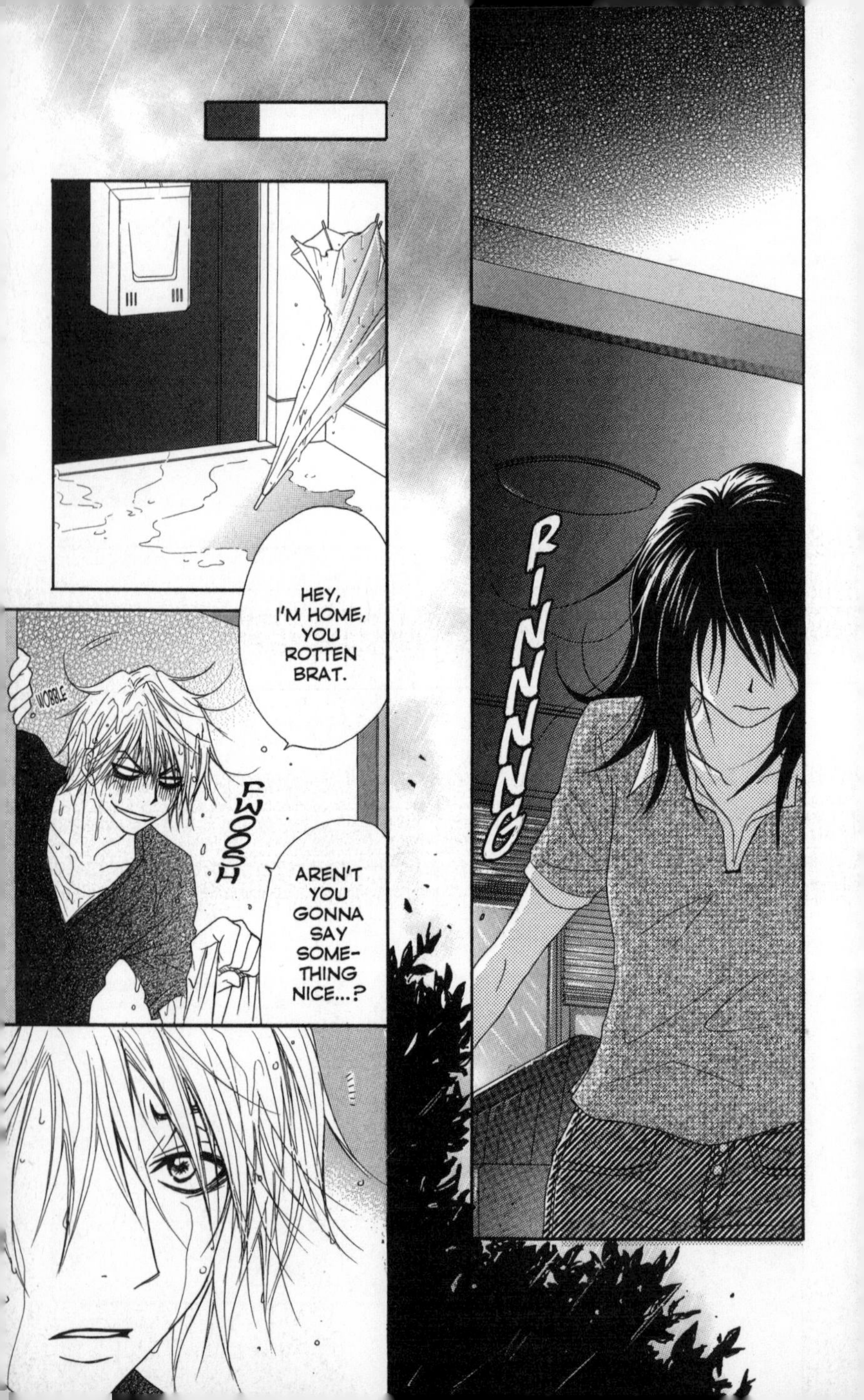
RINNNNG
HEY, I'M HOME, YOU ROTTEN BRAT.
WOBBLE
FWOOSH
AREN'T YOU GONNA SAY SOME-THING NICE...?

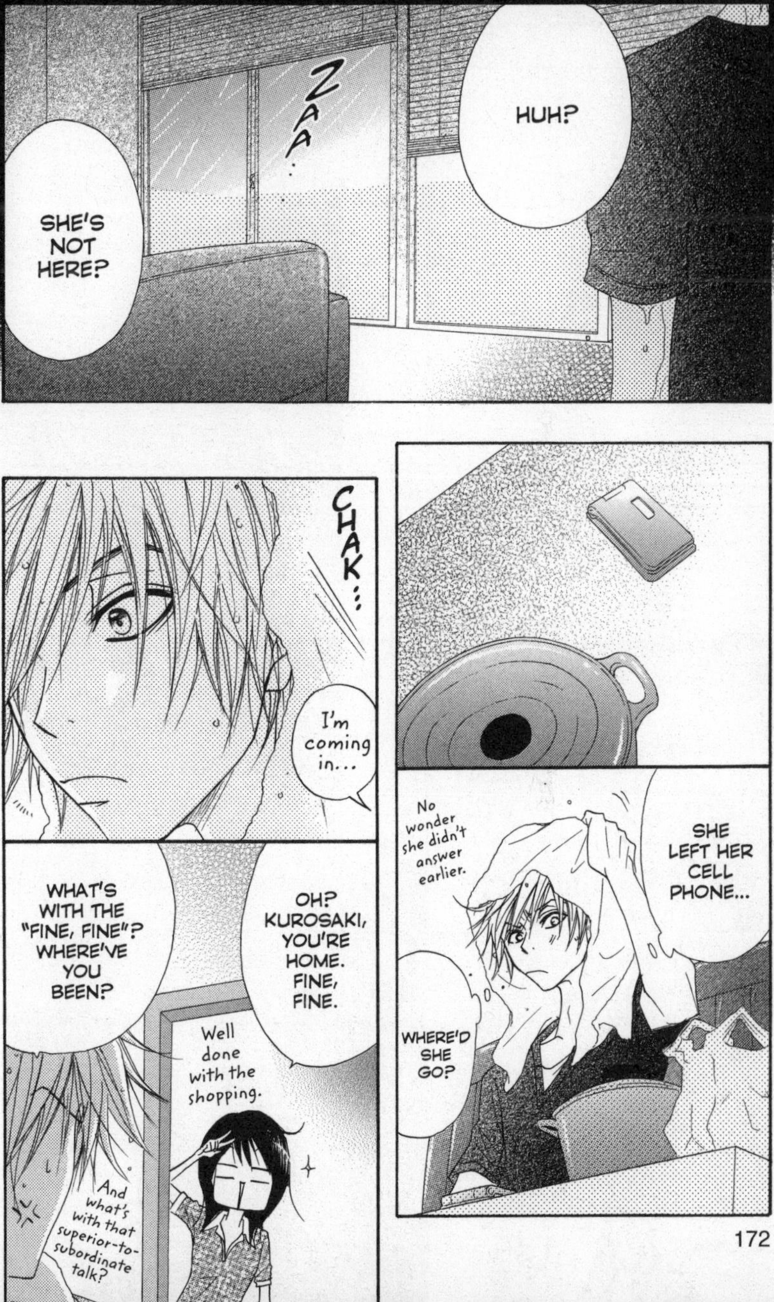
HUH?
ZAAA...
SHE'S NOT HERE?
CHAK...
I'm coming in...
SHE LEFT HER CELL PHONE...
No wonder she didn't answer earlier.
WHERE'D SHE GO?
OH? KUROSAKI, YOU'RE HOME. FINE, FINE.
Well done with the shopping.
WHAT'S WITH THE "FINE, FINE"? WHERE'VE YOU BEEN?
And what's with that superior-to-subordinate talk?

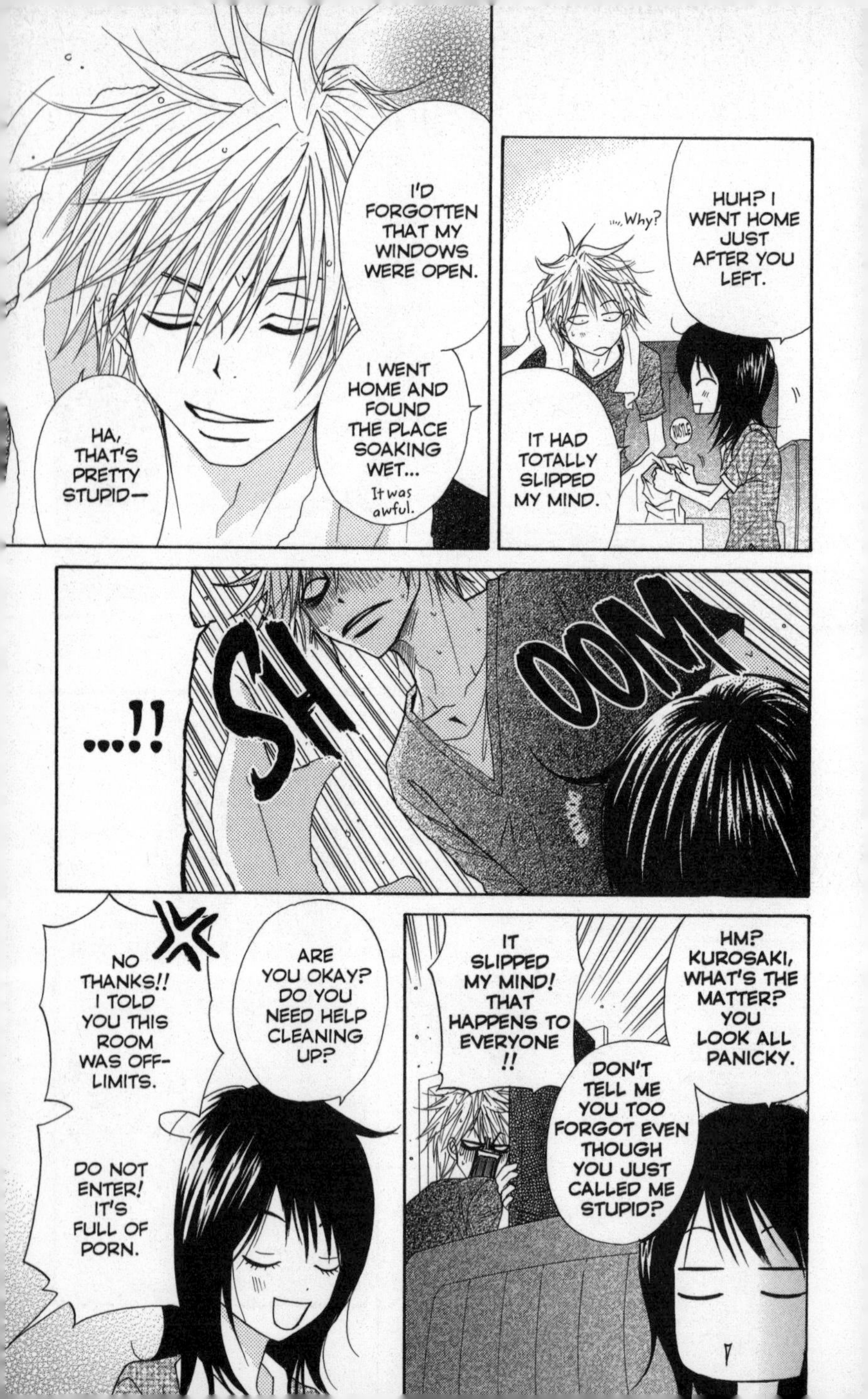
HUH? I WENT HOME JUST AFTER YOU LEFT.
...Why?
IT HAD TOTALLY SLIPPED MY MIND.
I'D FORGOTTEN THAT MY WINDOWS WERE OPEN.
I WENT HOME AND FOUND THE PLACE SOAKING WET...
It was awful.
HA, THAT'S PRETTY STUPID—
SHOOM
...!!
HM? KUROSAKI, WHAT'S THE MATTER? YOU LOOK ALL PANICKY.
IT SLIPPED MY MIND! THAT HAPPENS TO EVERYONE!!
DON'T TELL ME YOU TOO FORGOT EVEN THOUGH YOU JUST CALLED ME STUPID?
ARE YOU OKAY? DO YOU NEED HELP CLEANING UP?
NO THANKS!! I TOLD YOU THIS ROOM WAS OFF-LIMITS.
DO NOT ENTER! IT'S FULL OF PORN.

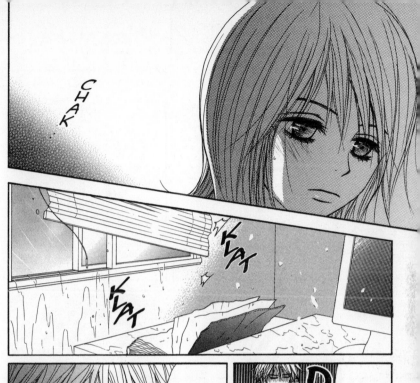

CHAK

KPAT

KPAT

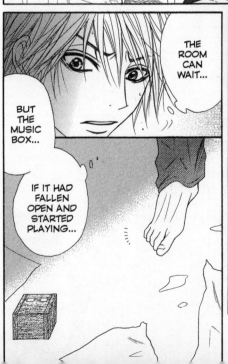

THE ROOM CAN WAIT...

BUT THE MUSIC BOX...

IF IT HAD FALLEN OPEN AND STARTED PLAYING...

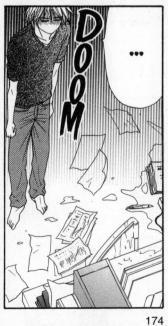

DOOM

...

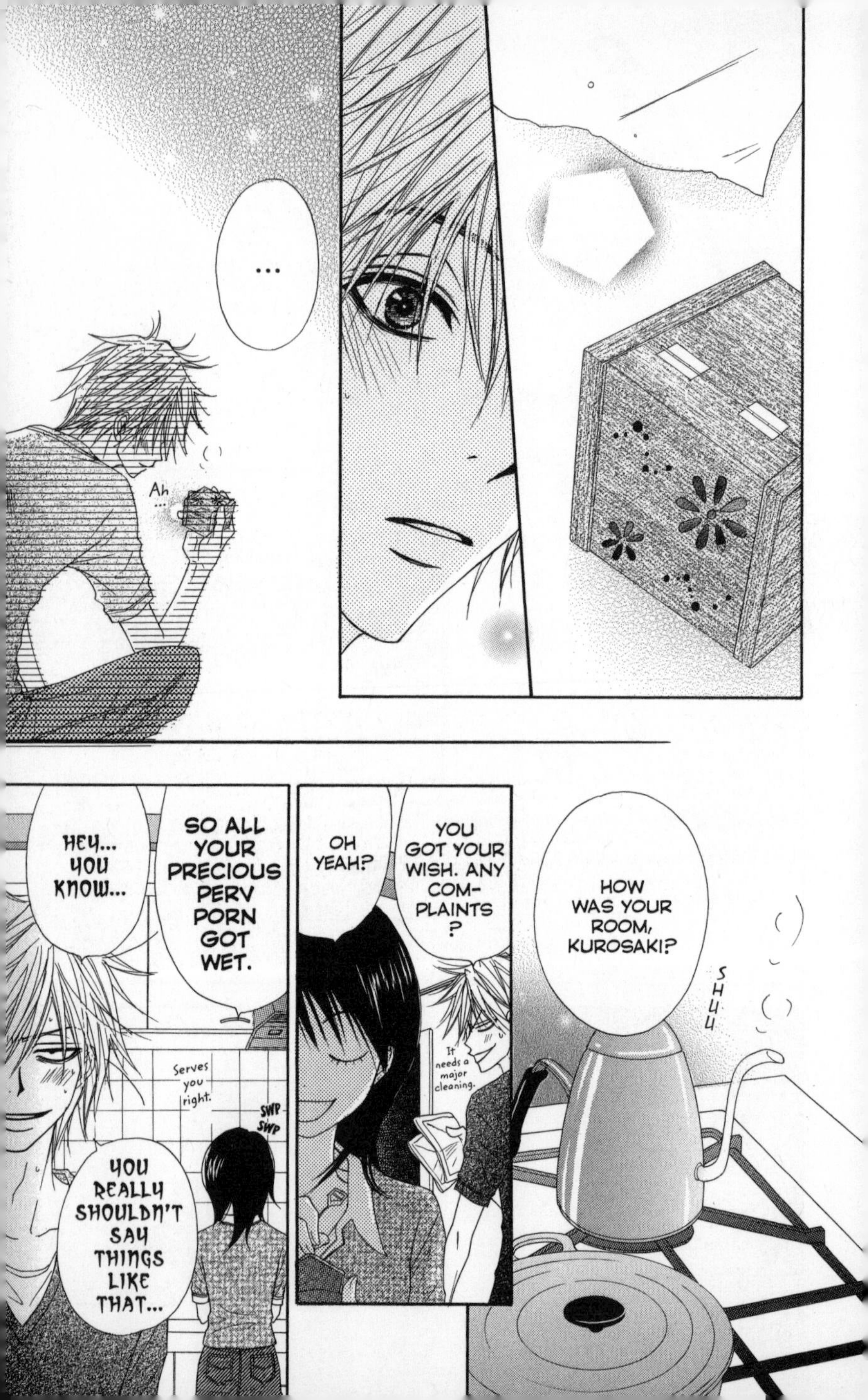
...
Ah...
HOW WAS YOUR ROOM, KUROSAKI?
SHUU
YOU GOT YOUR WISH. ANY COM-PLAINTS?
OH YEAH?
It needs a major cleaning.
SO ALL YOUR PRECIOUS PERV PORN GOT WET.
HEY... YOU KNOW...
Serves you right.
SWP SWP
YOU REALLY SHOULDN'T SAY THINGS LIKE THAT...

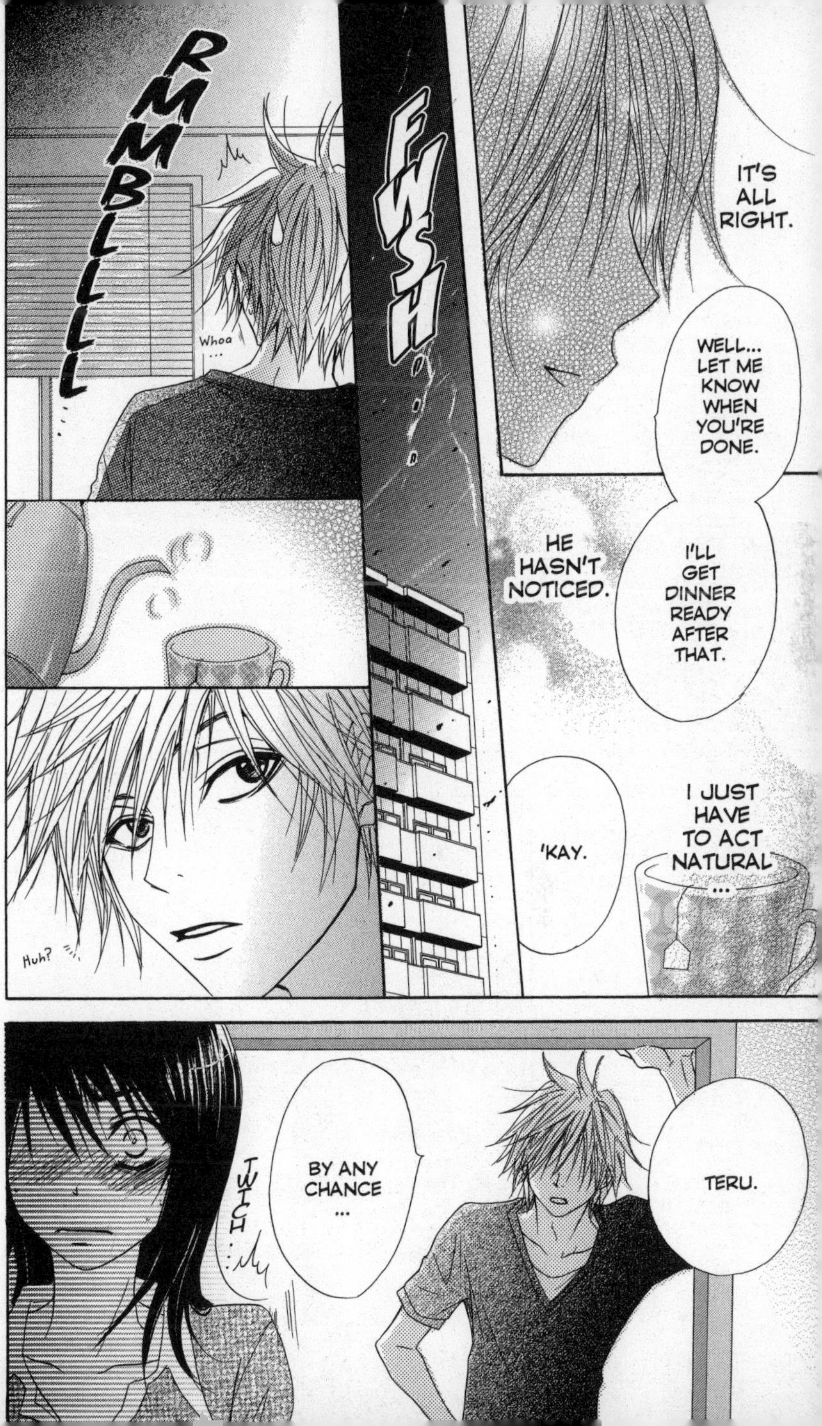
IT'S ALL RIGHT.
WELL... LET ME KNOW WHEN YOU'RE DONE.
I'LL GET DINNER READY AFTER THAT.
HE HASN'T NOTICED.
I JUST HAVE TO ACT NATURAL...
'KAY.
FWSH...
RMMBLLLL
Whoa...
Huh?
TERU.
BY ANY CHANCE...
TWITCH...

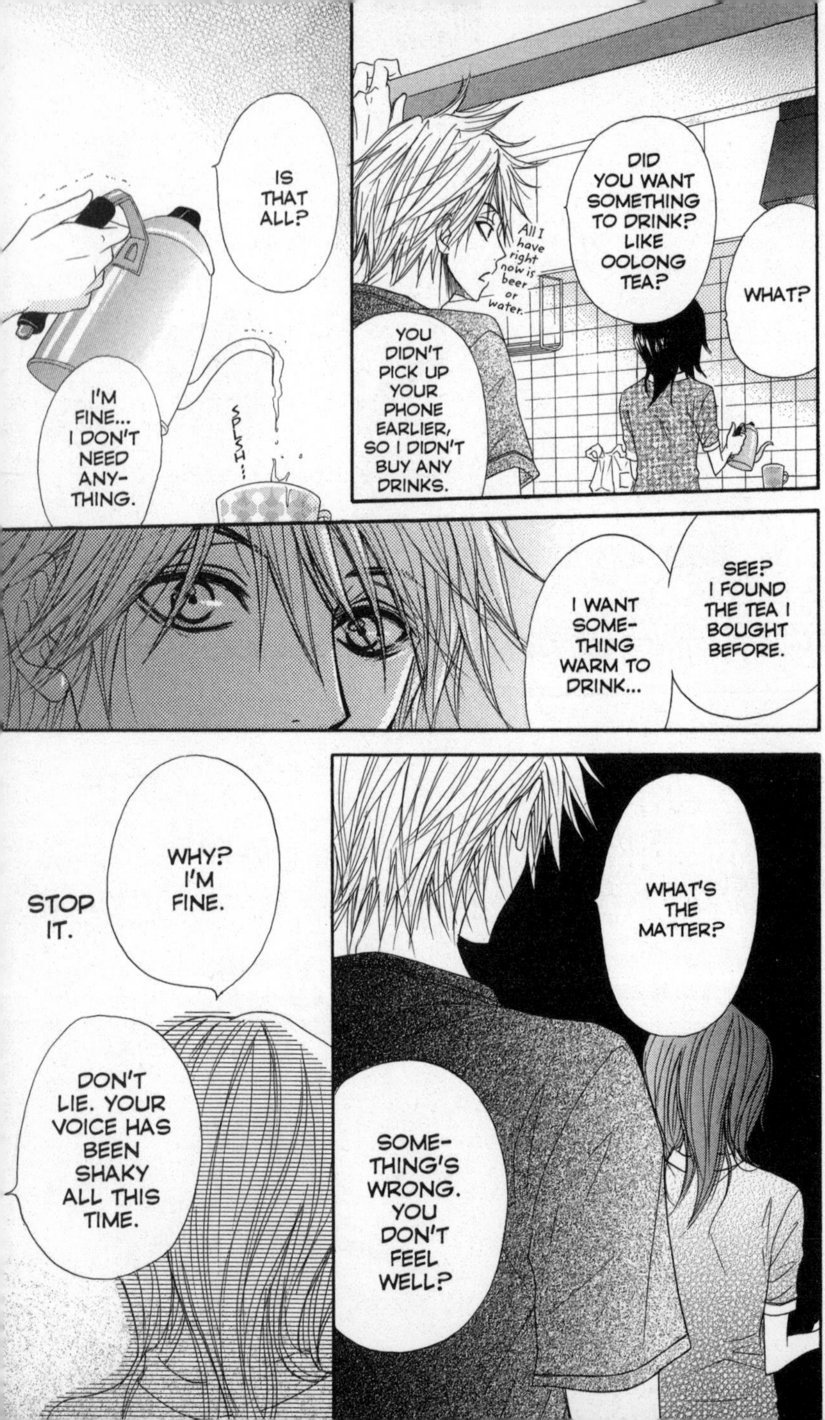
DID YOU WANT SOMETHING TO DRINK? LIKE OOLONG TEA?
All I have right now is beer or water.
WHAT?
YOU DIDN'T PICK UP YOUR PHONE EARLIER, SO I DIDN'T BUY ANY DRINKS.
IS THAT ALL?
I'M FINE... I DON'T NEED ANY-THING.
SPLSH...
SEE? I FOUND THE TEA I BOUGHT BEFORE.
I WANT SOME-THING WARM TO DRINK...
WHAT'S THE MATTER?
SOME-THING'S WRONG. YOU DON'T FEEL WELL?
WHY? I'M FINE.
STOP IT.
DON'T LIE. YOUR VOICE HAS BEEN SHAKY ALL THIS TIME.

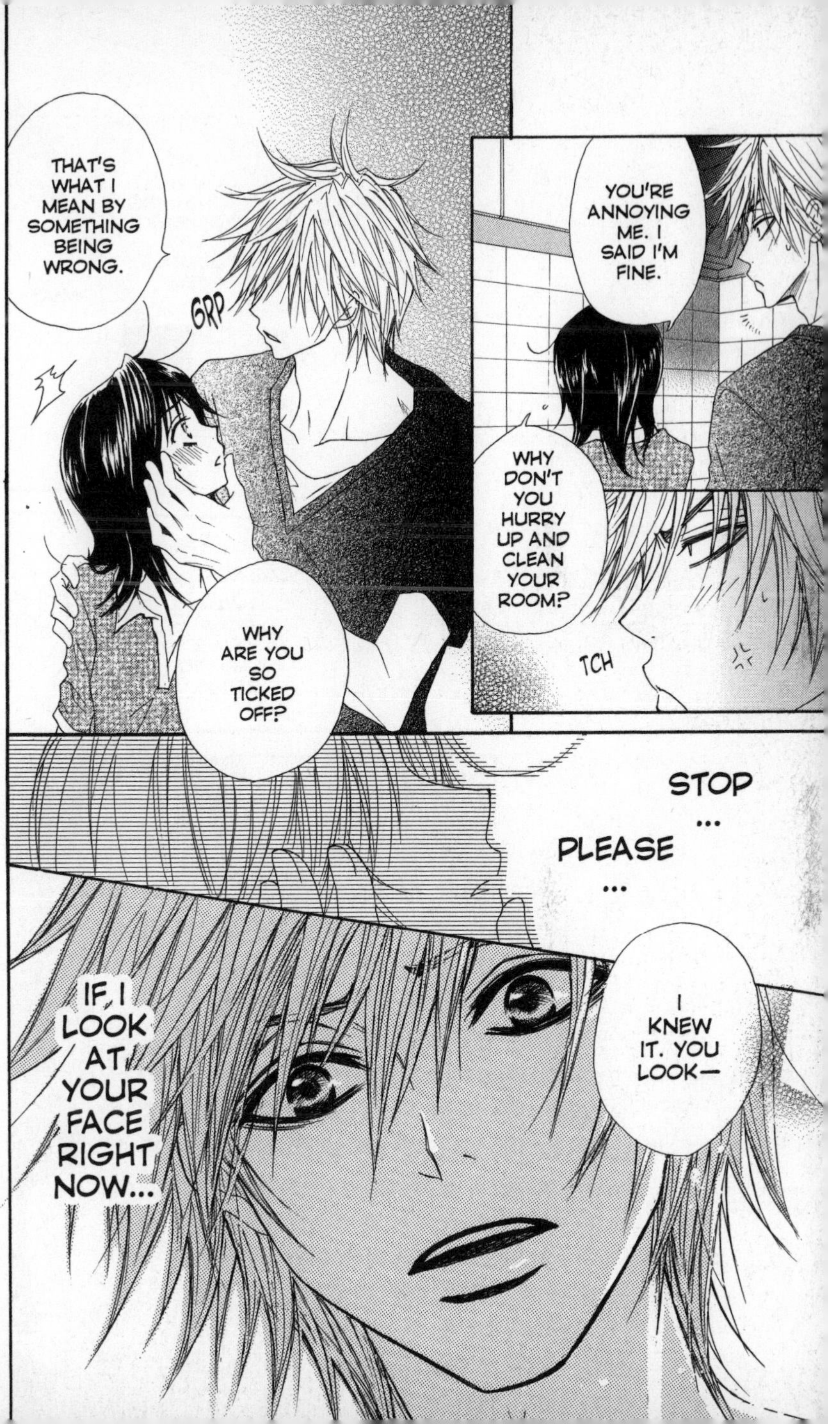
YOU'RE ANNOYING ME. I SAID I'M FINE.
WHY DON'T YOU HURRY UP AND CLEAN YOUR ROOM?
TCH
THAT'S WHAT I MEAN BY SOMETHING BEING WRONG.
GRP
WHY ARE YOU SO TICKED OFF?
STOP... PLEASE...
I KNEW IT. YOU LOOK—
IF I LOOK AT YOUR FACE RIGHT NOW...

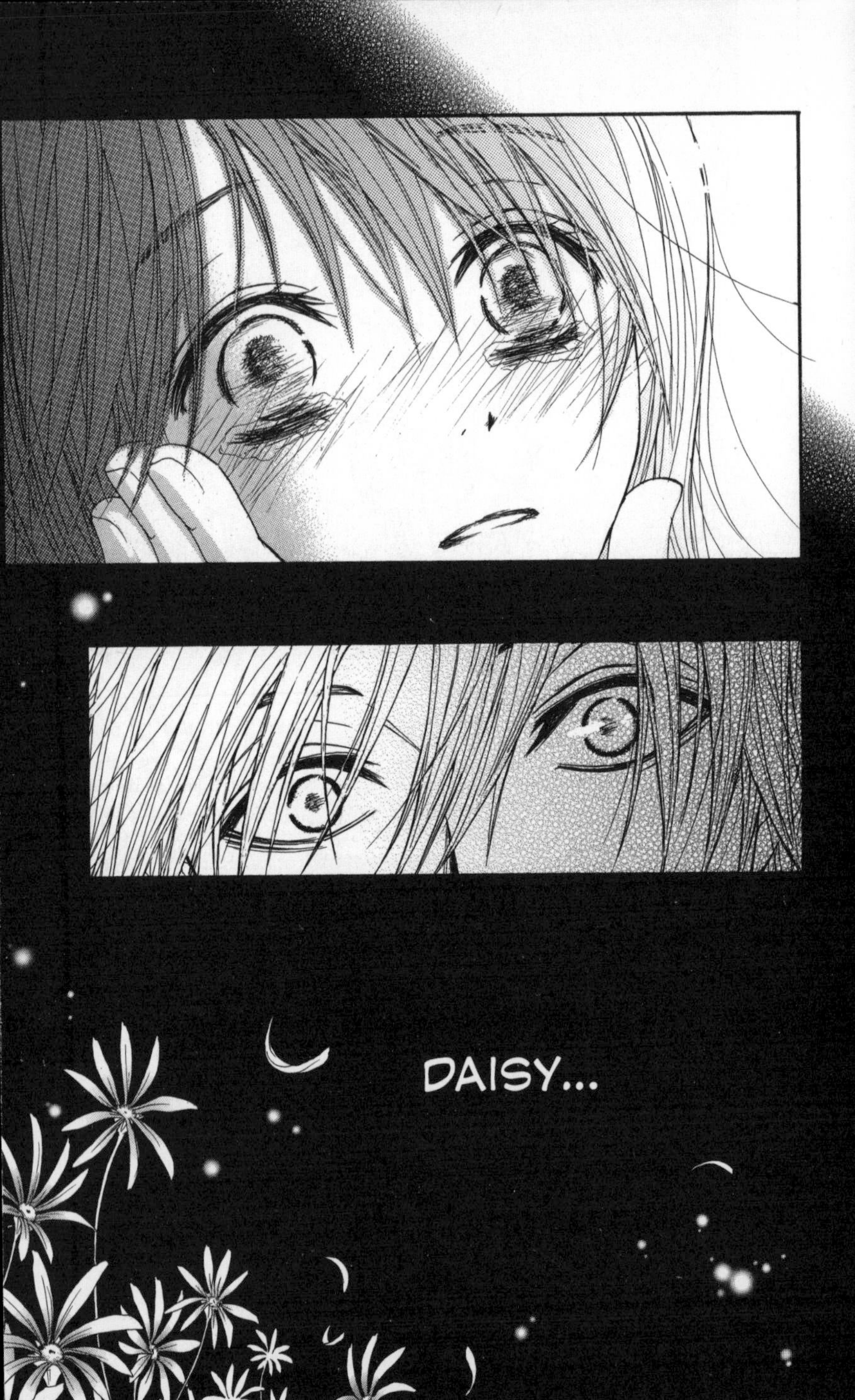
DAISY...

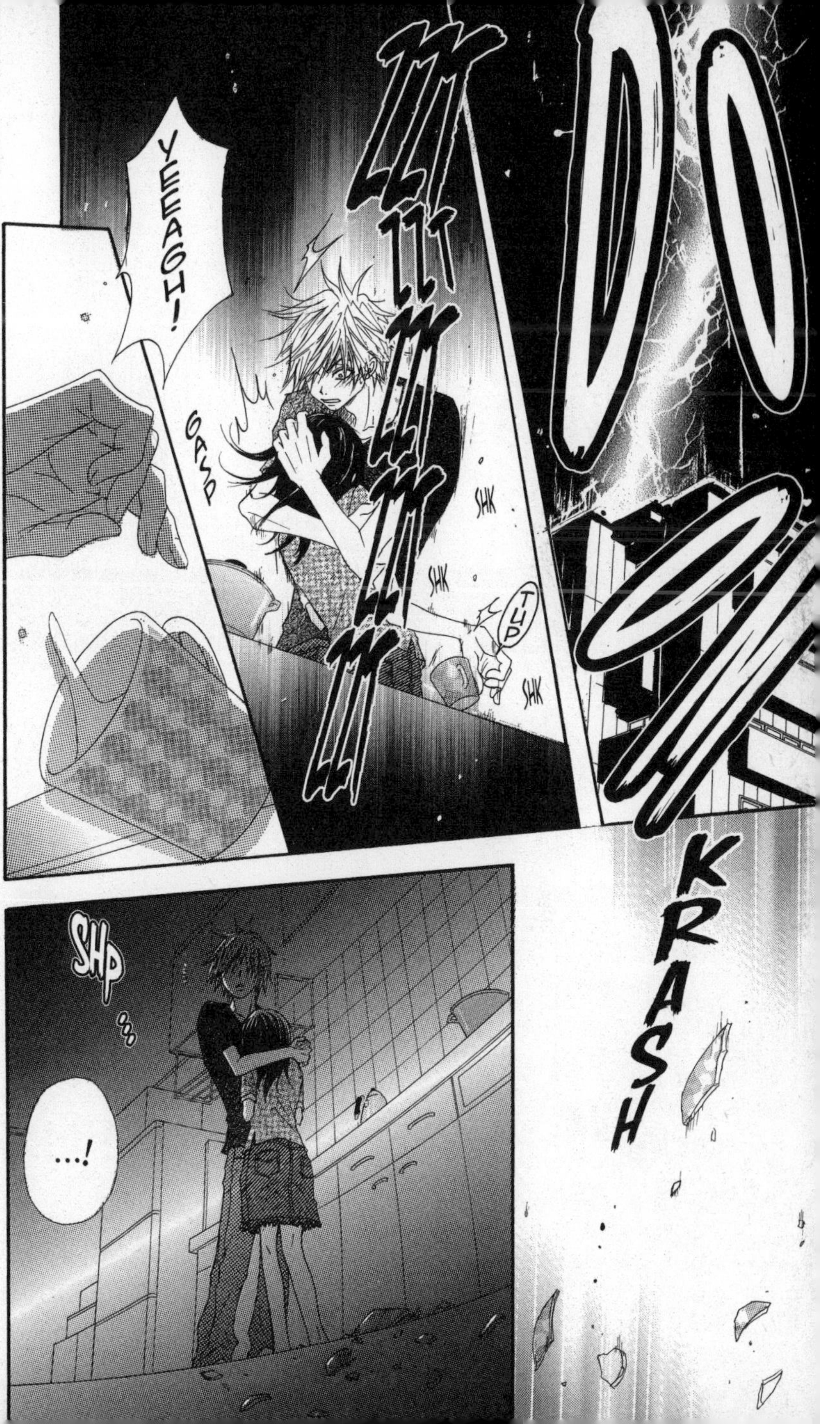
KRASH
SHK
SHK
TUP
SHK
GASP
YEEAGH!
SHP
...!

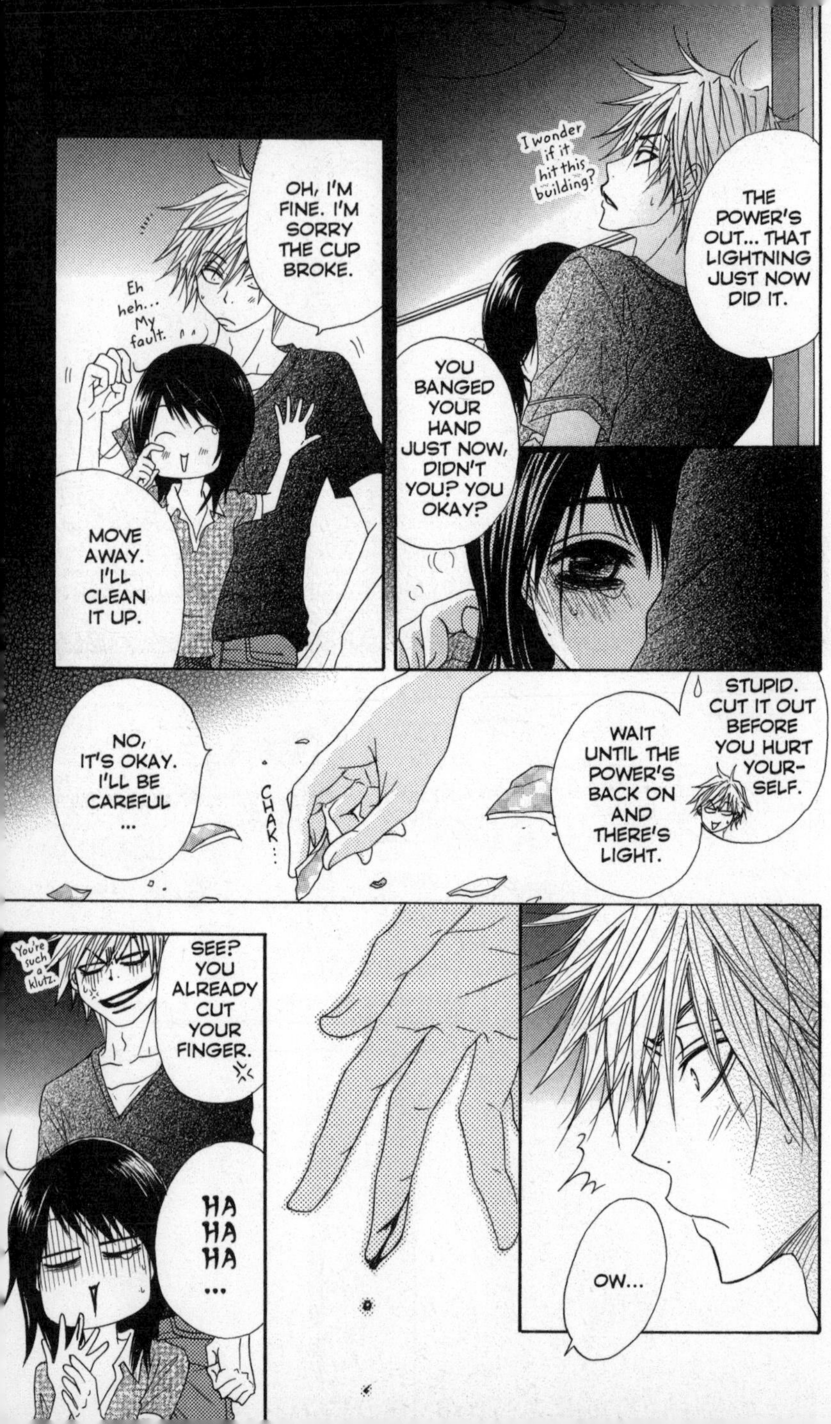
I wonder if it hit this building?
THE POWER'S OUT... THAT LIGHTNING JUST NOW DID IT.
YOU BANGED YOUR HAND JUST NOW, DIDN'T YOU? YOU OKAY?
OH, I'M FINE. I'M SORRY THE CUP BROKE.
Eh heh... My fault.
MOVE AWAY. I'LL CLEAN IT UP.
STUPID. CUT IT OUT BEFORE YOU HURT YOURSELF.
WAIT UNTIL THE POWER'S BACK ON AND THERE'S LIGHT.
CHAK...
NO, IT'S OKAY. I'LL BE CAREFUL...
OW...
SEE? YOU ALREADY CUT YOUR FINGER.
You're such a klutz.
HA HA HA...

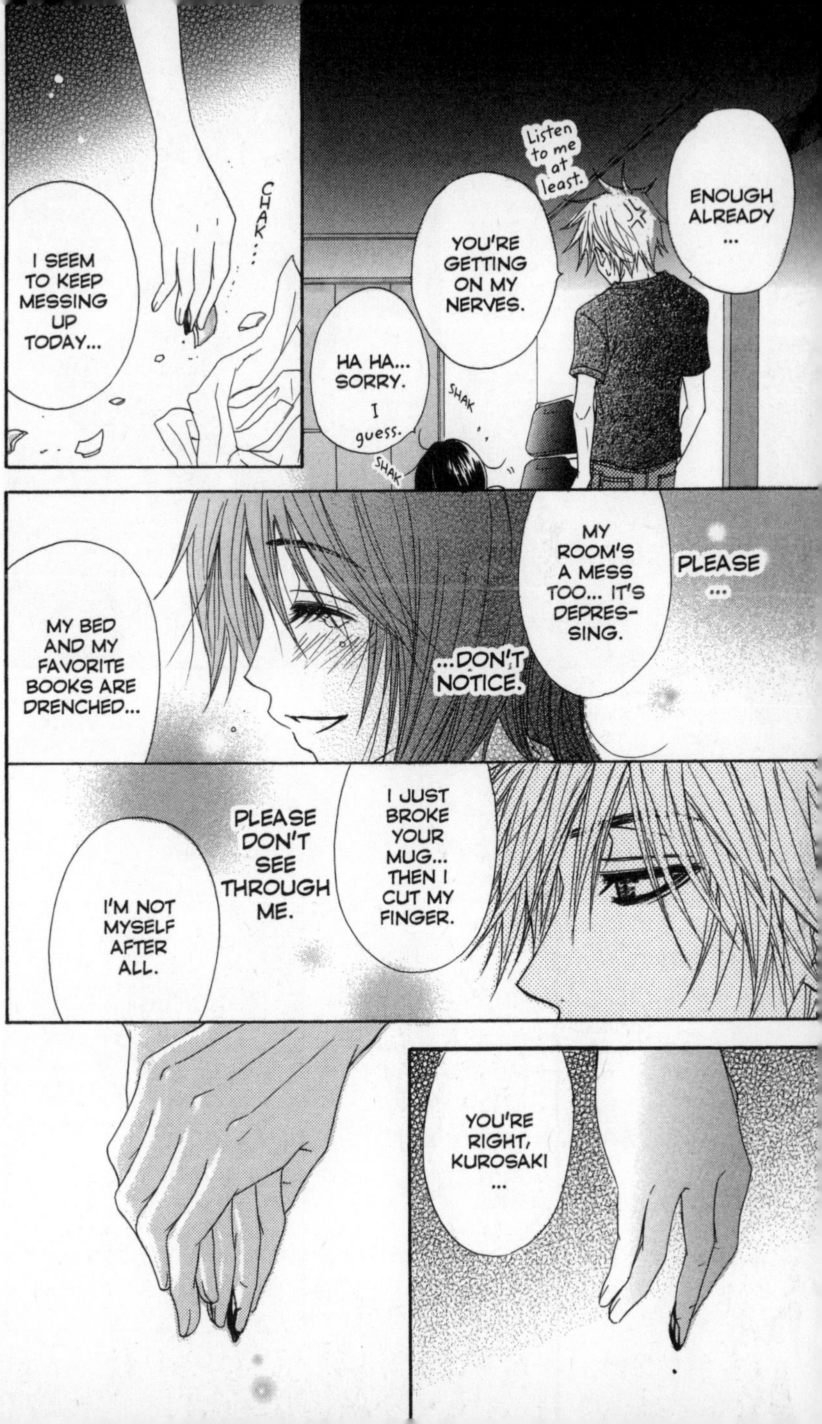
ENOUGH ALREADY...
Listen to me at least.
YOU'RE GETTING ON MY NERVES.
HA HA... SORRY.
I guess.
SHAK
SHAK
CHAK...
I SEEM TO KEEP MESSING UP TODAY...
PLEASE...
MY ROOM'S A MESS TOO... IT'S DEPRES-SING.
...DON'T NOTICE.
MY BED AND MY FAVORITE BOOKS ARE DRENCHED...
I JUST BROKE YOUR MUG... THEN I CUT MY FINGER.
PLEASE DON'T SEE THROUGH ME.
I'M NOT MYSELF AFTER ALL.
YOU'RE RIGHT, KUROSAKI...

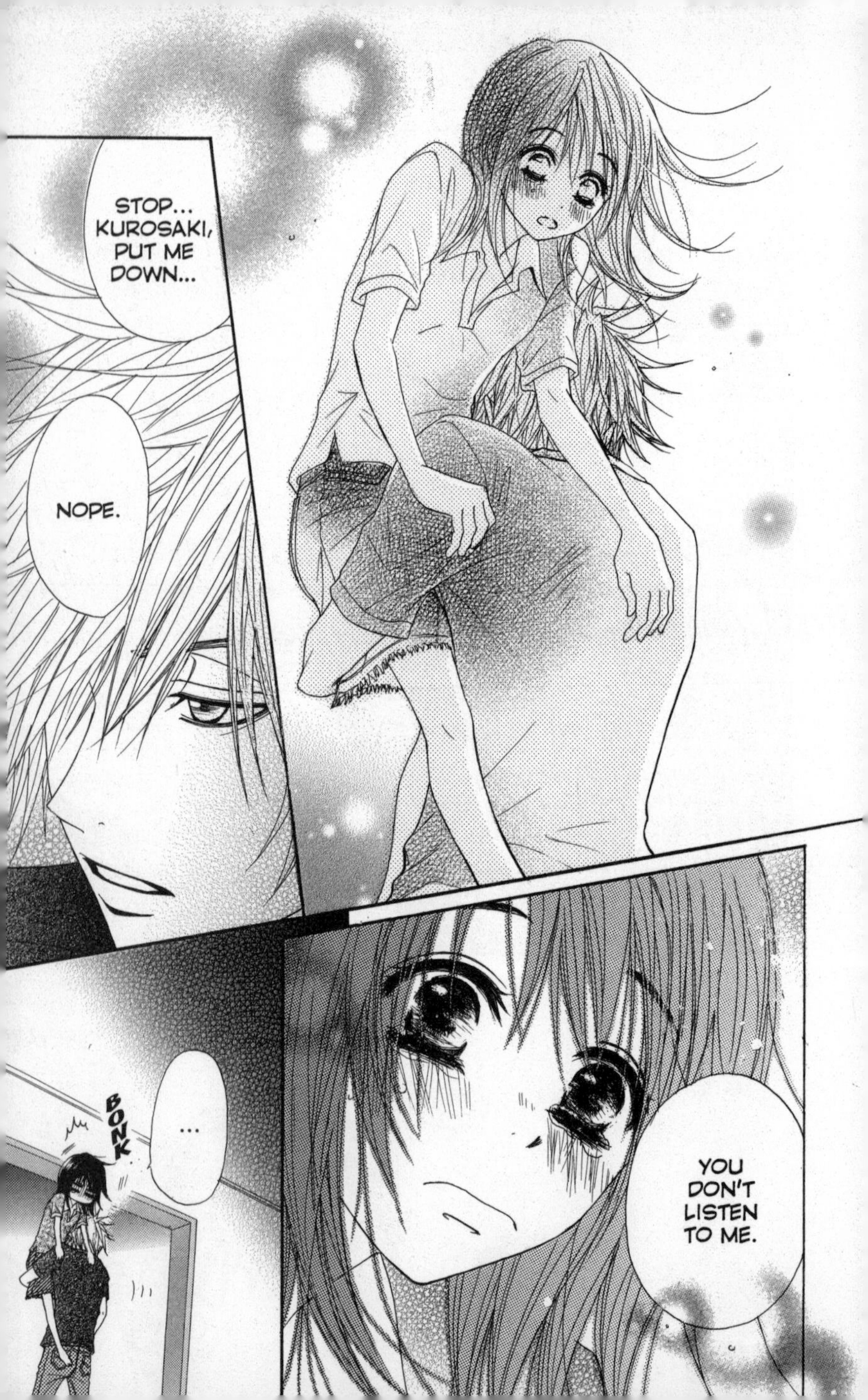
STOP... KUROSAKI, PUT ME DOWN...
NOPE.
YOU DON'T LISTEN TO ME.
...
BONK

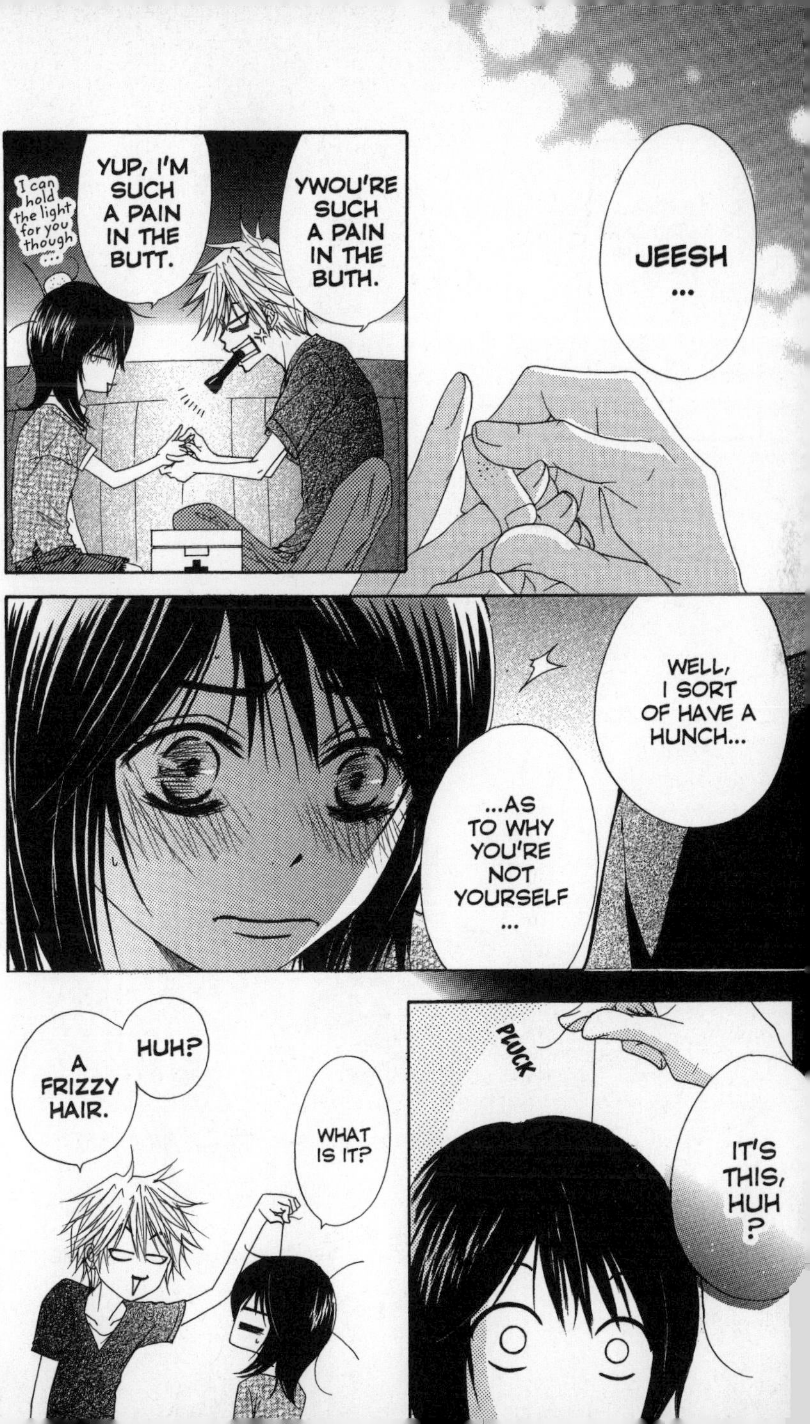
JEESH ...
YWOU'RE SUCH A PAIN IN THE BUTH.
YUP, I'M SUCH A PAIN IN THE BUTT.
I can hold the light for you though ...
WELL, I SORT OF HAVE A HUNCH...
...AS TO WHY YOU'RE NOT YOURSELF ...
PLUCK
IT'S THIS, HUH?
WHAT IS IT?
A FRIZZY HAIR.
HUH?

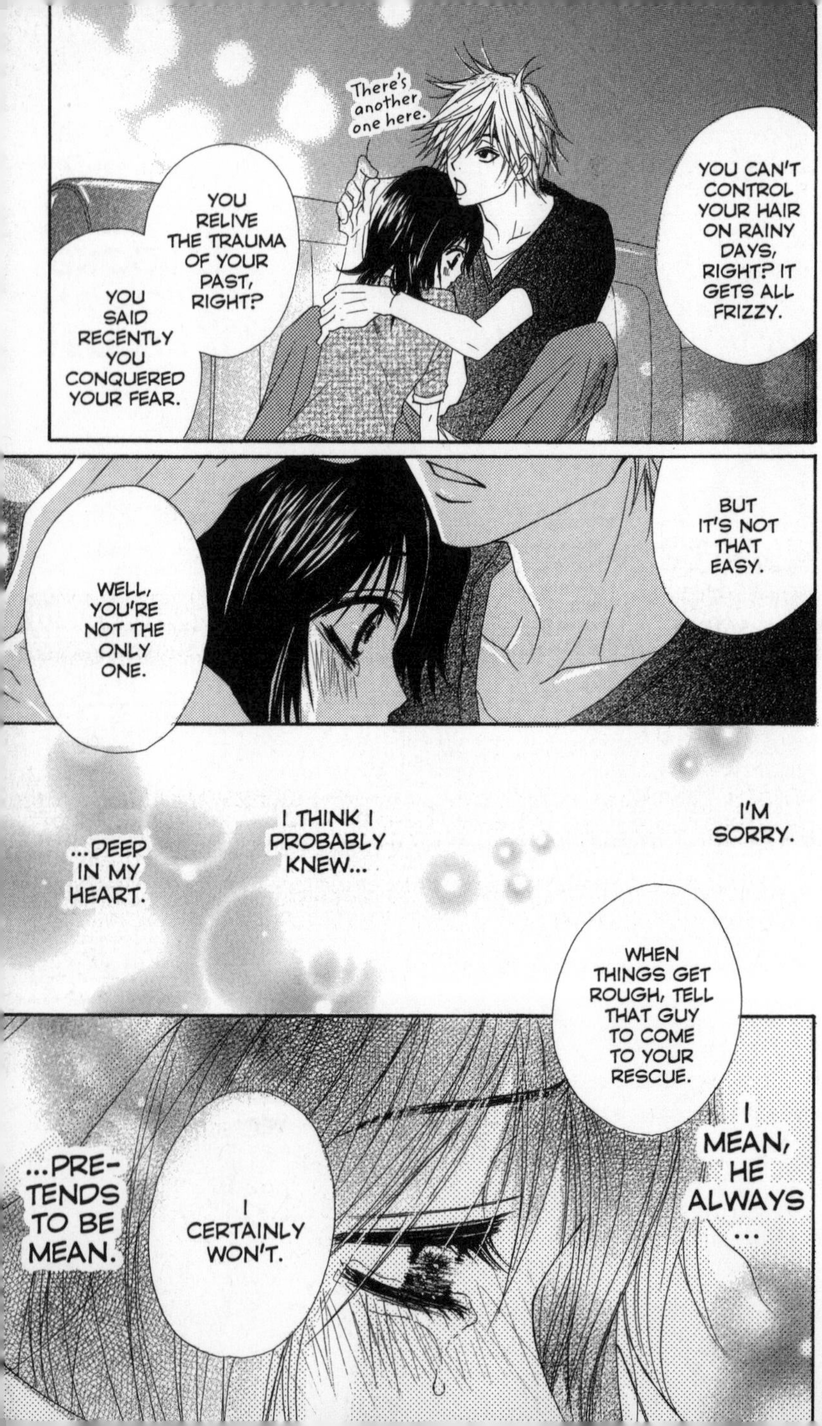
There's another one here.
YOU CAN'T CONTROL YOUR HAIR ON RAINY DAYS, RIGHT? IT GETS ALL FRIZZY.
YOU RELIVE THE TRAUMA OF YOUR PAST, RIGHT?
YOU SAID RECENTLY YOU CONQUERED YOUR FEAR.
BUT IT'S NOT THAT EASY.
WELL, YOU'RE NOT THE ONLY ONE.
I'M SORRY.
I THINK I PROBABLY KNEW...
...DEEP IN MY HEART.
WHEN THINGS GET ROUGH, TELL THAT GUY TO COME TO YOUR RESCUE.
I MEAN, HE ALWAYS ...
I CERTAINLY WON'T.
...PRE-TENDS TO BE MEAN.

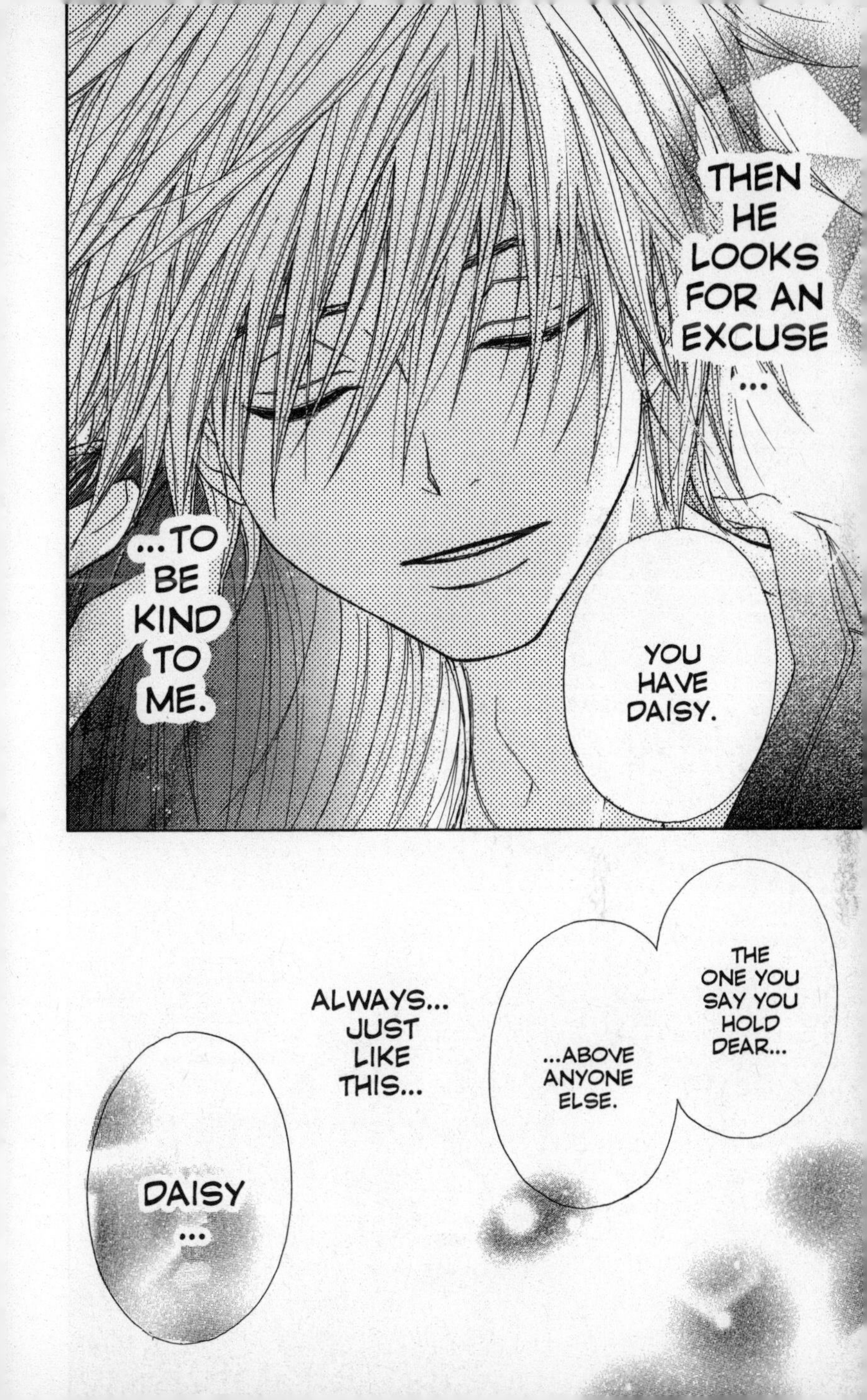
THEN HE LOOKS FOR AN EXCUSE ...
...TO BE KIND TO ME.
YOU HAVE DAISY.
THE ONE YOU SAY YOU HOLD DEAR...
...ABOVE ANYONE ELSE.
ALWAYS... JUST LIKE THIS...
DAISY ...

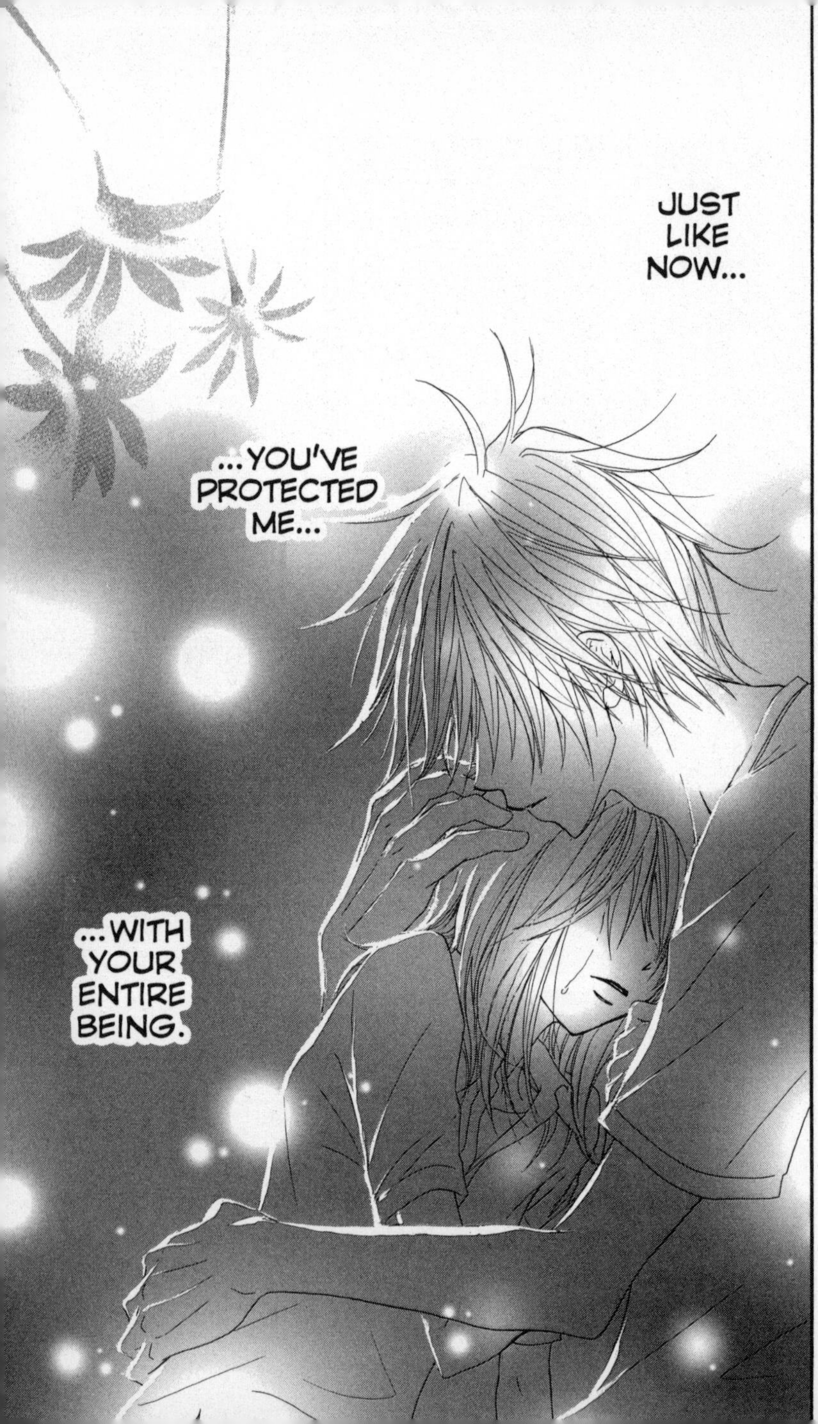
JUST LIKE NOW...
...YOU'VE PROTECTED ME...
...WITH YOUR ENTIRE BEING.

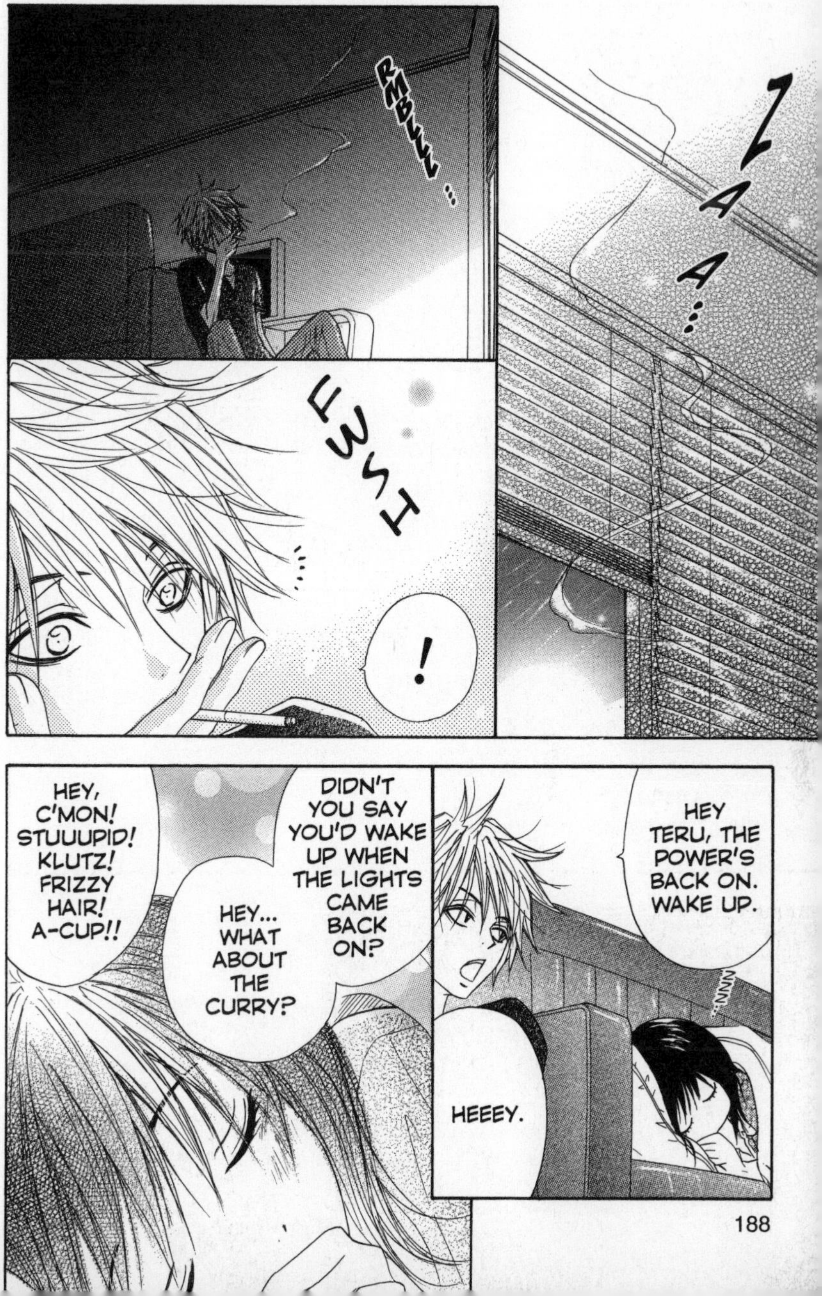
ZAAA...
RMBLLLL...
HISS
!
HEY TERU, THE POWER'S BACK ON. WAKE UP.
NNN...
HEEEY.
DIDN'T YOU SAY YOU'D WAKE UP WHEN THE LIGHTS CAME BACK ON?
HEY... WHAT ABOUT THE CURRY?
HEY, C'MON! STUUUPID! KLUTZ! FRIZZY HAIR! A-CUP!!

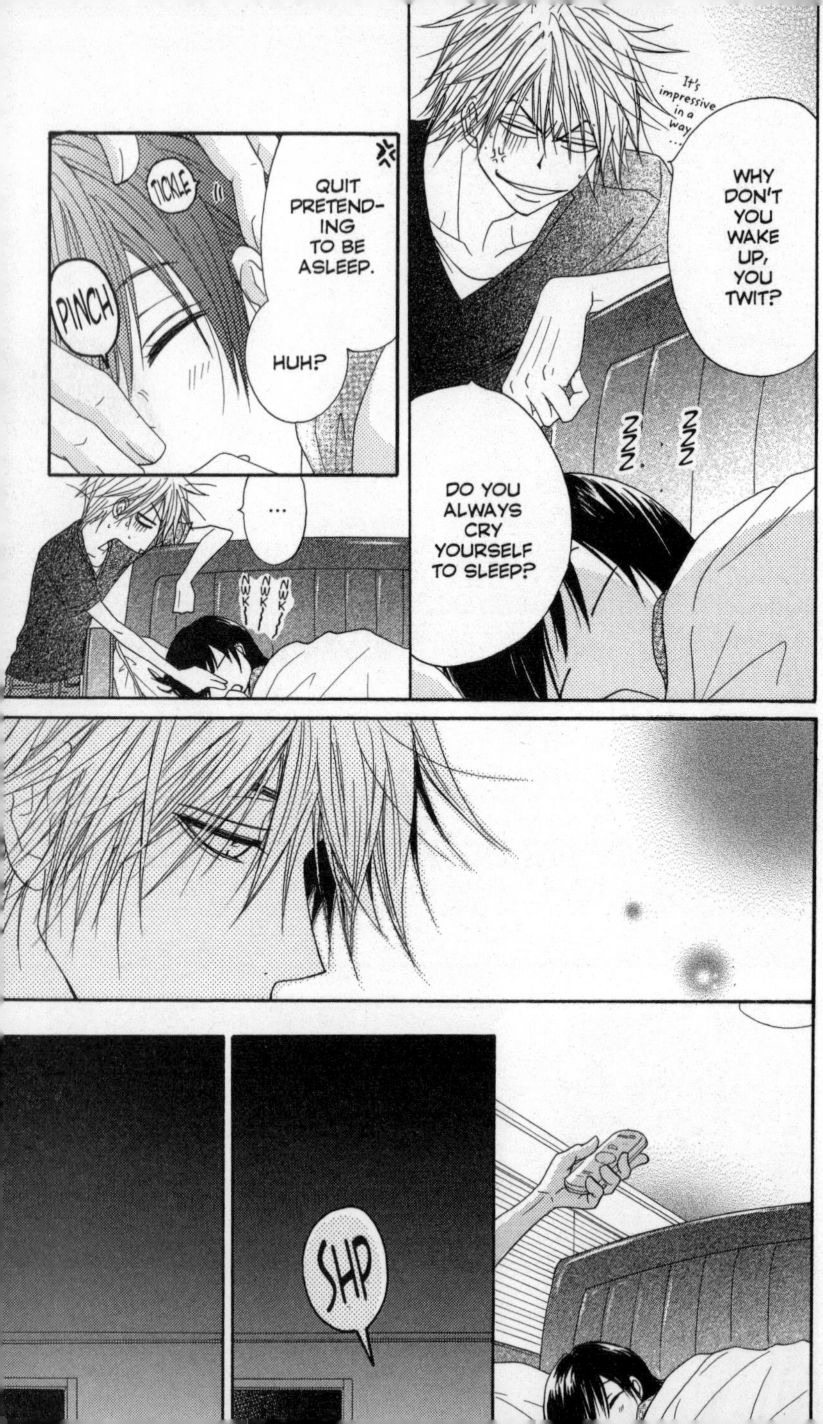
It's impressive in a way...
WHY DON'T YOU WAKE UP, YOU TWIT?
ZZZ ZZZ
DO YOU ALWAYS CRY YOURSELF TO SLEEP?
QUIT PRETENDING TO BE ASLEEP.
TICKLE
PINCH
HUH?
...
NWK NWK NWK
SHP

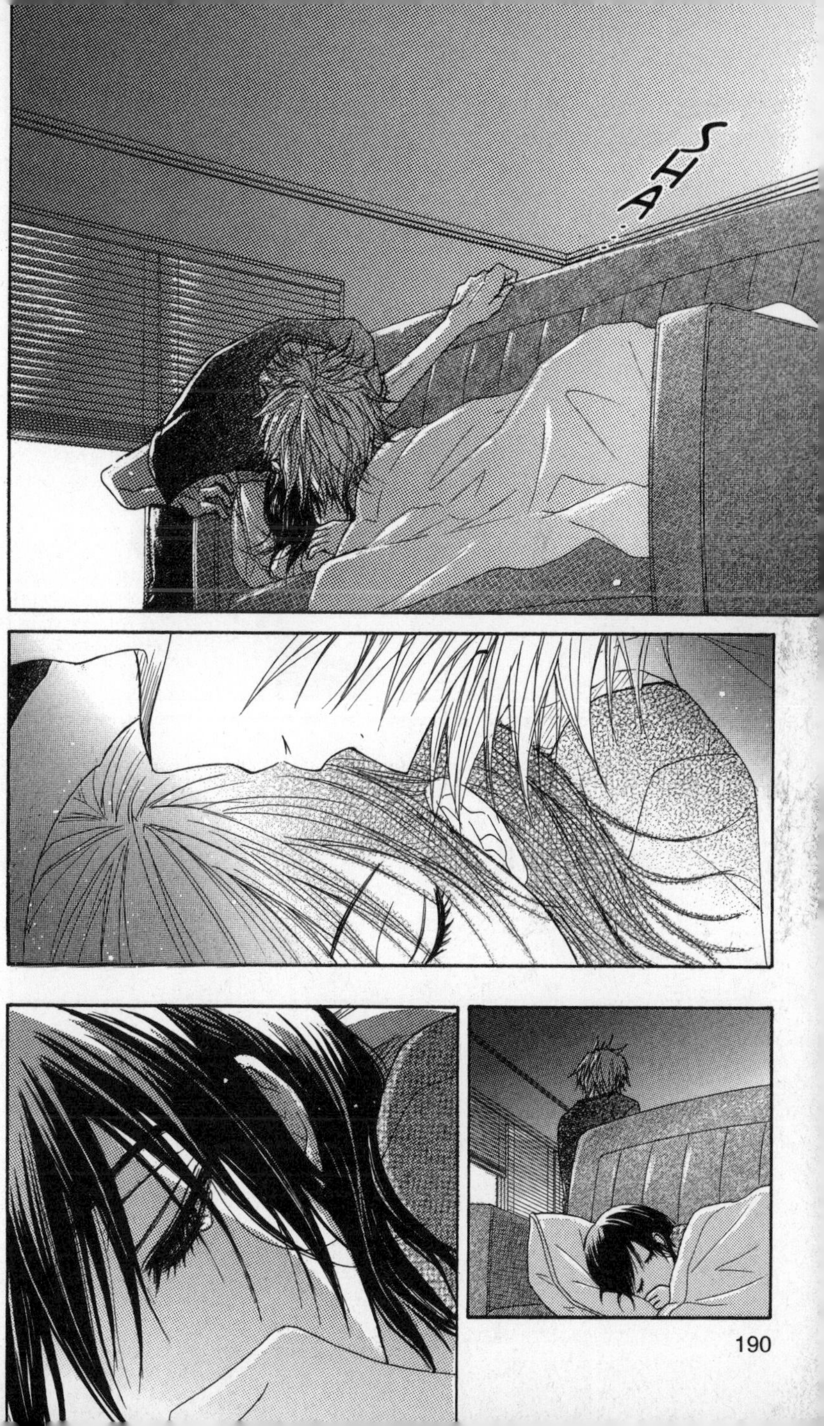
SHA...

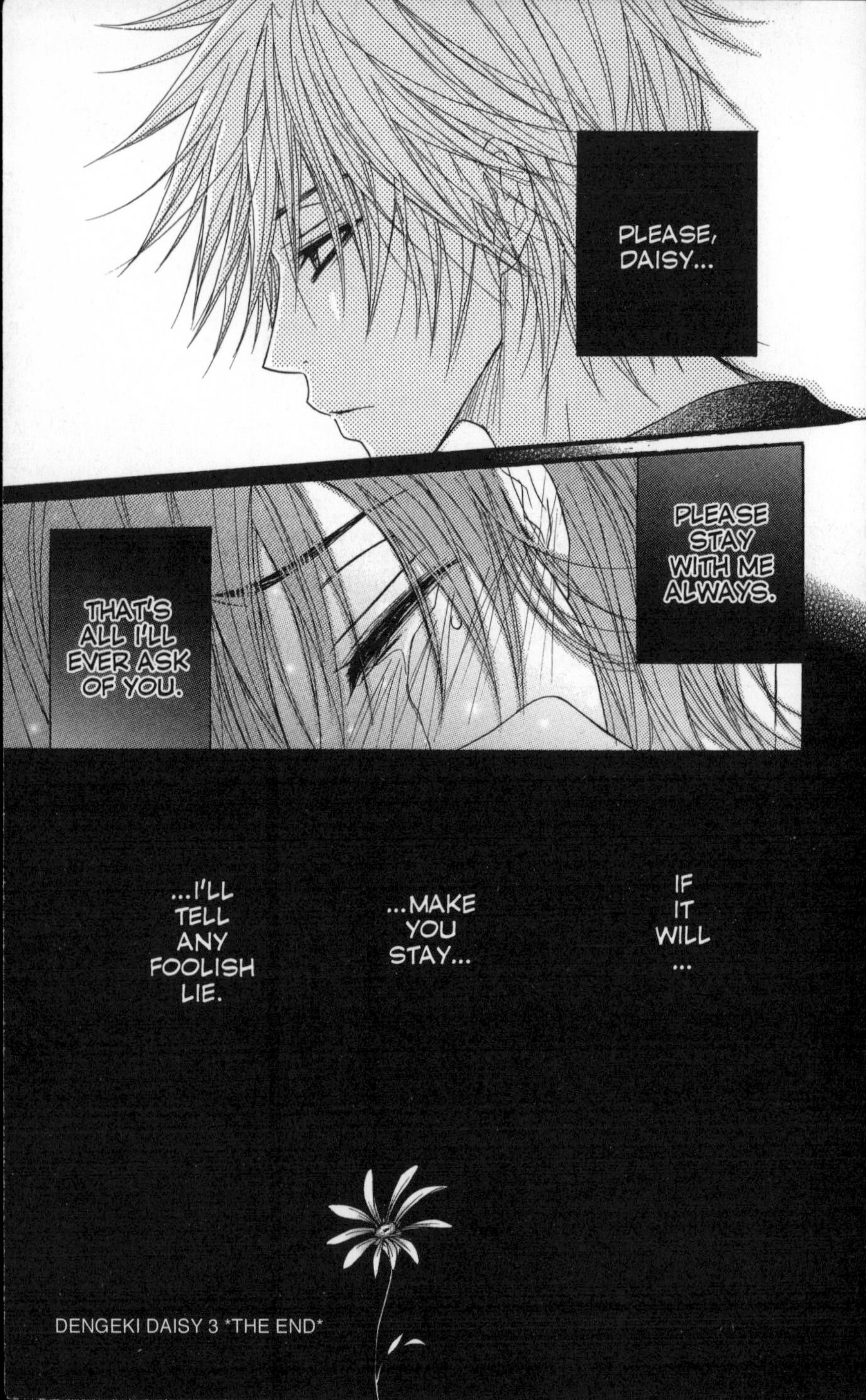

PLEASE, DAISY...

PLEASE STAY WITH ME ALWAYS.

THAT'S ALL I'LL EVER ASK OF YOU.

...I'LL TELL ANY FOOLISH LIE.

...MAKE YOU STAY...

IF IT WILL ...

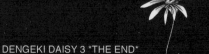

DENGEKI DAISY 3 *THE END*

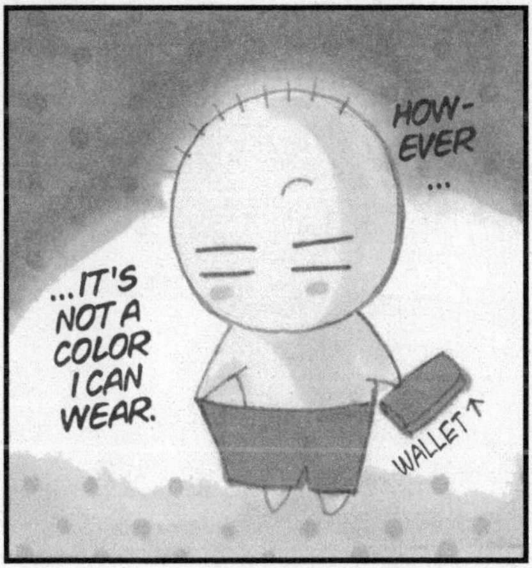
HOW-EVER...
...IT'S NOT A COLOR I CAN WEAR.
WALLET

Bright blue with a hint of green is one of my favorite colors. I get a bit excited when I see little items or shop signs around town in this color.

-Kyousuke Motomi

Born on August 1, Kyousuke Motomi debuted in *Deluxe Betsucomi* with *Hetakuso Kyupiddo* (No-Good Cupid) in 2002. She is the creator of *Otokomae! Biizu Kurabu* (Handsome! Beads Club), and her latest work, *Dengeki Daisy,* is currently being serialized in *Betsucomi.* Motomi enjoys sleeping, tea ceremonies and reading Haruki Murakami.

DENGEKI DAISY
VOL. 3
Shojo Beat Edition

STORY AND ART BY
KYOUSUKE MOTOMI

© 2007 Kyousuke MOTOMI/Shogakukan
All rights reserved.
Original Japanese edition "DENGEKI DAISY"
published by SHOGAKUKAN Inc.

Translation & Adaptation/JN Productions
Touch-up Art & Lettering/Rina Mapa
Cover Design/Yukiko Whitley
Interior Design/Nozomi Akashi
Editor/Amy Yu

Printed in the U.S.A.

Published by VIZ Media, LLC
P.O. Box 77010
San Francisco, CA 94107

10 9 8 7 6
First printing, January 2011
Sixth printing, November 2017

www.viz.com   www.shojobeat.com

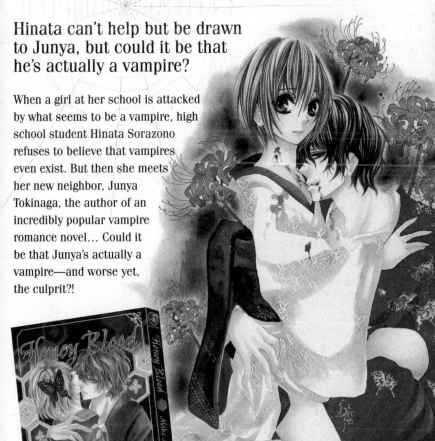

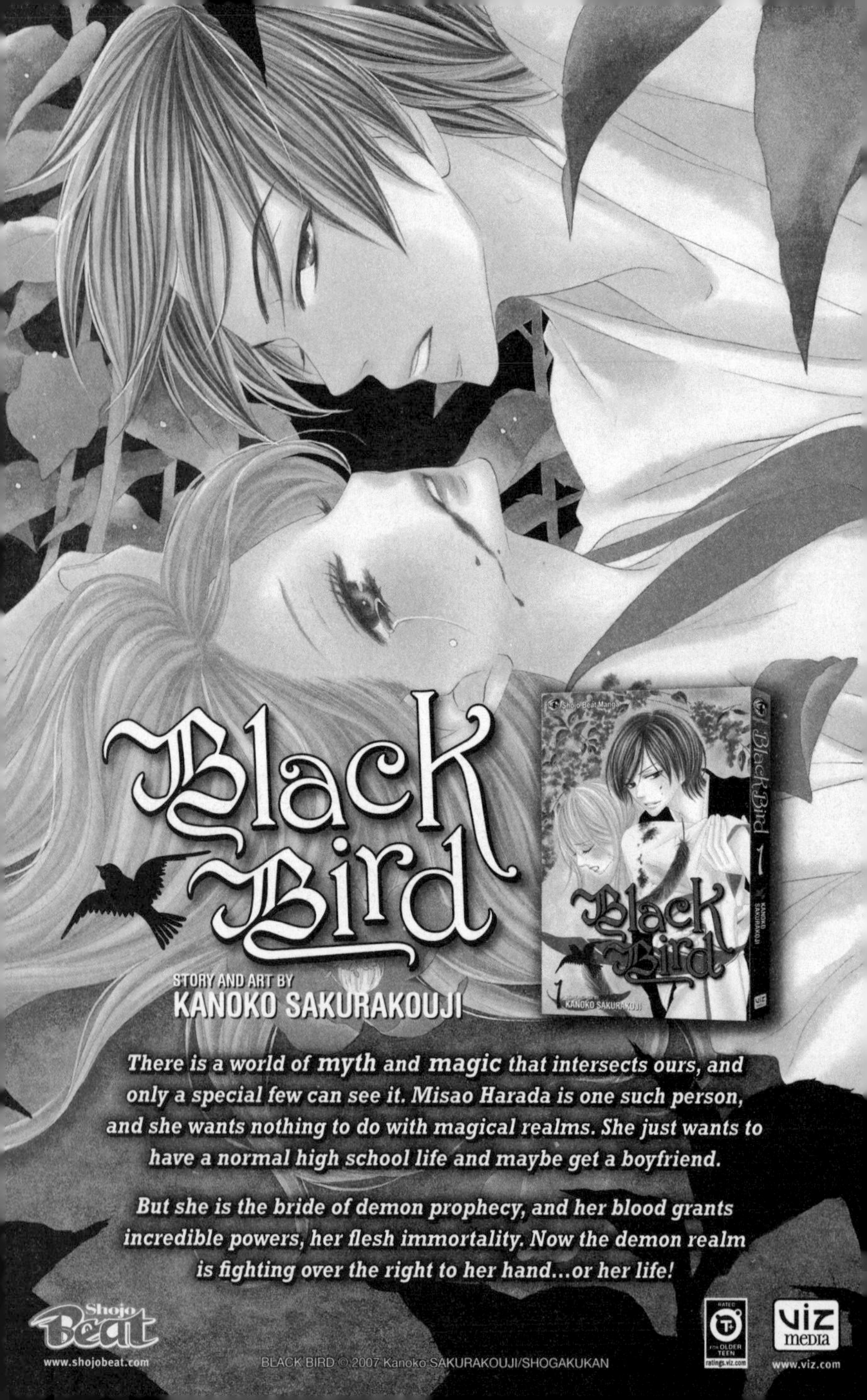
Black Bird
STORY AND ART BY
KANOKO SAKURAKOUJI
Shojo Beat Manga
Black Bird
KANOKO SAKURAKOUJI
There is a world of myth and magic that intersects ours, and only a special few can see it. Misao Harada is one such person, and she wants nothing to do with magical realms. She just wants to have a normal high school life and maybe get a boyfriend.
But she is the bride of demon prophecy, and her blood grants incredible powers, her flesh immortality. Now the demon realm is fighting over the right to her hand…or her life!
Shojo Beat
www.shojobeat.com
BLACK BIRD © 2007 Kanoko SAKURAKOUJI/SHOGAKUKAN
RATED T+ FOR OLDER TEEN
ratings.viz.com
viz media
www.viz.com

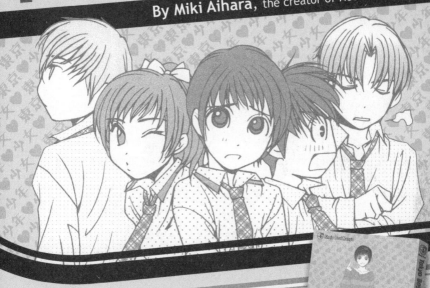
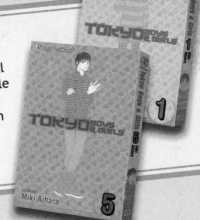
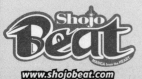

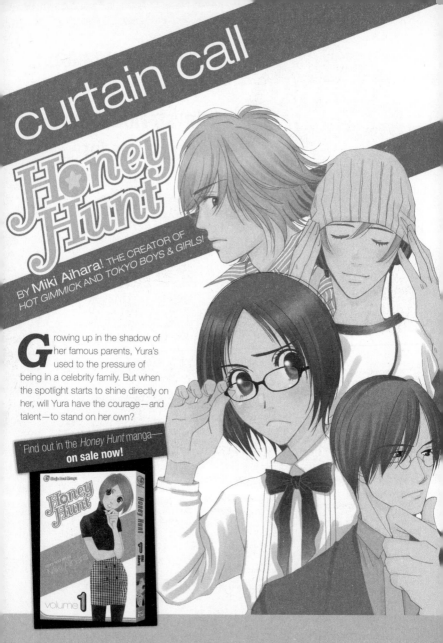

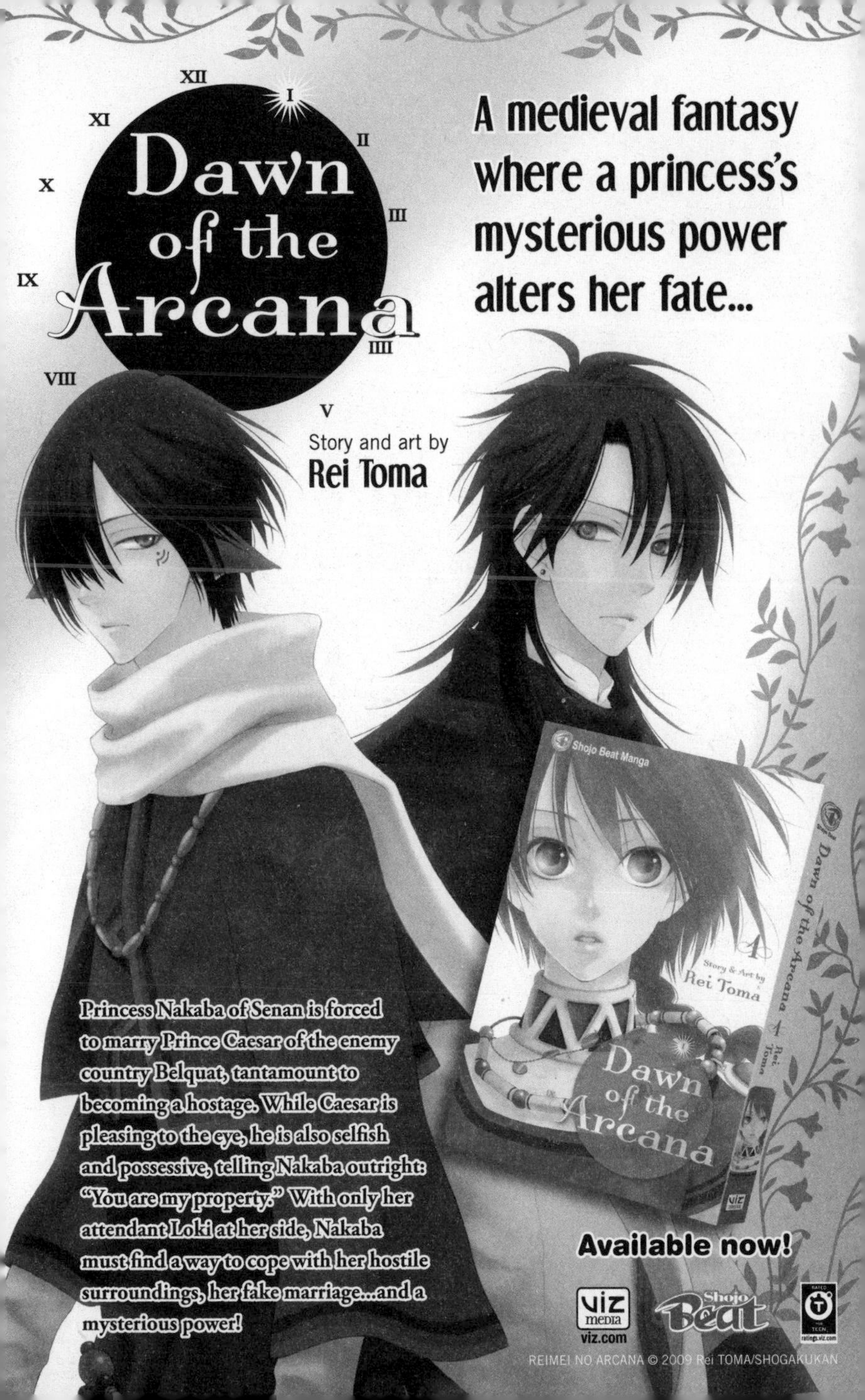
XII
I
XI
II
X
Dawn of the Arcana
III
IX
IIII
VIII
V
A medieval fantasy where a princess's mysterious power alters her fate...
Story and art by
Rei Toma
Shojo Beat Manga
Dawn of the Arcana
1
Story & Art by
Rei Toma
Princess Nakaba of Senan is forced to marry Prince Caesar of the enemy country Belquat, tantamount to becoming a hostage. While Caesar is pleasing to the eye, he is also selfish and possessive, telling Nakaba outright: "You are my property." With only her attendant Loki at her side, Nakaba must find a way to cope with her hostile surroundings, her fake marriage...and a mysterious power!
Available now!
viz media
viz.com
Shojo Beat
ratings.viz.com
REIMEI NO ARCANA © 2009 Rei TOMA/SHOGAKUKAN

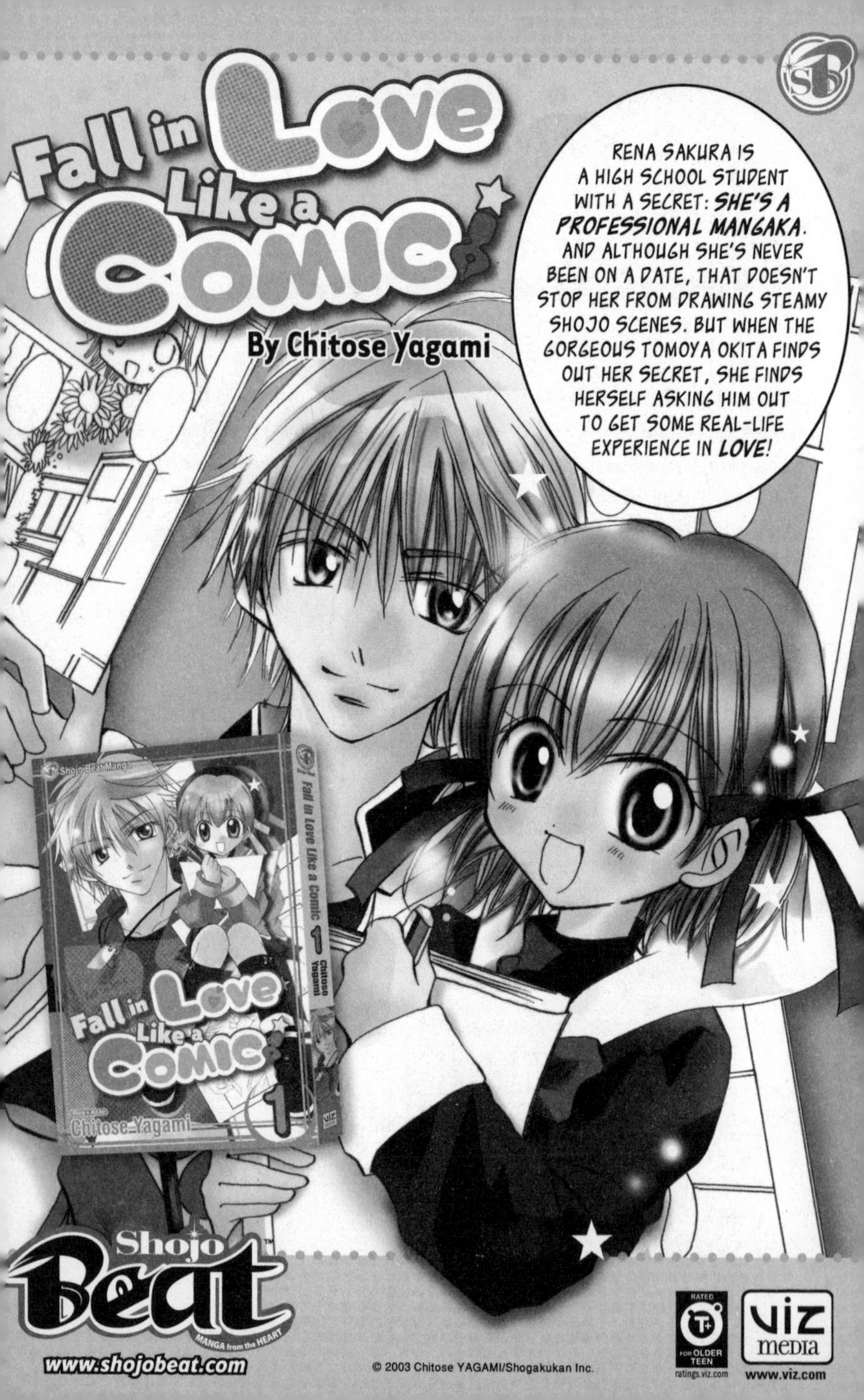
Fall in Love Like a Comic
By Chitose Yagami
RENA SAKURA IS A HIGH SCHOOL STUDENT WITH A SECRET: ***SHE'S A PROFESSIONAL MANGAKA***. AND ALTHOUGH SHE'S NEVER BEEN ON A DATE, THAT DOESN'T STOP HER FROM DRAWING STEAMY SHOJO SCENES. BUT WHEN THE GORGEOUS TOMOYA OKITA FINDS OUT HER SECRET, SHE FINDS HERSELF ASKING HIM OUT TO GET SOME REAL-LIFE EXPERIENCE IN ***LOVE***!
Shojo Beat Manga
Fall in Love Like a Comic 1
Chitose Yagami
Shojo Beat™
MANGA from the HEART
www.shojobeat.com
© 2003 Chitose YAGAMI/Shogakukan Inc.
RATED T+ FOR OLDER TEEN
ratings.viz.com
VIZ media
www.viz.com

This is the last page.

In keeping with the original Japanese comic format, this book reads from right to left—so action, sound effects, and word balloons are completely reversed. This preserves the orientation of the original artwork—plus, it's fun! Check out the diagram shown here to get the hang of things, and then turn to the other side of the book to get started!

1
1
2
2
3
4
3
5
6
4
7
8
5
9
142

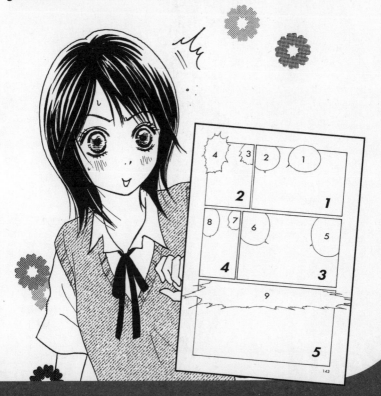